THE AUTHOR OF HIMSELF
THE LIFE OF MARCEL REICH-RANICKI

THE AUTHOR
OF HIMSELF

THE LIFE OF MARCEL REICH-RANICKI

Marcel Reich-Ranicki

Translated from the German by Ewald Osers

With a foreword by Jack Zipes

Princeton University Press

Princeton, New Jersey

For Teofila Reich-Ranicki and
Andrew Alexander Ranicki

Published in the United States and Canada by
Princeton University Press, 41 William Street, Princeton,
New Jersey 08540

First published in English by Weidenfeld and Nicolson and in German under the title *Mein
Leben* Copyright © 1999, Deutsche Verlags-Anstalt GmbH, Stuttgart

Library of Congress Control Number 2001088229

ISBN 0–691–09040–8

This book has been composed in 10.75 Times New Roman

Typeset at Selwood Systems, Midsomer Norton

www.pup.princeton.edu

Printed in Great Britain by
Butler & Tanner Ltd, Frome and London

1 3 5 7 9 10 8 6 4 2

CONTENTS

v

FOREWORD:
HOLOCAUST SURVIVOR AS
LITERARY POPE OF GERMANY

It appears that miraculous forces have worked wonders in Marcel Reich-Ranicki's life. After all, how is it possible that a young Jewish boy from a small town in Poland, who was raised in Berlin, then forced by the Nazis to live in Warsaw in 1938 and experience the uprising of the Warsaw Ghetto, could have survived not only the terrors of the Holocaust but also the malicious police state of Poland to become the most successful and controversial literary critic in postwar Germany?

In fact, Reich-Ranicki is today a cultural institution in Germany, and his word can make or break a writer's career. For years he has served on prestigious national and regional committees that award literary prizes. He has published reviews in all the leading newspapers and magazines in Germany, including *Die Zeit, Frankfurter Allgemeine Zeitung*, and *Der Spiegel*, as well as numerous books on literature. He has hosted popular radio and television shows and captivated participants and audiences with his bold pronouncements, his hyperbolic and very peculiar manner of speech, and with his comprehensive knowledge of German literature, art, and music from the eighteenth century to the present. Wise and astute, he also plays the clown and is as much an entertainer as he is a serious critic. Indeed, he can be formidable and ferocious in defending his views, witty and sovereign in repartee, and has come to represent the epitome of the cultured German. Yet, Reich-Ranicki refuses to call himself a German.

This is one of the great ironies of postwar German history. A Jew became and still is the literary pope of the German nation and yet refuses to assume a German identity. How this could happen is the focus of Reich-Ranicki's autobiography, which has become a veritable best-seller in Germany. Just as Reich-Ranicki writes in wonderment about the course of his life, German readers are intrigued by his marvelous story that reads like a *Bildungsroman*, a typical German novel of development. But, of course, his development has not followed a straight and easy path.

In 1929, when Reich-Ranicki was nine years old and about to move from the Polish city of Wloclawek, one of his favorite teachers told him that he was going to travel into the land of culture, and his mother nodded her approval. And yes, Reich-Ranicki did soak up German culture in Berlin and did develop a great love affair with German literature. But as an 'alien Jew,' the Nazis compelled him and his family to return to Poland. In 1938 Warsaw became his home, and he held various jobs until he was forced to live in the ghetto, where he was employed as a translator and interpreter by the Jewish Council. At the beginning of 1943 he became a member of the Jewish resistance and managed to escape the ghetto with his wife after their parents and relatives had been sent to concentration camps where they were murdered. Reich-Ranicki's account of the sordid and humiliating conditions of life in the ghetto is an important document of the barbarism of the Nazis and the valor of the Jews, especially because he worked in the offices of the council and was privy to major encounters with high-ranking officials on both the German and Jewish sides. Moreover, he experienced the daily deprivation as most of the Jews did and worked clandestinely with members of the resistance. Once he and his wife managed to get outside the ghetto, they were hidden by simple Polish peasants in a crude cellar for close to two years, an incident that Günter Grass fictionalized in his novel, *From the Diary of a Snail* (1972). After they were liberated by the Russians, Reich-Ranicki and his wife made their way to Warsaw where he joined the Communist Party and began working for the Foreign Ministry. But since he did not adhere to the strict policies of the CP, he was eventually imprisoned and dismissed from the party. This dismissal led to his work as a journalist and his return to German culture, and it enabled him to turn his love for German culture into a profession. From 1950 to 1958, Reich-Ranicki became the foremost Polish literary critic of German literature from the East and the West, and he befriended some of the most important writers and critics of the times, such as Anna Seghers, Bertolt Brecht, Hans Mayer, Siegfried Lenz, Heinrich Böll, and many of the members of the famous Group 47. When anti-Semitism reared its ugly head in Poland during the 1950s, Reich-Ranicki fled in 1958 to West Germany – another one of the striking twists in his development. Thanks to his connections with numerous German writers and key people in the mass media, he was able to establish himself quickly on the cultural scene. In fact, it is astonishing to see how fast he became famous if not notorious. Through his reviews, books, and radio and television shows, he focused all his efforts on re-establishing the great humanistic tradition of German literature and became the spokesman for the renewal of this tradition on the contemporary scene. However, he also had a knack for making enemies, even out of those writers who had befriended him, such as Böll, Grass, and Martin Walser. Reich-Ranicki was always and still is a troublemaker and compulsive writer who felt himself to be on a mission in postwar Germany. At one point in his autobiography he asks himself: 'Why then the great trouble, the constant strain? Because of the literature? Yes, certainly. Was it my ambition to continue, perhaps in a very demonstrative manner, the tradition of Jews in the history of German literary criticism to which I had long since adhered in a leading position and in great public view? Certainly. Did my passion have anything to do with my yearning for a home country, that home country which I was lacking and which I had believed to have found in the German literature? Yes, and possibly in a much greater degree than I was even aware.'

It is both the self-awareness in his autobiography and also his stout refusal to compromise his position as a non-German writer who feels that he has a claim on German culture that makes Reich-Ranicki such a fascinating figure. In this respect, he differs from writers like the literary scholar Victor Klemperer, whose diaries and autobiographical writings were published in Germany and the United States in the 1990s and became best-sellers. Klemperer felt himself more German than Jewish and could never really surmount or deal with this dilemma, despite his terrible experiences during the Holocaust. Reich-Ranicki has become more German than most Germans but holds onto something indelibly 'Jewish,' probably because of the Holocaust, and refuses to be called a German. His survival as irascible critic and literary pope of Germany is truly one of the most noteworthy stories of postwar history, and it is a story well worth reading.

Jack Zipes
University of Minnesota
February 2001

PART ONE

1920–1938

1

'WHAT ARE YOU REALLY?'

It happened towards the end of October 1958, at a meeting of the Group 47 in Grossholzleute, a small village in the Allgäu region of south-west Germany. I did not know many of the writers assembled there – small wonder as I had only been back three months in the country from which the German authorities had deported me in the autumn of 1938. Anyway, I felt isolated at the conference, and so I did not mind a young German author, with whom I had spoken in Warsaw the previous spring, coming over to me in the lunch break. I did not then know that the prize he was to receive from the group the following day would mark the beginning of his rapid rise to world fame.

This vigorous young man, self-assured and a little rebellious, now engaged me in conversation. After a brief exchange, he abruptly confronted me with a simple question. No one as yet, since my return to Germany, had ever put it so directly and with less embarrassment. He, Günter Grass from Danzig, wanted to know: 'What are you really – a Pole, a German, or what?' The words 'or what' clearly hinted at a third possibility. Without hesitation I answered: 'I am half Polish, half German, and wholly Jewish.' Grass seemed surprised, but he was clearly happy, even delighted, with my reply. 'Not another word. You would only spoil this neat bon mot.' I, too, thought my spontaneous reply was rather clever because this arithmetical formula was as effective as it was insincere. Not a single word of it was the truth. I was never half Polish, never half German – and I had no doubt that I would never be either of these. Nor, even to this day, was I ever wholly Jewish.

3

When, in 1994, I was invited to take part in a series of lectures – 'Talks about one's own country' – I accepted the invitation but found myself in a somewhat delicate situation. I had to start with the admission that I lacked what I was supposed to talk about – I have no country of my own, no homeland, no fatherland. On the other hand I am not an entirely homeless person, a person without a country. How is that to be understood?

My parents had no problem at all with their identity. I am sure that they never gave this matter any thought. My father, David Reich, was born in Płotsk, an attractive Polish town on the Vistula, north-west of Warsaw. At the beginning of the nineteenth century, when Płotsk belonged to Prussia and was at the centre of the province known as Neu-Ost Preussen, a government official was working there: a gifted young lawyer, E. T. A. Hoffmann. Not long before he had held a post as *Assessor* in a larger and more interesting place – the city of Posen. But as he had produced caricatures which his superiors regarded as particularly malicious, he was transferred, or actually banished, to Płotsk.

I know virtually nothing about my ancestors on my father's side. This is certainly my own fault because my father would have been only too ready to impart extensive information if I had shown the least interest. All I know is that his father had been a successful merchant who had acquired some wealth. He owned a substantial block of flats in Płotsk. He had not stinted on the education of his children. One of my father's sisters became a dentist, another studied singing at the Warsaw conservatoire. She had hoped to become an opera singer, but did not quite succeed – although she was allowed to appear as Madame Butterfly in Łodź. When, a little later, she got married her proud parents acknowledged their daughter's artistic success by having her entire trousseau, and especially her bedlinen, embroidered with butterflies.

My father, too, was musical and played the violin when he was younger. He must have given it up rather soon because in my childhood his instrument lay on top of the wardrobe. As his ambition was to go into business, his parents sent him to Switzerland. There he studied at a commercial college, but soon dropped out and returned home. So nothing came of that either because, even in his youth, he lacked staying power. In 1906 he married my mother,

Helene Auerbach, the daughter of an impoverished rabbi. At the wedding reception, held in a hotel in Posen, the bridal music from *Lohengrin* was played, followed by the wedding march from Mendelssohn's music for *A Midsummer Night's Dream*. Among Jews in Poland, at least among educated ones, this was nothing unusual; indeed it was part of the ritual. The young couple's honeymoon was to Germany: after visiting Dresden they travelled on to the spa of Kudowa.

Had Günter Grass, or anyone else, ever asked my father what *he* really was, his response would likewise have attracted remark. Of course, he would have replied simply that he was a Jew. No doubt my mother would have given the same answer. She grew up in Prussia or, more accurately, in the border area between Silesia and the province of Posen. She only came to Poland when she married.

Her ancestors on her father's side had been rabbis for centuries. Some of them can be found in major Jewish reference works because they had published scholarly books which, in their day, had commanded great respect. They were concerned not so much with theological as with judicial problems – which, incidentally, was quite common among Jews. Rabbis in the past were not only spiritual leaders and teachers but, at the same time, also judges.

Even though only the eldest of my mother's five brothers became a rabbi – a post he held first in Elbing, then in Göttingen, and finally, until his emigration just before the Second World War, in Stuttgart – it may be said that they were all emancipated and accepted in the community, even though, in their way, they kept up the family tradition; three became lawyers, the fourth a patent agent. Thus the religious aspect became a matter of indifference to them, apart from the rabbi, the eldest.

And my mother? She did not want to know anything about religion and had little interest in things Jewish. In spite of her origin? No, probably because of it. I believe that her unmistakable turning away from the spiritual world of her youth was a quiet and gentle protest against her reactionary parental home. Nor was she at all interested in anything Polish. When, every year, I wished her a happy birthday on 28 August, she asked me if I was aware of who else had that day as his birthday. She was born on the same day as Goethe. This, she liked to think, was in some way symbolical. In conversation with me she was fond of quoting from the classics. If I disliked my food I was told:

Can I by stamping on the ground raise armies?
Will a lieutenant grow in my outstretched hand?

Later, when I read *The Maid of Orleans*, I discovered to my surprise that in Schiller's play it was not a lieutenant growing in the out-stretched hand, but fields of grain. Be that as it may, my mother's store of quotations came from German literature, especially that which was taught in schools towards the end of the nineteenth century – chiefly Goethe and Schiller, Heine and Uhland.

My father, on the other hand, remained closely linked to Judaism. Did he believe in God? I do not know, it was not something one ever talked about. Probably the existence of God was a matter of course for him, like the air he breathed. On feast-days and on the sabbath he would go to the synagogue, and also later when we were living in Berlin. But this was not necessarily a religious act. The synagogue, to Jews, is not only the house of God but also a social centre. One would meet there to chat, with one's friends and acquaintances, and possibly also to God. In short, the synagogue served as a sort of club.

It was not religion that moulded the life of my father, but tradition. At an early age, like countless other Polish Jews of his generation, he had been deeply impressed by Zionism. He was fond of recounting that he had taken part in the Third Zionist World Congress in Basel. But that was a long time back, in 1905. I never heard of any subsequent involvement with Zionism by my father or of any activity within any kind of Jewish organization.

Unlike my father, who spoke several languages – Polish and Russian, Yiddish and, as nearly every educated Jew in Poland, German – my mother was not a good linguist. To the end of her life, to the day she was gassed at Treblinka, she spoke faultless, and indeed elegant, German; her Polish, on the other hand, despite having lived for some decades in that country, was faulty and rather elementary. She did not know Yiddish, and if she tried to speak it – for instance when shopping at the market in Warsaw – indulgently

6

smiling Jewish stall-keepers would observe: 'Madam comes from Germany.'

In the town where my parents settled, in Włocławek on the Vistula, my mother almost felt as E. T. A. Hoffmann had done in nearby Płotsk – in exile. Poland was, and remained, alien to her. Just as Irina Sergeyevna in Chekhov's *Three Sisters* yearned for Moscow, so my mother yearned for the metropolis which, in her eyes, symbolized happiness and progress, and where the other family members were living – her elderly father, her sister and four of her brothers – as well as a few of her school friends. She yearned for Berlin.

Meanwhile she had to be content with Włocławek, a rising industrial town which, until the restoration of the Polish state in 1918, belonged to Russia. The German–Russian frontier then ran in the immediate vicinity. In the 1920s the town had some 60,000 inhabitants, about a quarter of whom were Jews. More than a few of these had a conspicuous hankering for German culture. Every so often they would travel to Berlin or to Vienna, especially when they wished to consult some famous medical man or even undergo an operation. In their bookcases, along with the works of the great Polish poets, they would often have the German classics. And most of these educated Jews read German newspapers as a matter of course. We subscribed to the *Berliner Tageblatt*.

There were four Catholic churches in the town, one Protestant church, two synagogues, several factories, including Poland's oldest and largest paper factory, and three cinemas – but no theatre and no orchestra. The most important feature of Włocławek, to this day, is the fourteenth-century Gothic cathedral with a sarcophagus by Veit Stoss. Among the disciples of the priests' seminary near the cathedral, from 1489 to 1491, was a young man from Toruń – Nicholas Copernicus.

I was born in Włocławek on 2 June 1920. Why I was given the name Marcel never concerned me at the time. Only much later did I discover that this was no accident. My sister, thirteen years older than me, had been named Gerda by my mother – she alone concerned herself with such matters. My mother had not the slightest suspicion of what she had done: Gerda was considered in Poland to be a typically German name. Yet hostility to anything German was an old tradition in Poland, going back to the Teutonic Knights. During the First World War and subsequently, the Germans were equally unpopular. Thus my sister was often derided at school because of her German name: it was not easy to decide whether anti-German sentiments or anti-Semitism played the major part here.

My brother, who was my senior by nine years, fared a little better in that respect. He, too, had been given a decidedly German first name – Herbert – by my unworldly mother but he also had a second name – Alexander. According to tradition, Alexander the Great had treated the Jews well and granted them all kinds of privileges. Out of gratitude the Jews had, even during Alexander's lifetime, often named their sons after him. As a matter of fact, my own son is called Andrew Alexander, though this has less to do with the King of Macedon than with the Jewish custom of honouring dead family members by giving their names to one's children. Thus the daughter of my son is called Carla Helen Emily – the names of her grandmother who perished in Treblinka.

It was only a few years ago that I discovered that the date of my birth, 2 June, is, in the Catholic calendar, the day of Saint Marcellus, a Roman priest and martyr from the reign of the emperor Diocletian. I am sure that my parents were totally unaware of the existence of this saint when they gave me a name that was scarcely customary in Poland at the time. Maybe the choice of name was suggested by a Catholic maid or nanny. Whoever was responsible – I bear him or her no ill will. On the contrary, I am grateful. Because, unlike my sister Gerda, I never suffered as a result of my first name.

If I was sometimes mocked by my peers as a child, this was due to a trifling circumstance which, however, I have not forgotten to this day. I was five or six when my mother, during a short visit to her family in Berlin, saw, in a department store, some children's clothes with the slogan 'I am a good boy'. She thought this amusing. Without considering the possible consequences, she had these words translated into Polish and embroidered on my own clothes. Inevitably I soon became the object of the other children's mockery – and reacted to it with fury and defiance. By screaming and fighting I wanted to prove to those mocking me that I was anything but a good boy. This earned me the nickname 'Bolshevik'. Could this have been the beginning of my characteristic defiance?

One day my father, surprisingly, brought home a man with a beard. He had exceptionally long side-locks and wore a caftan, that black cloak-like coat which was the customary garb of Orthodox Jews. This quiet man, who seemed a little weird to me, was to become my tutor. He would, my father explained, teach me Hebrew. But that was all my father was able to say because at that moment my mother appeared and immediately intervened: I was, she said resolutely, too young for tuition. The disappointed teacher was sent on his way with the promise of employment at some future date. This was my father's first attempt to intervene in my education; it was also his last.

My mother never explained to me why she would not hear of any education in the Jewish tradition. When the time came to send me to school she decided that, unlike my brother and sister, I was to attend the Protestant, German-language, primary school. Was this, possibly, a protest against Judaism? Not necessarily. She simply wanted me to be educated in the German language.

However, there was a problem from the start. I knew too much already. That would not have mattered, but unfortunately I also knew too little. A nursemaid who looked after me had amused herself by teaching me how to read, casually and without any fuss. I learned very quickly, except that no one showed me how to form letters. However, in our apartment there was an ancient typewriter and I did not find it difficult to transfer individual letters to paper. I was soon able to type a short letter to my sister who was then studying in Warsaw.

So my mother took me to the German school. She explained the situation, which she thought unusual, to the headmaster, a particularly strict gentleman who, if I am correctly informed, was executed by the Poles as a German spy during the first few days of the Second World War. He appeared to have encountered such problems before. He immediately tested me: I read fast and correctly. But this was not the end of the matter. A decision would have to be made. He said, not without some humour: 'Either we put him in the first form, then he'll be bored during reading lessons, or he goes straight into the second form, but in that case you'll have to see to it that he learns to write at home.' My mother did not hesitate for a moment: 'Straight into Form Two! I have an older daughter. She'll teach him to write. He'll learn soon enough.' When, nowadays, I recount this episode to German writers I usually add: 'And he hasn't learned to this day.' Our authors, often blessed with a childlike mind, take a lot of delight from this remark.

My mother never suspected what the consequences of her decision would be. No one in my form was interested in the fact that I could not write. But that I was the only one who already read books and occasionally reported on them during lessons, proudly and boldly, aroused the envy of my classmates. From the outset I was different from them, I was an outsider. I could hardly know that I would always remain one. Whatever school I attended, whatever institution I worked in, I never quite fitted into my surroundings.

But all in all I did not have many problems at that Protestant school, especially since I was treated kindly by one of the women teachers, a young German called Laura. There was a reason for this: my mother used to lend Laura the latest German books, which she ordered regularly from Berlin. I well remember one book which the young woman, whose massive bosom greatly impressed me, was awaiting with such impatience. It was not one of the great literary works of the day, but a novel which had shaken the whole of Europe – Remarque's *All Quiet on the Western Front*.

There was nothing original about my own reading matter. I read a lot, but more or less the same books as other children. I best remember Dickens's novel *Oliver Twist* and Defoe's *Robinson Crusoe* – both books no doubt in the versions for 'more mature young readers'. I was even more fascinated by a book of a totally different character – a multi-volume German encyclopaedia. It was mainly the illustrations which I could not tear myself away from. It was here that my liking for reference books of all kinds had its beginnings.

But my most enduring impressions came from music. My sister played the piano and I frequently heard Bach and, even more often, Chopin, in our apartment. At the same time I was enthusiastic about another instrument – the gramophone. We had a lot of records, chosen by my father who was much more musical than my mother. In addition to popular symphonic works, which were modern in my father's youth – from Grieg's *Peer Gynt* suites to Rimsky-Korsakov's *Sheherazade* – there were operas such as *Aida*, *Rigoletto* and *Traviata*, *Bohème*, *Tosca* and *Madame Butterfly*. There was also a Wagner record, just one – Lohengrin's 'Grail Story'. I never tired of hearing the same arias, duets and overtures again and again. My slight aversion to Grieg and Rimsky-Korsakov goes back to those childhood experiences, as does my indelible love of Italian opera, mainly by Verdi but also by Puccini, to which I have remained loyal to this day.

In the spring of 1929 all kinds of things happened in our family. I observed the tears of my mother and the helplessness of my father, I heard them lament and complain. Their anguish and despair increased by the day. We were all heading for a terrible disaster – even we children sensed this. The catastrophe occurred soon enough. It had two causes – the economic slump and my father's temperament. He was reliable and undemanding, kind and lovable, but he had not the slightest commercial talent. He was a businessman and entrepreneur whose businesses and enterprises usually yielded very little or nothing. Of course he should have realized sooner that he had chosen the wrong occupation and looked around for another job. But for that he lacked all initiative. Application and energy were not among his virtues. His life was unhappily marked by weakness of character and a passive disposition.

Soon after the First World War my father had started a business in Włocławek – presumably with his father's money – a small factory manufacturing building materials. He was fond of describing himself as an 'industrialist'. But in the late 1920s there was less and less building in Poland and bankruptcy could no longer be avoided. The fact that this was nothing unusual at the time was small consolation to my mother. If her husband had manufactured coffins, she used to say, people would have stopped dying.

My mother suffered a lot at this time. She was ashamed to walk in the street because she anticipated the sneers or contemptuous looks of neighbours and acquaintances. These were probably exaggerated fears, since my mother enjoyed great popularity in the town. People admired her quiet, distinguished manner, which they attributed to her origins in the world of German culture. But perhaps she feared not so much the contempt of her fellow citizens as their pity.

Needless to say, she was entirely innocent of the disaster. No one could blame her for having failed to recognize her husband's incompetence. But one thing is certain: whatever positive qualities my mother had, she was – in this respect very much like my father – totally impractical. No doubt, when the crisis arose, she found it difficult to do what needed doing to avert the worst consequences of bankruptcy and thus to save the family. Money had to be found. And there was only one source. One of her brothers in Berlin, Jacob, was a particularly successful lawyer, the wealthiest member of the family. Overcoming her reluctance to telephone him, she implored Jacob to wire a substantial sum of money. He sent her half the sum she requested.

I was nine at the time and, naturally enough, did not understand what was happening around me. But there were too many tears being shed for me to be unaware of the family tragedy. My father's failure was both deplorable and pitiful, but this cast less of a shadow on my youth than did the economic consequences of the collapse in the longer term. Later, as a teenager, I was all too aware of my parents' dependence on the relations who were helping them. Fear that I might one day find myself in such humiliating circumstances influenced many a decision in my life for years to come.

Initially, however, this catastrophe worked to my advantage. Amid the dramatic and fateful consequences of the disaster, my mother's long-standing wish was suddenly fulfilled. As there was no future for our family where we were, it was decided to move to Berlin. There, my parents were hoping, it would be possible to make a new beginning, even though, as emerged later, there were no definite ideas about my father's future occupation. I was sent ahead to Berlin and was to spend the summer holiday with the family of the affluent Uncle Jacob – he had three children of roughly my age – at Westerland on the island of Sylt.

Before leaving, so my mother believed, I had to say goodbye to my teacher, and I shall always remember the words with which she sent me out into the world. Fixing her gaze on the distance, Miss Laura of the billowing bosom announced seriously and solemnly: 'You're going, my son, to the land of culture.' I did not quite understand what this was about, but I was aware of my mother nodding approvingly.

Next day, under the supervision of an acquaintance of my parents who also happened to be travelling westwards, I found myself on the

Berlin train. Strangely enough, I had no fear of what was awaiting me in the unknown city, nor was I scared of the relations whom I had never met. Was this a child's recklessness or a lack of imagination? There was, I suspected, something else. I had heard such a lot about Berlin – the trains there were alleged to run under the ground or up above the houses; buses, so I had been told, had seats on the roof; there were endlessly moving staircases on which one only had to stand to be carried up or down.

It was a long journey and it would be evening before I reached the fairy-tale city which my parents had described, the dream land they had promised me. With great curiosity I awaited the end of the journey – and it was this curiosity that displaced all doubts and fears. Thus, feverish with expectation, I thought of the miracle I was about to experience – the miracle of Berlin.

2

'HALF DRAGGED,
HALF PLUNGING,
SO HE SANK...'

At the Zoologischer Garten railway station in Berlin I was met by an elegant, dark-haired lady of about forty. This was Aunt Elsie, my Uncle Jacob's wife. It must have been late in the evening because, when we got to the apartment, there was no sign of my cousins, two male and one female; they had already gone to bed. And my uncle was not there either. So I sat alone with my aunt at the large circular dining table which could have seated ten or even twelve persons. But there was someone else in the room – an attractive, pleasant-looking young woman, wearing a black dress and a white apron and – to my amazement – also white kid gloves. In dignified silence she served the evening meal. A little overwhelmed, understandably, by this strange new world, I answered the questions put to me timidly and monosyllabically. Thus an awkward silence soon descended.

Of course, I could not know what was concealed behind this genteel façade. But I soon sensed that the deliberate, contrived style of the household was not genuine. There was a marked artificiality about it – cool and solemn. Uncle Jacob, who came from a poor background, was a sought-after, almost a prominent, attorney and notary, and proud of his very remarkable success. His brothers, too, were well-off, living in an affluent style, but he alone was anxious to demonstrate his social rise. He needed status symbols, he depended on them. The glamour of the 'Founders' Period' suited his taste, he was impressed by the pomp of the turn of the century.

I do not believe that my uncle actually enjoyed riding. Nevertheless, two allegedly very valuable riding horses were part of his establishment – one called Avanti and the other, significantly, Aristokrat.

Every morning he would go riding with his wife in the nearby Tiergarten, as was the done thing. The neighbourhood in which he had settled was, at least in his opinion, aristocratic: the family who had kindly received me, the son of a bankrupt businessman from a small Polish town, did not live in the fashionable west of Berlin, or in Dahlem or Grünewald, but on Roonstrasse, immediately next to the Reichstag. Now and again we children were reminded that Bismarck had for a time resided in our immediate neighbourhood.

In the apartment, which was huge to my eyes, I was astonished to find a room of exotic appearance, crowded with plants of all kinds. That, it was explained to me, was the winter garden. There one could hear a continuous soft splashing noise: in a corner there was a pale-blue, by no means small, ceaselessly playing fountain. Between the dining room and the sitting room, called the music room, there were two marble columns extending from floor to ceiling. On a wall in this room, among many other paintings, there was a picture of a woman in oriental attire lying on the floor. She was gazing, longingly and challengingly, at the face of a man whose head lay on a silver salver. Later my girl cousin informed me, not without pride: 'That's Mama as Salome.' Before marrying my mother's brother, Aunt Elsie had been an actress in her native Cologne. Perhaps that was the reason why everything in the apartment seemed theatrical.

That first evening in Berlin, when I sat alone with my aunt at the massive table, I had a soft-boiled egg. No sooner had I eaten it than Aunt Elsie picked up the shell and established that, as she had evidently expected, some egg remained inside. 'This is not how one eats eggs in Germany,' she informed me concisely and severely. That was probably the first time I heard the word 'Germany' – and it did not sound very friendly.

A little later I was in bed, crying bitterly. Because I was lonely and overtired? Because Aunt Elsie had treated me harshly and frightened me? Certainly, but I was more scared of a large oil painting hanging above my bed. It seemed to me uncanny and horrible. It was a copy of a picture much admired and popular in those days – Arnold Böcklin's *Triton and Nereid*.

The following morning I had breakfast with my cousins. Then, led by a spindly governess, we took a walk in the nearby Tiergarten. But first we were allowed to jump about on some steps and chase each other around a splendid column. These were my earliest contact with Prussian history – the steps of the Reichstag and the Victory Column which, at that time, stood in front of the building. I did not then suspect that things Prussian would, if not exactly mould me, at least accompany me throughout my life – mainly Kleist and Fontane, and also Schinkel.

I did not remain in Berlin long, because soon the family left for their holiday at Westerland. Travelling with us were the governess, the cook, the maidservant and, needless to say, the two horses. And there were many, many trunks, especially cabin trunks. For me, the stay on the North Frisian island of Sylt proved most useful. When, a few months later, my mother came to Berlin and addressed me in Polish I answered her in German. After a while my German was a lot better than my Polish. But she still found my linguistic knowledge inadequate and she made me read to her every day for at least half an hour, unfortunately from a book someone had given me that I did not much care for. It was a travel book, then very popular, by the Berlin journalist Richard Katz.

So I read aloud and suffered in silence, but gradually started groaning and complaining. My mother tried to pacify me: 'Be patient – the day will come when you will read German books from choice and with pleasure.' 'No, never!' I screamed. Evidently I was wrong, because I have spent by far the greatest part of my life reading German books, though not always voluntarily. But perhaps it is Richard Katz's fault that later in life, with rare exceptions, I never particularly warmed to travel books.

When the rest of the family arrived in Berlin that autumn, Uncle Joseph installed us in the rather drab flat that belonged to my grandfather, the long-retired rabbi Mannheim Auerbach, not far from Charlottenburg station. Within two or three weeks in my new surroundings – this was still 1929 – I was sent to school. As was the custom in elegant families, the children of Uncle Jacob and Aunt Elsie were taught at home by a tutor, but there could be no question of that in my case – for financial reasons. When my mother met me after my first day at school she saw tears in my eyes. No, nobody had done anything to harm me at my elementary school in Berlin-Charlottenburg. But I had witnessed an incident of a kind until then unknown to me.

A pupil who had committed some offence had been called to the front of the class by our teacher, Herr Wolf. Immediately there was a short command: 'Bend over!' The culprit did as he was told – and received several vigorous blows with a cane that stood in the corner of the classroom for this purpose. After that, the crying child was allowed to return to his place. This was, as I soon discovered, a perfectly normal occurrence. No one else in the class was surprised, let alone shocked, by it but I had never experienced anything of the kind in Poland.

Adorning the invisible gateway to this new phase in my life – probably the most influential one – were three images – Miss Laura's sentimental and friendly vision of the land of culture, Aunt Elsie's severe reminder of German orderliness, and the punishment delivered so vigorously and efficiently by Herr Wolf, the teacher. Quite so, there must be order and discipline. But was that possible? Should schoolchildren receive such harsh treatment in the land of culture? Something was not right there.

Of course I did not understand, or even suspect, that contradiction at the time. However, on my first day at school in Germany I experienced something that I never quite managed to shake off, something that accompanied me all my life. Perhaps I should say 'has accompanied me'. I mean fear – fear of the German cane, of the German concentration camp, of the German gas chamber, in short, fear of German barbarism. And what about the German culture which Miss Laura had so emphatically and longingly promised? That was soon revealed to me. Quite quickly I fell under the spell of German literature, of German music. Fear was joined by happiness – fear of things German by the happiness I owed to things German. Here, too, the present tense is appropriate – the happiness I still owe.

I did not have a bad time at the Charlottenburg elementary school: I was neither flogged nor picked on. But while the teachers did not make things difficult for me, my classmates did. They saw in me, not surprisingly, the foreigner, the stranger. My clothes were a little different from theirs, their games and pranks were unfamiliar to me. Hence I was isolated. In other words, I was not one of them.

Everything in that school was new to me, even the fact that in the first German lesson one of the boys – the form monitor – was told by the teacher to take a large number of books from a bookcase and distribute them. Every pupil received a copy, from which he was made to read about half a page. I managed this more or less, but the book did not grip me, the author did not appeal to me – and does not to this day. It was Peter Rosegger's *When I Was Still a Backwoods Boy*. Böcklin and Rosegger – life was not overly kind to me.

In the spring of 1930 I was to enter the Werner von Siemens-Realgymnasium, the secondary school in Berlin-Schöneberg, not far from Bayerischer Platz and in the part of the city where we were then living. Because I had only been at my elementary school for four months I was one of those pupils who had to sit an entrance examination – first a written exam and then an oral – in German and arithmetic. My mother was due to collect me at eleven. But at ten o'clock I was waiting for her outside the school on Hohenstaufenstrasse, patiently and in high spirits. I had done so well in the written exam that I was exempted from the oral. My mother was proud of me.

A generous reward followed. First I was allowed to choose a cake in the *Konditorei* opposite and then I was taken to the circus by my father. The famous Sarrasani circus was then performing in Berlin – I think on the Tempelhofer Feld. Yes, I liked it all right. The next time I was at a circus was a quarter of a century later, when the Soviet State Circus visited Warsaw in 1955. On that occasion I wanted to give my six-year-old son Andrew Alexander a treat.

Neither in 1930 nor in 1955 could I have known that one day I would owe an unusual success to a circus. In 1968 the German periodical *Der Spiegel* carried a review of Alexander Kluge's film *Artistes at the Top of the Big Top: Helpless*. Here the reviewer complimented me for having 'most convincingly impersonated the director of the Soviet State Circus. I was delighted, for it does not often happen that a beginner in the art of acting receives such unstinted praise from a *Spiegel* reviewer. However, I was completely unaware of ever having impersonated anybody, either on the big screen or elsewhere. Perhaps I should explain how my successful performance as an actor came about. In the spring of 1968 Kluge had filmed a meeting of Group 47 at the Pulvermühle tavern in Franconia and used those shots for his much-discussed *Artistes at the Top of the Big Top: Helpless*. Omitting the soundtrack, he had presented the writers' conference as a congress of circus directors. In later years I have indeed been occasionally offered minor parts in films. Evidently the producers thought it would be amusing to cast me as a literary critic. I have invariably declined these offers, sometimes with the honest explanation that I was finding it difficult enough to act the role of a critic 'convincingly' in real life.

My secondary school career also began with an incident which, trivial though it was, I have not forgotten to this day. In the first lesson we were all called upon, in alphabetical order, to give the date and place of our birth. When my turn came, the teacher accepted the date without surprise, but he was amused when I mentioned the place. So there was a boy in his class who was born in some remote or, what was worse, unpronounceable, town. The teacher made heavy weather of attempting to pronounce this peculiar name, Włocławek. The whole form roared with laughter – and the more the boys laughed, the more did the teacher try to entertain them with new variants, from 'Lutzlawiek' to 'Wutzlawatzek'.

How I envied my classmates who were born in Berlin, Breslau or Eberswalde. I clenched my fist, though only in my trouser pocket, and said something cheeky. For that I received a vigorous box on the ear. Yes, one got boxed on the ear, not only in the lower forms, but also in senior ones in Prussian secondary schools. After this punishment, which my classmates regarded as quite normal and perhaps even called for, I swore vengeance. If I wanted to be accepted and even respected, I realized, I would have to excel in class. That was not going to be easy because until then I had only been a mediocre pupil.

Before long – and defiance may have played a part in this – I became top in a subject which was then called arithmetic but soon renamed mathematics. Maybe those days left some trace after all – because my son became a mathematician, indeed a very good one. He is now a professor at the University of Edinburgh and his work appears in the lists of the most prestigious international publishing houses. Several of his books have received prizes but unfortunately I am unable to read them, let alone understand them.

My love of mathematics did not last long. When I was thirteen or fourteen, a different subject fascinated me – a subject, moreover, which seemed to me even more suitable for getting my own back on those of my classmates who had mocked me. Yes, I had my revenge –

I became, and remained until graduation, the form's stop student in German. From defiance? Perhaps, but this, of course, is not the whole story.

There was another motivating factor – one that cannot be over-rated. Reading stories, novels, and soon also plays gave me more and more pleasure. And before I realized it, I was totally taken over. I was happy – perhaps for the first time in my life. An extreme, an uncanny sensation had come over me and enthralled me. I was in love. '*Half dragged, half plunging, so he sank . . .*' – I was in love with German literature.

3

HERR KÄSTNER: 'TO BE APPLIED TO THE SOUL'

At first, following the mostly casual suggestions and occasional advice of my teachers, I read the same books as my classmates. At a very early age I was interested in popular historical novels – the bestseller *Ben Hur* by the American author Lewis Wallace, *Quo Vadis* by the Polish Nobel Prize winner Henryk Sienkiewicz, *The Lion of Flanders* by the Flemish writer Hendrik Conscience, and *The Last Days of Pompei* by Edward Bulwer-Lytton.

In addition, dutifully but a little bored by them, I read Fenimore Cooper's *Leather-Stocking* novels. For a time I was also excited by the works of that German author who was not ashamed of employing the cheapest means to capture the reader's interest, who did not flinch from either primitivism or sentimentality – Karl May. But once I had read a few of those green-coloured volumes I no longer wished to know any more about him – maybe because his hero, Old Shatterhand, was a little too strong and brave for my taste and, moreover, unselfish to an excessive degree. What is more, he was what seemed most despicable to us Berlin schoolboys – intolerably pompous and a terrible show-off.

'*And perhaps from what is German / once the world will regain its health*' – these lines written by the now forgotten Emanuel Geibel were certainly not known to me then. But I was becoming irritated by the fact that it was invariably a German who, in Karl May's novels, saved those in trouble and treated the villains as they deserved, who dispensed order and justice – if not with his bare fist then with a miracle weapon.

In January 1967 I had a discussion in Tübingen with the aged writer and music critic Ernst Bloch – it was a broadcast recording. We talked about this and that, but soon Bloch mentioned Karl May, whom he admired. May was, he said, one of the most thrilling and colourful narrators in German literature. Cautiously I ventured to contradict him, criticizing the poor style of the author of *Winnetou*. Bloch disagreed. Here, he believed, the language of the narrator was entirely appropriate to his subject, his characters and their motives. But this seemed to me a somewhat ambiguous remark, not necessarily one of praise – and I ceased to contradict him.

The German historical novels of the nineteenth century, those regarded as particularly commendable, were all characterized by a marked patriotic tendency – such as Joseph Scheffel's melodramatic *Ekkehard*, Gustav Freytag's solid *Die Ahnen* [*Our Forefathers*], or Felix Dahn's novel *Ein Kampf um Rom* [*A Struggle for Rome*], a huge panorama brilliantly employing contrasting effects, whose characters engraved themselves, certainly not accidentally, on my memory. It was not the reckless Belisarius, always heroically fighting at the head of his army, who impressed me most in Dahn's novel, but the physically weak and paralysed general Narses, a strategist vastly superior to all the rest.

However, I read all these books with mixed feelings, and certainly without enthusiasm. The world of heroes and knights, of fencers and fighters, of powerful kings and valiant swordsmen, mostly of rather simple minds – that was not my world. I was fascinated by a totally different book, Erich Kästner's *Emil and the Detectives*, a 'novel for children'.

While he was alive I repeatedly, perhaps somewhat defiantly, wrote that Kästner, this singer of small freedoms, this poet of little people, was one of the stars of German literature in our century. Did I lay it on too thick? Kästner's novels, including the most important one, *Fabian*, are little known today. He had no luck with anything he wrote for the stage. His essays are mostly to the point, but they are occasional writings without special significance. What remains? Unquestionably a few of his poems and perhaps one or two of his books for children.

Emil Tischbein and his friend Gustav with the klaxon – these were incomparably closer to me than the Red Indian gentleman Winnetou or the noble Old Shatterhand, closer than the generals Cethegus,

Narses and Belisarius fighting for Rome. The story of the Berlin children who succeed in catching a thief, the villain who had robbed Emil on the train, the children who, rather like Old Shatterhand, ensure that justice takes its course and that order is restored – it is not entirely without sentiment, but, unlike the work of Karl May, it is free from the exotic, from the grand gesture, from bombast. Kästner's story took place not in a distant time and country, it happened here and now, in the streets and backyards of Berlin, in a setting familiar to us. The characters spoke in the way we, who grew up in the big city, did. The credibility of this book, and hence also its success, was due chiefly to the authenticity of its everyday language.

I liked Kästner's later novels for children, mainly *Pünktchen und Anton*, but they did not impress me quite as much. Soon, however, his name ceased to be mentioned. When on 10 May 1933, in the square in front of the Berlin State Opera, his books were burned, he was among the crowd who wished to witness this unique spectacle in modern history. Nevertheless he remained in Germany. If Kästner is listed as an emigré, in some reference works on literature by German exiles, this is incorrect, but nevertheless true in a sense. In the period from 1933 to 1945 he, the man who fell between two stools, had made his decision. He did not emigrate, but his books did – they could only be published in Switzerland. Erich Kästner was Germany's honorary author-in-exile.

Thus I only rarely came across his writings during those years. They were not to be found in municipal libraries or in bookshops – though one might pick them up in some second-hand shops for a few Pfennigs. The politically incorrect titles were secretly pulped. By then I was no longer reading Kästner: I think I had outgrown him, even his poems. However, I could not forget him.

This was brought home to me in a surprising manner a few years later – in the Warsaw ghetto. I was visiting an acquaintance in whose flat I found something I had not expected – German books. Suddenly a neat little volume caught my eye: *Doktor Erich Kästners Lyrische Hausapotheke* [*Doctor Erich Kästner's Lyrical Medicine Cabinet*], published in Zurich in 1936. I immediately turned to the poem which opened the collection: *Eisenbahngleichnis* [*Railway Parable*]. It began: *Wir sitzen alle im gleichen Zug / und reisen quer durch die Zeit* [We are all sitting in the same train / travelling through time]. And it ended: *Wir sitzen alle im gleichen Zug / Und viele im falschen Coupé* [We are all sitting in the same train / But many in the wrong compartment].

I desperately wanted to own this book. I would have bought a copy if this had been possible but it was not to be found in any of the second-hand bookshops in the ghetto. However, I was allowed to borrow it – naturally only for a limited time. A girl whose name was Teofila but who was called Tosia – who will play an important part in this book – copied Kästner's *Lyrical Medicine Cabinet* for me by hand. She even illustrated the poems and stitched the pages together with great care. I received this hand-made book on my twenty-first birthday – 2 June 1944 – in the Warsaw ghetto. Had I ever been given a more beautiful present? I am not sure. I had certainly never received one on which more care had been lavished – or more love.

So there we sat together, Tosia and I, in the dark night, with poor light, slowly and thoughtfully reading the German verses she had copied for me. Now and then, we heard German shots and Jewish cries from a nearby ghetto entrance. We started, we trembled. But we continued to read the *Lyrical Medicine Cabinet*. We, who had not known love for long, were enchanted by the slightly sentimental yet wonderful *Sachliche Romanze* [*Businesslike Romance*]. We read about the couple who, after eight years, had suddenly lost their love, 'the way other people lose a stick or a hat', and who simply could not understand it. We thought of our future together, which, we were convinced, could not be – except perhaps in some concentration camp. We read the irritating questions *Kennst du das Land, wo die Kanonen blühn?* [Do you know the land where the cannon bloom?] – that witty persiflage of Goethe's *Kennst du das Land, wo die Zitronen blühn?* [Do you know the land where the lemons bloom?] – and *Wo bleibt das Positive, Herr Kästner?* [What's happened to the positive, Herr Kästner?]. We smiled at the characterization of the climber: *Die Ahnen kletterten im Urwand / Er ist der Affe im Kulturwald* [His ancestors climbed in the primeval forest / He is the ape in the cultural forest]. We were alarmed by the warning: *Nie dürft ihr so tief sinken, / von dem Kakao, durch den man euch zieht, / auch noch zu trinken* [Never must you sink so low / as to drink / from the cocoa through which they drag you]. And in the midst of the hardships of the

24

Warsaw ghetto we were struck by the two verses entitled 'Moral', by those eight words: *Es gibt nichts Gutes / ausser man tut es!* [There is nothing good / unless you do it!].

I know that Kästner's 'lyrics for daily use' do not fall into the category of great German poetry. Nevertheless his intelligent, ingenious and perhaps slightly sentimental poems affected and moved me, indeed delighted me. What was taking place around us every day could not fail to affect my reading matter. At a time when death was to be expected any day, I found it hard to read novels or even short stories.

Over the five-year span of the German occupation of Poland I never read a single novel, not even the one which enjoyed unexpected success in the ghetto, being passed from hand to hand – Franz Werfel's *Die vierzig Tage des Musa Dagh* [*The Forty Days*], the story of the persecution and murder of the Armenians during the First World War. In that book many Jewish readers believed they discerned parallels to their own situation.

But I did read poetry, most often Goethe and Heine. Despite the miserable everyday situation their work still interested me. Admittedly some other poets, who were not among my favourites anyway, became alien to me, if not unbearable at this time. These were the poets with the hieratic gestures, the prophets, the secret whisperers, the 'custodians of the sacred fire'. The oracular diction of such poets as Friedrich Hölderlin, Stefan George and to some extent Rainer Maria Rilke, got on my nerves; their sometimes magnificent verbal music had lost its magic – although not for ever, as would emerge later.

It is of course incongruous to mention Kästner in the same breath as Rilke and George, let alone Hölderlin. But in some situations in life one has a weakness for Gershwin and no patience with Bruckner's symphonies. That is why, for a time, the scepticism and humour of Erich Kästner's big-city poetry was infinitely closer to me than the poetry of the seers.

There was another reason why I was drawn to the work of Kästner, but I did not give it much thought in the Warsaw ghetto. The *Lyrical Medicine Cabinet* reminded me of the spirit and climate of that Weimar Republic culture (the often misused word is correct here) which had so fascinated me in the last few years before Hitler – even though I was still a child – and during the first few years after the Republic's collapse, when I could scarcely tear myself away from the books and gramophone records, the periodicals and programme leaflets of the 1920s. Of course it was pure chance that I discovered Kästner's poems in 1941. They could just as well have been verses by Bertolt Brecht or feuilletons by Kurt Tucholsky, or journalistic reports by Joseph Roth or Egon Erwin Kisch, book reviews by Alfred Kerr or Alfred Polgar, the songs from *The Threepenny Opera* or from *Mahagonny*, or those from *The Blue Angel*, the voices of Marlene Dietrich, Lotte Lenya or Ernst Busch, of Fritzi Massary and Richard Tauber, the drawings of George Grosz or the photo-montages of John Heartfield. All these evoked the world which had moulded me and which, until recently, I had felt to be my own, the world I had loved and from which I had been expelled and exiled.

The thought never struck me that I might one day make Kästner's acquaintance. Apart from the fact that my chances of surviving the war were microscopically small, if anyone had predicted that I would meet Kästner I would probably have replied that this was as absurd as meeting Wilhelm Busch or Christian Morgenstern. However, in the autumn of 1957, when I was once again living in Poland, I visited the Federal Republic. My journey began in Hamburg and took me via Cologne and Frankfurt to Munich. I immediately tried to find out Kästner's telephone number. That was by no means easy, but I got it eventually. When Kästner learned that I was a critic from Warsaw – such visitors were rare in Munich then – he did not demur. He suggested meeting at the Café Leopold in Schwabing.

His work was popular again, just as in the old days, prior to 1933. He was esteemed, even though, I believed, still underrated. He had recently been awarded the Büchner Prize. A seven-volume edition of his *Collected Writings* was in preparation. Yet the impression he made was less of a dignified gentleman than of an exceedingly charming one, slim and good-looking, smart and elegant. Considering that he was now fifty-eight, he seemed surprisingly youthful.

When he had politely answered my questions Kästner asked how I had fared during the war. As concisely as possible I told him about the Warsaw ghetto, about discovering his poems, and I showed him the handwritten, by then somewhat tattered, copy of his *Lyrical Medicine Cabinet*. He was surprised and fell silent. He had been able

26

to imagine a lot of things, but not that his verses were read in the Warsaw ghetto, or that they were copied by hand the way literary texts were copied in the Middle Ages. He was moved and I believed he had tears in his eyes.

I did not see Kästner again until the autumn of 1963, when we were both members of a jury for a 'German Raconteur Prize', endowed by *Der Stern*. The jury met at the Schlosshotel Kronberg near Frankfurt. I happened to be by the reception desk when Kästner arrived. He greeted me amicably and immediately turned away to order a double whisky. Only when he had downed it was he ready to fill in the hotel registration form. During the jury sessions, too, which he attentively followed without saying much, he drank alcohol at regular intervals.

The third and last time I met Erich Kästner was towards the end of January 1969. North German Radio had asked me to interview him for television on the occasion of his seventieth birthday. The recording was made in a café, one of whose regular customers Kästner had been during his time in Berlin and which he was fond of mentioning in conversation – the Café Mampe on Kurfürstendamm between Joachimsthaler Strasse and the Gedächtniskirche. At that time the café still looked much as it had before the war. Kästner arrived punctually and looking, at least it seemed to me, as lively as ever. One might have taken him for a man of sixty. But in fact his condition was sad and pitiful. Even during our preliminary conversation he found it difficult to concentrate. His replies were vacuous and slightly confused: they were little more than clichés and I was shocked. I probably feared the impending television interview even more than he did.

I tried to prepare him for all the questions I was going to ask him. But most of these perfectly simple questions seemed to him too difficult; he would not, he said, be able to answer them. I felt sorry for him in his scarcely concealed helplessness. I wanted to help him, to make matters as easy for him as possible. The people from North German Radio were also very patient – maybe because, as we discovered later, they had all read *Emil and the Detectives*. The phrases which Kästner eventually spoke into the microphone made it clear that his memory was scarcely functioning any more. Altogether we managed to record fourteen minutes. Ultimately no more than two or three of these could be used – and they were rather poor. Having drunk alcohol throughout the interview, he was now totally exhausted. We could no longer understand his babbling. When he tried to stand up, he had to be supported. The waiters were watching him in silence. We got him into a taxi. When I shook hands with him in parting he tried to smile.

A few days later I received a letter from Kästner. In the envelope was a harmless occasional poem, *An die Gratulaten*. It ended with the verses: *Bin gerührt und trotzdem heiter. / Danke sehr. Und mache weiter* [Am touched, yet cheerful. / Many thanks. Am going on]. Evidently he had wanted to add a personal word, and so he wrote under the poem: *Dear expert, Mampe is a pleasant place and we are charming people. Yours Kästner.*

On 29 July 1974 – by which time I had become responsible for the literature section of the daily newspaper *Frankfurter Allgemeine* – our no-longer-young office boy brought me a note from the German Press Agency, putting it on my desk with his usual resigned remark: 'Another corpse for you.' I read it quickly: the German poet Erich Kästner had died in a Munich hospital. As always in such cases I glanced at the clock. Yes, the obituary could just be managed before the deadline. But it had to be done in a hurry. Before I started work on it I telephoned Tosia who, in the Warsaw ghetto in 1941, had copied his poems. Her reaction was: 'Oh no!' Then the line went quiet. If I remember rightly, my eyes were moist – and I imagine hers were too.

In 1998 we, Tosia and I, received a rather unusual request. The author and publisher Michael Krüger wanted us to edit a volume of Kästner's lyrical poetry. Tosia was to choose the poems and I was to write the epilogue. We gladly complied. As a title for the book we chose a formula of Kästner's: '*To Be Applied to the Soul.*'

4

REVERENCE FOR WRIT

The National Socialist regime had an immediate impact on the pupils of the Werner von Siemens-Realgymnasium in Berlin-Schöneberg. On the morning of 28 February 1933, during the main break towards ten o'clock, we were engaged, as usual, in a game we called 'baseball' but which had little in common with the real thing: we had to make do with 'balls' cunningly twisted from sandwich paper. We scarcely noticed that the senior pupils were standing about in groups in the school yard, talking excitedly.

It was not until after the break, when one of our teachers stood outside our classroom and curtly directed us to the assembly hall, that we suspected that something unusual had happened. The head-master, a quiet man, then addressed us – clearly and factually, without displaying any emotion. The Reichstag, he informed the assembled students, had been set alight during the night and was presumably still burning. This was stale news to me because, at five or six in the morning, the telephone in our flat had rung and woken us all. My Uncle Max, the patent agent, a cheerful and jovial person who was always on the lookout for news, especially if it concerned Hitler and the Nazis, could hardly control himself. He had an irresistible urge to give us some sensational news. It was not 'The Reichstag is on fire', but 'The Nazis have set fire to the Reichstag.'

The headmaster's address hinted at the same thing, though indir-ectly. 'I forbid all pupils', he said, 'to suggest that the National Socialists have set fire to the Reichstag.' Many of us pricked up our ears. This prohibition gave us an idea that would probably not otherwise have occurred to us. Why had our headmaster said this?

Was he simple-minded, or did he intend to be provocative? We certainly did not see much more of him. He soon disappeared from the school – for political reasons, it was said. Things were sometimes that simple.

The spirit of the new rulers did not at first make itself felt in our lessons. But now and again there were incidents which had been unknown before 1933. During a handball game pupil R. believed he had been the victim of a foul by pupil L. They were both good players, but one was a Hitler Youth leader and the other a Jew. In the heat of combat R. shouted at L.: 'You filthy Jew!' In 1934, such insults were not customary in our school. Thus the incident grew into a minor scandal.

The matter came to the ears of our form teacher, Dr Reinhold Knick. In his next lesson he made a somewhat solemn speech; his voice seemed to shake a little: 'As a Christian I cannot condone that ... Let us never forget that our Saviour was a Jew too.' We all listened in silence, including the Hitler Youth leader R. But outside school R. ceased to be silent. A few days later Knick was summoned to the regional office of the Hitler Youth (or some such authority) and shortly afterwards he was interrogated by the Gestapo. He pleaded his Christian conscience, which did not help him much: he was warned, even threatened. The consequences were not slow in coming. At the end of the academic year he was transferred – to the Hohenzollern-Gymnasium, also in Berlin-Schöneberg.

To none of my teachers during the years 1930 to 1938 do I owe as much as I do to Dr Knick. I do not know whether he came from the Youth Movement, as was reported, but there was always something of that movement about him. He was in his early or mid-fifties, tall and slim, with fair, thinning hair and pale-blue eyes. He was an enthusiast, one of those who believed that life had no meaning without literature or music, without art or theatre, and, to older students, he was known as 'the blond romantic'. He was marked by the poetry of his youth – by Rilke, Stefan George, and by the early work of Gerhart Hauptmann, which he loved although with some reservations. Stefan George's verses: *Wer je die Flamme umschritt / Bleibe der Flamme Trabant!* [Whoever walked round the flame / let him remain the flame's adherent!], sounded not like a reminder but like an avowal when spoken by him.

Reinhold Knick was not only a multi-faceted and outstanding teacher – he taught mathematics and physics, chemistry and biology, as well as German. He was also an artist, a producer, an actor and a musician. He was fond of presenting literary texts whether the syllabus provided for them or not, especially humorous ones, and we often benefited from his skill at recitation. For instance, he amused us with Wilhelm Busch's poem *Balduin Bählamm*. When he read the first act of Hauptmann's *Biberpelz* to us, the whole class roared with laughter. More than that: we instantly understood what the concept 'naturalism' meant. Simultaneously Knick influenced my choice of reading matter. Enthusiastic about *Biberpelz*, I immediately read half a dozen of Hauptmann's plays. I understood that literature could be – and should be – entertaining. I have never forgotten this.

Even in my day a theatrical production which Knick had staged in the school assembly hall in the early 1920s was still remembered with enthusiasm. The successful Berlin theatre manager and producer Victor Barnowsky had found it so remarkable and original that he immediately invited the amateur to produce a play at his Lessing Theater. Knick finally allowed himself to be persuaded and Barnowsky was sure he had made a sensational discovery.

But after a few rehearsals Knick asked to be released from his contract. The rehearsals, he said, had shown him that he was unable to realize the theatre he had in mind with professional actors. Most of these were too anxious to score effects. He therefore preferred to continue to work with amateurs.

I only saw one of his productions, Shakespeare's *Tempest*, in 1936, by which time I had moved on to the Fichte-Gymnasium and Knick was teaching at the Hohenzollern-Gymnasium. He himself played Prospero. I was deeply impressed but had a number of reservations, which concerned more than just details. I wanted to talk to him openly about these, so I arranged to visit him at his flat in Steglitz.

Knick had extensively adapted the text and, among other things, made Prospero's epilogue end with the final line of Hebbel's *Nibelungen*: '*In the name of Him who died on the Cross*'. Such a Christianization of Shakespeare seemed to me not only a stylistic offence, but altogether inadmissible. To my astonishment he immediately agreed with me. But he added that, in view of what was happening

31

in Germany, it was not enough to produce good theatre. It was also necessary to remind the audience of ideals, which were now more important than ever. That was why he had accepted the price of a stylistic offence.

I permitted myself another objection. In *The Tempest*, I argued, two worlds confronted one another – a gentle and noble, reflective and melancholy one, with Prospero, his daughter Miranda and the aerial spirit Ariel at its centre, and the rather vulgar, partly plebeian and partly animalistic world of the misshapen slave Caliban, the jester Trinculo and the ever drunk master of the wine cellar Stephano. I was interested, I explained, in the poetical, intellectual world; I had no patience with the other, the coarse and primitive one, indeed it repulsed me. But Knick, in his production, had unfortunately given free rein to the simple and common elements of the play, thereby establishing an equilibrium which did not benefit *The Tempest* but damaged it.

Knick was in no way impatient with this presumptuous fifteen-or sixteen-year-old. Instead he listened carefully to everything I said, and his response went something like this: 'I understand you, but you mistake reality. Human society consists not only of representatives of the spirit like Prospero with his large library; it also includes such beings as Caliban, much as you may dislike them. They are two sides of the same coin, and both are important. Take care – especially nowadays – not to perceive just the one side and overlook the other. I believe you have a great weakness for intellectuals. There's nothing to be said against that, except that this weakness should be kept in check – one should be careful not to disregard everything else.' I have since seen *The Tempest* on the stage many times; the best production was probably in Hamburg in 1960, with Walter Gründgens as Prospero. But nothing had changed: I felt respect without warming to the play. One has got to face it: there are world-famous works which one reveres rather than loves.

I was allowed to visit Knick many more times at his Steglitz flat – always at 5 p.m., and invariably at 6 p.m. his wife would knock at the door as a sign that I was to take my leave. To make the most of the time available to me I always prepared myself thoroughly for these visits. I would make a list of many names and titles. I would report to him about my reading, and he would confirm or correct my impressions and judgements. Why, I have since wondered, did he take so much trouble with me? Did it amuse him to answer my questions about literature? I believe there was an additional reason: the attention he devoted to me had something to do with the Third Reich and the persecution of the Jews.

I often thought of Knick during the war, of his recommendations and warnings. When I returned to Berlin, in 1946, I immediately went out to Steglitz. Of course he asked me how I had managed to survive and how my family had fared. He listened in silence to my scanty report. He was reluctant to speak about what the Nazis had done to him and his family. At the end of the war he was promoted and became a secondary school headmaster.

Casually he remarked that many of his visitors now wore American or British uniforms. These were his former Jewish pupils. They all – he said – spoke a lot about gratitude. But he really did not know what they should be grateful to him for. I had a pretty good idea, but I can only speak for myself: he, Reinhold Knick, was the first person in my life who represented German idealism and personified that which, until then, I had only known from literature – the ideals of the German classics.

That the reality of the Third Reich called these ideals into question and refuted them, in the most brutal and barbaric manner, is obvious. No one, apart from the communists, came to experience this so painfully as the Jews. They were being continually harassed and discriminated against: not a week, not a day, passed without new regulations and decrees – in other words, without the Nazis inflicting all kinds of new humiliations. The Jews were being systematically excluded from the German nation – the term now, increasingly, was the 'people's community'.

During the first few years after the Nazi seizure of power, quite a few of those humiliated and persecuted sought protection and asylum in Judaism. What had long become a matter of indifference to them, something from which they had even deliberately turned away, now acquired new significance for them. Vastly more people attended services in the synagogues – and these were obviously not just believers. Jewish organizations recorded an unmistakable increase in membership. This was particularly true of the younger generation, of teenagers. Did it also apply to me?

My grandfather, that provincial rabbi whose flat we shared, was by then over eighty, frail and blind. It was part of my duties to keep him company each day for about a quarter of an hour. He told me all kinds of stories and anecdotes about his learned ancestors. These conversations were neither useful nor particularly interesting to me, the less so as he often repeated himself and no longer perceived the world around him.

One day, however, he surprised me by asking me what I wanted to be. I answered truthfully that I did not know yet. At that, he gave me a surprising piece of advice: our conversations had convinced him that I was well suited for the profession of rabbi; that was the occupation which, in line with family tradition, I should take up. To make the idea more palatable to me, he added that being a rabbi was a good job for a lazybones. Clearly he was a matter-of-fact man with a sense of humour. But as a rabbi's principal function is that of teacher, it may be that my grandfather did not misjudge me all that much. Because in the profession which, after a good deal of hesitation, I eventually chose, the profession of critic, the pedagogical element also predominates – or should do so.

Grandfather's livelihood was financed by his sons – and, as they were not tight-fisted, their subsidies were also sufficient to cover our – admittedly modest – needs. Throughout my secondary school years I never had a new overcoat and well beyond my school-leaving exam I had to wear cast-offs of my elder brother. But I never found this a hardship and I never protested against it. The fact that my classmates were better dressed never bothered me. When my sister was taken to a casino by an acquaintance and there won fifty or a hundred marks, she made me a present of a fine jacket – known in Berlin as a *Sakko*. It was an experience that, evidently, I never forgot.

The person who should have been responsible for our livelihood, my father, was only in his mid-fifties during my time at school, but already he impressed me as being tired and resigned. All his attempts to make a living in Berlin failed miserably. Whenever we were asked about our fathers' occupation at school, I would envy my classmates, mostly the sons of well-off professional men. While they replied: 'Chemist', 'Lawyer', 'Architect' or, most impressively of all, 'General manager', I, still a child then, was silent and embarrassed. Eventually

I would mumble: 'Businessman', but that was not enough. The teacher wanted more detailed information, and this I could not provide.

My father went to the synagogue regularly, probably more frequently than in Poland, presumably because he felt lonely and isolated in Berlin. He wished me, then eleven or twelve, to accompany him. I was bored during the services because, in all those prayers, I understood only a single word, 'Israel'. So I read the German translation of the texts, which irritated me because, or so it seemed to me, there was only a single sentence endlessly repeated in a variety of forms: 'Praised be the Lord our God'. I could not understand adult men mumbling more or less brainless texts and actually regarding this as a personal dialogue with God. Having attended synagogue with my father a few times I simply refused to go any more, offering the simple explanation that I had absolutely no interest in the divine service and that it sent me to sleep. Weak and benevolent as my father was, he accepted this. I never had any violent arguments with him about it, let alone a quarrel.

Later too, when we were living in the Warsaw ghetto, my good-hearted and good-tempered father was a failure. I wanted to help him. When the ghetto management, the Jews' Council, was looking for temporary office staff I tried – without success – to recommend my unemployed father for one of these jobs. There were worse things in the ghetto, certainly, but I did feel a sense of shame in front of my colleagues because, at the age of twenty, I had to try to find a miserable job for my father, then aged sixty. I therefore never experienced that almost traditional conflict between father and son. Besides, how should such a conflict have arisen? After all, I never hated my father. Unfortunately, I never respected him either; I always simply felt sorry for him.

According to an age-old tradition a Jewish boy, on reaching the age of thirteen, is solemnly accepted into the community of the faithful. I too was expected to submit to that ceremony, called bar mitzvah. Why I did not resist, even though by then I did not want to have anything to do with the Jewish religion, I no longer know – possibly because all my Jewish classmates accepted it without protest. And perhaps also because I wanted to be the centre of attention and receive presents. Nor do I know why the whole business was delayed

35

by a year. The ceremony took place in the (long vanished) synagogue on Lützowplatz.

According to a Jewish maxim, a Jew can live with or against God, but not without God. To make it perfectly clear: I have never lived with or against God. I cannot recall a single moment in my life when I have believed in God. The rebellion of Goethe's Prometheus – '*I pay homage to you? For what?*' – is totally alien to me. During my school days I occasionally endeavoured – unsuccessfully – to grasp the meaning of the word 'God', until one day I came across Lichtenberg's enlightening aphorism: the concise observation that the phrase that God had created man in his image meant, in reality, that man had created God in his image.

When, many years later, I told a friend, a believing Christian, that for me God was no reality at all, but rather a not entirely successful literary figure, comparable perhaps to Oedipus or King Lear, he replied without hesitation that there could be no stronger reality than Oedipus or King Lear. I liked this diplomatic answer, but was not convinced by it. Thanks to Lichtenberg, I found it even easier to live without God.

What I object to most in the Jewish religion is suggested by these verses from Goethe's *Faust*:

> *Statutes and laws, inherited*
> *Like an old sickness, passed on by the dead*
> *Through endless generations, creeping down,*
> *From land to land, from town to town.*
> *Sense becomes nonsense, good deeds dangerous...*

That is what I cannot bear about the Jewish religion – its reluctance and inability to abolish, or at least to reform, countless injunctions and prescriptions which have existed throughout human memory but which have long become nonsensical. In the Ten Commandments it states: '*Six days thou shalt labour and do all thy work. But the seventh day is the sabbath of the LORD, thy God: in it thou shalt not do any work...*' Even as a child I experienced a consequence of this. There were two students in our class from observant Jewish families. They attended class with us on Saturdays because, within the meaning of the observance and sanctification of the sabbath, Jews are allowed, or indeed advised, to devote themselves to learning on the seventh day of the week. Writing, on the other hand, was regarded as work, and the two students were exempt from it.

How then, I asked myself, was one to concern oneself with learning? No one was able to explain that to me. And because strict Jews are not permitted to carry any object whatsoever on the sabbath, these two could not, on Saturday, bring along any exercise or text books, indeed they were not even allowed to have a coin or bunch of keys in their pockets. Those who lived at a distance from the school had to travel by tram or by bicycle. But the religious pupils were not allowed to do this either: Jews are forbidden to ride on a Saturday, on whatever means of transport. These rules outraged me, especially the one which forbade Jews to write on the Sabbath. Very early on, I doubted the good sense of those who strictly observed these regulations.

There was another injunction of the Jewish religion that seemed highly questionable to me at an early age. My grandfather, who of course obeyed all the rules, would call me to his room on a Saturday. He would simply say: 'It's dark in here' – nothing more. My parents explained to me that a pious Jew must not light a fire on a Saturday, and this applied also to turning on the electric light. Grandfather, however, could not ask me to switch on the light because this would have been tantamount to an invitation to commit a sin. That was why he confined himself to the statement that it was getting dark in the room. When I ventured to remark that this was sheer hypocrisy because in effect he was inviting me to commit an alleged sin, I was told that I should accept that this was so. No, I have never accepted that those rules which, in remote prehistory, may have had some validity should continue to be observed. I stuck to Goethe's words: *Sense becomes nonsense, good deeds dangerous.*

But I am also aware, and will never forget, that the Jews have built neither castles nor palaces, erected neither towers nor cathedrals, founded no empires. They have merely strung words together. There is no religion on earth which reveres the word, and writing, more than Judaism. It is more than sixty years now since I stood next to the tabernacle – the cabinet in which the scrolls of the Torah are kept – in the Lützowplatz synagogue, expectant and a little nervous. I cannot forget the moment when the prayer leader carefully took out, and then raised, the parchment scroll with the Five Books of Moses high above the congregation. The believers froze in reverence and bowed to the Writ. I was moved, I held my breath. And whenever I recalled that moment in later years I thought to myself: It is quite right that this moment deeply impressed the child and engraved itself on his memory. Things like this could not fail to interest a literary man, and would stay with him all his life.

Even so, that was the last time, towards the end of 1934, that I took part in a religious service. No, that is not quite correct. I attended a Jewish service at the end of 1990 – in the Old-New Synagogue in Prague. But on that occasion I was a tourist. Besides, paradoxical as it may be, I owe whatever I learned about Judaism in my youth chiefly to the Prussian *Gymnasium* during the years of the Third Reich.

For how long Jewish religious instruction was allowed to continue in Berlin schools I cannot recall – but it was certainly still taught in 1936 and perhaps even in 1937. Twice a week one of the well-known rabbis from the west of the city came to the school. I believe he was not allowed to enter the staff-room, but we, the few remaining Jewish students, had a classroom at our disposal in which perfectly ordinary Jewish religious instruction could take place.

I still have a clear memory of one of those teachers of religion. This was Max Nussbaum, who was both very elegant and exceptionally young: he was only twenty-six, but had taken his doctorate three years previously and was a popular preacher and witty teacher. In 1940 he emigrated to the United States, became a rabbi in Hollywood and rose to be one of the most important Jewish figures in North America. Some publications gave him special credit for having accepted into Judaism three famous actors – Marilyn Monroe, Elizabeth Taylor and Sammy Davis jr.

On the evening of my bar mitzvah in 1933 there was the customary dinner party for the entire family at our flat – there were about fifteen guests. But I was disappointed. Not only was I not the centre of attention, no one took any notice of me. The conversation at table was very excited, but it was about a different subject. The Reich radio had reported that a conspiracy against Adolf Hitler, headed by the SA chief of staff, Ernst Röhm, had with Hitler's participation been savagely crushed by the SS and the Gestapo. No one yet knew how many people had been murdered – the term 'Röhm putsch' had not yet been coined.

By now, many Jews had already left the Reich. Those especially endangered – Social Democrats and communists together with many writers and journalists who had, during the Weimar Republic, engaged themselves against the National Socialists – fled during the first days or weeks after the Reichstag fire. Others were able to prepare their departure and take at least some of their possessions with them.

At once two conflicting attitudes emerged among the Jews. One stated: After what has happened there is no longer any place for us in this country; we should not indulge in any illusions but emigrate as soon as possible. The other held: Let us not lose our heads, but rather let us wait and see; nothing is eaten as hot as it is cooked. Quite a few tried to convince themselves that the anti-Semitic agitation was directed against the eastern Jews and not against the Jews who had lived in Germany for centuries. Those who had served in the First World War, and had even been decorated for their bravery, believed that nothing could happen to them. Frequently their non-Jewish friends and acquaintances tried to reassure them, with the best possible intentions: surely an inhuman regime such as the Nazis was unthinkable in Germany in the long run. After two, or at most three, years the party would be overthrown. So it made no sense to dispose of one's possessions and abandon one's home.

At the festive bar mitzvah dinner in our flat, both views were expressed. Even though the brutality and evident lawlessness of what had happened horrified everybody, the latest news was also viewed as evidence of the regime's weakness. Those who considered it right and possible, in spite of discrimination, to remain in Germany, those who therefore hoped to survive the Third Reich in situ, saw Hitler's barbaric handling of the opposition from within his own ranks as a confirmation of their optimism.

From today's perspective it is astonishing, to say the least, that the number of Jews leaving Germany did not increase despite their systematic persecution, despite the introduction of monstrous measures such as the Nuremberg Laws in September 1935. Whereas some 37,000 emigrated in 1933, the figures for 1934, 1935, 1936 and 1937 remained between 20,000 and 25,000. What kept the overwhelming majority of Jews from emigrating for so long is easily explained – it was their faith in Germany. That faith was only shaken by the night of the German pogroms in November 1938, the Kristallnacht – and, this was by no means true of all the Jews living in Germany.

My parents had neither money nor contacts, they lacked initiative, energy and efficiency. They did not even think of emigrating. My brother, nine years older than me, a quiet and reticent person, had completed his secondary school education while still in Poland and then studied dentistry at the University of Berlin. Because he had Polish citizenship he was able to continue and complete his studies despite the Third Reich. He took his degree in 1935 with a doctoral thesis which was graded '*Summa cum laude*'.

What about me? Private contacts or even friendship between Jewish and non-Jewish pupils, until then perfectly normal, gradually ceased in 1934 and 1935. We were excluded from school ceremonies, excursions and sporting events. Each of the dwindling number of Jewish pupils tried to cope with this exclusion in his own way. This, together with the fact that I felt lonely anyway, was probably the reason why I sought, and expected to find, contact in a Zionist youth organization, the Jewish Pathfinder Association of Germany. That was a mistake, though not a regrettable one.

The regular excursions, known as outings, sometimes took up several days and, during holidays, also took place on Saturdays – because this Jewish association was unconcerned with anything religious. We slept in barns or in tents. It was then that I came to know that part of eastern Germany which I have always been fond of, the Mark Brandenburg, the heartland of Prussia.

Of course we sang songs, but not Jewish hiking songs because these did not exist. So we sang '*Prinz Eugen, der edle Ritter*' and '*Vom Barette schwankt die Feder*', '*Görg von Frundsberg führt uns an*' and '*Dem Frundsberg sind wir nachgerannt, der Fahne haben wirs geschworen*' – in other words, traditional German *Landsknecht* songs. We sang '*Wildgänse rauschen durch die Nacht*' without realizing that these verses were by Walter Flex, and we liked songs like '*Die Glocken stürmten vom Berwandsturm*' and '*Jenseits des Tales standen ihre Zelte*', unperturbed by the fact that their author, Börris von Münchhausen, was now a follower and indeed an admirer of the Nazis. In short, the songs of the Pathfinder movement included those which were also being sung by the Hitler Youth, where, incidentally, 'Jenseits des Tales' was prohibited after the Röhm putsch, presumably because of its homoerotic associations. Thus, surprisingly, I also came to know this branch of the German tradition.

The 'home evenings' of the Jewish Pathfinder Association, however, directed my interest to quite different subjects, chiefly to an intellectual whose writings and diaries I read at once and for whom, regardless of their ideological and political aspect, I still have a lot of sympathy. This was Theodor Herzl, an Austrian Jew who has achieved the unprecedented – he had helped to change the world by a novel.

At first Herzl was nothing other than a typical, if exceptionally intelligent, Viennese coffee-house writer, a good columnist and the author of mediocre comedies which, nevertheless, were staged by the Burgtheater. He had little in common with Judaism, and nothing with Jewish religion. It was the Dreyfus trial in Paris in 1894, which he attended as a reporter, that brought about a change in him. Herzl became a statesman, albeit without a state, a prophet whose utopia has become reality. Being a man of letters he chose a novel for his vision of the state of Israel. It was published in 1902 under the title *Altneuland* [*Old New Land*].

It is paradoxical that the modern Jewish state had its origins in a work of German literature, an artistically insignificant novel with truly enormous consequences. Of course I did not appreciate this at the time, or even suspect it. I was probably impressed by the author's magnificent fantasy, by the assimilated, German-speaking Jew with his unusual boldness and grandiose talent for organization.

But neither the Mark Brandenburg, nor the songs of the Pathfinders, neither Theodor Herzl nor the vision of the state of Israel made me feel at home in this youth organization. There seemed to be no outlet there for my great passion, literature. Yet there was one home evening which delighted and disturbed me and made me reflect whether my place was not, after all, in that organization.

One of our leaders, probably little over twenty, switched off the ceiling lights and pulled a lectern from the wall into the centre of the room. Then, to our surprise, he withdrew into another room. A few minutes later, awaited by us in silence, he slowly and solemnly re-entered the nearly dark assembly room. He was wearing a long military greatcoat from the First World War; in one hand he held a

41

torch and in the other a slim book. It was a green-and-white-patterned volume of the Insel-Bücherei. The young man began to read: '*Riding, riding, riding. And the spirit is grown so weary, the longing so great.*'

Not only was *The Lay of the Love and Death of Cornet Christoph Rilke* unfamiliar to me; the theatrical way in which the writing of the young Rilke was presented by that costumed amateur in the half-darkened room probably contributed to my almost falling in love with the poetry. '*Begun a banquet, it became a ball – one can't tell how*' – these words have never lost their charm for me. Nor has the magic of the rhythm: it was '*a meeting and retreating, a pleasure without measure in the splendour, a choosing of partners but to lose and find them once again*'. And I still hear the final line: '*There he saw an old woman weep.*'

I realize of course that this poem is not one of Rilke's important works: it is as questionable as it is successful, as notorious as it is famous. There is no shortage of the sickly or sentimental, of the precious and the pretentious. Without doubt, anything Rilke wrote in his early years is easily mocked. If I wished to write a damning review of Rilke's *Cornet* I would certainly not find it difficult.

Nevertheless I still have a liking for this poetic prose. I admit as much without feeling ashamed. In Schiller's *Don Carlos*, the Marquis Posa requests the Queen to tell his friend, the Infante:

> *That he should hold in his esteem his dreams*
> *Of youth, if he will be a man one day*
> . . .
>   *That he not stray, e'en if the voice of wisdom*
> *Speak out from muddy depths its calumny*
>   *Against enthusiasm, heaven's daughter.*

Literary works which overwhelmed us because they touched us at the right moment, and therefore remain unforgettable, are an essential part of the dreams of our youth. When one reaches the age of puberty, one is particularly receptive to the emphatic, the highly strung, if at times over-strung, tone of the *Cornet*. Thus it is one of those works of literature about which, in the course of one's life, one has read all kinds of disapproving comment, and perhaps even indulged in it oneself, but to which one nevertheless remains loyal. This is not only because we hold in esteem the dreams of our youth but also because we look back wistfully to the time when enthusiasm, heaven's daughter, inspired and delighted us.

I never again saw the young man, in his army greatcoat, who recited Rilke's rhythmical prose to us. Shortly after that evening, so I was told, he left Germany and emigrated to Palestine. Not until the 1960s did I learn that he had joined the Israeli army and subsequently become one of the best pilots in the air force of the young state. He piloted the plane which brought Adolf Eichmann to Israel in 1960.

After the *Cornet* evening I came up with an idea which was received as a little odd. I proposed that a literary circle be established within the Pathfinder association. This would concern itself with German poetry, especially with that which then interested me most – classical German poetry. Not many teenagers exhibited much interest in literature. There were only five of us, just enough to read Goethe's *Iphigenie auf Tauris*, each part being allocated to one of us. I chose that play because I had heard it on the radio and been impressed by it. Ever since, I have been convinced that *Iphigenie* is not a stage play but a radio play. In other words, it is a work which does not need visual presentation.

However, not even the existence of a literary circle could change my determination to leave the Jewish Pathfinders as soon as possible. I learned quite a few things in that organization but, when all was said and done, it was not the place for me.

5

RACIAL THEORY

'My son is a Pole and a Jew. How will he be treated at your school?'
my mother asked the headmaster of the Fichte-Gymnasium in Berlin-
Wilmersdorf. This was in the winter of 1935. Incidentally, she somewhat exaggerated: I certainly did not consider myself a Pole, but
rather a Berliner. However, I still had Polish citizenship. My parents,
admittedly, had applied for German citizenship and, since my mother
had been a German citizen before her marriage, they had been
promised a favourable and quick decision. But that was in 1932. In
1933, naturally, nothing came of it.

My mother, however, had achieved exactly what she had hoped to
achieve with her somewhat provocative question. The headmaster
assured her, most politely, that her anxieties were quite unnecessary.
After all this was a German, a Prussian, school and that justice was
the supreme principle was a matter of course. For a student to be
discriminated against because of his origins – that was unthinkable
at the Fichte-Gymnasium.

Over lunch, on her return, my mother reported this conversation
to us with obvious satisfaction. It had reinforced her belief that,
despite everything that was happening, there were still upright men
in Germany who practised justice and order.

When, after the Easter holidays, in 1936 I first set foot in the
building of the Fichte-Gymnasium, the headmaster whom my mother
had liked so much was no longer to be seen. Why? They did not
disclose that kind of thing to us students. But there were rumours of
compulsory retirement. His successor was called Heiniger. On
national holidays he appeared in an elegant brown uniform with gold

44

trimmings: he was a 'Golden Pheasant' – the popular term for the senior officials of the National Socialist German Workers' Party (NSDAP).

My change of schools was made necessary by the closure of my former school, the Werner von Siemens-Realgymnasium, in 1935. That was an unusual measure. Not so long ago, in the much-maligned Weimar Republic, schools used to be founded, not closed down. Its dissolution, as may be guessed, was linked to the political situation. In Schöneberg, especially in the neighbourhood of the Bayerischer Platz and the Viktoria-Luise-Platz, there lived a relatively large number of Jews. Some had already emigrated, others were no longer able to afford to send their children to secondary schools, largely because Jews had been deprived of the right to apply for exemption from, or a reduction in, tuition fees. In consequence, the number of students at the Werner von Siemens-Realgymnasium dropped dramatically soon after the Nazi seizure of power. Moreover, the school was said to have a particularly bad reputation in the eyes of the new regime: it was regarded as liberal, if not actually 'left wing'.

As the next few years would prove, I was lucky: the teachers at the Fichte-Gymnasium, whether they were Nazis or not, on the whole treated the Jews decently and correctly. As every lesson opened with the words '*Heil Hitler*' we knew at once, the moment a teacher entered the classroom, where he stood politically.

The salute gave it away. Some teachers would salute smartly and with military precision, while others would utter the words softly and give a careless salute. But although nearly all the staff with whom I had any dealings could be divided into two categories, I do not mean Nazis and non-Nazis. The demarcation line lay on a different plane. One lot were honest, dutiful civil servants – no more and no less. Whether they taught Latin or mathematics, German or history made no difference. They came into class well prepared and followed the prescribed syllabus. Provided they did not annoy us or make excessive demands on us, we behaved correctly towards them. There was something like indifference on both sides.

The other teachers were likewise not necessarily passionate educators. But one did feel some kind of passion in them. Perhaps they had dreamed of a different profession in their youth: maybe they had wanted to become scientists or writers, musicians or painters. Their ambitions had not materialized, whatever the reasons, and so they had found themselves trapped in the education system. But this did not diminish their love of music or literature, art or science, or lessen their admiration of the French ésprit or the English mentality.

This love, this yearning, this admiration gave them the strength, in their daily dealings with young people, to repress their bitterness and overcome their resignation. Admittedly, this second group of teachers was not always well prepared, and they did not hesitate to deviate occasionally from the official syllabus. Because what they imparted to us, on the margin of teaching, as it were, was not boring and stimulated our imagination, we were mostly grateful to them for that.

There was one teacher, no longer young, who explained to us at length that all past interpretations of *Hamlet* were inadequate or even incorrect. A book by him would shortly come out, presenting a new, definitive interpretation. I saw a copy of it in the window of a bookshop near our school soon after publication. However, not a single paper so much as mentioned this allegedly pioneering work. I have long forgotten the name of this teacher, but his committed expositions, even though they frequently led down blind alleys, enhanced my interest in Shakespeare and triggered my own ideas.

Some teachers succeeded, apparently effortlessly, in inspiring us. One such enthusiastic teacher was Fritz Steineck. He had a single passion – music. No matter whether he was discussing a Haydn oratorio, a Schubert *Lied* or a Wagner opera, he always spoke with great commitment. It was enormously important to him – or so it seemed to us – to convince us that a particular passage by Mozart or Beethoven was superb, and to explain why. He seemed to be genuinely grateful to those who were seriously interested in music – including the Jews. Indeed, he was particularly fond of Jewish pupils because most of them were musical and many played the piano or the violin. I do not recall any Nazi songs featuring in his lessons.

When, with shining eyes, he spoke to us about *Tannhäuser*, playing or singing to us the more important scenes, he drew our attention to a situation which he believed was often underestimated. At the beginning of the second act, immediately following Elisabeth's entrance aria, the stage directions read: '*Tannhäuser, accompanied by Wolfram, enters from the stairs in the background*'. When Elisabeth

46

catches sight of Tannhäuser, Wolfram sings: *'There she is, approach her undisturbed.'* This is followed by the direction: *'He remains backstage, leaning against the balustrade.'* This, according to Steineck, was a moving moment. Because Wolfram loves Elisabeth, but – and this emerges here for the first time – withdraws in favour of Tannhäuser. This was a case of noble self-denial. Whenever you see *Tannhäuser*, Steineck prophesied, you will think of me at that point. He was right – at least as far as I am concerned.

When those students who played an instrument were asked to perform something, one of them – a Jew – hammered out a miserable hit-song, unlike the rest who always played classical pieces. We were afraid that Steineck would severely reprimand him. But the incident had not outraged him, only saddened him. He said quite softly: 'That was bad music. But even bad music can be played properly.' He asked for the sheet music, picked it up with his finger-tips to indicate his distaste, and sat down at the piano. It was not beneath his dignity to play the song to us. He was a brilliant teacher, a lovable person, and I owe a lot to him.

As a postscript I should mention something I did not learn until many years later, in 1982. That music teacher, Steineck, had been a long-serving member of the Nazi Party, not just a fellow traveller. Ever since the late 1920s he had been an enthusiastic follower of Hitler. There is something else I discovered about him: at the Fichte-Gymnasium it was customary to bid farewell to the graduates each year with the song '*Nun zu guter Letzt*', sung by the school choir. This song, dating back to 1848, its words written by Hoffmann von Fallersleben, now had a fatal flaw, one which until then had escaped notice: its music was composed by a Jew – Felix Mendelssohn-Bartholdy.

Steineck found a way round this delicate situation. He simply wrote a new tune to the old text. He, who had spent years convincing us that there was nothing finer and nobler on earth than music, felt no inhibitions, no shame, about 'dejudaizing' or 'aryanizing' that song. Why did he lend himself to such a shameful deed? What was behind it? Certainly neither ignorance nor love of music; more probably ambition and vanity. Or did he wish to please the powerful headmaster, Heiniger, the 'Golden Pheasant'?

This Heiniger was the only member of staff who, if I remember correctly, frequently revealed himself as an ardent Nazi during lessons. But on no account should he be confused with the often vulgar SA men in the street. There was nothing military about the appearance of this fifty-year-old man with his bald pate. He did not behave like an officer inspecting his company or battalion. Instead he was anxious to convey to us students the relaxed manner of a general. At times he allowed it to be understood that he knew infinitely more about the new state than could be read in the papers. Not a minor Nazi therefore, but one of the powerful and initiated élite – that was how we were meant to see him.

Heiniger taught our form history. He talked a lot and examined rarely, regarding himself as a professor, not as a crammer. He treated us courteously, as if we were already at university. Nor had the Jewish students any cause for complaint – myself least of all. He was pleasant to me and never – I was grateful to him for that – asked me about historical facts or dates. He believed I was good, primarily, at interpreting history and would sometimes converse with me during lessons as though with an adult, an equal. That, of course, was merely tactics. He wanted to hear my views so that he could the more effectively refute them from the National Socialist point of view – in which he succeeded effortlessly.

One day he surprised the class with an announcement that the Jewish pupils would be 'exempted' from the next history lesson. The lesson, as it emerged later, was devoted to a discussion of 'world Jewry'. That, at least, the Jewish pupils were to be spared. But his views on Jews had no effect on the marks he handed out. He always gave me a 'Good' – the highest grade ever given in our form for history – and did likewise in my school-leaving certificate.

He was a fair man, Heiniger. If, however, his superiors had ordered that Jews had to stand during lessons or only enter the school barefoot, he would undoubtedly have carried out the instruction and in fine, well-chosen words justified it as a historical necessity. No, we did not have to enter the school barefoot – but our skulls were measured, including those of some non-Jewish students. This happened in 'racial theory' lessons, a new subject introduced in the Third Reich, the sole purpose of which was to convince the pupils of the inferiority of the Jews and the superiority of the 'Aryans'. The subject was taken over by the biology masters, in our case by an elderly, sensible man named Thom, whose name led pupils each year to perform the same prank. At the beginning of the autumn term, the door of the form for which he was responsible was always decorated with a notice: '*Uncle Thom's Cabin*'.

Evidently this teacher was not impressed by the new science. He bored us with detailed stories about Neanderthal man and other prehistoric humans. One reason why he was not keen on discussing the issues of Jews may have been the surprising results of the skull measurements. These were performed in accordance with an instruction in the Textbook of Racial Theory and were expected to prove with scientific accuracy the race of the measured individual.

It turned out that only one of our classmates had the typically northern, racially best skull – and he was Jewish. Herr Thom seemed embarrassed by this but by no means put out. With a smile he asked the student whether there might have been some Aryans among his ancestors. His answer was: 'No, only Jews.' Everyone laughed. Incidentally, this classmate – tall and slim, with fair hair and blue eyes – was to have been one of the standard-bearers for the inauguration of the 1936 Olympic Games. When, at the last moment, it was discovered that he was a Jew he was quickly replaced.

It was inevitable that the distance between Jewish and non-Jewish pupils should widen all the time, and this was mainly due to the world outside rather than the teaching of racial theory in schools. The non-Jews were all members of the Hitler Youth, some in an allegedly more distinguished formation, the Naval Hitler Youth, which would exercise on the Havel River. One of them was a senior Jungvolk leader. They often came to school in uniform and were fond of discussing their experiences and adventures, but did not do so when talking to the Jews. I still remember a classmate who, having been allowed to take part in one of the Nuremberg Party Rallies, excitedly boasted in class: 'I stood quite near the Führer. I saw him. I shall never forget his blue eyes.'

From none of my classmates did I ever hear a word against the Jews. Certainly most of them, if not all, believed in the new Germany. They listened to the radio, they read the newspapers more or less thoroughly. Day after day they were exposed to a highly aggressive anti-Semitic propaganda, which was noticeably toned down for the 1936 Olympics, but resumed with increased violence in 1937 and, even more so, in 1938. On our way to school we had to pass the red display cabinets exhibiting the current issue of the anti-Semitic magazine *Der Stürmer* with its notorious cartoons. During the Olympic Games these boxes disappeared. Foreigners were to be given the impression that the Third Reich was a civilized state. Some Jews also made themselves believe that the worst was over and they would now be treated more humanely.

A minor incident seems to me typical of the atmosphere in our school. A young teacher, undoubtedly a Nazi, entered the classroom after the break a little earlier than usual. 'You're making as much noise as in a Jew school,' he said, by no means kindly. Instantly there was silence – an eerie silence. Then the lesson began, but after a few minutes the teacher became aware of the frosty atmosphere. 'What's the matter?' he asked. One of the pupils rose and replied curtly that the remark about the Jew school had not been necessary. The teacher was clearly uncomfortable. He did not understand, he said, why the class should react with such hostility to a phrase in common use in the German language.

Clearly, anti-Semitic remarks were not customary in lessons – at least not in our school or in our form. Did we owe this to the Prussian spirit so revered by the Jews since their emancipation? Or did we pupils of the Fichte-Gymnasium benefit from what was left of the ethos of the West Berlin bourgeoisie? What is certain is that we were treated fairly, even by the Nazis among our teachers.

And our classmates? Why did they not harass us Jews, why did they never give us any trouble? In 1963 we met in Berlin – the survivors of the 1938 graduation class, including four medical men. It went the way such reunions usually go: 'Do you remember?' harmless anecdotes were related, all kinds of reminiscences were exchanged. Some of them spoke, though rather casually, of their professional attainments, of their numerous and far-ranging holiday trips. The cars they drove were also mentioned. The atmosphere was pleasant and lively.

Once or twice, when it was remembered that there were Jews present, the merriment was a little clouded, and a silence fell. This happened when someone mentioned an incident during a school festivity or outing and suddenly broke off in embarrassment because, at that time, the Jews were excluded from them. It was only twenty-five years later that I learned that there had been a high-spirited farewell party following our school-leaving exam, at which some of the teaching staff and some of the students had pledged brotherhood to each other in a rather intoxicated state. The behaviour of some of our classmates was criticized, but only of those who were absent because they had been killed in action.

Casually – but seriously – I was asked how I had survived the war. Surely it would be proper, my classmates no doubt felt, to show some interest. It was a polite question, no more. I replied briefly and concisely. No one wanted to hear details. They were grateful to me when I quickly changed the subject. All of them, educated and thinking people, had been officers in the Wehrmacht, in the east and in the west. They must have experienced horrible and brutal things. Had they been involved in the persecution of Jews? I do not know. That they were aware of what had happened to the Jews, at least in broad outline – of that I am quite certain. Had they ever thought about it – during the war or afterwards, when the German guilt was increasingly emerging? For those two days – that was how long the reunion lasted – my schoolmates betrayed no sign of it, not even during private conversations.

That none of them felt a share of guilt I can understand. Nothing is further from my mind than to hold them guilty. But did they not accept some responsibility for what had been done in the name of Germany? No, nothing was said, they did not wish to speak about it. My well-brought-up classmates who had once worn brown or black uniforms, and subsequently those of the Wehrmacht – they were, I believe, typical representatives of the generation of 1919 and 1920. I had no intention of pursuing the subject. After all, we had not come to Berlin to hear unpleasantnesses; better to let things continue on an amicable note. But I could not restrain myself from disturbing the harmony a little – with a question which concerned not the war years but, our time at school together.

Over the past quarter of a century, I told them, I had often asked myself why, despite the monstrous anti-Semitic propaganda in the Third Reich, our classmates never acted offensively towards us. For a moment they were all silent. Eventually someone said, a little hesitantly: 'Good Lord, how could we believe in the theory of the inferiority of the Jews? Our star pupil in German was a Jew and one of our fastest one-hundred-metre sprinters was also a Jew.'

I was baffled. The answer disappointed me, I found it ludicrous. If I had not been the best student in German and my friend one of the best runners – would it then have been permissible to treat us badly? Was the persecution of the Jews despicable only because the Jews had this or that achievement to their credit? I believe I could easily have convinced my old classmates that they were trying to fob me off with a nonsensical reply. But I felt that I had sufficiently upset the genial atmosphere and let it pass.

The truth was probably different. The behaviour of our teachers – who always treated us Jews politely and decently – may also have played a part in the example they set. Moreover, our fellow pupils came from middle-class homes where the upbringing of children has always been a major concern. Our class was well-behaved; vulgar expressions – the kind that are nowadays continually used even in German literature, especially in a sexual context – were not customary among us. Manners were friendly and polite.

Most importantly: did these teenagers believe official propaganda? Were they convinced that the Jews really were the misfortune of the German nation and of mankind? Quite possibly. But I still believe that in the eyes of these students the National Socialist propaganda was ultimately concerned with an abstract concept (such as 'world Jewry') and was not necessarily applicable to those with whom they shared a desk, from whom they would occasionally copy test papers while offering similar services in return – in short, to the boys they had known and respected for years, their Jewish classmates.

The fact that more and more Jews were disappearing from our school and that those who remained came to be discriminated against and ostracized – this our classmates, the sons of good families and members of the Hitler Youth, probably regarded as a matter of course. They never talked to us about it, they never uttered a word of surprise, let alone of regret. That is what it was like at the Fichte-Gymnasium in Berlin. At other Berlin schools, especially those in the northern and eastern districts, attended chiefly by children of the lower middle and working class, things are said to have been considerably worse. But, according to the recollections of both Jews and non-Jews, it was in the provincial towns that Jewish children had the hardest time. Here they were not infrequently tormented, brutally and sadistically, both by their teachers and their classmates.

I have a particular fond memory of one fellow pupil. He was pleasant and his behaviour towards the Jews was impeccable. When I saw him for the first time after the war – he had by then become a doctor – he told me that in 1940, near the Stettiner railway station, he had caught sight of our old classmate T. among a large group of Jews under police escort. He had looked miserable. 'So I thought T. would feel very embarrassed if I saw him in such a pitiful state. I felt awkward, and I quickly looked the other way.' Yes, that is exactly what happened: millions looked the other way.

6

SEVERAL LOVE AFFAIRS
AT THE SAME TIME

When did my passion for literature begin? I am not quite sure, but my mother must have become aware of it at a very early date. Because when I was twelve she gave me, I forget on what occasion, a very unusual present – a ticket to a performance of *Wilhelm Tell* at the Staatliches Schauspielhaus in the Gendarmenmarkt.

That evening, towards the end of 1932, when for the first time I attended a real stage performance and not just a children's play, was also significant because it marked the beginning of several important love affairs. I mean my love of German literature, my long-lasting love of the theatre, even though this wore off a little over the years, my love of Schiller, which was often severely tested, and finally my love of Schinkel's Schauspielhaus, which has remained my favourite building in Berlin.

The great Jürgen Fehling was the producer of that performance of *Tell*. Who were the actors on the stage during those final months of the Weimar Republic? Does this matter to us today? Perhaps it does a little. The role of Arnold von Melchtal was played by a young, vigorous, rapidly rising actor, already well known and a few years later to become a highly successful film director, showered with praise by the German press. His name was Veit Harlan, and he later produced the vilest, the most infamous, German film that was ever made about and against the Jews – the film of *Jew Süss*.

The part of Tell was played by Werner Krauss, probably the greatest actor of the day. He too was later involved in *Jew Süss*: at his own request he acted not one but several Jews, and it was hard to decide which of them was the most revolting. Tell's wife, Hedwig, was Eleonora von Mendelssohn, a great-granddaughter of Joseph, the eldest son of the philosopher Moses Mendelssohn. She emigrated in 1933 and later committed suicide in the United States.

The actor playing Konrad Baumgarten, who in the first act of *Wilhelm Tell* flees from the henchmen of the Landvogt, was likewise a Jew – Alexander Granach. Soon he had to flee in real life. The part of Johannes Parricida was taken by Paul Bildt. His wife, who was Jewish, was not registered with the authorities in order to escape deportation to Theresienstadt (Terezín). When she died, shortly before the end of the war, she was secretly buried in a park. Bildt and his daughter became totally confused and decided to commit suicide together. Only Bildt survived.

The role of Ulrich von Rudenz was played by Hans Otto, who had never made a secret of being a communist. As soon as the National Socialists came to power he joined the underground resistance and, in November 1933, was murdered while in detention. In the days of the German Democratic Republic a theatre in Potsdam was named after him – it is still called the Hans Otto Theater. And finally, a curiosity: Gessler, the Reich Governor, was brilliantly played by a young character actor whom we were still able to admire on the stage in the 1990s – Bernhard Minetti.

This performance of *Tell* in the Gendarmenmarkt instantly transformed my reading matter. In my parents' rather modest library I found a set of Schiller's works. I was in bed with a slight cold and did not have to go to school, so I simply started on page one of volume one, with the play that opened this edition, *Die Räuber* [*The Robbers*]. No sooner had I read the words *Are you quite well, father?* than I was hooked. All I was interested in was a single question: what was going to happen to those robbers, how would the plot be resolved? I found the play enormously exciting. I read it with flushed cheeks and red ears, and I could not stop reading until I had reached the sentence: *That man may be helped.* And I was happy. Karl Moor fascinated me infinitely more than Old Shatterhand; his robbers were more exciting than all the Red Indians of Karl May.

Over the years I have repeatedly seen this play on the stage. They were more or less successful productions, but I never experienced a really good one. Is *Die Räuber* still stageable? I am not sure. About half a century after this reading in bed, I was invited by Hesse Radio to introduce the film versions of various Schiller plays, including *Die Räuber*. I discussed the weaknesses and faults of this play in detail – which is not difficult as they are all quite obvious. The departmental head responsible was present in the studio: he did not welcome my vehement accusations and criticisms and only breathed again when I said: '*That's it then. All I have to explain now is why I love Die Räuber more than most plays in world literature.*' And, to this day, this has not changed.

My first success as a student of German was also connected with Schiller. I was still at the Werner von Siemens-Realgymnasium. One of my classmates was to give a lecture on *Wilhelm Tell*, but ran out of words after five minutes. The teacher, who had evidently expected more, asked whether anybody else had something to say about the play. I put up my hand and was off. *Tell*, I argued, glorified political assassination and individual acts of terrorism. In order to explain and justify this view I must have used a lot of words, because forty minutes later, when the bell went, I was still on my feet. But the teacher allowed me to conclude my arguments and then curtly commanded: 'Sit down!' Silence descended on the class, everyone expected me to be found guilty of criticizing a classical work. In fact, our teacher said that what I had argued was not sufficiently documented and, in part, also wrong. On the other hand – he added cheerfully – it was not bad at all. To the surprise of the form I was given the best grade – One. I learned two things then – first, that in discussing literature one had to take some risks, and second that one should not let oneself be intimidated by the classics.

I do not wish to conceal that my early weakness for Schiller's play was soon joined by another – a weakness for his popular and often derided ballads. True enough, some of them cannot nowadays be taken altogether seriously, but there are some which I have always read with pleasure. I consider *Die Kraniche des Ibikus* to be one of the most beautiful ballads in the German language.

Then something happened in 1966 which made me disbelieve my eyes. In Volume 3 of an edition of Schiller's Works, the volume devoted to his poetry, the editor, evidently a barbarian, had failed to include *Die Kranich des Ibikus*, as well as *Das Lied von der Glocke*, *Die Bürgschaft*, *Der Graf von Habsburg*, *Der Kampf mit dem Drachen*, *Das verschleierte Bild von Sais*, and other well-known poems. This edition, brought out by a reputable publishing house with a rich tradition, once again demonstrated that the Germans – unlike the French or the English, the Spanish or the Italians – have a fractured and profoundly disturbed relationship with their greatest poets. Incidentally, the barbarian who endeavoured to kill off those Schiller poems was a man of exceptional poetic talent – Hans Magnus Enzensberger.

In our German lessons – and this may seem surprising – little account was taken of the effect of the Third Reich, at least not at our school. This should not be understood as opposition by the teaching staff; as a rule it had nothing to do with politics or ideology, but far more with our teachers' reluctance to deal with a literature they hardly knew. A few things, of course, were sidelined in the new era. Our books still contained poems by Heine, but these appeared without explanation. Classic works that contained Jewish characters or motives, or indeed centred on them, such as Lessing's *Nathan the Wise*, Droste-Hülshoff's *Die Judenbuche* [*The Jew's Beech*], or Hebbel's *Judith*, were no longer mentioned.

As for the authors who were promoted by the new regime – Agnes Miegel and Ina Seidel, Hans Grimm and Hanns Johst, Eberhard Wolfgang Moeller, Hans Rehberg and Hans Friedrich Blunek – our German teachers did not want to know about them. They stuck to what they had read and learned prior to 1933: Schiller's *Kabale und Liebe* and *Wallenstein*, Goethe's *Goetz von Berlichingen* and *Faust*, Theodor Storm's *Der Schimmelreiter* and Gottfried Keller's *Die Leute von Seldwyla*. They knew their way about these books and could teach them most effectively.

'I can't bear the classics, my school spoilt them for me' – one often hears this said. The opposite was true for me. My school, along with the theatre, aroused my interest in literature, from Lessing to Gerhart Haputmann, and more particularly Goethe, Schiller and Kleist, enormously enhanced it, and sometimes directed my enthusiasm to areas unknown to me. The syllabus, admittedly, was a little one-sided, with a marked bias towards northern Germany. Thus our German lessons offered more Kleist and Fontane than Hölderlin and Jean Paul, more Hebbel and Storm than Mörike and Stifter.

Within a period of three years, from 1935 to 1938, I had had three German masters at the Fichte-Gymnasium. They represented – that, of course, was purely accidental – three political trends. The first was a German Nationalist, the second a Liberal, and the third was a Nazi.

What the German Nationalist told us about his experiences during the first post-war years was as patriotic as it was narrow-minded. But when he spoke about Kleist's *Prinz von Homburg* – fairly dividing his sympathies between the Prince, the Elector and Kottwitz – or when he explained to us through the example of Storm what a short story was, then it was obvious that he was a sound German scholar. He respected me and treated me impeccably – without particularly liking me.

Carl Beck, the Liberal, was quite different. This pleasant, jovial man was surely one of those who became teachers because they failed to realize their professional ambitions. Having obtained his doctorate with a dissertation on Gottfried Keller, he was probably a literary man rather than a teacher. It is possible that I was his favourite pupil. We happened to go the same way to school. When I met him I greeted him, as demanded by the school rules, with '*Heil Hitler*' – yes, even the Jews were expected to do so. Beck likewise raised his arm, as one could not be sure that one was not observed by another teacher or student. But he did not say '*Heil Hitler*'. He mumbled '*Good morning*', and then we talked about literature, including Heine.

I nearly always had a One for my essays. My star turn was called 'Mephistopheles – a Characteristic'. On one occasion, however, I only expected an indifferent grade. This was an interpretation of Schiller's poem *Pegasus im Joche*. I had committed a blunder: at the last moment, as we were about to hand in our work, I suddenly realized that a lengthy passage of my carefully structured essay was a bold, but incorrect, thesis. On the spur of the moment I crossed out that part and renumbered my sections. But that, I realized, was an unforgivable sin.

To my extreme surprise, however, Beck awarded my essay a '*Very Good*'. I only mention this incident because of his justification, which impressed me at the time and which I still like. He said something like: 'I'm giving you a One for two reasons. First, for your idea in the deleted passage and secondly because you eventually rejected the idea. It was an original idea, but wrong.'

On one occasion I was very sure of my ground. My essay on

Georg Büchner filled three exercise books – that exceeded the require-
ments and was inappropriate – and it seemed to me a masterpiece.
But I was bitterly disappointed. It was only marked '*Good on the
whole*', a Two minus. I was told to report to Beck in the break –
which was unusual. As students were not allowed into the staff-room,
he came out to speak to me. My piece, he told me, was beyond the
scope of a school essay, but as a literary essay it was not yet good
enough. Hence only '*Good on the whole*'. He looked around to make
sure no one overheard us and added under his breath: 'But when
you've become a critic in Paris, send me a postcard!' Paris then was
the centre of a German exile literature.

I decided to start writing reviews at once. I wanted to review every
production I saw. I acquired a massive ledger and first of all wrote
an extensive account of a production of Ibsen's *Hedda Gabler*, starring
Hilde Hildebrand, who was perhaps better known as a film actress.
I no longer remember what my second review was about, but I am
certain that there never was a third.

In the winter of 1937 my mother went to see Beck to inquire about
my progress and returned home delighted. He had received her very
cordially and given her a surprising piece of advice: 'Dear lady, do
not allow yourself to be confused by the present temporary conditions – and make it possible for your son to study German literature
at the university.' Later I learned that during the war Beck had been
in the habit of always raising his hat in the street to Jews, just as
though they were acquaintances of his, even though, as the law
prescribed, they were identified by a yellow star. Was he a political
person? I did not think so. But he had read the German classics and
taken them seriously. He had taken them to heart. Today when I
think of Carl Beck it is I who feel an urge to raise my hat.

Finally, in my last year at school, I was taught German by a young
Studienassessor who, upon entering the classroom for the first time,
shouted a particularly loud '*Heil Hitler*', thereby proclaiming himself
as a decided Nazi. He was unpopular with nearly all the boys.
Because he belonged to the Nazi Party? No, of course not, but
because he boasted about it. That was what aroused suspicion.
Opportunists were not liked. Soon it emerged that this German
master was not among the most intelligent of our teachers. Unlike
his predecessors he felt under an obligation to include in his lessons

some National Socialist literature. We therefore had to buy a small, recently published selection of National Socialist poets. The class was not very happy about this and the verses were ridiculed, which still amazes me. Evidently my classmates had had enough of such songs. No doubt they had to sing them a lot in the Hitler Youth.

For our written school-leaving examination we had a choice of four subjects. I had expected two, or perhaps even three, of these to be in the Nazi spirit. But it was worse: all four were, more or less, inspired by it. I opted for a rather vile quotation from the – by now forgotten – Nationalist Socialist cultural philosopher, Paul Lagarde.

In addition, each student had to pass an oral examination in the subject of his choice: indeed he was expected to shine in it. Only two students chose German for this test – both of them Jews. A subject had to be proposed several weeks before the examination and had to be accepted by that unpopular *Studienassessor*. Mine was rejected by him immediately and without explanation. My choice had been Georg Büchner who was not much liked in the Third Reich – a circumstance I must have missed. *Woyzeck* was not allowed to be performed at all, and *Danton's Death*, at least in Berlin, only during the war. This play, in particular, contains a lot that could be, or indeed was bound to be, understood as applying to the Third Reich.

My other proposals were likewise viewed with suspicion by the *Assessor*. He would have nothing to do with Lessing (because of *Nathan*), he did not like Hebbel, whose biblical dramas (*Judith* and *Herodes and Mariamne*) were thought 'inopportune'. Franz Grillparzer's *Jüdin von Toledo* was likewise out of the question. After a lot of hesitation he accepted the young Gerhart Hauptmann. Shortly before the test, one was given a piece of paper with the question one was to speak on. Then one was entitled to half an hour in a locked room, to prepare oneself. On my sheet of paper was a thesis of Arno Holz: '*Art tends to become nature again. It becomes nature to the extent of its conditions of reproduction at the time and in the way these are handled. (Derive from this a characterization of naturalism.)*' As can be seen, the Fichte-Gymnasium was a very demanding school. But the German master seemed to regard the task chosen for me as too abstract. He had added by hand: *G. Hauptmann as a naturalistic poet. (Vor Sonnenaufgang, Einsame Menschen, Weber.)*

This note neither surprised nor intimidated me. But I had no sooner uttered a few introductory sentences about *Vor Sonnenaufgang* than I was sharply interrupted by our headmaster, the 'Golden Pheasant' Heiniger, who acted as chairman of the examining board. He wanted to know about the National Socialist attitude to Gerhart Hauptmann. That was a question I was not prepared for.

I might have said that, on the occasion of his seventy-fifth birthday, only a few months earlier, Hauptmann had been widely celebrated throughout the Reich – by all the state theatres and also by others. Or I might have quoted remarks by Third Reich dignitaries, suggesting that they were claiming him as their own and occasionally even wooing him. But I never said any of this – either because it did not immediately occur to me or because I feared my answers might annoy the chairman of the board. Instead I declared that the Reich particularly appreciated the fact that Hauptmann had placed the social issue at the centre of his work. After this they did not wish to hear anything else from me. With an unpleasant 'Thank you' I was dismissed. Could the 'Golden Pheasant' have regarded my answer as irony?

In my school-leaving certificate I did not, as in all the previous years, receive the grade '*Very good*' for German, but only '*Good*'. Dr Beck, the German master, later told me in confidence that the chairman had not even allowed a discussion of my performance, but had declared that, for reasons which had nothing to do with the subject, the grade '*Very Good*' would not be appropriate in the case of this student – meaning a Jew.

I am ashamed to admit that I was disappointed and really angry. The decision of the 'Golden Pheasant' was petty, but my reaction to it was ridiculous. Was the whole business trivial? No doubt, but it was also revealing. It revealed that even after leaving school I was still secretly hoping to prepare for a profession which had at least something to do with literature.

I have never read as much as I did during my secondary school days. There was a municipal library in every district of Berlin, and they were all of them fairly well equipped. Anyone with an interest in literature could find anything they wanted there, including the latest books by contemporary authors. Admittedly you could not borrow more than two books at a time. This was not enough for me, but the problem was easily got around: I joined two municipal libraries, one in Schöneberg and the other in Wilmersdorf.

I have a fairly good memory of what, upon my deportation from Germany in the autumn of 1938, I knew of world literature. I find it difficult to explain today how I managed, within a span of five or six years, to read all the plays of Schiller and most of those by Shakespeare, nearly everything by Kleist and Büchner, all the short stories of Gottfried Keller and Theodor Storm, some of the great and mostly voluminous novels of Tolstoy and Dostoevsky, of Balzac, Stendhal and Flaubert. I read the Scandinavians, especially Jens Peter Jacobsen and Knut Hamsun, all of Edgar Allan Poe, whom I admired, all of Oscar Wilde, who filled me with enthusiasm, and a great deal of Maupassant, who amused and stimulated me.

Probably my reading was often cursory and certainly there was a lot I did not understand. But even so: how was it possible? Did I know of a method for rapid reading? Certainly not – I do not know of any such method to this day. On the contrary, I tend to be a slow reader. Because if I like a text, if it is really good, I savour every sentence, and that takes time. And if I dislike a text? Then I get bored, am unable to concentrate and suddenly notice that I have failed to understand a whole page and have to read it again. Good or bad, I am a slow reader.

There were probably special circumstances which enabled me to cope with the quantity of my youthful reading matter. I was able to spend several hours reading each day because I finished my homework very quickly: I only devoted enough time to it to ensure the grade of 'Satisfactory'. In consequence I neglected the science subjects and unfortunately also foreign languages. Sport – regrettably – occupied very little time. And I did not attend a dancing school – a matter I greatly regret. I certainly never learned to dance.

My reading matter was determined not only by my studies at school and my love of the theatre, but also – strangely enough – by Nazi cultural policy. The extensive printed catalogues of the municipal libraries continued to be in use, except that the titles withdrawn were crossed out in red ink. The names and titles of Jews, communists, socialists, pacifists, anti-fascists and emigrés may have been deleted, but they continued to be easily legible – names like Thomas, Heinrich and Klaus Mann, Alfred Döblin, Arthur Schnitzler and Franz Werfel,

Carl Sternheim, Carl Zuckmayer and Joseph Roth, Lion Feuchtwanger, Arnold and Stefan Zweig, Bertolt Brecht, Õdön von Horváth
and Johannes R. Becher, Anna Seghers and Else Lasker-Schüler,
Bruno and Leonhard Frank, Tucholsky, Kerr, Polgar and Kisch,
and many others.

It does occur to me, though, that at that time I had not heard a
name of supreme importance – Franz Kafka. Of the six-volume
edition of his *Collected Works*, four volumes still appeared on the
list of a Jewish publishing house in Berlin in 1935, but the last two –
since Kafka had of course been placed on the 'list of harmful and
undesirable authors' – were published in Prague in 1937. But it seems
that none of my contemporaries knew of Kafka either. He was still
a treasure to be discovered.

The numerous red deletions were most welcome to me. Now I
knew what I had to read. Of course, I had first to get hold of these
undesirable and prohibited books. But this was not all that difficult.
In the book burnings in Berlin in May 1933 some 20,000 volumes
were allegedly thrown into the flames – predominantly from public
libraries. In other towns the number of books destroyed was probably
less.

Be that as it may: these improvised actions, with their mainly
symbolical significance, only resulted in the destruction of part of the
stock of proscribed books. Many survived in bookshops, in publishers' warehouses and in private homes. Most of these sooner or
later found their way into Berlin's second-hand bookshops where, of
course, they were not to be seen in the windows or on display. But
the shopkeepers, especially if they knew their customers, were willing
enough to produce them, and they were cheap. Moreover, my
relations and the friends of my parents, as was customary in middle-
class families, had bookcases containing a lot of the titles now deleted
from the official catalogues.

My Uncle Max, the cheerful patent agent who never ceased to
believe that the Third Reich would shortly collapse, perhaps even
next year, had such a bookcase and I often had an opportunity of
making use of this gold-mine. My uncle had a delightful young son,
then about five years old, and I was frequently needed as a babysitter.
Those were wonderful evenings: I not only amused myself with
countless books but was also generously recompensed. I received one

mark for each evening and sometimes, when my uncle had no change, even two marks. The child I had to look after during those evenings never woke up once. An exemplary charge, and now one of the most famous painters in England – Frank Auerbach.

I badly needed the money, but chiefly for theatre tickets, not for books. A person emigrating could only take a few things with him and books were not usually among them. And if one did take books into exile, these were generally not novels or volumes of poetry, but specialized literature and, above all, dictionaries. What had to stay behind was given away.

A friend of this uncle, a research chemist in Berlin-Schmargendorf who was getting ready to emigrate, allowed me to help myself to his books. He advised me to bring a small suitcase along, or a rucksack. Instead I arrived with a large suitcase. I had not been able to find a smaller one, I lied. The amiable, though evidently dejected, chemist opened his bookcase and said casually, or even resignedly: 'Take whatever you like.'

What I saw took my breath away. I remember to this day what I spotted immediately – the *Collected Works* of Gerhart Hauptmann and Schnitzler, as well as those of Jens Peter Jacobsen whom Rilke had recommended so warmly and emphatically. I quickly took what I could fit into my case, unconcerned about its weight. I could barely carry it, but eventually managed to get it to the nearest tram stop.

The heavy load did not impair my happiness, nor did the elegiac warning of the friendly chemist: 'You have nothing to thank me for. I'm not making you a present of these books; they're only a loan – as are these years. You, too, my young friend, will be driven out of here. And all these books? You will be leaving them behind just as I am doing now.' He was right. I piled up many more books from many other bookcases, but when I was deported from Germany two years later I was only allowed to take one volume with me.

Occasionally I also profited from the journals displayed in the reading rooms of the municipal libraries. I would find articles there which interested me and which were not without influence on my reading. Thus, in 1936, the arresting title of a literary essay in the *Nationalsozialistische Monatshefte* caught my eye – 'An End to Heinrich Heine!' I read the article with growing attention and, what was more, with satisfaction.

The author, a philologist, had mainly picked on two poems which were among the most popular of Heine's repertoire – *The Lorelei* and *The Two Grenadiers*. Both, he argued, were typical of Heine's inadequate and shallow knowledge of the German language and represented 'not yet cast-off Yiddish'. This was proved, another German scholar wrote at the time, by the very first line of *The Lorelei*: '*Ich weiss nicht, was soll es bedeuten*'. A German would have written: '*Ich weiss nicht, was es bedeuten soll*'. It did not worry me that the Nazis, who vituperated Heine, were dishing out such nonsense. That issue of the *Nationalsozialistische Monatshefte* made me a passionate Heine reader.

What I could not find anywhere, of course, was the literature of the emigrés. Naturally we wanted to read what the expelled or escaped authors were now writing, but this was not obtainable. Germans travelling abroad would not have run the risk of bringing books or journals back with them, and sending them by post was out of the question. But there were two significant and memorable exceptions, two excited evenings I shall never forget. On these evenings two widely differing examples of German exile literature – both letters – were read aloud.

My sister, who had broken off her studies in Warsaw in the early 1930s and had moved to Berlin, there made the acquaintance of Gerhard Böhm, a German Jew whom – he has long been dead – I gratefully remember. Böhm, soon to become my brother-in-law, was one of the few people who, in my youth, interested themselves in my education, especially my literary education. He worked as an export merchant, but basically he had no occupation. Making money – to put it mildly – was not his strong suit. Maybe the fact that he was not very tall explained why he was fond of bragging. He would talk, most vividly, about his many trips around the world – except that he never made them. He was fond of boasting that, during the Weimar Republic, he had written under a pseudonym for *Die Weltbühne* – but that, too, was an invention.

Yet this Gerhard Böhm, a short man and a tall story teller, was a likeable person, intelligent and articulate. What he told me, in extensive conversations, proved that the entertaining can also be instructive, and that the instructive need not necessarily be importunate. He was extremely well versed in literature, especially in the new German literature, and – as letters written much later were to prove – he was a good stylist.

He had an important and lasting influence on my choice of reading matter. He loved Kurt Tucholsky and had not only collected his books but had also hidden, behind harmless volumes on his shelves, the small red volumes of *Weltbühne*, of which I found at least ten complete years in his flat. I owe my early love for Tucholsky to him.

He, my friend and brother-in-law Gerhard Böhm, was the only person close to me who not only interested himself in my reading, but was also disquieted by it. He was afraid that, being fifteen or sixteen then, I might become so fascinated by literature as to neglect my life. More than once he quoted to me the ancient dictum *Primum vivere, deinde philosophari* [First live, then philosophize]. He saw a danger that the intellectual element might displace everything else in me. When he made me a present of Friedrich Gundolff's monograph of Goethe (which, incidentally, greatly disappointed me), he wrote as a dedication on the fly-leaf the wise and wonderful quotation from *Faust*:

> *I say*
> *A philosophic ponderer*
> *Is like a poor beast led astray*
> *By some malignant sprite, to graze on desert ground*
> *When fine green grass is growing all around!*

My brother-in-law had been politically active in the Weimar Republic. For a while he was a member of the Communist Party but was soon regarded there as a Trotskyite, no doubt rightly so, and expelled from the Party – a fortunate circumstance which probably saved him from arrest in the Third Reich. He also instructed me – in rough outline only – about communism and about aspects of Soviet art, about Lenin, and mainly about Leon Trotsky. Through him I met some pale and monosyllabic people wearing new, but unmistakably cheap, suits. These were his old communist friends, recently released from prison or concentration camp.

Not until much later did I learn that my brother-in-law had worked in the political Resistance. I too was involved in these activities – the occasional carrying of messages and similar tasks. Modest as these

66

missions were, I was flattered by the confidence placed in me. They made me feel very important, although I certainly did not underrate the danger. No, my brother-in-law did not make me a communist, but he prepared me for communism.

Those two unforgettable literary evenings were likewise connected with him. It must have been in early 1936 when about ten of us, mostly young people, met in a spacious and well-appointed apartment in Grunewald. It belonged to a slightly older friend of Böhm, who had organized the meeting and at whose request I had been invited.

I did not know what was going to happen so I was greatly surprised when I saw two copies of the SS journal *Das schwarze Korps* lying on the table. Without any kind of introduction my brother-in-law read out a longish article from one of these. Its title, if my memory serves me right, was 'Declaration of Bankruptcy by an Emigré'. It was Kurt Tucholsky's letter to Arnold Zweig of 15 December 1935, a letter of farewell.

At first we were stunned, and then we were horrified. The letter contained an outburst of anger, evidently dammed up for many years, against the German Left and against the German Jews. We could not believe that these implacable and occasionally hate-filled remarks, now and then turning into open abuse, could have been written by Tucholsky. But soon our doubts were allayed. His style was unmistakable. The SS journal, it turned out later, had shortened and mutilated the letter and supplied it with sneering subtitles – but the text was not a forgery. Yes, the emigré Tucholsky had actually written about the Jews with revulsion and disgust, even employing primitive and malicious anti-Semitic clichés.

No one doubted that his painful squaring of accounts with the Jews was a squaring of accounts with himself. This letter had been written by a man in whose life the pain of Jewishness, and an uncanny self-hatred, had played a major, possibly the decisive, part. We also knew that a few days after writing this letter he had committed suicide. What we did not know was that, in exile, he had resolutely dissociated himself from his political ideals and turned to Catholicism, which fascinated him. Nor did we know that he was then a sick man, probably incurably so.

We admirers of Kurt Tucholsky left the grand, if somewhat gloomy, apartment in Berlin-Grunewald still in a state of shock. While we

67

had attempted to discuss the letter immediately after reading it, but in effect only babbled helpless words, out in the street we were silent, each of us busy with our own thoughts. Then our ways parted, some got on a tram, but I wanted to walk home in order to be alone.

Should that letter, I asked myself, be viewed as more than the collapse of a great German writer of our century? I was walking fast, almost hurrying. Was I anxious to get home? Or was I trying to get as far away as possible from the place where a reading had so unexpectedly turned into a terrible experience? I do not know. But I remember clearly what I felt as I walked in the direction of Halensee – fear, almost panicky fear, of what probably awaited us.

The other unforgettable evening was in February 1937. It was a cool, dull and rainy day. We met in the same apartment in Grunewald, but the circle was smaller, probably for reasons of security. Only seven or eight people had been invited. The owner of the apartment, who we knew had all kinds of contacts in Germany and abroad, had again not told us the purpose of the meeting. He switched off the lights, except for a standard lamp next to my brother-in-law's chair. Then he handed Böhm a small package of paper, very thin and written on both sides.

Everybody was silent, there was an eerie atmosphere in the half-darkened room. I recalled the reading of Tucholsky's letter a year previously and wondered nervously what was in store for us this time. My brother-in-law read out a piece of prose which had evidently got to Berlin illegally. Again it was a letter, written by an author in exile – Thomas Mann. It was his reply to the withdrawal of the honorary doctor's degree awarded him, years earlier, by the University of Bonn.

Whenever the authors of the Third Reich pilloried the writers in exile – and that happened often enough – they nearly always named and attacked Heinrich Mann, whereas his brother Thomas Mann was usually spared. I had by then read a number of books by both of them. I esteemed Heinrich Mann, especially his *Professor Unrat* and *Der Untertan* [Man of Straw]. But I admired and revered Thomas Mann after reading his *Buddenbrooks*.

The formative effect on me in those early years, however, came from another book, an imperfect and perhaps even questionable short story. Tonio Kröger, who dreams of the '*bliss of the commonplace*' and fears that *'life in its seductive banality'* might escape him, who suffers from not belonging anywhere and who lives like a stranger in his own house – in him I recognized myself. His lament that he was often *'sick to death of being a portrayer of humanity and having no share in human experience'*, affected me profoundly. The fear of living only in literature, of being excluded from the human world, the yearning for the fine green grass which is growing all around and yet remains unattainable, has never entirely left me. This fear and this yearning belong to the leitmotifs of my life.

I have remained faithful to the story of Tonio Kröger. When I was awarded the Thomas Mann Prize in 1987 it was obvious to me what I would talk about in my acceptance speech – about this poetical compendium of all who cannot come to terms with their non-belonging, about the bible of those whose only home is literature.

The question of what Thomas Mann, then resident in Switzerland, would do in view of the events that were unfolding in Germany assumed – I am not exaggerating – a vital importance for me. That evening, in February 1937, when I heard the opening words of his letter, I was so nervous, I think I was trembling. After all, I had no idea what to prepare myself for, what Thomas Mann had decided, how far he had gone. But the third sentence removed all uncertainty. Because in it he spoke of the *'despicable powers which are devastating Germany morally, culturally and economically'*. There was no doubt left: in this letter Thomas Mann had, for the first time, very clearly taken up his stance against the Third Reich.

That dark evening in Grunewald, hearing the words of Thomas Mann, read slowly and thoughtfully, with the monotonous and continuous beat of the rain against the window panes and the breathing of those present being audible in the silence – what did I feel? Relief? Yes, certainly; but more than that – gratitude. Subsequently, in the most varied conversations about Germany, in Berlin, in Warsaw, and in the ghetto, I have time and again referred to the central idea of that letter. *They* – meaning the National Socialists – *have the incredible temerity to confuse themselves with Germany! At a time when, perhaps, the moment is not far off when the German people will give its last not to be confused with them.*

I could not have known, in 1937, that during the Second World War Thomas Mann would play an international role which had never before fallen to a German writer. He became the representative, highly prominent counter-figure. If I were asked to suggest two names which epitomized Germany in the twentieth century, I would answer unhesitatingly: Adolf Hitler and Thomas Mann. These two names still symbolize the two sides, the two possibilities, of Germandom. There would be disastrous consequences if Germany were to forget or repress one of these two possibilities.

After the final sentence of the letter no one dared say a word. My brother-in-law, who had read the text, suggested we had a break before discussing Thomas Mann's letter. I used that break to thank my host and take my leave. I did not wish to get home too late, I said, I had an important test paper to write the following day. That was a lie. In reality I wanted to be alone – alone with my happiness.

7

MY MOST WONDERFUL REFUGE – THE THEATRE

Although the programmes of the Berlin state theatres were adorned with swastikas, we nevertheless experienced a real flowering of German theatrical art. To avoid any misunderstanding: those who had seized power in 1933 did not, as a result, appear in a more favourable light; nor was the gulf which had opened between the civilized world and the country ruled and terrorized by the Nazis in the least narrowed by the achievements of the artists who persistently ignored National Socialist cultural policy, or even cautiously opposed it. Naturally, the performances in Berlin's opera houses, at the Schauspielhaus am Gendarmenmarkt and some other theatres, or the concerts, especially those of the Berlin Philharmonic under Wilhelm Furtwängler, did not diminish the tyranny. But they made the lives of many people more tolerable – including my own.

What did I expect from the theatre which, during those years in Berlin, accounted for a substantial part of my life? Bertolt Brecht, who never tired of repeating that he wished, through the theatre, to enlighten and educate the people, knew very well why, at the same time, he laid provocative emphasis on the theatre's principal business – which was to entertain the people. Did I, too, hope that the theatre would provide me with entertainment and distraction at a time of gloom? Nothing more? Did I perhaps seek asylum? But that would mean that my enormous enthusiasm for the theatre had something to do with the new regime. I urgently needed a refuge not in spite of, but because of, the fact that barbarians were in power in Germany.

It has been suggested that I entered the world of literature through the stage door. That is not quite correct. In fact, it was a reciprocal process: literature had driven me to the theatre and the theatre had driven me to literature. The two together offered me what I urgently needed, and on which I became dependent to an increasing degree – help and refuge. Thus, amidst the Third Reich, German literature, along with the Berlin theatre, proved to be the ivory tower of the Jewish teenager.

At the Gendarmenmarkt theatre the advance sales of tickets always began on Sunday in the morning at ten o'clock. However, to get one of the few cheap tickets one had to start queuing at eight, or, at the latest, at nine – especially if one wanted to see a première. For the première of a work with Gustaf Gründgens in it, one had to start queuing even earlier. At the Gendarmenmarkt, a seat in the third tier cost two marks, in the 'gods' it cost one mark. The acoustics in this building were so good that one could hear better up there than in the stalls – including even the prompter. At the State Opera, a seat in the fourth tier cost two marks fifty, a standing-room ticket one mark. Stand through *Rigoletto*? No problem. But through *Götterdämmerung*? As far as I recall, I did not get any pocket money at all but what I earned from my uncle, as a babysitter and messenger carrying documents to the Patent Office, was enough for two or three theatre or opera performances per month.

As for the cinema, I visited it far less often; my interest in film was limited even then – probably because words as a rule affected me more strongly than images. My first film, which I saw while still in Poland, was Charlie Chaplin's *Circus*; I saw my first talkie in 1930 in Berlin, at the UFA Palast am Zoo. It was *Die Drei von der Tankstelle*, featuring the then exceptionally popular Lillian Harvey and Willy Fritsch, along with a young comic actor, Heinz Rühmann. One of my most exciting cinema experiences was Willi Forst's *Maskerade* with Paula Wessely. This film was reputed to be a masterpiece and I was determined not to miss it. But the reason for my excitement had nothing to do with its artistic merit. It was due to the fact that *Maskerade* was banned for those under eighteen, by order of the police. And in 1934 I was only fourteen.

The box offices of the smaller Berlin cinemas were, as a rule, manned by the proprietors. They were not bothered about the age of the visitors; they simply wanted to sell as many tickets as possible. But to be on the safe side I wore my only suit with long trousers, together with a tie. It was rumoured in school that there were sometimes surprise police checks at the cinemas, and that juveniles who dared to disobey the police orders were severely punished. How, I wondered, would under-age offenders be treated if, moreover, they were Jews? Thus I watched *Maskerade* both in fear and with delight. I was lucky: neither then nor later – and from then on I was interested exclusively in films passed only for adult audiences – did I ever experience those police checks I was so afraid of. No doubt the police had other tasks than checking cinema audiences during those years.

Paula Wessely's co-star in this particularly fine film was Anton Wohlbrück, an actor of Jewish origin who was living in Austria but who shortly afterwards emigrated to England, where he was successful as Anton Walbrook. He was one of the many outstanding directors and actors whom the German theatre now had to do without. Max Reinhardt, Leopold Jessner and Erwin Piscator, Marlene Dietrich, Elisabeth Bergner and Lilli Palmer, Albert Bassermann, Ernst Deutsch and Fritz Kortner, Tilla Durieux, Lucie Mannheim and Grete Mosheim, Therese Giehse, Helene Weigel and Rosa Valetti, Ernst Busch, Alexander Granach, Peter Lorre and Max Pallenberg – all of these, and many others whose names have since been forgotten, had to emigrate. Either because they were Jewish or of Jewish extraction, or because they did not wish to live in the Third Reich.

In the Weimar Republic the number of original and outstanding producers, actors and stage designers had been unusually large. Those who remained in Germany immediately attracted the interest of the Nazis, regardless of whether they had a left-wing or even a communist past – such as the actor Heinrich George, the director Erich Engel, the stage designers Traugott Müller and Caspar Neher – or if they had Jewish relations – such as the actors Hans Albers, Paul Bildt, Theo Lingen and Paul Henckels.

The Third Reich was most anxious to maintain the high standards of Berlin's pre-1933 theatrical life and in this they only partially succeeded. What most Berlin theatres had to offer after 1933 was usually mediocre. But at the Schauspielhaus am Gendarmenmarkt and the attached 'Small House' theatre, both under the management of Gustaf Gründgens (whom Max Reinhardt had brought to Berlin in 1928), as well as at the Deutsches Theater and the Kammerspiele, which were managed by Heinz Hilpert (until recently Reinhardt's closest collaborator and leading director), the theatrical culture of the Weimar Republic was being impressively and often brilliantly sustained. Much the same is true of the Unter den Linden state opera, where – a most unusual situation – the Jew Leo Blech was allowed to continue as General Musical Director until 1937.

What was happening at the theatres had, with very few exceptions, nothing in common with the wishes of the cultural politicians of the Third Reich. Gustaf Gründgens, to his great credit, had turned the Gendarmenmarkt theatre into a haven which, during the years of terror, offered asylum to the best theatrical talent, especially to those whom the regime (mostly with good reason) mistrusted. Thus – to confine myself to one example – the producer Jürgen Fehling, who was a practitioner of the now discredited and proscribed expressionism and had worked with Leopold Jessner, found an outlet for his exceptional gifts in Gründgen's theatre. Thus the spirit of the 1920s continued to predominate in the foremost Berlin theatres.

What had changed, however, was the programme. The work of most of the newer German playwrights could no longer be performed – either because they were Jews or of Jewish extraction (like Hugo von Hofmannsthal, Schnitzler and Sternheim, Ferdinand Bruckner, Walter Hasenclever and Ernst Toller) or because they were emigrés and opponents of the Third Reich (such as Brecht, Horváth and Georg Kaiser) or because they were considered 'degenerate' (like Frank Wedekind, Ernst Barlach and Marieluise Fleisser). And because the authors approved of, or promoted by, the Nazis usually wrote very weak, if not atrocious, plays, managers like Gründgens and Hilpert had no choice but to draw on the repertoire of the past. They staged the dramas of great literature from Aeschylus through Shakespeare to George Bernard Shaw, and of course the German classics from Lessing to Gerhart Hauptmann.

I therefore had an opportunity to become acquainted with world theatre not only as a reader of plays. I was intensely interested in everything I saw, I positively soaked it up. Theatre performances moulded my existence and dominated my life. But many a famous play disappointed me or left me cold. I acknowledged the importance of Molière, but he bored me a little and I never came to love him. Goldoni seemed to me remarkable but a little silly. My attitude to Beaumarchais and Gogol was respectful, but rather remote. Ibsen, who was – astonishingly – only rarely staged seemed to me old-fashioned. Shaw's comedies, which were frequently performed, amused me without touching me profoundly.

The difficulty of finding performable plays meant that theatre managers did not shrink from delving into their archives and producing such dust-covered hits as *A Glass of Water* by Augustin Scribe or *La Dame aux camélias* by Alexandre Dumas (fils), giving them new life with virtuoso performances. Within a short span of time it was possible to see all four comedies of Oscar Wilde, three of which were moreover made into films in 1935 and 1936.

All this amused and excited me. I admired the great actors who could bring even weak plays to life. But it did not move me. What really affected and thrilled me were, time and again, predominantly Shakespeare's comedies and, even more so, his tragedies. And such playwrights as Lessing, Goethe and Schiller, Kleist, Büchner and Grabbe, Raimund and Nestroy, Grillparzer and Hebbel, and eventually Gerhart Hauptmann. Was I perhaps, in the Third Reich, looking for the other Germany? No, this idea never occurred to me. However, surrounded by a hostile, or at best chilly, world I was longing, consciously and subconsciously, for a counter-world. And I found this in the German theatre.

After the war, many productions in the leading Berlin theatres were hailed as gestures of resistance against the Nazis. Was this really the case? In 1937 the Deutsches Theater staged Schiller's *Don Carlos*: Albin Skoda was Carlos and Ewald Balser was the Marquis Posa. Much was said and rumoured about that production at the time. But what caused a sensation was not its outstanding quality, which was questioned by no one, but an eerie circumstance. Each night, after Posa's words: '*Grant freedom of conscience*', there was such thunderous applause that it was impossible to continue with the performance. The actor playing the King had to wait for the audience to quieten down before he could utter the words: '*Peculiar dreamer*'.

Was this anything more than applause for Schiller's verses and Balser's fine acting? Was it really a demonstration against the Nazi state? Yes, very probably. It would be ludicrous, however, to assume that those in power had been unaware of this. Goebbels, in his diary, commented very favourably on this production, and the 'Reich dramaturgist' Rainer Schlösser is reported to have said that, even in

Schiller's lifetime, the audience vigorously applauded after Posa's much-quoted words. At any rate, there were thirty-two performances of this production of *Don Carlos*.

The climax of the confrontation of the State Theatre with the Nazi regime was believed to be Jürgen Fehling's production of *Richard the Third* with Werner Krauss. I was present at its première on 2 March 1937. I shall never forget that performance – neither the acting of Krauss nor Fehling's radical concept of the production. He produced the story of the cynical and power-hungry criminal in a way that allowed it to be applied to Hitler and to conditions then prevailing in Germany – the more so as certain passages were especially emphasized, such as: '*Bad is the world; and all will come to naught, / When such ill dealing must be seen in thought.*'

The bodyguard of the villainous king wore black-and-silver uniforms suggestive of those of the SS, and the murderers of the Duke of Clarence wore brown shirts and riding boots reminiscent of the SA. The finale was magnificent and stunning. After the words '*The day is ours, the bloody dog is dead*' there was suddenly total darkness, both on the stage and in the auditorium. A few moments later all the lights suddenly came on. The soldiers on the stage sank to their knees and intoned a powerful Te Deum, to be heard in all parts of the theatre.

There can be no doubt about what Fehling was aiming at with this production, without seeking to alter Shakespeare's text or using some new translation. More questionable is whether his intentions were understood by the audience as a whole, or perhaps only by those who were opponents of the regime. They would derive satisfaction and often considerable secret pleasure from the anti-Nazi allusions, both in *Richard the Third* and also in the productions of other classical plays. But were these mostly witty acts of defiance, often reminiscent of cabaret practice, really worth the risks involved?

I am not quite sure, especially as – and this should not be overlooked – these attacks on the Nazis had undesirable consequences. The fact that some anti-regime performances were tolerated has often been interpreted as evidence of the self-assurance, or even generosity, of the new party. One thing is absolutely certain: it would be absurd to believe that the Nazis were oblivious to these undercurrents. What the censor fails to understand – and this applies to all dictatorships – the public understands even less. It is just that the police state sometimes considers it opportune to turn a blind eye.

Of course I was not indifferent to these secret and eerie protests against tyranny, but having known people who had been put in concentration camps for lesser offences, the risks which these some-what rebellious theatre people took upon themselves seemed to me disproportionate to any real results. Creditable as these protests were, I did not think they succeeded in bringing about the slightest change. What could the theatre in the Third Reich offer the public? Certainly not political enlightenment, but perhaps something which – among other benefits – I gained from it myself. One might call this inner strength.

When I reflect today on which productions of the classics, apart from *Don Carlos* and *Richard the Third*, most affected me in the 1930s, I am tempted to name a great many. Was there really a theatrical flowering that ignored, or even opposed, the spirit of the age, or am I still viewing what delighted me then through the eyes of an enthusiastic, impressionable, and still very young person?

I remember Lessing's *Emilia Galotti*, produced by Gründgens, as an exciting and stirring, intimate drama. As the floor of the stage was covered with stone slabs, the steps of the men rang out and echoed, creating a tense or even aggressive atmosphere. All the roles were superbly cast, but my most powerful recollection is of Käthe Dorsch: she acted a Countess Orsina who, sensitive, nervous, alter-nately melancholy and elated, fluctuated between relentlessly clear vision and a moving insanity.

Goetz von Berlichingen never interested me; it seemed no more than a document of literary history. But when I now think of the play, or reread it, I still see and hear Heinrich George. He was magnificent in the title part, which he had grown into to the extent that no one else dared to try his hand at it, at least not in Berlin. It was said that whenever George played Goetz, he was slightly drunk. Nor did I like the *Jungfrau von Orleans* [*The Maid of Orleans*], but I can still see Luise Ullrich in the almost unbearable scene when Joan declaims: '*Farewell, ye mountains, ye beloved meadows, / Ye old familiar quiet vales, farewell ... Joan goes and never comes again.*' Ullrich spoke the lines undramatically and softly, almost as a stammer, as if engaged in an inner monologue.

Goethe's *Egmont* was much closer to my heart as a boy and I still have a weakness for the play. Unfortunately it is seldom staged these days. During the Berlin production of 1935 I fell in love with the actress playing Klärchen. This was Käthe Gold, who also enchanted me as Gretchen and Käthchen, as Ophelia and Cordelia, filling me with happiness. And I was happy when I saw her on the stage again for the first time after the war. This was in Zurich in 1945. She was then forty-two and still played the part of Gretchen.

No actress left such an enduring impression on me as Käthe Gold – not even Elisabeth Bergner, whom admittedly I only knew during her later years, or Paula Wessely, whom I saw all too rarely on the stage. But I still remember Wessely in Grillparzer's *Des Meeres und der Liebe Wellen* [*Hero and Leander*] and as Shaw's Saint Joan. She was also an outstanding film actress, which cannot be said of Käthe Gold. This may be due to the fact that Gold's strongest talent was her diction, which as a rule is not so evident in the cinema.

In Fehling's 1937 production of *Käthchen von Heilbronn* – he staged it as an intimate, poetic play combined with a romantic spectacle of knights amid thunder and lightning, and perhaps too much fire and noise – Käthe Gold in the title role was like a young girl out of a fairy-tale, dainty and magical, modest but also a little rebellious. She was perfect for any part that was young and feminine – from the dreamy girl in Hauptmann's *Und Pippa tanzt!* [*And Pippa Dances*], to a teenager in his comedy, *Die Jungfern vom Bischofsberg* [*The Maids from Bischofsberg*].

The première of this comedy, written in 1907, had alarmed and depressed me – even though the production, with Marianne Hoppe playing alongside Käthe Gold, was excellent. This was staged in November 1937, in honour of Gerhart Hauptmann's seventy-fifth birthday. The Nazis did not like Hauptmann; time and again, he fell foul of them whether he wanted to or not. But they urgently needed a representative writer of the older generation, a living classic – and since Thomas Mann had emigrated, there remained only Hauptmann.

That was also the reason why the propaganda ministry tolerated, and sometimes even recommended, new productions of his old plays. In view of the increasing shortage of plays, the theatres welcomed this. *Die Weber* [*The Weavers*], however, was not allowed to be staged in the Third Reich. This was because Hauptmann was not prepared to comply with the Nazis' request for a new, optimistic ending, suggesting that in Hitler's state the weavers were well off.

Hauptmann personally attended many of the productions on the occasion of his birthday, including that of *Die Jungfern vom Bischofsberg*. I had a cheap seat in the second tier and had a good view of the state box, where he sat with Hermann Gœring. The applause after the play was tempestuous, clearly intended not only for the actors but also for the two prominent gentlemen. As I saw with my own eyes, they acknowledged it with the Hitler salute. Gerhart Hauptmann, the author of *Die Weber* and *Die Ratten* [The Rats], who largely owed his rise to fame to Jews (especially Otto Brahm and Max Reinhardt, Alfred Kerr and Siegfried Jacobsohn) did not shrink from raising his arm in the Hitler salute.

One of the most important productions that year was *Michael Kramer* with Werner Krauss. In this part Krauss looked like Johannes Brahms. His opposite character, Kramer's wastrel son Arnold, played by Bernhard Minetti, seemed more interesting to me. Today we can hardly imagine the glory of Werner Krauss, the less so as, after his death and that of Gründgens and Kortner, we no longer have any actors of comparable stature. His adaptability was boundless. In the 1930s he would, within a single week, play Faust, Wallenstein and Kandaules in Hebbel's '*Gyges und sein Ring*', Richard III and King Lear, and in between also Professor Higgins in *Pygmalion*, one of Shaw's best comedies which has been shamelessly eclipsed by *My Fair Lady*.

If I were asked in which of these parts Krauss had most impressed me, I would hesitate between Wallenstein, Kandaules and Richard III. Many years later, in Hamburg, I saw Gründgens as Wallenstein and as Kandaules. He was profoundly moving and a virtuoso in both parts, but he was not the equal of Werner Krauss. He lacked Krauss's immediacy and elemental power, which were so strong, so overwhelming, that they made one forget his professional skill and brilliance. When Gründgens appeared on the stage he immediately began to act: from his glances and movements, from his way with language, from the sudden pauses and unexpected bursts of speech, there miraculously emerged on an original, compelling character. When Krauss stepped on to the stage, the character he acted was instantly present – without him having said or done a thing.

79

As King Lear, Krauss slightly disappointed me. Was this because of his acting, or the play, or perhaps myself? The story of an evidently senile old man, no longer capable of perceiving the world, let alone of rational judgement, who frivolously gives away his kingdom and is dependent on the mercy of two wicked daughters, who, alone and insane, blunders about the heath (to make matters worse, during a thunderstorm) – no, that story hardly convinced me.

But surely *Lear* is one of the most famous tragedies in world literature? I had read a good deal about the play, but nothing was able to convince me of this – until, to my surprise and joy, I came across the following sentence in a review by Alfred Kerr, dating from 1908: '*This work is almost unbearable to me on the stage today, with those childish awkwardnesses, those pleonasms, which it displays alongside its greatness.*' That settled the *Lear* issue for me – or so I thought.

After the war I saw the play repeatedly, in different languages. Gradually the old fairy-tale ceased to be a matter of indifference to me. I was beginning to understand why it was famous. Why had my attitude to this play changed so much over the years? I did not know – until I came across a late poem by Goethe which starts with the line: '*There's a King Lear in every old man.*' Goethe was seventy-eight when he wrote that poem.

Does one have to be old to understand and admire *Lear*? Does one have to be young to be enthusiastic about *Romeo and Juliet*? I was thirteen or fourteen when an aunt, who knew of my enthusiasm for the theatre, suddenly telephoned me. Would I like to go to the theatre? She had a free ticket, but I would have to set out at once: it was *Romeo and Juliet*. The play was being staged in a theatre which, over the years, found itself repeatedly compelled to change its name. In the Germany of Wilhelm II it was the 'Theatre on König-grätz Street,' during the Weimer Republic it was the 'Theatre on Stresemann Street', and in the Third Reich the 'Theatre on Saarland Street'. After the Second World War a name was chosen which was no longer dependent on German history – Hebbel Theatre.

Romeo and Juliet was not one of the Shakespeare plays I already knew. And as I only acquired that free ticket at the last moment there was no time to read the play, or even read about it in a theatre guide. Perhaps it was due to this unpreparedness that *Romeo and*

Juliet almost unnerved me, that it almost struck me speechless, that it affected me as deeply as only one other Shakespeare tragedy – *Hamlet*. This was hardly due to the quality of the performance. The production, if I remember rightly, was respectable rather than outstanding. Romeo was played by Wolfgang Liebeneier, who was to become famous during the next few years as a director and film actor. Why, then, did this evening at the theatre stir me so deeply?

I had by then read many novels and stories, poems and plays which had love at their centre. To me however, who had not as yet had the slightest erotic experience, it had remained something abstract. Not until that evening did I understand what love was. Because theatre is more sensual and persuasive than the text of even the most beautiful short story or ballad? Not only that. I sensed what made *Romeo and Juliet* different from other literary works. It was, above all, Shakespeare's uncanny radicalism, the absoluteness with which he treated this subject.

For the first time I understood, or perhaps only surmised, that love is an urge which knows no bounds, that the exaltation of those made happy or unhappy by it leads to a madness that defies the whole world, or tries to do so. I felt that love is a blessing and a curse, a grace and a doom. I discovered that love and death belong together, that we love because we must die.

At the time, over sixty years ago, I would not of course have been able to explain the overwhelming effect which Shakespeare's *Romeo and Juliet* had on me. I could not know that only a few years later I would myself experience the menacing proximity of love and death; that an experience awaited me that was as wonderful as it was terrible – to be in love without being able, even for a moment, to forget the supreme danger of death, to live with the threat of death while loving. What remains of art? Robert Musil asked this question and answered it in plain terms: '*We remain, as changed persons*'. I say without hesitation that *Romeo and Juliet* changed me – just as did the tragedy of the intellectual, the story of Hamlet, Prince of Denmark.

In the course of my life *Hamlet* has crossed my path more frequently than any other drama of world literature. At school we read *Hamlet* in our English lessons. I am surprised that our teacher chose Shakespeare's longest and, in many respects, most difficult play, but I am grateful to him to this day. For foreign-language texts, especially Latin ones, many of us used the strictly forbidden cribs – small, thin booklets which were easily concealed. They contained literal translations and saved one looking up words in the dictionary. For *Hamlet* I too, disregarding the prohibition, used a crib – admittedly a noble one, Schlegel's translation. I have loved and admired the play ever since, and this love has not been diminished by the many newer translations, even though in places, these present the English original more accurately.

I must have seen *Hamlet* on the stage at least ten times – in four languages (German, English, French and Polish) and with such great actors as Laurence Olivier and Jean-Louis Barrault. Added to this are several film versions. I mention all this for two reasons. First: it would be embarrassing to boast of anything I have written in my life. But perhaps it is permissible to boast of something one has failed to write. Thus I have resisted every temptation and never written even the shortest essay on *Hamlet*; I did not dare. Second: whenever I think of that play, or what I experienced in connection with *Hamlet*, I think of Gustaf Gründgens.

I admired Werner Krauss, I venerated Käthe Dorsch and I was in love with Käthe Gold. But Gustaf Gründgens virtually hypnotized me. This is not to say that he was the greatest actor of my youth – that, probably, was Werner Krauss – but no one was as close to me, no one interested me as much as Gründgens. This was due to the circumstances of the period. In 1934, at the age of barely thirty-four, Gründgens was appointed by Göring to the post of *Intendant* of state theatres in Berlin. In a comparatively short time he succeeded in making the Gendarmenmarkt theatre the best theatre in Germany. By doing so beyond any doubt, he served Adolf Hitler's state. But at the same time – and this is a fact – he served those who suffered under the Nazi regime and, in the midst of the Third Reich, were looking for solace and strength from the theatre, especially from the dramatization of classics. And, last but not least, he saved the lives of people who were in great danger at the time.

What excited and stirred me was not Gründgens's impressive work as *Intendant* and producer, but his performance as an actor. Gründgens was younger than the other great actors of the day – Werner Krauss, Emil Jannings, Eugen Klöpfer, Heinrich George,

Friedrich Kayssler, Paul Hartmann – who had all begun their artistic careers in imperial Germany. He had been moulded not by the Germany of Kaiser Wilhelm but by the Weimar Republic, and seemed to me incomparably more modern.

Whenever the Nazis wished to characterize something they thought corrupt, despicable or worthy of condemnation, they used the term 'asphalt'. They spoke of the 'asphalt press', of 'asphalt culture' and, most often, of 'asphalt literature'. Although it was Goebbels who either invented, or at least popularized, this concept, I like it, it pleases me. If anyone nowadays were to describe me as an 'asphalt man of letters' I would be delighted rather than offended. Great literature has always been created in the great cities. The writers I love come from Stratford, Neuruppin, Auteuil or Augsburg, but they rose to fame in London, Berlin or Paris.

I viewed Gründgens as a typical representative of the culture of the twentieth century, the 'asphalt culture' to which he remained loyal in the Third Reich. Gründgens the actor, who until not long before had been married to Thomas Mann's daughter, Erika, and had been a friend of her brother, Klaus, had nothing in common with the National Socialists. On the contrary, I regarded him as the anti-type of his age. He personified not blood and soil, but what was morbid and suspect, a twilight world. He did not play heroes or believers, but broken and degenerate characters, scintillating figures: he preferred parts which allowed him to elucidate and accentuate the narcissistic and the neurasthenic.

His concept of art, his anti-heroic attitude, his predilection for the doubters, the scoffers and the sceptics – all this was the exact opposite of what the Nazis were aiming at, what they were loudly proclaiming. Whenever I saw Gründgens on the stage – especially as Don Juan in Grabbe's *Don Juan and Faust* or as the Prince in Lessing's *Emilia Galotti* – I believe I sensed just that. But nowhere did it emerge more powerfully than in his Hamlet.

The peak of Gründgens's artistic career was unquestionably his Mephisto in both parts of Goethe's *Faust*. Certainly no other actor of our century can be compared to Gründgens in that role. But to me, a Jew living in the Third Reich full of fear, his 1936 Hamlet was even more important. It has often been said that each generation seeks and finds itself in *Hamlet*, which it sees as a reflection of its own questions and difficulties, its own defeats. I too recognized features and outlines of my existence in Nazi Germany in *Hamlet* – thanks to Gründgens.

He played a young solitary intellectual, '*sicklied o'er with the pale cast of thought*'. Here was a passionate reader of books and a theatre enthusiast who has become an outsider. Hamlet's words '*The time is out of joint*' and '*Denmark's a prison*' were – or so at least it seemed to me – especially emphasized by Gründgens. In this kingdom of Denmark, a police state, everyone is spied on by everyone else – the minister Polonius does not trust his son Laertes who has gone to Paris: he sends an agent after him to spy on him. The queen too cannot be trusted by the state: when speaking to her son Hamlet, the minister personally eavesdrops on their conversation.

Most suspect of all is Hamlet: he reads and thinks too much and has, moreover, just returned from abroad. Two courtiers, Rosencrantz and Guildenstern, are sent for: they grew up with him and are therefore thought suitable for 'spying him out'. Hamlet is a man whose existence, unlike that of his contemporaries, is determined by his mind, by his conscience. He complains that '*conscience doth make cowards of us all*' and declares: '*I will speak daggers to her, but use none*' – yet he stabs Polonius. He is, simultaneously, superior to the world he inhabits and not equal to it.

After seeing Gründgens in this play I read every scene of *Hamlet* differently from before – as the tragedy of the intellectual in a cruel society and a criminal state. Did the audiences of this performance feel the same? Probably only a small minority. But could the Nazis, especially their cultural politicians and journalists, miss the fact that this *Hamlet* might also be understood as a political manifesto, as a protest against the tyranny in Germany? Of course not.

The Nazi Party's daily *Völkischer Beobachter* carried a full-page article in which Gründgens's interpretation of Hamlet was described in terms then regarded as insults ('decadent', 'neurasthenic' and 'intellectual') and condemned as anti-National-Socialist. Gründgens immediately fled to Switzerland, fearing persecution – also in connection with his homosexual inclinations and practices. But Gœring asked him to return, guaranteeing him his personal safety. Soon Gründgens was back in Berlin.

There is yet another memory, a very different one, attached to that

Hamlet performance of 1936. It concerns Ophelia's famous mad scene, played by Käthe Gold with restraint and tenderness. I was affected not only by her, the demented young woman, but also by the situation of a helpless witness to her behaviour – her brother Laertes, the young man who is totally shattered by the emotional and mental collapse of his sister. As he cried out in despair: '*Do you see this, O God?*', I was suddenly seized by fear that this might happen to me – having to watch helplessly as a person very close to me is gripped by insanity, screams and babbles. Paralysed by fear in the auditorium of the Gendarmenmarkt theatre, I thought to myself: May I be spared this. But I was not spared it.

Of all the actors I was able to watch in my youth I was therefore most fascinated by the one who was Gœring's protégé and who in 1936 was appointed a Prussian State Councillor. It may be thought equally surprising that, in my early days, I was most profoundly affected by the composer who must be counted among the most infamous anti-Semites in the history of culture – and not only German culture.

I was only thirteen when, after appropriate preparation on the piano, my sister took me along to a performance of *Die Meistersinger von Nürnberg*. In spite of Nazi propaganda I was instantly charmed by this opera – possibly because it is a work about music and literature, about the artist and the public, about critics. To this day no opera gives me greater pleasure, greater happiness, than *Meistersinger*. And none moves me more deeply and excites me more strongly than *Tristan und Isolde*.

Late one evening, after a garden party in the grounds of a hotel, a television reporter surprised me with a simple question. He wanted to know how I came to terms with a Jew-hater like Richard Wagner. I replied spontaneously: 'There were, and there are, many fine people on earth, but none of them has written *Tristan* or *Meistersinger*.'

Does that mean that he should be forgiven his essay 'On Jewry in Music'? Certainly not. Yet among the leading conductors of Wagner there has always been an astonishingly high proportion of Jews – from Hermann Levi, who conducted the première of *Parsifal* through Bruno Walter and Otto Klemperer to Leonard Bernstein and Georg Solti, Lorin Maazel, Daniel Barenboim and James Levine. The musicologists to whom we owe the principal studies of Wagner

85

likewise include many Jews. Does it speak in favour of those conductors and scholars, or against them, that they regarded Wagner's
music as more important than his journalism, especially as these
essays are ultimately only the angry outbursts of a muddle-head?

In March 1958, shortly before my return to Germany, I had a
lengthy conversation in Warsaw with the composer Hanns Eisler. He
had come to Poland from East Berlin to finish writing his music for
Brecht's play *Schwejk in the Second World War* and to conduct it for
a tape recording. Along with my friend Andrzej Wirth I had translated
it into Polish and the première was imminent. We spent an evening
together. Eisler, a cheerful and articulate person, was chatting away
to us in high spirits. He related all kinds of anecdotes, not at all bad
ones, mostly about musicians.

Thus he told us about his farewell visit to his teacher Arnold
Schoenberg, in Los Angeles at the beginning of 1948. When Schoenberg heard that Eisler was about to return to Germany he was
sad; when he heard that his beloved pupil intended to settle in East
Berlin he was disquieted. Eisler tried to explain to him that, as a
communist for many decades, he belonged where his comrades were
in power. He could understand that all right, Schoenberg said, but
there was the danger that the Russians might abduct him. Why
him in particular? The unworldly master answered quite seriously:
'Because they don't have a single Schoenberg pupil in the Soviet
Union.'

It was not long before Eisler began to talk about Wagner – or,
more accurately, to berate him. He called him a complete charlatan,
a kitsch-monger of the worst kind, a tasteless show-off. I did not
dream of taking the accusations seriously. They amused me. Besides,
it was clear to me that anyone attacking a composer of the past with
so much fervour was betraying himself. He probably owed Wagner
a lot. He was linked to the person he attacked, if only by love–hate.

So I let Eisler speak without contradicting him. Why should I? It
was clear to me that I would easily win this good-natured dialogue.
Because I had a name up my sleeve, which, like a joker in a game of
cards, would decide everything. I only had to play it and Eisler, a
splendid musician, would surrender at once.

Finally the moment arrived when I had had enough of his tirades.
I said: 'Yes, Herr Eisler, what you are saying may well be right. I

quite agree. But this terrible Wagner' – now I came to my joker – 'has written *Tristan*.' Eisler fell silent. It was quiet in the room, deathly quiet. Then he said very softly: 'That's something entirely different. That is music.' Four years later, in 1962 – I had long returned to Germany – I read in the papers that Eisler had died. And I also read that the great Jewish musician, Hanns Eisler, had asked for the score of *Tristan und Isolde* on his deathbed.

In another conversation about Wagner, my game with *Tristan* as a joker was less successful. This took place at the offices of West German Radio while I was waiting to appear in a talk show, whose participants included the composer Karlheinz Stockhausen. As our conversation began to flag I resorted to the most reliable means of instantly reviving a conversation with musicians. I asked politely: 'What, dear Herr Stockhausen, is your attitude to Wagner?' He replied in a bored manner that quite recently he had again heard *Die Walküre* and also *Lohengrin*. That was music totally beyond discussion. I accepted this and softly – and, I admit, sanctimoniously – asked the simple question: 'And what about *Tristan*?' For a moment Stockhausen was silent and then he said hesitantly: 'The overture' – he really said 'overture' and not 'prelude' – 'the overture is good, the rest is superfluous.' This is the most original judgement I have ever heard on Richard Wagner's *Tristan und Isolde*.

8

A SUFFERING WHICH
BRINGS HAPPINESS

In my youth there was no such thing as sex education, either at home or at school. When I was ten I believed that babies came into the world through their mother's navel, widened for that purpose. When I was eleven or twelve I occasionally tried, in conversation with classmates during breaks between lessons, to learn something about sex. Some of them, I hoped, might be able to tell me a fact or two. But although these boys knew a few rude words, they actually knew even less than I did. And I was surprised to find that many of them were not greatly interested in the subject – or so they pretended. We were all rather repressed. No doubt things were different in the proletarian districts of Berlin.

One day someone lent me a brochure. It was written in bad German and printed on poor paper, sixteen pages in all. But what disappointed me was not the style or the quality of the paper of this 'Facts of Life' brochure, but its subtitle: '*For Young Men*'. In other words, nothing for or about girls? Nothing about the phenomenon which appeared to me and my friends mysterious and enigmatic, which was supposed to have something to do with the moon and which differentiated us from girls? In short, nothing about monthly bleeding?

Instead the brochure was focused on two theses. The young readers were implored to abstain from any sexual intercourse before marriage. Otherwise they would run the risk of incurable diseases with which they might infect their future wives and perhaps their future children. Secondly, readers were emphatically warned against masturbation: it led to horrible skin diseases, or even to deafness and blindness.

More productive than this brochure or conversations between lessons, was a find I made in the street. In a rubbish container I caught sight of a condom packet. It seemed to be empty, but it was not – it contained a thin, folded sheet of paper. This was, as one might expect, the directions for use, in small print and in great detail. I took it home to read carefully – not because I wished to know how to use condoms, but because I hoped to find some hard information about sexual intercourse. But this was not so simple. The text was difficult and some passages totally incomprehensible. It was full of foreign words I did not know.

Fortunately, there was the multi-volume Brockhaus Encyclopaedia at home. I got down to work and looked up all the foreign terms contained in those scientific or pseudoscientific 'instructions for use' – vagina, clitoris, penis, erection, coitus, orgasm, ejaculation, sperm. There was no end to my reading because each of these keywords led me to further words I wished to find out about – masturbation, uterus, menstruation, syphilis and many more.

Thus the Brockhaus Encyclopaedia became my textbook in matters of sex – a textbook whose factual control pleased me but whose dryness disappointed me. But it was not long before I discovered that the information which I sought and urgently needed was also to be found in a very different kind of publication, and that the subject was dealt with there less factually, but all the more colourfully.

It occurred to me that I might impress my girl cousin with these directions for use – a pretty and lively girl, only two years my senior, and by no means prudish. She was most grateful for the printed slip of paper which I showed her and, in a fit of generosity, made her a present of. Fortunately she felt she should repay my kindness in an appropriate manner. Clearly she wanted to prove to me that she was not living in the backwoods and that, at the age of fourteen, she was almost an adult. She gave me a fattish book and allowed me to take it home, but she advised me to read only the passages she had marked.

Back home, expecting the book to be something improper, I locked myself in the bathroom with it. But it soon turned out that there was no need for that. This was a serious novel, with admittedly some passages touching on sexual matters. I began by reading only the marked bits. I liked them, I found them instructive and, at the same time, charming and even poetic. I was stimulated both by *what* was said and by *how* it was said.

Having, with flushed cheeks, read everything that had struck my cousin I decided to disregard her advice and read the whole book. I did not regret it. Maybe it was then that I realized what mattered in literature – that meaning and presentation, content and form, cannot be separated. The book that provided me with those early insights into sexuality and some elementary insights into literary problems was Hermann Hesse's novel *Narcissus and Goldmund*.

When I reread this book in the 1950s my early impression did not prove enduring. That rather strong mixture of German romantic tradition and unworldly inwardness, of gentle sentimentality and angry contempt for civilization, no longer appealed to me. I had a similar experience with another, surely a more important, novel by Hesse, *Steppenwolf*. I read it, not entirely from choice, three times: in the 1930s I was enchanted, in the 1950s disappointed, in the 1960s horrified.

But there is one book by Hesse whose 'soul food' suited my generation and which I found moving and impressive even later – his novel *Unterm Rad*, published as early as 1904. Although I did not myself suffer greatly at school and was never tormented by my teachers, gloomy schoolboy novels were among my favourite reading matter – especially *Freund Hein* [*Friend Hein*] by Emil Strauss, Musil's *Verwirrungen des Zöglings Törless* [*Young Torless*] and, of course, the final part of Mann's *Buddenbrooks*. No doubt what attracted me then was the literary quality of these books, and more especially their surprisingly strong identification appeal to teenagers.

In attempting to extend and deepen my information on sexual matters, I was helped not so much by the intellectual Narcissus as by the artist Goldmund. That Faust got Gretchen pregnant I had known for a long time, but unfortunately I could not find the scene in Goethe's play when this happened. Then, probably for the first time, I began to suspect that in literature the most important things are contained between the lines or between the scenes. In Schiller's *Die Räuber* I was startled by Spiegelberg's crude account of the raid on a convent of nuns. How, I wondered, would our German teacher cope with this scene? He made it easy for himself – he skipped it.

My youthful fantasy was greatly fired by the novels of Jakob

Wassermann. He was a moralist with a weakness for shallow pomposity, an impassioned psychologist with a bent for trashy writing. He was fond of the demonic and the decorative, the problematical and the piquant. His books attracted countless readers but only a few serious critics. But I admit that in my teens I rather liked his verbose and overblown novels, perhaps because of their sexual motifs.

I was so deeply affected by one situation in Wassermann's *Gänsemännchen* [*The Goose-Man*] that I remembered it many years later. A man wants to see his girlfriend naked. She turns out the light. She undresses – he hears the rustle of her clothes. She opens the stove door – the red glow makes her abdomen, especially her pubic hair, shine dark red ... I have now looked for that passage in *Das Gänsemännchen*. It turned out that I preserved it accurately in my memory for sixty years – except that the pubic hair does not exist in Wassermann: it was the product of my thirteen- or fourteen-year-old imagination.

I was just as excited by a passage in Flaubert's *Madame Bovary*. The estate owner Rodolphe Boulanger, returning from a visit to the Bovarys, meditates on what he experienced there. '*Time and again he saw Emma before him, in the same room and dressed as he had just seen her, and in his mind he undressed her.*' These few simple words – '*and in his mind he undressed her*' – alarmed me and imprinted themselves on me for ever.

Today I know why they had that effect on me: I discovered, to my surprise, that my occasional fantasies were by no means uncommon, that there had been men before me who had thought of undressing a woman in their mind. I understood that there was something to be discovered and recognized in literature which was of an importance that could not be overstated – one could discover oneself there, one's own emotions and thoughts, one's hopes and inhibitions.

Around the same time I read in a novel by Zola how a young girl feels about her first menstruation. That interested and excited me greatly. But I regretted that nothing of the kind was to be found in literature about the experience of boys having their first erection or ejaculation. Alfred Döblin, who had grown up in the nineteenth century, reports that the first time he saw a naked woman was as a medical student at the age of twenty-three – it was a female corpse in the dissection room. Things were not quite as bad for me, but even so I was not granted my first view of a naked woman until shortly before taking my school-leaving exam.

My grandfather, the rabbi, died in 1936 at the age of eighty-eight. For at least five years he had been blind. Nevertheless he insisted that the heavy volumes with the Hebrew writings of his ancestors should lie on the table before him, so that he could touch them. As he was unable to read the newspapers, and as he had not left his flat for some time, we did not find it difficult to spare him the reality of the Third Reich. Whoever visited him was asked to avoid the subject.

When he was buried at the Jewish cemetery in Weissensee – this was the first time I attended such a ceremony – I was surprised to see that my grandfather was not, as I had expected, buried in a coffin, but in an ordinary box. The reason was explained to me: all men were equal before God, and for that reason it was not permissible for some to be buried in fine decorated, or even luxurious, coffins while others, those from poor families, were buried in simple or even shabby ones. That was why it had been the custom for thousands of years, at least among believing Jews, to treat their dead equally and to bury them in plain, unadorned wooden boxes of rough planks. With my mind having been made receptive to symbols by literature, I like this archaic custom and felt respect for this humility in the face of death.

Of my mother's six siblings only her youngest brother, then thirty-six, was absent from the burial. He was a handsome, elegant man, in the opinion of some of the family a little too elegant and something of a show-off. He was an attorney with an office on Unter den Linden, which the family regarded as inappropriate, as a sign of his hubris. He had broken the mould in two respects. He had a weakness for horse-racing and his bets occasionally landed him in serious financial trouble. Secondly, unlike his four brothers, he had a liaison with a non-Jewess, whom he later married, an impressive lady who claimed to be an actress. Except that no one had ever seen her on the stage or the screen.

This uncle left Germany immediately after the Nazi rise to power – moreover, in a great hurry, allegedly because of some debts. With a Mexican passport he had moved to France where he survived the war as a member of the Foreign Legion. That sounds rather more adventurous and dramatic than it actually was. But he did not have such a bad time in the French Foreign Legion. He was in charge of the library.

After my grandfather's burial my mother's brothers reflected on who was to be their father's heir. But the poor rabbi had left nothing, absolutely nothing – only a gold watch, a present on his bar mitzvah in 1861. The brothers decided that as he had loved none of his grandchildren more than me, the watch should be mine. I received it with some pride. I still owned it in the Warsaw ghetto. There I had to sell this beautiful old-fashioned watch, much as it hurt, because I needed money urgently – to pay for an abortion.

The death of my grandfather changed our lives. The monthly subsidies from my mother's brothers stopped and financially we were worse and worse off. His spacious room was therefore quickly refurbished and let. The woman who moved in disturbed me, I have to confess it, from the start. She was nearly thirty, tall, slim and blonde and, if I remember correctly, came from Kiel. Her appearance certainly betrayed her north German origin. She was, in the language of those days, an Aryan. She usually dressed a little extravagantly – she was fond of long, close-fitting black trousers of velvet or artificial silk, and a dark-red or purple jacket down to her knees, reminiscent of a tail-coat. This wardrobe probably owed much to the example of that actress who had fascinated a whole generation of men and women but whose name could no longer be mentioned in public in the Third Reich – Marlene Dietrich. By profession our blond lodger was a photographer; she worked in the publicity department of a large firm. Her name was by no means extravagant – she was, like the most famous lover in German literature, called simply Lotte.

What is love? In 1991 I was asked, by a German illustrated journal, to define the concept. But it had to be done in a single sentence. The task tempted me, but the fee offered seemed much too low. I told the editor that I was willing to write what they wanted, but it would have to be at least two typewritten pages. A single sentence on this subject was far too much trouble and would be worth five times the fee offered. In other words, the shorter the text the higher the fee. They agreed. I wrote: '*What we call love is that extreme emotion which leads from affection to passion and from passion to dependence; it throws the individual into a state of intoxication capable, at times, of diminishing his or her soundness of mind. It is a happiness that gives rise to suffering and a suffering which brings happiness.'*

Did I love Lotte? I am not sure. But for the first time in my life my interest in a woman soon turned into a steadily increasing sympathy, an intense affection which was not yet passion and did not lead to dependence, but which nevertheless agitated me to a degree until then not experienced. There was no intoxication, yet I surmised what love is, or, more exactly, what it can be.

I conducted lengthy conversations with the attractive and somewhat shy photographer – usually in her room or on our balcony. I am still astonished that she had so much time for me. Why? Perhaps because she found herself in a life crisis and needed someone who would listen to her. When Tolstoy felt the urge to talk from the heart he hired a carriage and had himself driven through the town. What he absolutely had to tell, he would now tell – the coachman. So maybe I was the coachman for Lotte: she liked the receptiveness and curiosity of a sixteen-year-old, she welcomed his cautious questions. That he quite obviously admired her did not bother her in the slightest.

I was flattered by Lotte's confidence. Anything she told me or, more frequently, hinted at about her past, seemed a generous gift to me. For the first time I realized that speaking about oneself can be an exceptional gift, something equalling or approaching surrender. Moreover, Lotte, as no one before her, took me entirely seriously and, without any fuss, treated me as an equal, as an adult. Like all teenagers, presumably, I urgently needed that recognition and it made it easier for me to bear my isolated existence. For this I was grateful to her. I began to understand that love also always has to do with the need for self-confirmation and that there is no love without gratitude. It need not arise from gratitude but it leads to it – or else dies.

We talked a lot about literature, especially about the French and Russian novelists of the nineteenth century, whose work she knew well. Of course we also spoke about German writers, often about those who were forbidden or at least unwelcome at that time – about Arthur Schnitzler and Franz Werfel, about Thomas and Heinrich Mann. It was some time before I noticed that, whether we were talking about Stendhal or Balzac, about Dostoevsky or Chekhov, Lotte's attention was mainly focused on the female characters and

on erotic motifs. That was probably the secret of our relationship –
we needed to talk about love, but for entirely different reasons.

She had not been spared disappointments. Some time ago she had
parted from a friend – or, as she emphasized, had had to part from
him. A little later, a lover had abandoned her. She was seeking
consolation and protection – in literature. And I? I believed I
knew about love because I had an excellent and reliable source of
information. From this inexhaustible source I could draw the most
beautiful and most intelligent words about love – but only words. In
short, the north German blonde came from love to literature, while
I wanted to escape from literature to love. We met halfway.

Our balcony talks made me realize again that we – the quiet
photographer and the restless student – were reading books mainly
to understand ourselves. As we were both on a quest for ourselves a
partnership arose which gave our dialogue an unmistakably erotic
tone though by no means a sexual one. I never touched the woman
I talked to about love in literature; it never occurred to me – as
Rodolphe Boulanger did to Emma Bovary – to undress her in my
mind. Her words and glances, her confidences and understanding,
were enough for me. And the more clearly she revealed herself, and
perhaps exposed herself, while speaking of characters in novels –
always speaking very softly – the more I felt enlightened and enriched.

It was not long before – inevitably, as it seemed to me – a name
cropped up in our conversation, a name which deepened the already
perceptible intimacy – the name of Fontane. At that time I only
knew *Effi Briest* and *Irrungen, Wirrungen* [*Entanglements*], whereas
she knew nearly all Fontane's novels. But very quickly she homed in
on one of them and frequently returned to it – *Der Stechlin*. Her
interest, however, was not in the landed aristocrat Dubslav von
Stechlin, or in his son Woldemar, or any other male character, but
chiefly in Melusine, the Countess von Barby.

The good-looking, clever and witty Melusine – whose marriage
was soon to end in divorce – had been, as Fontane put it, married
and perhaps not married. This sounds mysterious but can scarcely
be misunderstood. The allusion is to her husband's sexual failure: it
is this which has deeply offended and hurt her. This is probably the
reason for Melusine's unusual nature. Just as she loves what is
striking, so she personifies it herself. Longing for love and happiness,

she arouses, deliberately or not, the longings both of men and of women. She is a proud woman, reserved and provocative, cool yet warm-hearted. Melusine's emphatic self-assurance possibly hides nothing other than insecurity. Is it these contradictions which enhance her character, which heighten her attraction?

Perhaps it was a good thing that I did not then know *Der Stechlin*. I was thus able to let the story of Melusine affect me without worrying whether it really corresponded to the text of the novel or whether the narrator had, knowingly or unwittingly, enriched what had remained in her memory with new features and nuances. I was able to learn from our dialogue how one could talk about oneself without exhibitionism – and quite certainly I also learned a thing or two about love.

Our conversations were getting ever longer and, as it seems to me today, ever more beautiful. But this idyll on the balcony overlooking Güntzelstrasse in Wilmersdorf came to an abrupt end. Our attractive tenant gave notice: she was in a great rush, she was in a panic. She was clearly embarrassed about explaining to us why she had to leave. The reason was that she was afraid – and this had something to do with me.

A few months previously, in the autumn of 1935, laws had been enacted by the Reich government which revoked the emancipation of the Jews. On pain of heavy prison sentences the 'Nuremberg Laws' prohibited marriage, as well as extramarital relations, between Jews and 'Aryans'. By 1936 sentences on Jews and non-Jews for 'racial defilement' were a daily occurrence and the press reported on the brutal public maltreatment and pillorying of those accused of having infringed those laws.

Yet the north German photographer, the 'Aryan', had had no misgivings about moving in with us. Because she despised the Nazis? There may have been a touch of recklessness in it. My father and my brother were by then living in Warsaw, but I was still in Berlin and subject to the racial laws. I might have become a liability to our tenant. She had now been expressly warned and, quite rightly, was drawing her conclusions. She left our flat the very next day.

I did not see her again until 1952, in Warsaw. She was living in East Berlin, married to a communist who had spent several years in prison in the Third Reich. Now we were again face to face – she, no longer working as a photographer but holding some post in the GDR administration, and I, after some roundabout wanderings, having returned to literature. In the presence of our (mostly silent) spouses we recounted to each other what we had been through. Then the talk turned to communism, to conditions in the GDR and in Poland, to our disappointments and to our disillusionments.

She spoke as softly as in the past, and it seemed to me that, as before, she was yearning for love and happiness, as though this yearning was, as before, personified in her own manner – attractively and charmingly, though now with clear traces of resignation. Suddenly she asked me a question which must have astonished our respective partners. What about Fontane? I answered factually that Fontane was not known in Poland at all: not one of his books had been translated. But perhaps this would change before long as I had recently succeeded in arranging for a Polish edition of his *Schach von Wuthenow* [*The Shah of Wuthenow*]. This, at least, was a start.

She nodded, with a smile which was slightly ironical. She had understood that I had evaded her question. So she repeated it more clearly: she would like to know my present attitude to Melusine. To those present, the question must have seemed unworldly or at least irrelevant – as perhaps also my reply. Whether I still loved Melusine – I said – I really did not know. But I knew perfectly well that I would never forget her.

97

9

THE DOOR TO THE
NEXT ROOM

I no longer remember her name. Nor do I know how it came about that she invited me to dinner. Perhaps she wished to please someone, maybe my sister or my brother-in-law. She had probably been told that there was a young man living near her who was passionately interested in the theatre and would enjoy talking to her about her experiences. She was an actress.

She had graduated from a drama school in Berlin and had been employed for nearly two years – in Hildesheim or perhaps in Braunschweig. She had had an opportunity of working in Hanover, but nothing came of it. Because this was 1933 and she was Jewish. Afterwards she married an evidently prosperous businessman who was not a Jew. The marriage soon ended in divorce. Then, at the beginning of 1938, she was living on her own, as it happened quite near us, in a pleasant but simply furnished apartment. That was also how she dressed. A tight beige sweater, a blue scarf round her neck, a wide dark-brown skirt – everything seemed carefully chosen and yet was inconspicuous.

What she told me about the theatre sobered me up a little – that provincial theatres did not want to know about art, that they were stuck in a routine, that no première was adequately rehearsed, that the actors ceaselessly had to learn new parts and that beginners had a particularly difficult time. I knew all that. Instead of listening to her attentively I was, perhaps a little too obviously, interested in her sweater. Of course she noticed it. But whether her smile meant encouragement or rejection I was unable to judge.

She told me she was getting ready to leave Germany and would do so quite soon. When did I plan to emigrate and where to? I must first take my school-leaving exam, I replied, and that would be in two months' time. And then? Beyond that I had no plans. I was ashamed of my vagueness. She was evidently touched by the fact that the, until then, rather voluble young man had suddenly become monosyllabic. She remarked, not at all unpleasantly, that I was clearly more interested in Shakespeare than in my future.

We were both silent and an uncomfortable pause ensued. To bridge it, I asked her if she would like to speak a part for me. She was not at all bashful and agreed immediately. With quick movements she switched off the ceiling light and rearranged a small standard lamp. She was standing in front of the corner fireplace, deep in thought. Before long she had decided on a text which, evidently, she thought suitable for me. It was the scene of a young lover, written by a nineteen-year-old, from Hofmannsthal's little play *Death and the Fool*. It started like this:

> *Yes it was lovely ... Have you quite forgotten?*
> *It's true, you hurt me, hurt me, oh, so much...*
> *But, after all, what doesn't end in pain?*

Admittedly, this monologue of the girl lover is not, to put it mildly, free from sentimentality, it is certainly not the best literature. And yet I love these verses as I love Rilke's '*Cornet*'. That they never fail to move me is due to the young woman from whom I first heard them in a half-darkened room.

After the words 'dim pleasure', with which the monologue concludes, she stepped up to me and regarded me silently and sadly. I was waiting, but nothing happened. Suddenly she said she would also like to recite a poem by Hofmannsthal, the most beautiful poem she knew. She meant the *Tercinas on Transience* with the wonderful second stanza:

> *This is a thing that mocks the deepest mind*
> *And far too terrifying for lament:*
> *That all flows by us, leaving us behind.*

When she had finished I risked some observations on Hofmannsthal's poetry. They were probably banal or even foolish. She ignored my efforts with the brief sentence: '*Lord, it is time*'. I no longer remember whether I recognized the Rilke quote. I nodded and we went out into the hall. As I was trying to take my overcoat off the hook she stopped me with a gesture and opened a door – not one leading to the staircase but into the next room. It was rather dark in there: the light came from a small lamp standing next to a wide couch.

As I was walking home through the deserted streets a single verse kept going through my head, always the same one: *This is a thing that mocks the deepest mind*. The next day I wrote her a short letter. It remained unanswered. Three weeks later I received a slim packet through the mail – posted in Paris but without a sender's address. It contained the small Insel volume with Hofmannsthal's *Death and the Fool*. The dedication read: '*What doesn't end in pain?*' As I could find no address I was unable to thank the sender of this book. But I still thank her in my mind.

The inevitable shock was soon overcome. Studying for my school-leaving exam took up much of my time. And soon a new friendship began which, without exciting or confusing me, became important to me. Friends of my parents had a daughter called Angelika. She was fifteen or sixteen, was interested in literature and the theatre, and had already written a few things which had actually been published – in the periodical *Jüdische Rundschau*. This soon turned out to be an exaggeration: her poems and prose pieces had indeed appeared, but in the children's supplement of the journal. I found them rather insignificant, but I was impressed by the fact that they had been published. But most of all I liked the girl's seriousness.

Now and again we would meet in the Stadtpark Schöneberg. We had long talks about the plays of Schiller and Kleist, on which Angelika Hurwicz was quite well informed. Next I introduced her to Shakespeare, which was fun for me. Eventually we arrived at Heine's erotic poetry. That was the only erotic thing there was between us. What had brought us together was not just love for literature, but also the similarity of our situations. Asked how she pictured her future, she answered unhesitatingly. She wanted to attend a drama school and become an actress. I too had a clear and decisive answer: I wanted to do German studies at the university and become a critic.

We both realized that our plans were impossible, that they were absurd daydreams. After all, we were living in the Third Reich, where Jews were excluded from studying and could have no professional prospects whatsoever. But why should we not dream and fantasize? She spoke of the parts she hoped to play; I spoke of the poets I wanted to write about. Later, when I was in Warsaw, I quoted to her, in a letter, the verse from Heine: '*My child, yes, we were children . . .*' Soon afterwards war broke out and contact with Angelika was severed.

When I was in Berlin in the winter of 1946 the Deutsches Theater staged *Hamlet* with Horst Caspar in the title role. In the programme the name Angelika Hurwicz caught my eye. I felt sure that this must be her. So she had survived, she had realized her intention, and was now on the stage of one of the best German theatres. Admittedly only as a lady at court, a silent part. But that was how acting careers usually began. I did not recognize her – probably because she was heavily made up and wore a wig.

After the performance I waited at the stage door. The situation was a little strange. I was wearing the uniform of a Polish officer and it was almost dark by then. Would she recognize me? Would there be a stiff, rather awkward, conversation between two people who had become strangers to each other? A cool reunion with one of the few girls I had known well before the war, and who was now back in Berlin, would disappoint me more than a cordial meeting would please me. I wanted to see Angelika Hurwicz, but I was scared. Cowardice won: I did not wait, I went home. And although I remained in Berlin for a few more months I did not seek her out.

At the beginning of the 1950s, however, her name started appearing in Warsaw and I found it more and more frequently in newspapers from the GDR. There were no other German papers in Warsaw. So, in the meantime, she had become an established and successful actress. She owed her exceptional success primarily to the part of the silent Kattrin in Brecht's *Mother Courage*.

In December 1952 Brecht's theatre, the Berliner Ensemble, brought three plays to Warsaw, including *Mother Courage* – with Helene Weigel and Angelika Hurwicz in the main roles. On this occasion there was a reception at the GDR embassy – mainly for critics. They were to be given an opportunity to talk to the principal actors. I was in a virtually empty room, where my chief interest was the bookcase. But I had no time to inspect the neat rows of books on the shelves, for Angelika Hurwicz, escorted by one of the GDR's Warsaw diplomats, entered the room. As he politely enquired: 'May I introduce you', we both answered simultaneously: 'No need.' Then we started talking – and we talked a lot during the following days.

We went for walks, as we used to do in Berlin. I felt none of the awkwardness that I had been afraid of. She told me what had happened to her, how she had managed to survive the war. She had been taken on by a small Sudeten German travelling theatre, an old-fashioned family enterprise. As an actress? Oh yes – and she had to study new roles all the time. In addition she had to do whatever needed doing – act as a prompter, a scene shifter, raise the curtain, sit in the box office, and so on. It had not been easy, but no one had asked to see her personal documents, no one had been interested in whether she was Jewish. Then it was my turn to report on what had happened to me during those years. Suddenly Angelika Hurwicz seemed a little embarrassed: 'Forgive me,' she said, 'I don't even know what you do. What your profession is.' I replied briefly: 'Well, I have become a critic: I write about German literature.'

She paused and I was not quite sure how to interpret her silence. After a while she began to speak slowly and thoughtfully: 'In the midst of the Third Reich, in a hopeless situation, the two of us, two Jewish teenagers, spoke of a future in which we could not seriously believe for a moment. How could a Jewess become an actress or a Jew a critic? But we nevertheless allowed ourselves the luxury of dreaming of a life in the theatre or literature. It was probably our dreams which brought us together. And it seems scarcely believable – our dreams have actually come true. While our people were being murdered we were spared. We were not shot or gassed. We have survived without deserving it. We owe it to pure chance. For incomprehensible reasons we are the chosen children of horror. We are marked people and will remain marked to our final days. Do you realize this?' 'Yes,' I said, 'I do.'

10

WITH INVISIBLE LUGGAGE

The closer the final exams drew, the greater was my fear. It was not the examinations I was afraid of, nor possible harassment by teachers, let alone classmates. Nor did I fear that, readily recognizable as a Jew as I was, something might happen to me in the street or on public transport. Surprising as this may sound today, I never suffered any hostility in Berlin, and never witnessed any.

What I was in permanent fear of were further anti-Jewish decrees by the authorities; these could have made my life hell. Each day I searched the paper – we took the *Deutsche Allgemeine Zeitung* as the *Berliner Tageblatt* had ceased publication – for any new measures directed against the Jews. These were frequently to be found but not, so far, those which would concern me most. I was tormented by the thought that Jews might be excluded from German schools, or at least from the school-leaving exam. Not getting my school-leaving certificate, my *Abitur*, would – I was convinced of this then – have been a major calamity for me.

In the end, the few Jewish students who remained at the Fichte-Gymnasium were not expelled. We were allowed to take our exam. Why was that? I did not discover the reason until half a century later. It was due to a personal decision by Hitler. Towards the end of 1936 his education minister, Rust, submitted to him the draft of a 'Jewish school law', providing for the segregation of Jewish pupils on racial grounds. But that would have meant that children of the Christian faith, who were Jewish within the meaning of the Nuremberg Laws, could have attended only Jewish schools – against which the Primate of the Catholic Church in the Reich, Cardinal

Bertram of Breslau, protested. Not wishing to put any further strain on relations with the Catholic Church, Hitler chose to postpone the 'Jewish school law' for the time being.

What I feared almost as much was that Jews would one day be prohibited from going to theatres and opera houses. This would have meant expulsion from my wonderful refuge, from my ivory tower. As a matter of fact, from 12 November 1938, Jews – by order of the Reich Chamber of Culture – were banned 'with immediate effect from visiting theatres, cinemas, concerts, lectures, artistic events, dance performances and exhibitions of a cultural kind', but by then I was no longer in Berlin.

What was to become of me? This question weighed on me throughout my school days, most heavily of course in my final year and more heavily still after my school-leaving exam.

For the other, non-Jewish pupils, the school-leaving exam was the longed-for release from school discipline. And for me? Of course I dreamed of all kinds of professions. To be a *Dozent* [lecturer] or a professor of German literature – that seemed to me a wonderful vocation. Or perhaps work as a dramaturgist? That also seemed attractive because it combined the two areas of my principal interest – literature and the theatre. However, the profession to which I was most strongly drawn, and one that was discredited in the Third Reich, was that of critic. These were dreams which I did not dare to discuss with anyone. I asked my family what was to become of me. No one had an answer. My father, by then in Warsaw, was unable to look after me and my mother was equally helpless.

My five Berlin male and female cousins, all of them roughly of my age, were being sent to colleges in England. There they survived the Second World War. I too could have been sent to England, but that needed money – a certain, not even excessive, amount per month, but it had to be guaranteed. There could be no question of that in our family.

Every student who wished to sit the school-leaving exam had to submit an application in which he was required to state what he intended to do after school. I said I wished to study German language and literature. On my 'certificate of maturity' it stated accordingly: 'Reich wishes to study at the university.' In point of fact, my mother did not entirely rule out the possibility that, as a Polish citizen, I might be able at least to begin my studies at the University of Berlin. This was a naive, unrealistic idea, possibly due to the fact that my brother had been able to obtain his doctorate in Berlin as recently as 1935. I therefore submitted a matriculation application and, as was to be expected, received a rejection notice from the Friedrich Wilhelm University.

To crown this unworldliness, I yielded to my mother's urgings and requested an interview with the Rector of the university. It was – and this astonishes me to this day – immediately granted. The Rector received me and was exceedingly polite. Evidently he did not wish to say that Jews were no longer admitted, so he pleaded a shortage of university places.

I was never able to make up for what was denied me then – I never studied at a university. Not until some decades later did I see the interior of a university lecture theatre. That was in Göttingen in 1961, when I was invited to give a lecture there. I therefore know lecture theatres only from the lectern end. Since that useless visit to the Rector in the spring of 1938 I have never set foot inside the building of what, after the Second World War, became the Humboldt University.

In the end there was a job for me, but one which had nothing in common with the things I was interested in. I found a position as a trainee in an export firm in Charlottenburg, whose owner was a Jew but which, for some reason or other, continued to operate. The work was exhausting and boring, but I did not mind. Even this kind of work seemed better to me than none.

When I asked my boss what I would be qualified to do if I managed to complete my apprenticeship, he replied curtly: 'If you're lucky, go into business.' This is just what I never learned. However, there were two things I did gain from my brief traineeship – it saved me from getting depressed and it taught me how a well-organized office functions.

Meanwhile my mother, too, had moved back to Warsaw. I was living in a tiny furnished room on Spichernstrasse in Charlottenburg, where Brecht had once lived with Helene Weigel. Over the years the situation of the Jews had drastically changed for the worse. In 1933 and 1934 they might still have expected friendly and reassuring words from non-Jewish neighbours and acquaintances, to the effect that things would soon change for the better: 'You'll just have to hang on.' The Jews liked these reassurances, except that in 1938 they were no longer to be heard.

Arrests, abuse and torture soon reduced the number of incorrigible optimists and increased the number of emigrés. In 1938, to the horror not only of the Jews, identification by name was officially introduced. Jewish women had the additional first name 'Sara' forced upon them and men the name 'Israel'. In addition, the passports of Jews had a large 'J' stamped on every page.

Added to these dramatic and mostly cruel measures were others designed not so much to terrify as to humiliate. In the parks there were now yellow benches labelled 'Jews only' – needless to say, these were few in number and in the least favourable locations. In many restaurants and cafés, in hotels and bathing places, notices were displayed: 'Jews not welcome here' or 'No admission for Jews'. Some cafés preferred to dispense with such notices, but if a Jew ventured inside he would have an empty cup placed before him, sometimes with a slip of paper saying 'Jews out!' In some places these notices were erected even at the entrance to the towns.

The plight of the Jews at that time was made worse by the Reich government's foreign successes. After the *Anschluss* of Austria in March 1938 the regime seemed as though it would be in power for a long time to come. Nevertheless the number of Jews preparing to emigrate rose only slowly. Eventually my sister and her husband, Gerhard Böhm, decided to leave Germany. They wanted to go to England. It was a vague plan which lacked the slightest basis. If they succeeded, they hoped that I would join them. However, the German authorities had other plans for me.

In the early morning of 28 October 1938, it was not yet seven o'clock, I was vigorously awakened by a policeman who looked no different from those who controlled the traffic in the streets. Having carefully examined my passport, he handed me a document. It said that I was being expelled from the German Reich. The policeman ordered me to get dressed at once and to come along with him. But I asked to be allowed to read the document again. This was allowed. I then took the liberty of objecting, a little timidly, that the paper said I had to leave the Reich within a fortnight – and, moreover, I had the right to appeal. Such subtleties did not move the rather impassive policeman. 'No, come along at once.'

Needless to say, I had to leave behind everything that I had in my little room. I was only allowed to take five marks with me, as well as a briefcase. But I did not quite know what to put in it. In the hurry I put in a spare handkerchief and something to read. I was reading Balzac's *Woman of Thirty* – so I packed that. I was clearly not very nervous because I thought of making a present to my landlady of a ticket for the next première at the Gendarmenmarkt – Shaw's *Doctor's Dilemma* with Gründgens and Werner Krauss in the leading roles. Incidentally, I did not miss much: in spite of the star casting it was, as I subsequently learned, only a mediocre production.

The policeman walked alongside me through the still dark streets at a comfortable pace. People were hurrying to their jobs, the trams ran as usual, the shops were being opened, Berlin's daily routine was just beginning – but I was excluded from it. Someone must have been telling lies about me, for without having done anything wrong I was under arrest. Yes, I was actually being led away. Before long the policeman and I had reached our destination: the district's police headquarters.

Here I immediately found myself among ten or perhaps twenty fellow victims. They were Jews, all of them older than me, the eighteen-year-old. They were speaking perfect German and not a word of Polish. They had either been born in Germany, or had come to Germany as small children and attended school there. But like me they all, as I soon discovered, had Polish passports.

We were kept waiting for an hour or two and were then taken in a Black Maria to an assembly point, a police precinct on Sophie-Charlotte-Platz. Hundreds of Jews were already standing there, in the open – likewise, as it turned out, Polish citizens. Now I realized that my assumption had been wrong. No one had denounced me. I merely belonged to a group which was condemned, initially, to deportation only. There were some 18,000 Jews in all. This was the first officially organized mass deportation of Jews. In Berlin only men were expelled; in other German cities women were expelled too.

Not until the late afternoon, when it was dark, were we taken to a siding of the Schlesischer Bahnhof. There a long train was waiting. Everything had been carefully prepared, there was no shouting and no shooting. Clearly the operation was not to attract attention. We were not told where the train was going, but it was soon clear that it was going east – to the Polish frontier. We were freezing, the carriages were not heated, but everyone had a seat. Compared to subsequent transports these were humane, indeed almost luxurious, conditions.

I read the Balzac novel, which seemed bad to me and did not interest me at all. Was this, I wondered, because of the apprehension I was feeling? Evidently I had no serious worries yet. At the German frontier we had to get off the train and form up in columns. There were shouted commands, many shots, shrill screams in the darkness. Then a train arrived. It was a short Polish train, into which the German police now brutally drove us.

The carriages were crammed full. The doors were immediately slammed shut and sealed, and the train pulled out. Now we, the expelled, were among our own, including women from different towns. Most of them had been arrested in the middle of the night and many had not been allowed to dress. They were wearing nightdresses beneath their overcoats. Close to me stood a dark-haired girl from Hanover: she might have been twenty. With tears in her eyes she asked me questions I could not answer. The crush became ever tighter. Suddenly she stroked me and pressed my hand against her breast. I was taken aback, I wanted to say something. But somebody pushed me aside. She called out two or three words to me, perhaps an address, but I did not catch them.

What would happen to me in Poland? The closer we got to our (as yet undisclosed) destination, the more the simple question as to my future troubled me. It seemed to me just as gloomy, just as impenetrable, as the forests through which we were slowly travelling. The train jerked to a stop. We had arrived at the Polish frontier station but were not allowed to leave the train. Not until several hours later were the sealed doors opened.

What was I to do in a country which was completely strange to me, whose language I understood but only spoke badly and with an effort? What was I to do in Poland without a profession and without the chance of learning one? My only luggage was the briefcase containing the Balzac novel and my spare handkerchief.

But I had brought along something else on this journey, something that, admittedly, was invisible. However, I did not think of that in the cold train on which I was being deported from Germany. I could not then suspect what a role this invisible luggage – which I then thought of as useless and superfluous – would play in my future life. Because from the country from which I had been expelled I had taken a language with me, the German language, and a literature, the German literature.

PART TWO

1938–1944

11

POETRY AND THE WAR

So I was now back in Poland – the land of my birth, which had become my place of exile. Everything was strange to me, and Poland has always remained a little like that. But my situation, initially, was not at all bad, certainly better than that of most of the Jews expelled from Germany in the autumn of 1938. My brother and my parents shared a flat in Warsaw, which additionally housed my brother's dental practice. Small as the flat was, there was of course room enough to put up a camp-bed for me. And I was able to make myself understood in Polish.

But I did not know what to do. Nobody knew. There could be no question of studying at the university, if only for financial reasons. And who was going to give me a job? I was unemployed, a superfluous person. At least the one thing I knew – German – proved useful. I gave German tuition to students who had difficulties at school. I did not earn a lot, but enough to afford fairly frequent theatre and concert tickets – needless to say, the cheapest available.

My first fine moment in Warsaw was in a concert hall. It was a symphony concert conducted by a young man who came from Vienna and who is still well known today, though perhaps more as a musicologist – Kurt Pahlen. The concert began with Mozart's *Eine kleine Nachtmusik* – which was not nearly as hackneyed then as it is today – and instantly I felt a little better, though still lonely. When, nearly fifty years later, in 1995, the distinguished figure of Kurt Pahlen approached me in the foyer of the Great Festival Building in Salzburg during an interval, politely introduced himself and immediately tried to thank me for something I had written somewhere, I stopped him short and said: '*If anyone has to thank anyone, then it is me. Your concerts helped me then and I have never forgotten you.*' It was a moving moment for the two elderly gentlemen in dinner jackets who stood facing each other.

Joyful and sorrowful at the same time – that was how I felt in Warsaw then. I had what the unemployed always have – a lot of time on my hands. I could therefore set out on a search. But for what? In Poland, too, I decided to search for German literature. My library, containing many, not particularly good, editions of the classics, countless banned books and those which the friendly chemist had 'lent' me before his emigration, had remained in Berlin.

I soon found what I now wanted: I was anxious to discover what Thomas and Heinrich Mann, Arnold and Stefan Zweig, Alfred Döblin and Joseph Roth, Werfel, Feuchtwanger and Brecht had written in exile, since 1933. That was not difficult because there were many private lending libraries in Warsaw, some of them well stocked with German books. A friend of my brother's, a failed lawyer with a secret love of literature, proposed a deal to me – in return for having German conversation with him two or three times a week, he would introduce me to the history of Polish literature. I agreed at once and I have never regretted it.

To this day my knowledge of Polish literature is neither solid nor thorough. But the failed lawyer's hints and comments had a certain system about them, and my command of the Polish language, which is melodious and seductive but by no means easy, was improving all the time. Soon I was in a position to make an unexpected discovery which, before long, was to play an important part in my life. During the first months of 1939 I discovered contemporary Polish poetry.

I was astonished by its elegiac and melancholic tone which was never weakened, let alone challenged, by its wit or irony. I was charmed by what characterized and ennobled this poetry – its insistent passion and winged perfection. I was delighted by its natural, unassuming combination of vitality and musicality. To my surprise, something in the verses of those Polish poets was closer to me than Rilke and George, apart from a few of Rilke's poems, which I had admired rather than loved. Maybe this was due to the fact that the Poles, who were simultaneously lyrical and satirical poets, often reminded me of Heine and occasionally of Brecht. Reading their verses – and this seems so obvious I am almost ashamed to say so – I was reminded also of Chopin's mazurkas and polonaises, of his preludes and ballads.

In fact, next to the works of Chopin, poetry is the Poles' finest contribution to European art. I still believe this. Unfortunately Europe was never much concerned about Polish poetry. This is as regrettable as it is understandable, but it is a misfortune for Polish literature. Because Polish novels, with few exceptions, do not rise above mediocrity and the same is true of Polish drama, unless it is verse drama. Polish poetry, however, stubbornly resists attempts to translate it into another language. While we have respectable German translations, really good ones are exceedingly rare.

What I found particularly enchanting and attractive was the work of the poets who became known shortly after the First World War and were called in Poland, after the journal founded by them, the 'Skamandrites'. The greatest among them was a poet of incomparable versatility – Julian Tuwim, born in 1894, the son of a Jewish bookkeeper in Łódź. In the 1920s he became one of the most highly esteemed and praised poets and satirists in Poland, but also the most frequently attacked. Only the fact that he succeeded in fleeing to France in time, and thence to the United States, saved him from the gas chamber.

In the early 1950s I was occasionally able to have a chat with him in the café of the Polish Writers' Union in Warsaw. Tuwim was a quiet and exceedingly charming person. But the more modest his manner – and it was a rather too pointed, somewhat coquettish modesty – the more I felt that this slim, handsome man in his late fifties, was acting a part.

I am pretty sure that I would have had the same impression in conversation with Heine or Rilke, with Stefan George, and certainly with Else Lasker-Schüler. Could it be that lyrical poets, more than dramatists or novelists, have a tendency to play-act in everyday life? This is a speculation which, while not entirely incorrect, is also somewhat risky. Gerhart Hauptmann and Thomas Mann certainly were no lyrical poets, but in both one could not fail to notice a readily forgivable vanity and touch of play-acting.

In one of our conversations I asked Tuwim about his attitude to German literature. Unusually for him, he answered somewhat reticently. The language of the Germans, he said, was incomprehensible to him and their literature unknown. This was quite untrue. I thought of some lines from *Faust*: '*I hear him, hear him twice distinctly / Nevertheless he does not convince me.*' After all, educated Jews who grew up in Łódź before the First World War nearly all spoke German. Moreover – I ventured respectfully to remind him – he had translated various things from German himself, such as poems by Hebbel and Gottfried Keller, comedies by Nestroy and, especially beautifully, lyrical poems by Heine. That, he replied coldly, was in an entirely different era – and quickly changed the subject.

A woman friend to whom I related this conversation observed: 'I am surprised that this astonishes you. Many of Tuwim's family were murdered by the Germans, including his mother. That may be no reason for him to speak contemptuously of the German language or of German literature. But he no longer wishes to have anything to do with it. He didn't say so more explicitly because he is a tactful person and he knows where your interests lie. He didn't wish to hurt you. Maybe he was even a little astonished at you. That's all.'

While drinking coffee with Tuwim I could not forget for an instant that the distinguished gentleman opposite me was a poet of genius, moreover one to whom I owed a lot. Only on one other occasion did I have the same feeling – in conversation with Bertolt Brecht. Tuwim died towards the end of December 1953 while on holiday at the spa of Zakopane in the High Tatra mountains – he was not yet sixty. His funeral took place in Warsaw. His coffin, on an open carriage, was driven slowly through the gloomy city. It was followed by a procession of cars carrying Tuwim's few relations and a striking number of representatives of the state and the authorities. Finally there came a bus filled with members of the Polish Writers' Union, who wished to attend the burial.

It was no organized cortège and yet, despite the frost, the streets were lined with people, most of them women. All of them – and this seemed strange to me – had brought their children along. This was because Tuwim's work included over thirty poems for children, which were exceptionally successful. There were, and are, few children in Poland who do not know one or another of his poems by heart. Now they were paying their final respects to the dead poet.

At the cemetery hundreds, if not thousands, of people had assembled. The orator was Poland's prime minister. As I was standing some way away I could not make out much of what he said, but I noticed that the writers with whom I had come by bus had tears in their eyes. They made no attempt to conceal them – even though it is more usual in their métier not to display emotion but to create it.

Polish poetry, when I first began reading it along with German exile literature in 1939, saved me from depression. My brother's dental practice was going well; he was very busy and therefore able to provide for the upkeep of most of our family. My father was planning to start up a new business and was conducting all kinds of negotiations. Eventually the firm was established – at the worst possible moment, in July or August 1939. The result, as might have been expected, was expenses – and nothing else. My mother was running the household. But I was not doing anything, even though I was not exactly idling. I was ceaselessly reading novels and poetry – and I had no prospects for the future. Naturally this tormented me, but not for long. History came to my aid. What many had feared and some had hoped for had arrived – the war.

The extremely tense situation in August 1939 – the 'war of nerves' – seemed quite unbearable to us. But there were also calm and reasonable people who warned us: 'One day you'll look back with nostalgia to this war of nerves.' Improbable as this may seem, we received the news of the German attack on Poland with a sense of relief: we breathed freely again. And when, on 3 September, Britain and France declared war, the populace could scarcely contain its joy. The mood, and not only in Warsaw, was enthusiastic. I immediately sent a postcard to my sister and her husband, who for the past few weeks had been living in London: things would not be easy, perhaps far from it, but we were of good cheer because we had not the slightest doubt about Germany's defeat. The postcard never arrived.

Throughout the war I never for one moment doubted the ultimate victory of the Allies. Even during the sunny, though to us sad, days immediately after the occupation of Paris, my conviction never wavered. Was this just wishful thinking? Probably not. My certainty was largely due to my Prussian *Gymnasium*, which had taught me time and again, particularly in my German lessons, that in human history the final triumph went to the just cause.

Confident as I was that the war would end with the defeat of Hitler and his party, I greatly feared – and I told my friends so – that terrible things lay ahead for the Jews. I never predicted or even surmised what in fact subsequently happened, but I felt that a regime that had organized the Kristallnacht – it occurred a few days after my deportation – was capable of the worst horrors.

Our joy over the Allies' entry into the war soon gave way to panic. The Polish papers had recently stated that the German army was inadequately equipped, that many officers and men were opponents of Hitler and hence potential deserters. It was argued in all seriousness that the appalling condition of many Polish roads and tracks would make the advance of German tanks and armoured cars difficult if not impossible – thus favouring Poland. Everything turned out differently from the predictions of the incorrigible Polish optimists, however; the German armies triumphed and stories of the atrocities committed by the German troops quickly spread in Warsaw. In the occupied Polish towns and villages, it was said, they were cutting off the tongues, and often also the testicles, of the men, especially Jews. Few people believed these rumours, but even so they spread fear and terror.

On 7 September a colonel of the Polish general staff announced on the radio that German tanks were approaching Warsaw. He appealed to all men capable of bearing arms to leave the city immediately and make for the east. This was understood to mean that it was not intended to defend the Polish capital and that the Polish high command considered it wiser to withdraw and set up a line of defence somewhere east of the Vistula. The overwhelming majority of young men immediately obeyed the appeal – most of them without any luggage and without knowing which route they should take. The city was in the grip of hopeless chaos. It soon became known that the government and the high command of the army had already fled to Romania and that the colonel in question had acted irresponsibly and without authority. The city was by no means to fall into German hands without a fight; indeed, it was to be defended at all costs.

My brother and I had an unexpected opportunity to leave Warsaw by car. Some relatives and friends had hired a large truck on which they were intending to flee towards the east. They took us with them.

It seemed unimaginable that the Germans would occupy the whole of Poland; part of the country would presumably remain under Polish administration – and there one might hibernate until the end of the war. Everybody (including myself) believed that the Allies would finally defeat the Germans in the course of 1940, or in 1941 at the latest. We also believed that fleeing to the East would save us from the bombardment of Warsaw. Our parents remained in the city. The Germans, we thought, would surely not bother elderly people.

But wherever we arrived in our truck, those black birds of doom with their destructive load, the German aircraft, had been there already. And even if we did not see them or hear them for a while we certainly saw their work – dead bodies and ruins, decimated villages and destroyed towns. As fast as possible we drove through the burning and abandoned town of Siedlce, which was just then being bombed. Near the town of Brest we crossed the River Bug. We drove on and on until, eventually, we reached that desolate region known as the Pripet Marshes. There we halted in a small, miserable village.

Here there were no bombs, here there were only fields, forests and pastures, lakes and swamps and shabby peasant hovels. At least one could spend the night in them. Admittedly, there were no beds: the peasants slept on benches along the walls. Benches, stools and tables – that was the entire furniture. No wardrobes, no chests? No, these villagers had no need of them. They owned nothing that might be stored in wardrobes or chests. The discrepancy between the standards of civilization in the western and eastern parts of Poland was very great – everyone, of course, knew that. But I did not learn until September 1939 that there were regions in Poland where people lived just as in the Middle Ages.

There, in the eerie silence of this village, we were cut off from the world. No radios, no telephones, no newspapers. Looking for something to read, I asked the peasants if they had a Bible or a prayer book. No, they replied in astonishment, they had never had anything of the kind. I might perhaps find some books at the priest's, but he was living in the town, some twenty kilometres away. And what use would books be to them? Like a substantial part of the Polish population they were illiterate.

In our group there was a girl of my own age who had also recently passed her school-leaving exam. We would walk together, along narrow paths between the wet fields. We had to be careful not to fall into a swamp. But we were soon so taken up with ourselves that we no longer worried about the hazards around us, although we never strayed off our path. As she knew that I had come from Germany she told me that in her German lessons they had discussed a particularly beautiful short story, a love story, very tender and very sad. There was a poem in it which she particularly liked. It started like this:

> Today, only today
> I am so fair;
> Tomorrow, tomorrow
> All will be o'er!

The motif of transience, expressed very simply, seemingly artlessly, had moved the eighteen-year-old girl. This did not surprise me, because I knew from my own experience that those who had just discovered it for themselves were particularly susceptible to it.

Showing off a little, though not exaggerating, I remarked casually that I had read all the poems and stories of that author. She asked me to tell her something about him. He had – I told her – been a quiet lawyer, a minor official and a great lover, who was attracted to very young girls. On one occasion, when he was already engaged, he even made advances to a blond girl of thirteen, whom later, after his wife died, he married.

Thus, amidst the wasteland of the Pripet Marshes, we talked about Theodor Storm and *Immensee*. A verse came to my mind:

> No sound of our turbulent age
> Got through to our hermitage.

And we spoke about love. Quoting German and Polish verses as we walked along side by side, we did not mind the path getting narrower. It brought us closer to one another. Suddenly I looked into her eyes and saw tears there. So I did the simplest and most obvious thing: I kissed her, her moist eyes, and then probably also her lips. When I looked up at the clear blue sky I saw high up – no, not the white cloud Brecht remembered when he thought of Marie A., but three or four aircraft. They were flying so high we did not worry about them. But it was here again – the sound of our turbulent age.

However, and I felt quite sure of this, the aircraft looked different from those Adolf Hitler had sent against Poland. We returned quickly to our people in the village. They too were confused; they too did not think those were German machines. Perhaps they came from the Soviet Union. What was Stalin planning? Was he going to defend and protect Poland? Why else would he send up his planes? To help the Germans, the victors? In our miserable backwater it was impossible to learn anything. It was therefore decided to send three of our party by truck to the next, allegedly bigger, village in order to discover what was going on. One was chosen because he was thought to be the most politically aware person, another because he spoke good Russian, and finally myself, in case communication with Germans should prove necessary.

In the neighbouring village a surprise awaited us – a typewritten notice of the assassination of Hitler, Göring and Goebbels, the surrender of Germany and the end of the war. We enjoyed reading it but we were not happy because we did not believe a word of it. The villagers whom we questioned shrugged their shoulders. They told us that in another village, a little further on, a Russian detachment was stationed, having arrived two days before, and we might get some information there.

We drove on, but only found a sentry on duty outside a building which evidently served as a barracks. We tried to discover from this soldier in what capacity the Russians were there, whether they were on the side of the Poles or the Germans. But he was reticent and made a grim impression. Eventually he informed us, rather smugly as we thought: 'We are for the proletariat and for freedom.' We were no wiser than before.

On our way back we came across scattered Polish soldiers. They too told us of surrender – not of Germany but of Warsaw. The city was totally destroyed. And the Russians? Hitler and Stalin they said, were one heart and one soul and had divided up Poland between them. We quickly returned to our own village. Consultation with my brother only took a few minutes. We immediately agreed that there was no point in staying in eastern Poland or in fleeing further. In the new situation we had no alternative but to return to Warsaw as quickly as possible to see if our parents were still alive.

The following morning our truck brought our party to the nearest major road. From there, progress towards the west was slow – on horse-drawn carts, on transport vehicles of the disintegrating Polish army, and some of the way on foot. In Brest, one of the bridges over the Bug had remained intact; in the river drifted the swollen corpses of horses and cattle. On the highway, traffic was as dense as it had recently been on the main streets of Warsaw – traffic in both directions. Some were heading for home even though the Germans were there; others, it seemed, wanted to reach the by then Soviet-occupied part of Poland. The further we advanced towards the west, the more frequently we heard that Warsaw had been so badly bombed that many streets could no longer be found. The last part of the journey, nearly forty kilometres, we covered on foot.

Poland's former capital indeed looked like one huge field of rubble. Most buildings were destroyed; others, with no windows intact, also seemed wrecked and unoccupied. My brother and I were totally exhausted: we had had very little sleep for the past week, but we did not want to rest. Tired though we were, the closer we got to our destination the faster we walked. With every hour, with every minute, our excitement increased and so did our fears. At last we stood in front of the house where we had lived. The house was still there, although the flat below ours was rubble and ash.

Now we would learn whether our parents were alive or not. Our flat, as we could see now, had only been partially destroyed. Shaking, we knocked at the door, but no one opened up. Nervously we knocked again, more impatiently and more loudly. Suddenly we heard hesitant footsteps, the door was opened slowly and fearfully. Before us stood two – as we thought – very old people who did not recognize us in the darkness and who were evidently speechless with terror – my mother and my father.

12

HUNTING DOWN
JEWS IS FUN

No sooner had Warsaw surrendered, no sooner had the Wehrmacht entered the city, than the great entertainment of the victors began, the sport of the conquerors – hunting down the Jews.

After their speedy and magnificent triumph the euphoric and, understandably, adventure-minded German troops encountered an astonishing sight in the streets of some quarters of the Polish capital. What they had never seen before they were now seeing at every step – countless oriental, or oriental-seeming individuals with unusually long side-locks and bushy, unkempt beards. Their clothing was also exotic – long, plain black ankle-length caftans, and black, generally round, caps or hats.

On the other hand, it was easy enough to communicate with these dark yet lively strangers – unlike with the Poles. They spoke an idiom that sounded strange and rather ugly to German ears. But, unlike Polish, this language, Yiddish, if not spoken too fast, was fairly easy to understand. Why the language of the Jews, ugly though it might be, was comprehensible to German ears – that was not a question the soldiers asked themselves, unless there was a German scholar among them who was reminded by those, mostly guttural, sounds of the greatest German poets from a long-vanished epoch, of the verses of Walther von der Vogelweide and Wolfram von Eschenbach. The fact was that in their wanderings across Europe the Jews, in the Middle Ages, took with them and preserved the language of the German tribes among whom they had lived, Middle High German, albeit interspersed with Hebrew, Slav and other elements.

For the first time in their lives, therefore, the young soldiers saw orthodox Jews. These uncanny inhabitants of Warsaw aroused no sympathy in them, but rather disgust and perhaps revulsion. But maybe they also felt a certain satisfaction: whereas back home, in Stuttgart, Schweinfurt or Stralsund, they had as a rule been unable to distinguish Jews from racially pure Germans, or 'Aryans', they were at last able to see those they had so far only known as caricatures in German newspapers, especially in *Der Stürmer*.

Here they were then, those cunning and repulsive enemies of the German people, against whom the Führer so emphatically warned and of whom, even more frequently, the little doctor, Reichsminister Goebbels, would talk. Now the victorious troops understood what had been explained and preached to them for years – the many Jews in the streets of Warsaw were those terrible Asian hordes who threatened the lives of all Europeans and especially the Germans.

That these subhumans, who appeared frightened rather than hostile, should be carrying arms seemed highly unlikely – but one had better make sure. In October 1939 the round-ups in the streets were followed by raids on Jewish homes. These took place mostly after 8 p.m., when buildings were locked and one never knew which district would be next. Much as they tried, the soldiers were unable to find any weapons in the homes of religious Jews. But they owned something else that was most welcome to those Germans anxious to ensure order – rings and pocket-books, a little cash, and occasionally gold pocket watches.

However, it was not just a case of robbing the Jews. As the enemies of the German Reich, they were also to be punished and humiliated. That was not difficult. The soldiers soon discovered that orthodox Jews can be most painfully humiliated by cutting off their beards. To this end the enterprising occupiers equipped themselves with long scissors. But those cowardly Jews ran away and hid in courtyards and houses. This did not help them much: they were soon caught. By German soldiers? Certainly, but more frequently by those who immediately put themselves at the service of the new masters – by Polish rowdies and good-for-nothings, often by teenagers who were delighted to have found a new and amusing way of spending their time.

If they succeeded in catching one of the escaping Jews, they would drag him, noisily, to the Germans, who would immediately set to work vigorously – they cut off the long Jewish beards, occasionally setting them alight first with a burning newspaper. That was a particularly entertaining sight. As soon as the beard had dropped to the ground the many spectators cheered and clapped. The willing helpers did not end up empty-handed: now and again they would find a banknote or a ring.

Soon the assimilated Jews, those wearing European clothes, were robbed as well. And as the Germans found it difficult to tell them from non-Jews, their Polish helpers again made themselves useful. Most of them knew only a single German word – 'Jude' – but that was enough for their task. If an attacked man denied being Jewish, the command rang out: 'Trousers down!' – and it was soon established whether or not he was circumcized. The victims of such raids never knew when they would be able to return home – after a few hours, after a few days, or never.

Frequently the Jews – and Jewesses – picked up in the street were taken to a German office building which needed cleaning. If no rags were available for mopping the floor, the Jewish women, especially the prettier ones, were ordered to take off their knickers. These were then used as rags. For the soldiers this was tremendous fun – a game, incidentally, tried out by their comrades in March 1938 in Austria, especially in Vienna.

One evening we heard an unusually loud banging at the street door – the unmistakable practice of the Germans. The terrified concierge opened up at once, but soon discovered to his relief that these soldiers demanded admission only because they needed a Jewish dentist – meaning my brother. Their interest in his person, however, had nothing to do with dental treatment. The young men were looking for gold and assumed that a dentist would have some.

A moment later they were banging, just as noisily, at the door of our flat. That was their custom: they never used the bell because a vigorous knocking with a rifle-butt or some other weapon more effectively terrified those they wished to frighten. My brother opened the door and asked politely, if a little too loudly: 'How can I help you?' In the dim hallway we saw three soldiers in uniform, none of them more than about twenty years old. They shouted: 'Hands up!', aiming their weapons at us. Did any underground fighters hide out here? they asked gruffly. Our negative reply did not seem to surprise them. Then they grimly aimed their pistols at our wardrobe and ordered me to open it. Needless to say, there were no resistance fighters to be found inside. Next the military custodians of law and order looked behind the curtains, still with their pistols drawn.

Then they briskly came to the point. No longer shouting, but menacingly, they demanded to know where my brother kept his supply of gold and my mother her jewellery. One of them threatened my mother, and when my brother tried to protest, he was told: 'Shut your trap!' As if by way of apology my brother remarked that every son had only one mother. The soldier retorted: 'And every mother has only one son.' The situation was both comical and dangerous. None of us dared even to smile, let alone to point out to the soldier that this was not quite correct. Provoked by a cheeky Jew he might well have made use of his weapon. Whatever he did to us, he was not answerable to anyone.

Barely a minute later it was all over. The three soldiers had left our flat in a hurry, naturally with the booty they had demanded. I could not avoid the impression that our attackers had been beginners. Perhaps they had seen such a scene in a film and had acted it out afterwards? Anyway, the gold had gone and the fright had abated. What had not diminished was my mother's belief in German order and German justice.

In this respect she resembled a lot of Jews in Poland, especially the older and assimilated ones. They really believed that the German occupation would be no different from that in the First World War. Soon the occupiers would leave the Jews alone, and even treat them more or less civilly. And the raids and attacks during the first days and weeks following the conquest of Warsaw? Those were brutal, arbitrary acts, committed without the knowledge of their superiors, and would not occur again.

The following morning my mother set out to find the German *Kommandantur* and I accompanied her. She wished to lodge a complaint and demand the return of her wedding ring and the gold stolen from her son. She was genuinely convinced that she would succeed. However, we could not even set foot inside the *Kommandantur* building. A cheerful sentry advised us to get lost as fast as we could.

The soldiers who raided the flats of Jews wanted to enrich themselves. But they also acted from an entirely different motive. They were doing something that evidently gave them pleasure. Here in enemy Poland they had no need to suppress that inclination towards sadism which, back home, they had always been obliged to conceal – or so countless Germans in uniform were convinced. Here they did not have to consider anything or anybody, here they were not subject to any form of supervision or control. What they could not do on the Rhine or the Main and what they had always dreamed of, they could do here – let themselves go.

Towards the end of November 1939 German soldiers again turned up at our flat, this time between ten and eleven in the morning. Unlike their predecessors they wanted neither money nor gold, but manpower, especially young men. They immediately took us along with them – my brother, who had to cut short the dental treatment of a terrified patient, and myself. In the street there was already a column of thirty or forty Jews. As we were a little better dressed than the rest, we were commanded with sneers to the head of the column.

We marched off without knowing where or why. Our guards, most of them between twenty and twenty-five, amused themselves by bullying us and soon also by tormenting us. They ordered us to do whatever came into their heads – run fast, stop suddenly, and run some way back again. Whenever there was a large puddle in our way – and these were frequent in the ruined streets of Warsaw – and we tried to avoid it, we were immediately forced to run forward and back through the puddle several times. Soon our clothes looked pitiful – which was exactly what those soldiers wanted. Then we were told to sing. We sang a popular Polish marching song, but our guards demanded a Yiddish song.

Eventually they ordered us – and this idea was what they liked best – to yell in chorus: 'We are Jewish pigs. We are filthy Jews. We are subhuman' and more of the same kind. A rather elderly man pretended to be deaf. Certainly he did not shout along with us – perhaps because he was too weak or because he had the courage to protest against this humiliation. The soldier yelled at him: 'Run!' The old man ran a few steps, the soldier fired in his direction, the Jew fell and remained lying in the road. Was he wounded? Or dead? Or had he fallen from fright? I do not know, none of us was allowed to bother with him.

And me? Had this German barbarian in Wehrmacht uniform managed to offend or humiliate or chasten me? At the time I believed that he could not offend me; he could only beat me up or wound me or even kill me. I believed that it was more sensible to go along with that cruel circus, yelling and singing, rather than risk death. None of this was unusual. The same sort of thing was happening almost daily, in nearly every Polish town. What was unusual was what I experienced that morning immediately after this march.

After twenty or thirty minutes we had reached our destination, a splendid students' hostel built shortly before the war in Narutowicz Square. The large building now served as a German barracks. It was our task to give the whole basement, which unfortunately also contained a swimming pool, a thorough clean. Our guards informed us that if we did not work well enough or fast enough they would dispatch us into the pool with a hefty kick. I considered that entirely possible.

For some reason or other one of those cheerful and brutal soldiers wanted to engage me in conversation. I could hear at once that he came from Berlin. A chat with him might be useful. So I ventured to say boldly that I came from Berlin too. Shyly, I asked him where he lived. 'Gesundbrunnen,' he replied reluctantly. I had watched a lot of fine football matches there, I remarked. In my early school days I had indeed been greatly interested in football; it was a passing interest, but I still knew quite a bit about the major Berlin teams. His club, the soldier boasted, was Hertha BSC. Quickly I recited the names of the famous players at that time – and this saved me.

He was overjoyed at having found in Warsaw, a world so strange to him, someone to whom he could talk about Hertha BSC and its rival teams. The same young man who, less than half an hour earlier, had sadistically tormented us and forced us to shout that we were filthy Jewish pigs, who a few minutes before had threatened us with a drawn pistol that he would drive us into the icy swimming pool – that man now acted quite normally and almost amicably. I did not have to do any work at all, and my brother too profited from my surprising expertise. When this football fan from Berlin had chatted to me for about an hour we were allowed to go home, my brother and me.

That is how it was. Any German who wore a uniform and had a weapon could do whatever he wished with a Jew in Warsaw. He could compel him to sing or to dance or to shit in his trousers, or to go down on his knees and beg for his life. He could suddenly shoot him dead or kill him in a slower, more tortuous manner. He could order a Jewish woman to undress, to clean the street with her underwear and then, in front of everybody, to urinate. There was no one to spoil the fun of those German troops, no one to stop them from maltreating the Jews, no one to make them answerable for what they did. It revealed what human beings are capable of when they are granted unlimited power over other human beings.

German callers were becoming ever more frequent at our small flat. Towards the end of January 1940 two or three soldiers wished to see my brother; presumably they wanted to arrest him. By pure chance he was not at home. They said they would wait for him. This was clearly not one of those arbitrary raids or excesses, because the whole building was surrounded and no one was permitted to leave or enter. A little girl of nine or ten, the daughter of our concierge, was playing ball in the yard: she was the only person the soldiers took no notice of. But the little girl had been told by her mother to go out into the street inconspicuously, always bouncing her ball, and to run along to meet the *Herr Doktor* and warn him. This was exactly what happened. My brother instantly about-turned and hid in the flat of friends. Meanwhile the soldiers continued to wait for him patiently. After quite a long time, perhaps two or three hours, they withdrew. When my mother innocently asked if they were coming back later, they resolutely declared that they were not. In fact, they never returned.

A few days later we learned the background to this business. A young Pole of Jewish extraction, who had taken part in several successful operations of a patriotic resistance group, had dramatically succeeded in escaping from the Warsaw Gestapo prison. Thereupon over a hundred people – both Jews and non-Jews – were arrested as hostages, all of them professional people, lawyers and engineers, doctors and dentists. My brother's name had been on that list.

If the person searched for was not at home the Germans usually picked on a substitute – any man happening to be there, a family member or a visitor or even a craftsman doing some repair. All those arrested in such a sweep were executed. My brother was spared. The little girl playing with her ball had saved his life.

Why was I not arrested and murdered in place of my brother, as would have been the usual practice? A good question, or so it would have seemed before we had come to know the occupying power and its methods, before we realized that the Germans who controlled our fate were nearly all unpredictable creatures – capable of any infamy, any crime, any misdeed; before we made the discovery that wherever barbarism and cruelty are combined with chance and arbitrariness, any question about sense or logic is unrealistic and pointless.

13

THE DEAD MAN
AND HIS DAUGHTER

It was on 21 January 1940, shortly after 1 p.m., that my mother called me into the kitchen. She was looking out of the window and was visibly upset, but, as always, quite in control of herself. In the courtyard I saw several of our neighbours, perhaps eight or ten of them, gesticulating vigorously. Something exciting must have happened.

We were still at the window, alarmed and undecided, when someone rang our doorbell. The doctor should come at once – Mr Langnas had hanged himself; maybe something could still be done. But my brother was not at home. Before I could consider what to do my mother said: 'Go over at once. Langnas has a daughter, she's the one to be looked after now.' By then I was on the stairs, but I could still hear my mother's voice: 'Look after the girl!' I have never forgotten this admonition – 'Look after the girl!' – I can still hear it.

The door to the flat of the Langnas family, who had recently fled to Warsaw from Łódź, was half open. In the hall two or three people busied themselves with Mrs Langnas, who was lamenting loudly. Leaning against the wall, totally shattered, was the nineteen-year-old for whose sake I had come. We knew each other, though only casually. In those days the people who shared a block of flats soon made each other's acquaintance.

Everyone was anxious to know what was happening in the world: on that, we soon realized, our lives would depend. But there was nothing to be learned, other than the Wehrmacht High Command communiqué, from the only licensed newspaper in Polish, *Gazeta Żydowska*, a miserable and universally despised rag, and not much

131

more from the German *Warschauer Zeitung*. We had had to surrender our radios as early as October 1939. We therefore depended on word-of-mouth news, which was not always accurate, and on the circulating rumours, which were not always false.

The continuous need for news, which even if bad was at least reassuring, soon became a mania. This was the reason behind our nightly visits to each other's flats. We would meet in one of the neighbour's flats to learn the latest news. 'What's new?' was the routine question. I have retained the habit to this day. A few days earlier I had accompanied my father to the Langnas family's flat and spent an hour or two there. On that particular evening several people had met to confirm to each other that the Germans had serious worries and so perhaps they would not treat the Jews in the 'Government-General' too badly, that the triumph of the Allies was certain, and that the whole business could not last much longer.

That was when I had seen the nineteen-year-old girl for the first time. But as I wished to take part in the general conversation I only gave her part of my attention. However, it was enough to convince myself of two things: she knew German and she was evidently not indifferent to literature. That aroused my interest, but for the moment this was kept within bounds. It made me like her, but nothing more. Indeed, there was good reason for that – I was, at the time, heavily involved in another affair. An erotic and sexual one? Yes, certainly. I think back to it with mixed feelings. It is a banal story, a somewhat embarrassing one, and I find it difficult to talk about it – perhaps because it has happened a thousand times and been told countless times, most beautifully by Austrian authors, from Schnitzler, Hofmannsthal and Stefan Zweig all the way to Joseph Roth. But neither can I forget this experience.

A mature lady seduces the former school mate of her son, a young man of nineteen, who soon turns away from her – towards a younger woman. That is how it could be summed up. The lady was from St Petersburg, had escaped to Berlin in the early 1920s and in the summer of 1939 found herself in Warsaw. She was only just over forty, an original rather theatrical person and all the more striking in these mundane surroundings. Her clothes, mannerisms, her somewhat dramatic speech – all these were pure theatre. She was constantly acting a part – and, although occasionally over-acting, did it rather well. She had an urgent, barely concealed, need to impress everyone around her. Now she wanted to impress me. And although I saw through some of it, she succeeded at once.

Even her name was theatrical – Tatiana. Or rather, she had, without any sense of guilt, appropriated this beautiful name which had become popular in Germany through nineteenth-century Russian literature. Her light-blond hair was probably bleached, her pale blue eyes were striking because of their size. I have never seen more beautiful ones – or have they only become large and beautiful in my memory? She was fond of talking about the luxury amidst which she had grown up in St Petersburg and of the important men who had tried to win her favours in Berlin. Both claims were probably greatly exaggerated.

Her brother was in the Soviet Union, she told me with her hand over her mouth, a person of the highest rank, he was a member of the Central Committee or a minister, or both, but she would be putting her life on the line if she told me his name. I was fairly sure that this mysterious brother was an invention. What was no invention, however, was her exceptional charisma. Equally authentic was her remarkable ability to fascinate those around her, by no means only me, at least for a time.

I would visit Tatiana almost every afternoon, always between five and seven. She had concocted a pretext for my regular visits. She had a command of four languages, but her knowledge of the fifth, English, was only slight. I was therefore to read English prose with her. I suggested Joseph Conrad and Galsworthy. Anything was all right with her. This was not what mattered, and in the choice of literature she left the decision to me. In other matters she retained the initiative, briskly and energetically. I did not object.

Every afternoon followed the same pattern. First there was coffee and some excellent cake or other delicacies which were then very expensive in Warsaw, but still available. Then we would read English prose, but we did not concentrate on it fully. And our reading as a rule did not last long. '*That day we read no further*,' states Francesca da Rimini in the *Divine Comedy*. For us, the ill-matched couple, it should have been: '*Each day we read no further*.'

I owe a great many experiences to this seduction story. One day she told me that for a long time she had only had lesbian relationships, that her occasional experiments with men had changed nothing about that. I was the first who had enabled her to return to the male sex. That was intended to flatter me, but it missed its effect because I immediately suspected that it was an invention. I did not know then that women often try to satisfy their partners by such confessions.

After two or three months Tatiana's melodramatic performances, which I had to witness every day, began to get on my nerves and I gradually tired of what had at first been an exciting love affair. Not until later did I understand what I was then beginning to feel – I secretly longed for a very different relationship, with a younger woman, perhaps one of my own age. It may well be that I realized this on that day in January 1940 when I was suddenly faced with the task of looking after a weeping girl.

After that day, my visits to the woman who had made my first few months of the German occupation more bearable and more pleasant became less frequent and soon ceased altogether. A few weeks later I happened to meet Tatiana in the street. She said at once: 'You've left me for someone younger.' I was about to reply: 'That's life', but at the last moment checked myself and spared her the commonplace. She interpreted my silence correctly. I was startled. Because I saw tears in her large blue eyes.

'*He who loves most is the vanquished and must suffer*' – this simple and tough lesson from *Tonio Kröger* had engraved itself on my mind at a time when literature supplied me with my sole knowledge of love. Only now was I beginning to understand it. I did not know what to say to Tatiana. Disturbed and confused, I looked around in case there was any danger, such as a raid, which would have enabled me to escape. But everything was quiet. I could come up with no better excuse than that unfortunately I was in a hurry. She smiled sadly and understandingly, and perhaps with a trace of envy. I walked away quickly, but tried not to walk too fast. She should not notice that I was running away, that I was trying to escape.

Not until February 1946 did I meet Tatiana again – in Berlin, in a café on Kurfürstendamm. She was dejected. There were reasons for this, she said, about which she could not and did not wish to talk. Again she acted mysteriously. I asked no questions, and this may have disappointed her. In her decolleté she wore a fair-sized oval piece of jewellery, possible amber. It was on a gold chain which she had worn back in Warsaw. Suddenly she took it off and passed it across to me – with a slightly theatrical gesture. I looked at her questioningly. She said meaningfully: 'Look at the back.' To my surprise I saw, engraved on a gold disk, the words:

> *Plaisir d'amour ne dure qu'un moment,*
> *Chagrin d'amour dure toute une vie.*

But is it true what this verse asserts? Is the joy generated by love really brief and transient, and does its pain last a lifetime? Or is the opposite true? I was silent, the conversation did not get going again and, before long, I left; she wanted to stay on in the café. We parted entirely without ill feelings and indeed, as it seemed to me, with gratitude on both sides.

I was already in the street when she called me back. But we only exchanged a few more words. 'Are you remaining in Warsaw?' 'Yes.' 'And you really believe that politics is your profession?' 'Yes.' 'You are making a mistake. Your place is in Germany and not in Poland; your profession is literature and not politics.' 'Literature is not a profession at all, but a curse.' 'Stop quoting. I am not Lisaweta Iwanowna, and you are not Tonio Kröger. Let me advise you again: Leave Poland ...' I followed this advice, but not until twelve years after this conversation.

Without hurrying I walked down Kurfürstendamm in the direction of Halensee. Suddenly I realized that during the whole conversation with Tatiana I had been thinking of Tosia. And again, as countless times over the past few years, I recalled the day which changed my life – the 21st of January 1940, the day when her father, Mr Langnas from Łodź, put an end to his life.

He had been a child when his parents died. An uncle provided for his maintenance, otherwise he was left to his own devices. A self-made man, therefore, and an unusual one. Although quiet and reticent, he was a good businessman. He became a successful and affluent merchant, co-owner of a flourishing textile factory. Nevertheless, he lacked self-confidence – and perhaps his death was due to that.

Shortly after the invasion by the Wehrmacht Mr Langnas's business was expropriated. He was not permitted to enter his factory, which was now managed by a trustee. The following day a German soldier, a cheerful, strong young man, had slapped his face on Piotrkowska, Łódź's main street. Why? Perhaps he expected the Jew Langnas to give him the Hitler salute. But maybe it was nothing of the kind and he had only been annoyed by his superior officer and felt the need to beat someone up. Thus began the psychological breakdown of Mr Langnas. As soon as he got home he announced that there was nothing left to him now except suicide – and talked about it more and more frequently during the next few weeks.

Later, when Łódź was renamed Litzmannstadt and attached to the 'Reichsgau Wartheland', the family, in common with a lot of other Jews from Łódź, fled to Warsaw. But there, too, Mr Langnas exhibited signs of deep depression, although he no longer talked of suicide. It was thought he had got over his crisis. On 21 January his wife and daughter went into town to make some purchases. After less than an hour they returned home. It was too late. The man who had had his face slapped by a German soldier was found hanging from his trouser belt.

The two women had screamed but the daughter was quicker than her mother. She ran to the kitchen and got a knife. But her strength was not sufficient to cut the belt. Only the emergency doctor managed to do it, but that was all he could do. By then I was in the flat and taken into another room by the dead man's weeping daughter. I sat next to her, next to Teofila Langnas, who preferred the simple diminutive Tosia to her somewhat pretentious full name.

Our situations were not comparable – and we were both unable to deal with it, it was too much for us. She had known for ten minutes that she no longer had a father. She was crying, unable to speak. What was I to say to a girl who, ten minutes earlier, had tried in vain to cut her father loose from his belt? Both of us, nineteen years old, were equally helpless. I was conscious of the dramatic nature of the moment, but I could think of nothing other than stroking the desperate girl's hair and kissing away her tears. I doubt if she even noticed it.

In order to divert her attention, at least for a moment, I asked her what she had done in Łódź. She stammered her reply. I understood that six months previously she had passed her school-leaving exam and had intended to study graphic art and history of art in Paris.

Nothing, of course, had come of that because of the outbreak of war. I felt that I had to say something to her.

A few years previously, in Berlin, I had liked the film *Traumulus*, written shortly after the turn of the century by Arno Holz and Oskar Jerschke. This was chiefly because the main part, the schoolmaster called, not without reason, 'Traumulus', was played by Emil Jannings. Standing by the body of his favourite pupil, who had committed suicide, the teacher – this was how I roughly remembered it – states that we are here not to throw our life away but to conquer it. A pompous phrase, but it seemed to me more bearable than the uncanny silence or the customary phrase 'Life goes on.'

But then I did something improper, something that surprised me, something I would have thought almost impossible in this situation ten seconds earlier – I suddenly grabbed Tosia and, trembling, reached for her breast. She jerked, but she did not resist. She went rigid, but her glance seemed grateful.

The following day Tosia's father was buried. At that time Jews were still buried – soon there would only be *'a grave in the air'* for them, as Paul Celan says in his *Death Fugue*. Because suicides by Jews were not yet common, a lot of people had come to the cemetery, the more so as the quiet Mr Langnas had, in his home town, been not only a respected but also a popular merchant.

I accompanied and supported Tosia. By the open graveside I stood next to her. A friend of her father asked in some astonishment who the young man was who so obviously looked after the daughter of the deceased. Perhaps he considered it improper or unseemly. But the two of us, she and I, did not worry our heads about it. We regarded it as a matter of course that on this gloomy, rainy day in January 1940 we were together. And we have remained together ever since.

14

FROM QUARANTINE
DISTRICT TO GHETTO

The Final Solution had not yet been decided on, indeed the term was not yet known. But the arbitrary acts which made the lives of the Jews hell were further extended by systematic measures devised by the authorities. German bureaucrats were at work, busy desk-bound criminals. Although using different means, their aims were the same as those who attacked, robbed and tormented the Jews wherever they found them. There was a ceaseless string, in the Government-General, of new laws and decrees, new orders and ordinances, instructions and directives. We neither knew nor suspected what purpose all these measures were intended to serve, and if we had known we certainly would not have believed it. What they in fact prepared the ground for was the annihilation of all Jews, their 'extermination'.

Within a few weeks of the entry of the German troops into Warsaw the SS decreed that the Jews would, with immediate effect, have to live and remain within a certain part of the city. In other words, a ghetto was to be established. While this return to the Middle Ages could not be kept secret, it could be officially embellished and camouflaged. The term 'ghetto' was therefore carefully avoided – not only on the posters with instructions, but also in the press and in correspondence with the German authorities. What was to be established was always termed 'the Jewish Residential District'.

Within three days the Jews were to move into the northern, mostly dirty and down-at-heel, part of Warsaw. Simultaneously the non-Jews living there were to move out with all their belongings. Panic broke out among those affected, Jews and non-Jews; the city was in turmoil. Clearly the SS had been totally unaware of the consequences their decree would have.

In the districts earmarked for Jews there were offices and factories owned by non-Jews. What was to happen to them? That a modern city was a complex structure from which individual districts could not simply be lifted out or isolated – those who controlled the fate of the largest Jewish community in Europe had completely overlooked this fact. Their objectives could not be realized in a hurry: the SS leaders found themselves compelled to withdraw the ghetto decree.

The occupation authorities had publicly made fools of themselves. But the Jews drew no pleasure from this: it was clear that the German authorities would not give up their plan. The matter had simply been postponed, and it was fairly certain that the authorities would exact retribution from the Jews for their bungled decision.

What was the explanation for an obviously improvised decree, one that compromised the German rulers? The answer is simple. The SS leaders in Warsaw, equipped with extensive powers, were people of scant education. This emerged frequently even from the letters or notices drafted by them. Often they were just NCOs, or if they were officers, then only of ranks corresponding to second or first lieutenants in the Wehrmacht – and, as a rule, they were never promoted during their service in Warsaw.

For the time being, therefore, there was no ghetto in Warsaw. So the SS and the numerous German authorities had even more reason to identify, separate and humiliate the Jews. From 1 December 1939 all Jews over ten years old in the Government-General – in the Warsaw District the age limit was twelve – had to wear a white armband on their right sleeve, no less than ten centimetres wide, with a blue Star of David. The many Warsaw inhabitants, whether Germans or Poles, who felt a need to attack Jews in the street welcomed this mark of identification – and interpreted it correctly: the Jews were outcasts.

When a Jew encountered a uniformed German he had to make way for him immediately. This order was clear. Less clear was how a Jew should act beyond stepping out of the way. Should he give the German salute? On one occasion I failed to do so and was promptly beaten up by the soldier, who was no older than me. On another occasion, to avoid such chastisement, I saluted a soldier with raised arm – which did not worry me since I was used to that from my school days in Berlin. But the young member of the master race yelled at me furiously: 'Are you my comrade that you should greet me?' and hit me vigorously.

Specially marked food ration cards were then immediately introduced for Jews. Rations were considerably smaller than for the non-Jewish population. The consequences were predictable and planned – malnutrition and serious health conditions among most Jews were quick to appear. Soap rations were exceedingly small, and the soap contained a lot of grey sand. If you washed with it you were dirtier than before.

One of the many actions aiming at the complete segregation of the Jews was a special census. Every Jew had to fill in a very lengthy and detailed questionnaire. Why should the German authorities bother about such precise information – not only place and date of birth, but also about schools and knowledge of foreign languages, about military service, occupation, career and so on?

Questions as to the purpose of this census met with the same response: 'There has got to be order'. This was not very convincing since this 'order' was required only from Jews. But it gave rise to new fears – as it happened, without cause. The vast census may have cost the Jews a lot of effort and anxiety, but it did not really hurt anyone. As it soon turned out, the census was quite unnecessary: the German authorities never had the time or the inclination to evaluate the data. Why should they? In order to murder Jews they did not need to know their names or ages, their occupation or level of education, or all the other information requested in the questionnaires.

For me, however, the business had important consequences. In Warsaw, as in other towns of the Government-General, the survey had to be conducted by the Jewish Religious Community. In order to emphasize the fact that this was now no longer a religious institution, the German authorities renamed it the 'Jewish Council of Elders', and later, to give it a more contemptuous ring, the 'Jews' Council'. For the census, which took about two weeks to conduct, hundreds of office staff were needed, including some who knew German. On the suggestion of friends I applied, even though I had little hope of being engaged, given my age and the large number of unemployed applicants. However, I reported and found myself amidst a large number of candidates in the spacious hall of the municipal centre. Those who professed to know German were sent to an examiner. My examination took less than a minute – I was accepted, albeit only for two weeks.

A little later, however, this turned into permanent employment. I was engaged by the Jews' Council to conduct its correspondence in German. This Council had two general tasks – it had to administer the Jewish district which, a few months later, became the enclosed Warsaw ghetto. It was therefore a kind of municipal council, for which all the necessary communal services had to be established with lightning speed. Its other task was to represent the Jews and their different needs to the authorities, both German and Polish.

The volume of correspondence with the German authorities increased rapidly. More and more documents had to be translated each day – occasionally from German into Polish but mostly from Polish into German. A special department became necessary. It was called the 'Translation and Correspondence Bureau' and consisted of four people – a young lawyer, a fairly well-known Polish woman novelist, Gustawa Jarecka, a professional woman translator, and me. I, who was the youngest by some ten to fifteen years, was appointed head of this bureau. Because they thought I had organizational skills? More probably because – which was not surprising – I knew German better than those who were suddenly my subordinates.

For the first time in my life I was needed. Quite unexpectedly I had a job and a monthly salary, albeit a modest one. I was content – mainly because I was now in a position to contribute to the family's subsistence. And I was looking forward to what could be quite a tricky job. One question did not worry me at all: whether, with no previous experience, I would be up to my job. I could not then suspect that this precise situation would be repeated many more times in my professional life: time and again I was confronted with a task for which I was not in the least qualified.

So I started as an autodidact, a self-taught person, and I have been one ever since. After my school-leaving exam no one ever tried to teach me anything. Whatever I can do I have taught myself. I am not particularly proud of this and I do not recommend the method. I became a self-taught person through necessity, not from choice.

My life would probably have been a lot easier if I had spent a few years at a university. It is possible that certain peculiarities of my literary criticism – regrettable as well as positive ones – are linked to this self-teaching.

My work as head of the Translation and Correspondence Bureau was getting more revealing and exciting every day. As the entire correspondence between the Jews' Council and the German authorities passed through my hands I had a unique insight into what was happening. One of the most important topics of this correspondence were the sanitary conditions in the Jewish part of the city. As the Jews from nearby smaller towns were being systematically moved into Warsaw – mostly without belongings – the population increased rapidly. Soon it totalled 400,000 and later even some 450,000.

Before long the hospitals became seriously overcrowded and in a deplorable condition. Most medications were no longer obtainable; coal and coke were scarcely available or only for a lot of money – and the winter of 1940 was particularly severe. There was a lack of warm clothing. Besides, most of the Jewish population was undernourished. Not surprisingly, epidemics soon broke out, especially typhoid.

The Jews' Council immediately alerted the German health authorities. Numerous letters, applications and memoranda reported on the frightening spread of the typhoid epidemic. Statistics were included to convince the authorities that the epidemic represented a major danger, moreover, to the entire city of Warsaw. Help was urgently requested.

German reaction was incomprehensible, at least initially. Most of the letters I translated and wrote – I strove for a factual and clear account – remained unanswered. The German authorities did not wish to know about anything happening within that part of Warsaw, or about the matters which the Jews' Council persisted in pointing out to them. Did they not care about the spread of the epidemic? Not only did they not care, but they actually welcomed it.

In the spring of 1940 the Jewish-inhabited district was given a new name – 'Epidemic Quarantine District'. The Jews' Council was ordered to surround it with a wall three metres high, topped with a barbed wire fence another metre high. At the entrances to this district, which the Jews were not permitted to leave, notices were put up, announcing in German and Polish: '*Epidemic Quarantine District. – Only Through Traffic Permitted.*'

The authorities quite seriously maintained that they had ordered the erection of the walls on philanthropic grounds – their purpose was to protect the Jews from attacks and excesses. Simultaneously newspaper articles intended for the Polish population, as well as other publications, explained that the occupying power had been compelled to isolate the Jews in order to protect the German and Polish population of the city from typhoid and other diseases.

The desperate efforts of the Jews' Council to contain the spread of the epidemic produced few or no results. The German authorities refused any kind of help. Instead of combating the readily identifiable causes of the epidemic, they did not cease from stirring up the city's Christian population against the Jews. The main line of German propaganda was equating the Jews with lice. Very soon it became clear what the Germans intended – it was not the epidemics that were to be wiped out, but the Jews.

On 16 November 1940 the twenty-two entrances – later there would be only fifteen – were closed and from then on guarded day and night by details of six sentries. Two of them were German gendarmes, two were Polish police, and two were members of the Jewish militia which was called the 'Jewish Order Service'. This militia was not uniformed but easily recognizable. In addition to the armband mandatory for all Jews they wore a second, yellow, one as well as a service cap and on their chest a metal disc with a number. They were armed with truncheons.

Thus the Quarantine District, the part of the city officially called the Jewish Residential District, had become a huge concentration camp – the Warsaw ghetto.

15

THE WORDS OF A FOOL

Now and again a youngish man dressed in rags was to be seen in the ghetto, invariably accompanied by children and teenagers, running through the streets skipping and dancing. Passers-by were astonished but greeted him with applause. His identification mark was two Yiddish words, which he called out like a newsvendor: '*Ale glach*', in German: '*Alle gleich*', meaning 'All alike'. Whether this was a prediction or a warning, whether the man was mad or acted like a madman – that nobody knew. This bizarre person, whose name was Rubinstein but who was called 'Ale Glach', was the fool of the Warsaw ghetto.

But were all men really in the same boat? Renowned scholars and primitive bearers of burdens, outstanding doctors and miserable beggars, successful artists and common pedlars, wealthy bankers and small-time crooks, astute businessmen and solid craftsmen, orthodox Jews who did not for a moment question their ancestors' faith and others who did not wish to know anything about Judaism – all these were incarcerated in the ghetto, condemned to hardships and misery, suffering from hunger and cold, from dirt and filth, living through a thousand anxieties. Weighing upon them all, whether young or old, whether clever or stupid was a dark and terrible shadow from which there was no escape – the shadow of the fear of death.

It was not true, however, that these diverse people in the ghetto were all in the same position and had to share the same difficulties – at least not initially. Those who had some savings or possessions that could be sold, especially jewellery, gold or silver, old candelabra or other ritual items, could afford foodstuffs which were not available to most of the inhabitants, though they were equally indispensable to all since the official rations were barely sufficient to prevent people from starving to death.

A lot depended on a person's profession. Teachers, lawyers and architects had a particularly difficult time: there were no schools or law courts in the ghetto, and there was no building activity. Even so, many lawyers found posts in the ghetto administration or in the headquarters of the Order Service, the (very unpopular) Jewish militia. Doctors and dentists were much better off, there was always a demand for them. The same was true of craftsmen, especially carpenters, locksmiths, plumbers, electricians, and also tailors and shoemakers.

Simultaneously a new occupation emerged – smuggling. Every day thousands of Jews, men more often than women, and chiefly younger persons including teenagers, went to work in big German enterprises outside the ghetto. They did so voluntarily, even though payment was minimal. For they were able to take with them from the ghetto whatever was saleable, chiefly clothes, and occasionally watches and pieces of jewellery, all of which would be disposed of quickly at knock-down prices. From the proceeds the Jewish workers bought foodstuffs which they smuggled into the ghetto when they returned in the evening.

What would happen at the ghetto entrances was unpredictable. Sometimes the German gendarmes would brutally strip the smugglers of anything they were carrying on their persons – lard, sausages or even potatoes. There was a lot of shooting during these checks and no shortage of casualties. But there were also gendarmes who behaved differently, who did not care what those poor wretches, those amateur smugglers, brought into the ghetto.

An incomparably more important part was played by the professional smugglers – Jews of proletarian background, as a rule rough and massive fellows who, before the war, had earned their living as labourers or unskilled industrial workers. These were people who took calculated risks and were not afraid of death. They made common cause with Polish business partners of similar provenance, as well as with the German sentries at the entrances to the ghetto.

Gradually vast quantities of foodstuffs were shifted every night – hundreds of sacks of flour and rice, peas and beans, lard and sugar, potatoes and vegetables. The smugglers either quickly tossed these sacks over the wall or passed them through openings which were subsequently temporarily closed. Sometimes the deliveries were made by horse-drawn transport or by trucks which passed unchallenged through the official ghetto gates – in collusion with the German gendarmes who, needless to say, had been bribed to turn a blind eye.

Those participating in this smuggling racket made a lot of money. Prices of foodstuffs inside the walls were at least double those in the rest of Warsaw. The daring Jewish smugglers were thus able to live in conspicuous luxury: they were the customers of the not very numerous but very expensive restaurants in the ghetto. But they had to accept one major risk. Some day their German business partners might consider it undesirable to have Jewish accomplices. It might be wiser to get rid of them quickly, perhaps with a bullet.

One of Warsaw's principal exit roads, the East–West Axis, ran right through the ghetto. The Wehrmacht had a particular interest in this road, especially in the spring of 1941, before the outbreak of the German–Soviet war. All the traffic from the west to the east, via Warsaw, had to use this road. It was therefore separated from the ghetto, with the result that the residential district assigned to the Jews was divided. There was now the so-called 'big ghetto' and the 'little ghetto', linked by a wooden flyover bridge, financed incidentally by the Jews' Council.

The German sentries on duty on this bridge took a special delight in maltreating the Jews who had to pass that way – and there was no other way of getting from one ghetto to the other – in a particular manner. Many were allowed to pass unmolested. But if a bearded, and perhaps elderly, Jew came along he was commanded: 'Fifty knee-bends!' No one was up to that – they all fainted and collapsed after twenty or thirty. For a few months we were living immediately next to this wooden bridge and I was often able to watch this pitiful performance, an almost daily event, from my window. One soon became accustomed to shots and screams during the night, too.

Who would have thought it – there were even taxis in the ghetto. Not cars or horse-drawn carriages, but rickshaws. These were bicycles on which an inventive individual, usually a young technician, had mounted a wide seat, accommodating two persons. Admittedly only those few persons with money could afford a rickshaw ride. As for public transport, there was a tram inside the ghetto, hauled, as in the past century, by horses. It was always crammed full, and we therefore – my friends and I – never used it. We were afraid of lice, the principal carriers of typhus. We preferred to walk.

Admittedly, most streets were also crowded. Until the autumn of 1942 I never saw an empty street in the ghetto and only rarely a half-empty one. The dreaded contact with other pedestrians was therefore not always avoidable: even in the street one might pick up a louse and succumb to the almost invariably fatal epidemic. Death was encountered in the ghetto at every step. I mean this quite literally: in the gutter, especially in the early morning, scantily covered with old newspapers, lay the corpses of those who had died of debility or hunger or typhus and whose burial nobody wished to pay for.

Also part of the street scene were countless beggars who, leaning against a wall of a house or sitting on the ground, wimperingly begged for a piece of bread. Their condition suggested that soon they too would be lying covered by newspapers. There was a lot of shouting by the professional street vendors and poor people offering various articles for sale, such as pieces of clothing, in order to be able to buy food. Typical also were the muggers – teenagers hanging about the shops, lying in wait for passers-by who had bought something edible. They would suddenly snatch it from them and run off, or immediately bite into it regardless of the paper wrapping.

The impoverishment of the ghetto inhabitants rapidly worsened – and the German authorities attempted to accelerate this process. In 1941 all furs still owned by Jews were confiscated – not only fur coats but also fur collars and fur caps. Of course there were instances of theft in the ghetto, but not a single murder. There was, however, one case of cannibalism: a woman of thirty, crazed by hunger, had cut a chunk out of the buttock of her dead twelve-year-old son and tried to eat it. When I translated the report of this incident into German, it was pointed out to me that the matter had to be kept secret.

There was only one motor car in the ghetto – a small ancient Ford which was at the disposal of the chairman of the Jews' Council, the mayor of the ghetto, Adam Czerniaków. Otherwise, whenever a car was seen, the streets emptied. One could not rule out that the occupants of the car, Germans of course, might suddenly use their weapons and fire right and left into the crowd. Germans frequently came to the ghetto as tourists. They wanted to view that exotic world of the Jews, and quite often they also felt an urgent need to beat up and rob inhabitants.

There was often filming in the ghetto, both by German officers and soldiers who wanted to take home a souvenir and by professional film people. As the latter were probably members of 'propaganda companies', their favourite targets were beggars and cripples. Scenes would be stage-managed in which Jews of hideous appearance were taken by the film people to a ghetto restaurant. The owner of the establishment was ordered to spread a rich table for his uninvited guests. Producer and cameraman staged a feast: it was to show what a good life the Jews were having.

There was also some shooting of sexual scenes. At pistol point, German documentary film-makers forced young men to have intercourse with elderly and not exactly attractive women, and old men with young girls. These films, some of which were found in Berlin archives after the war, were not, however, shown publicly. The propaganda ministry and other German authorities were thought to have feared that such films might arouse pity instead of disgust.

Reality seemed increasingly to contradict the slogan of the ghetto fool, Rubinstein: 'All alike'. An exceedingly small minority, mainly the smugglers, had enough money to live almost as well as they had done before the war. Much greater was the number of those who, while not being able to eat their fill, found their hunger bearable, who looked after their clothes and regularly visited the hairdresser – who, in fact, resisted the general decline in living standards that was to be observed in the ghetto.

As a rule the assimilated Jews, who only spoke Polish, were a little better off than the orthodox ones and those who, whatever their attitude to religion, had remained faithful to the Yiddish-speaking environment. Contact between these two large groups was minimal even before the war, each had a low opinion of the other, even to the extent of despising their fellow Jews. The assimilated accused the orthodox of being backward, in almost every respect; the orthodox, in turn, believed that the assimilated had abandoned the faith and traditions of their ancestors, mainly for opportunist reasons. None of this changed after 1939: in consequence, there were two separate

Jewish worlds in the Warsaw ghetto. As for myself, I did not know anyone in the ghetto from the Yiddish environment.

My family and I did not belong to the privileged. None of us ever went to any of the notorious luxury restaurants. But our hardships were kept within limits. My brother had a good reputation as a dentist and therefore no shortage of patients. My work at the Jews' Council was not difficult and far from boring. Incidentally, I cannot complain: I have never in my life been bored by my professional work.

Many of the reports and petitions I had to check in translation, and many of the letters which I had to translate myself, enabled me to appreciate the extent of the hardships and misery in the ghetto. I soon realized that I was in an unusual position: I had access to documents of historic significance. One day a man, who has remained in my memory as one of the strongest personalities in the ghetto, entered my office and requested a brief talk with me. He asked if I was prepared to help him. I had already heard vague stories about him, the historian Emanuel Ringelblum, and his conspiratorial activities, and I was flattered by his confidence in me and request for assistance.

Even then there was an underground archive in existence, established and managed by Ringelblum. Here everything was collected that could provide evidence of life in the ghetto – public notices, posters, diaries, circulars, tram tickets, statistics, illegally published periodicals, scholarly and literary essays. It was hoped that future historians would draw on these sources. Reports based on these materials were also drawn up for the Polish underground movement and for the Polish government-in-exile in London. The correspondence between the Jews' Council and the German authorities was clearly of enormous importance for the archive. I was asked to prepare copies of all the more important letters and reports and hand them over to one of Ringelblum's collaborators in the secretariat of the Jews' Council.

The archive was placed in ten metal containers and two milk churns and buried in three different locations. Of these, only two were located after the war; the third is regarded as lost. Ringelblum was tracked down by the SS in Warsaw in 1944 and executed, along with his family, in the ruins of what had once been the ghetto.

He was a silent, indefatigable organizer, an open-minded historian, an impassioned archivist, a remarkably self-controlled and determined person. He was always in a great hurry, so our few whispered conversations were brief and to the point. Strictly speaking, I only knew him casually. But I still see him before me, Emanuel Ringelblum, the silent intellectual – just as I still hear the disturbing call of the skipping and dancing fool whose message consisted of only two words: 'Alle glach'.

16

'IF MUSIC BE THE
FOOD OF LOVE...'

The Jews in the Warsaw ghetto were tormented; they experienced terrible things. But from time to time they also experienced fine and wonderful things. They suffered. But they also loved. Except that love then was of a particular kind. A Viennese woman in a Schnitzler story says somewhere: '*Come, stay with me. Who knows if we'll still be alive tomorrow.*' Love inside the ghetto was clouded, every day and every hour, by the question of whether one would still be alive the following day. It was restless and quick, impatient and hasty. It was love at a time of starvation and typhus, at a time of terrible fear and deep humiliation.

People, especially the young, got together seeking protection and shelter from one another, and also help. They were grateful for a few hours or even just five minutes of happiness. I know the feeling well: the painful suspense which Goethe's Klärchen sings of, is always part of love, more often subconsciously than consciously – the fear that the unique, the inconceivable, might abruptly come to an end just as it had begun.

However, it was not the transience of love that worried lovers in the ghetto but the constant, ceaseless German threat: at any moment, even the most sublime, soldiers might suddenly come battering at the door with their rifle butts or even breaking it down. One was always afraid that they might brutally burst into the room. If all went well, we had an hour or two together.

What about that usual fear which, whether in peacetime or in war, weighed on young people living together – the fear of pregnancy? No one wanted a child in the ghetto. But not everyone succeeded in

151

preventing conception, especially as the condoms used had often perished – which one did not notice until it was too late. To terminate a pregnancy was not difficult. There were many gynaecologists in the ghetto, willing to help without charging exorbitant fees.

We, Tosia and I, were fortunate. She occupied a furnished room with her mother, who had the agreeable habit of spending the afternoons outside their home. So we were able to be alone. We told each other about our lives – and although we were barely twenty, we already had quite a lot to tell – we read poems by Mickiewicz and Tuwim, Goethe and Heine. She wanted to win me over to Polish poetry, while I tried to seduce her with German poetry. Thus we won each other's hearts, and sometimes we cut short our reading. Without knowing Freud's formulation, we learned the polarity of love and dying, the interlacing of happiness and unhappiness. Love was the narcotic with which we number our fear – our fear of the Germans.

Afterwards, when I left her and hurried to get home before the curfew, I could, amidst the misery and hardships, think only of what I had just experienced. *'Tis a dream, cannot really be true'* – these words, sung by Sophie at the very end of *Rosenkavalier*, went round and round in my head. I kept repeating them, I called them up silently without taking much notice of what was happening around me.

One evening on my way home I caught sight of the corpse of a man, probably a beggar starved to death – and saw, standing beside it on the pavement, a man, no longer young, clad in rags. Gazing at the dead man he said something, or, more accurately, mumbled something I did not understand. It must have been the Kaddish, the Jewish prayer for the dead. People walked past quickly, as if fleeing, and I did likewise, Hofmannsthal's verses still ringing in my head. I felt compelled to look back – the body had already been covered with newspaper. From nearby I heard shots and screams; I was afraid.

Later, when I was in bed and could still hear the German firing outside, I thought about Tosia and the poems I had read to her, the verses which enabled us to forget what was threatening us every day, what, amidst that barbarism, might be our fate at any moment. Yet there was something that affected us even more profoundly than poetry, something that both stirred and intoxicated us. It was music.

Jews have always been regarded as musical, especially those from Eastern Europe. The Warsaw Philharmonic, the orchestras of the Warsaw Opera and the radio, the many ensembles of light music, dance and jazz music – all included a fair number of Jewish players. These musicians were now in the ghetto and they were unemployed. As they mostly had no savings their hardships grew worse every day.

Surprising sounds could now and then be heard – Beethoven's violin concerto from one backyard, Mozart's clarinet concerto from another – both without accompaniment. I still picture a white-haired woman playing an instrument one would not have expected to see in a street in the ghetto: her head raised high, she played something French on her harp, perhaps Debussy or Ravel. Many passers-by stopped in surprise, a few put down a banknote or a coin.

Before long some musicians conceived the idea of organizing a symphony orchestra in the ghetto. To serve the noble art or to provide joy and pleasure to others? Nothing of the sort – they wanted to earn some money in order to assuage their hunger. It was soon clear that a large string orchestra could be created in the ghetto without much difficulty. There was no shortage of good violinists, viola, cello and double bass players. Wind instruments were a greater problem. Suitable candidates were sought by means of advertisements in the only newspaper in the ghetto and on notice-boards. Trumpeters, trombonists, clarinettists and percussion players from jazz bands and dance orchestras responded. It soon turned out that, even though they had never played in a symphony orchestra, they could sight-read Schubert or Tchaikovsky perfectly.

However, three wind instruments were still lacking. Soon further advertisements appeared: 'Horn, oboe and bassoon players urgently wanted.' As no one came forward, the oboe parts were played by clarinets and the bassoon parts by bass saxophones – and they did not sound bad at all. The greatest problem was the horns. A somewhat questionable solution was eventually found: they were replaced by tenor saxophones. There was no shortage of conductors. There were four in the ghetto, all of them competent, and one of whom was even an outstanding musician.

Simon Pullmann, born in Warsaw in 1890, had studied the violin at the conservatoire in St Petersburg, under the famous Leopold

Auer, and had later worked as a violinist, chamber music player and conductor chiefly in Vienna. The reason why he had failed to make it to the top was perhaps that he had never been pushy enough. In the summer of 1939 he was visiting his family in Warsaw – and was unable to get out of Poland in time. Thus Pullmann found himself in the ghetto and was soon, rightly, regarded as the most important of the musicians working there.

He was an exceptional person – self-confident and ambitious yet very quiet and reserved, and always exceedingly polite. During the orchestral rehearsals which I frequently attended I never once heard an impatient or loud word from him. The story goes that Bruno Walter once gently rebuked a flautist playing a false note with the words: 'Here I would recommend F sharp.' This was also Pullmann's style. He believed that it was the duty of Jews, even under these terrible conditions, to play good music well. He permitted no short cuts, he accepted no excuses, he rehearsed long and thoroughly, and thereby compelled the other conductors who might perhaps have been inclined to leave well alone – and who could have blamed them? – to work indefatigably and strive for a high standard.

As the strings were vastly superior to the winds, Pullmann naturally at first concentrated on music written only for them: Vivaldi and Boccherini, Bach and Mozart, and even Tchaikovsky's C Major Serenade. There were always some difficulties. Sometimes all the instrumental parts were available for a particular work but no full score, or else there was a full score but no parts for the instruments – so these had to be copied out by hand. But there was never any shortage of volunteers to do the job without reward.

Especially popular were five of Brahms's waltzes for piano duet. These were arranged for string orchestra by Theodor Reiss, a composer living in the ghetto, once he had obtained from Pullmann what the poor man could not afford himself – music paper. The première of this was most successful. Reiss was asked by the conductor to come up on the platform, but he was reluctant to do so. One could see at once that this was not the usual show of modesty. Eventually he did go up, bowed quickly and awkwardly, and hastily disappeared among the audience again. He had been ashamed of his clothes – he evidently did not own a jacket and wore an exceedingly shabby overcoat.

Pullmann also got his virtuoso string orchestra to play chamber music, especially quartets and quintets, and they played wonderfully – Beethoven's Great Fugue, op. 133, the Adagio from Bruckner's quintet, or the quartet by Verdi. Now and again the musicians, who would have preferred the traditional repertoire, complained that Pullmann was asking too much of them. In the end they always gave in – and never regretted it.

It is difficult to imagine now the dedication with which these musicians rehearsed and the enthusiasm with which they performed. In 1988, when we were preparing a series called *Literarisches Quartett* [*Literary Quartet*] for Germany's second TV channel, *Zweites Deutsches Fernsehen* (ZDF), I was asked what music I would like for the lead-in and lead-out. I asked for the first few bars of the Allegro molto from Beethoven's Quartet No. 3 in C Major, op. 59, which had been especially well performed in the ghetto by the string orchestra. Whenever I hear these bars of Beethoven I am reminded of the musicians who played them in the ghetto. They all perished in the gas chambers.

Much though the emphasis was on works for string orchestra, symphonic music was not neglected, despite the difficulties. Haydn and Mozart were played, Beethoven and Schubert, Weber and Mendelssohn-Bartholdy, Schumann and Brahms – in other words, predominantly German music, as throughout the world, although also Berlioz and Tchaikovsky, Grieg and Dvořák. In fact, everything was played that could be found, apart from modern music. Everything but Chopin.

A few months after the entry of the Wehrmacht into Warsaw the Fredéric Chopin monument was blown up by the German authorities. On 3 June 1940 the propaganda department of the Government-General of Poland prohibited the performance of music connected with Polish national tradition. The Decree was signed by State Secretary Josef Bühler, the deputy of Governor-General Hans Frank. It soon emerged that this prohibition applied to the entire oeuvre of Chopin.

In April 1942 the prohibition was lifted. Works of Chopin, as well as of Mieczysław Karlowicz, a composer esteemed in Poland with good reason – he lived from 1876 to 1909 – were permitted to be played again, but not, as the Decree expressly stated, within the

Jewish Residential Area. In the ghetto, therefore, not a single bar of Chopin was to be heard. But now and again some young pianist or other, rather recklessly, would play a less well known piece of his as an encore. When asked who the composer of that piece was, if it was not perhaps Chopin, he would, with an ironical smile, reply that it was Robert Schumann.

At first the concerts were held on the premises of the Melody Palace, an old variety and dance establishment which by chance bordered on the ghetto wall. Later a bigger and better hall was found – a modern cinema which had never been in operation because its construction was completed only just before the war. This Femina Theatre had nine hundred seats and was readily converted to concert use.

Chamber music – there were three string quartets in the ghetto and they were all good – and recitals by soloists were held in smaller halls, especially in one of the 'people's kitchens', where they took place in the afternoon almost as soon as the (miserable) soup had been dished out. A smell of cabbage and turnips still hung about the place, but this did not bother anyone listening to Schubert or Brahms. In winter the halls were frequently unheated, in which case audience and musicians alike were in overcoats. If there was a power cut, carbide lamps were resorted to.

There were also problems of a different kind. We were all of us hungry, nearly always. Violinists or cellists, even if hungry, can still produce beautiful music. Not so trumpeters or trombonists, whose physical effort is greater: hunger affects their performance. That was why an affluent doctor in the ghetto used to invite the whole orchestra for breakfast – the concerts usually began at twelve noon – so that the wind players should blow better and the strings be in a better mood.

In addition to soloists who had been known in Poland even before the war, many young violinists, pianists and singers made their débuts in the ghetto. I recall a particularly pleasant and intelligent musician of nineteen or twenty by the name of Richard Spira who played Beethoven's Piano Concerto in E Flat Major for the first time with the ghetto orchestra. His teacher, one of the most important Polish piano teachers, was living in Warsaw at the time – outside the ghetto, as he was not a Jew. Even though they were a mere two kilometres apart, Spira could not visit him, nor could the teacher visit Spira. But there were still a few telephones in the ghetto. Spira played the whole concerto over the telephone to his teacher and, in hour-long conversations, received exact instructions from him. The triumph of the pupil was shared by his teacher – despite the ghetto wall.

The most successful and popular figure in the musical life of the ghetto was a young dark-haired woman of girlish charm, a soprano whom no one had heard of before the war – Marysia Ajzensztadt, aged twenty. This beautiful and charming singer made her début with arias by Gluck and Mozart, with songs by Schumann and Brahms. To earn a livelihood she soon also appeared at a café – there was no coffee in the cafés but sometimes music – singing Johann Strauss and Franz Lehár. The audience in the regularly crowded café was enchanted – and so was the critic, Wiktor Hart.

The German-licensed *Gazeta Żydowska*, published twice weekly in Polish in the ghetto, also contained reviews of concerts. Wiktor Hart admired Marysia Ajzensztadt. Her singing, he wrote, 'testified to supreme art, to simplicity and measure: in a short time she has achieved true mastery.' Who was this enthusiastic critic, Wiktor Hart? If, today, his name appears in books dealing with that period, it is followed by a question mark or by the note 'unidentified'. But let us be open with each other: it was me.

An acquaintance, who was responsible for the signed columns in *Gazeta Żydowska*, knew that I was interested in music and had asked me if I could recommend a reviewer to him. I suggested a quiet man who was an excellent violinist and a great connoisseur of music. He wrote three or four excellent reviews and then fell ill. I was asked to substitute for him. I hesitated; after all, I had never in my life published any criticism. But the challenge attracted me so I agreed, initially only for two or three weeks. Things turned out differently and I wrote regular concert reviews for that paper – until there were no more concerts.

I did not feel entirely happy about doing it. True, I had heard a lot of music before the war (mostly on the radio or from records). I also had a fairly good knowledge of the history of music. But who was I to pass judgement on artists, many of whom had long been recognized? I was aware that this was not just bold but also impertinent, but I did it nevertheless. Reading my articles of that time, I

feel ashamed to this day. It is not a matter of the style, even though –
would you believe it? – I called Beethoven a 'titan' and Schubert a
'great master'. It does not matter that the twenty-year-old reviewer
was sometimes over-generous with his praise. But why did I have to
be so critical of this or that player? Why did I have to hurt musicians
who were doing their very best?

Perhaps I might plead in mitigation that – I am quite sure of this –
I never acted frivolously, and regularly sought the advice of the
expert whom I replaced. But when I consider what these Jewish
musicians suffered shortly after giving those concerts, I regret to this
day any critical or negative remarks that I made. Some of my
comments I no longer understand. Thus I wrote respectfully about a
performance of Haydn's 'Surprise' Symphony which, however, 'for
reasons unconnected with the Jewish Symphony Orchestra, could not
be played to the end'. What was I trying to suggest here? Did the
light fail? Or had some Germans walked in and dispersed us? I don't
think so – that I would not have forgotten.

But I can recall another concert which really was invaded by
Germans. Mozart's great G Minor Symphony was being played.
During the first few bars of the fourth movement two or three
Germans in uniform entered the hall. This had never happened
before. Everyone froze. The conductor saw them but went on conducting. Never before had I heard the final movement of this
symphony with such a marked tremolo in the violins and violas. This
was due not to the conductor's concept of the piece, but to the fear
of the musicians. No one could be sure what the Germans would do.
Would they yell: 'Raus, raus!' [Get out!]? Would they smash everything up? Would they consider it outrageous that Jews were making
music and would they even make use of their weapons?

But they just stood there and, for the moment, did nothing. The
orchestra played the symphony to its end. The audience applauded,
hesitantly and nervously. And now something quite unexpected,
something almost unbelievable, happened. The two or three men in
uniform did not shout, nor did they shoot. Instead they clapped and
amicably waved their hands. Then they withdrew without having
done any harm to anybody. They were Germans, yet they behaved
like civilized people. The incident was talked about in the ghetto for
weeks.

The concerts were always well attended, the symphony concerts usually overcrowded. In defiance of the general misery? No, it was not defiance that brought the hungry and wretched into the concert halls, but a longing for solace and elevation – however hackneyed these words, they are appropriate. Those who were ceaselessly fearing for their lives, those who were vegetating in the ghetto, were seeking shelter and refuge for an hour or two, searching for some form of security and perhaps even happiness. They needed a counter-world.

It was no accident therefore that among Beethoven's most popular works, along with the 'Eroica', the Fifth and the Seventh symphonies, was his 'Pastoral'. Where there were no fields and no woods, no streams and no bushes, many who normally did not care too much for Beethoven's music listened gratefully to the 'Awakening of serene feelings upon arrival in the countryside' and to other idyllic scenes – and they were grateful because these rural idylls had nothing in common with their surroundings.

It was not just the abandoned and the lonely who crowded into those concerts, but also the lovers. Those who had found each other felt confirmed by the music. And they quoted Shakespeare: *'If music be the food of love ...'* One day, after a particularly beautiful concert, I asked Tosia to promise me that, if she survived and I did not, she would always think of me during the Allegretto from Beethoven's Seventh Symphony. To my surprise she had no time for this flood of sentiment that suddenly swept over me. She would think of me, she said, not just during the Allegretto but during *every* piece of music we had heard together. That was the kind of sentimental talk we indulged in then.

What about poetry? There were also literary events in the ghetto, but much less frequently than concerts, and attendance as a rule was small. It is a fact – though possibly a commonplace – that music affects people in dangerous situations more directly than the spoken word, that it manages to arouse stronger feelings and stirs the imagination.

This happiness was of short duration. Soon the symphony concerts were stopped by the German authorities. Was the Commissioner for the Jewish Residential Area unable to bear the quality of the music? It was inadmissible – a letter to the Chairman of the Jews' Council stated – that works by 'Aryan' composers were performed in the ghetto. For that reason orchestral concerts were prohibited for two months, as from 15 April 1942. Recitals by soloists in a smaller framework could still be held, but had to be confined to the music of Jewish composers. From then on the programmes were mostly of Mendelssohn, Offenbach, Meyerbeer and Anton Rubinstein, as well as, of necessity, operetta composers such as Paul Abraham, Leo Fall and Emmerich Kalman.

In the circumstances I stopped writing reviews and turned towards another activity, which I believed to be infinitely more important. In the main building of the Jews' Council, which contained a large hall, I organized solo and chamber music performances. In the first half a pianist or a string quartet would play; in the second half there would be a woman singer or a violinist. Tickets, as for all concerts in the ghetto, were very cheap: the entire takings went to the musicians.

For us young people, this was not enough: we staged regular gramophone record concerts as well. Admittedly, the stock of records was limited, but the fact that they were old and scratched did not diminish our hunger for music. We would meet in small flats, some fifteen or eighteen people, however many fitted into the room. Strictly speaking, such meetings were forbidden but we were reckless enough to disregard this. Each guest brought along a gramophone record, a suite or a partita by Bach, a Mozart violin concerto, a Beethoven sonata or a Brahms symphony.

It seems to me that music has never played such an important part in our lives as it did in that gloomy period. Did Mozart charm and delight us all the more because we were hungry and in permanent fear for our lives? You had better believe it: in the Warsaw ghetto Mozart was never more beautiful. During that period of my life, German music forced German literature into the background. Soon things were to change again: instead of music, most unexpectedly, literature – especially German literature – would take on a renewed importance for both of us.

17

DEATH SENTENCES
TO THE ACCOMPANIMENT
OF VIENNESE WALTZES

The ban on symphony concerts not only saddened the musicians and their audiences, but also worried them. It soon emerged that this relatively harmless measure – after all, a large part of the population was not interested in concerts – was merely one of a number of regulations which, in the spring of 1942, testified to a planned change of conditions in the ghetto.

It was then, probably in March, that I first heard that somewhere in Poland the Germans were killing Jews with the exhaust gases of motor vehicles channelled into confined spaces. I did not believe these stories, and nobody I knew considered them even possible. The population of the ghetto was growing by the day. The new arrivals were Jews resettled – more accurately expelled – from villages in the Warsaw district. There were also transports of German and Czech Jews, chiefly from Berlin, Hanover and Prague. The boundaries of the ghetto were extended and some of the exits were closed.

During the night of 17/18 April uniformed Germans arrested fifty-three Jews in their flats and promptly shot them in the back, just outside their own front doors or in the immediate vicinity of their homes. They were chiefly political activists who had worked in the underground resistance and who were evidently, not without reason, viewed as potential leaders of a resistance movement. Further acts of terrorism followed in May and June 1942. Every night Jews, chiefly men, were being arrested and instantly executed. It was noted that these were mainly intellectuals, including many doctors. The ghetto was rigid with fear.

At the beginning of June another German film crew arrived and shot numerous posed scenes. Neatly dressed, attractive young Jewish women were picked up in the street and taken to the building which housed the Jews' Council. There they had to undress and were compelled to adopt obscene sexual poses and perform various acts. It was not clear whether the film crew had been instructed to shoot such scenes or whether they were merely amusing themselves.

A lot of contradictory rumours were circulating during those weeks. It was said that the administration of the Government-General of Poland had decided that 120,000 Jews should remain in the ghetto in order to serve the Wehrmacht by manufacturing uniforms and other items. It was also assumed that the German officials, especially those who worked in the office of the Commissioner for the Jewish Residential District, would be anxious to maintain the ghetto, so as not to lose their own posts and be sent to the front. In this way we all tried to reassure ourselves. Ultimately, however, no one took these optimistic rumours seriously: there was panic and there was fear of an impending disaster.

In mid-July Adam Czerniaków repeatedly intervened with the Commissioner for the Jewish Residential District, Dr Auerswald, on behalf of a large number of children (some 2,000) who had been caught smuggling foodstuffs and begging on the streets of Warsaw. They had been picked up by the Polish police and brought to the ghetto, where they were under arrest. Czerniaków, who had heard that Auerswald's wife was pregnant, believed that some advantage might be derived from this circumstance for the children under arrest.

He thought up a touching idea. He got Tosia, who was then trying her hand as a graphic artist, and whose work had been shown to him by his secretary on various occasions, to produce a special present for Auerswald – a photograph album for the as yet unborn child. The album, decorated with all kinds of illustrations, was to provide space for photographs illustrating the various stages of the child's life – the first tooth, the first birthday, the first day at school, and so on.

Tosia had to produce this album with lightning speed. She worked day and night and finished it at the very last moment, for a meeting on 20 July. Czerniaków was clearly satisfied: Auerswald was said to have been touched and had promised to authorize the release of the arrested children during the next few days. Tosia was happy at the thought of having played a part in saving the lives of so many children. Except that Auerswald no longer had any say in the matter: he had been deposed by the SS. His own child, whose passage through life Tosia had planned so colourfully, died shortly after birth.

By 20 and 21 July it was clear to everyone that evil things lay in store for the ghetto. Many people were shot in the street during these days and many were arrested as hostages, including several members of the Jews' Council and a number of its departmental leaders who, although the highest officials inside the ghetto, were by no means popular. Even so, the population was shocked: their brutal arrest was seen as a bad omen for all those who lived within the ghetto walls.

On 22 July several motor cars and two trucks drove up to the main building of the Jews' Council, carrying soldiers who wore German uniforms but, as was discovered later, were not Germans, but Latvians, Lithuanians and Ukrainians. The building was surrounded. Some fifteen men, including a few senior officers, got out of the staff cars. Some remained in the street, while the others quickly went up to the first floor. They did not make for the left wing which contained the large room housing the Translation and Correspondence Bureau, however, but for the right wing, the office of the chairman.

A sudden silence descended on the building, an eerie silence. We assumed that further arrests were about to be made. A moment later Czerniaków's assistant appeared and ran from room to room announcing the following instruction: all members of the Council were to report to the chairman at once. A little later he returned: all heads of department were also to report to Czerniaków. We assumed that not enough Council members were present to meet the number of hostages required, as most of them had already been arrested the day before.

Shortly afterwards the assistant appeared for the third time. Now I was summoned to the chairman. So my turn has come, I thought. But I was wrong. In any case I took a notepad and two pencils with me, as I always did when I was called to the chairman. In the corridors there were heavily armed sentries. The door to Czerniaków's large and – to my mind – over-pompous office stood open. He was standing behind his desk, surrounded by several senior SS officers.

Was he under arrest? When he saw me he turned to one of the officers, a corpulent, bald man – he was SS Sturmbannführer Höfle, the head of the Central Department Reinhard which operated under the SS and Police Chief and was commonly called the 'Extermination Commando'. Czerniaków introduced me to him with the words: 'This is my best correspondence clerk, my best translator.' So I had not been summoned as a hostage.

Höfle wanted to know if I could write shorthand. When I said no, he asked if I could write fast enough to take the minutes of the meeting that was about to begin. I curtly said yes. He thereupon gave orders for the adjoining conference room to be got ready. Along one side of the table sat the eight SS officers including Höfle, who was to chair the meeting. Facing them sat the Jews – Czerniaków and the five or six members of the Jews' Council not yet under arrest, the commander of the Jewish Order Service (the ghetto militia), the general secretary of the Jews' Council and myself.

I wanted to type the minutes straight on to the machine. As I knew that there was no relying on our old, rather clapped-out, typewriters, I had two machines brought over from the bureau, to enable me to go on writing even if, as happened frequently, the ribbon of one machine got tangled up. Sentries were posted at both doors to the conference room. I believe their sole purpose was to spread fear and terror. The windows overlooking the street were open on this warm and particularly fine day, but this did not seem to worry the Sturmbannführer or his men. Thus I was able to hear how the SS men waiting outside by their vehicles were amusing themselves. They evidently had a gramophone, a portable instrument, and were listening to music. And not bad music either. They were playing waltzes by Johann Strauss who, unknown to them, was not a pure Aryan. Goebbels had given orders to conceal the racially not quite pure origins of the composer he admired.

Höfle opened the meeting with the words: 'Today marks the beginning of the resettlement of the Jews from Warsaw. You all know that there are too many Jews here. You, the Jews' Council, are instructed to implement this programme. If it is carried out with precision, the hostages will be released again. If not, you'll all be strung up – over there.' He pointed to the children's playground across the street, quite a nice little park, given ghetto conditions, which had been solemnly opened a few weeks previously. There had been a band, the children had danced and given a gymnastics display, and the usual speeches had been made.

Now Höfle was threatening to have the whole Jews' Council and all the Jews present in the conference room hanged in this children's playground. We felt that this chunkily-built person, whose age I estimated to be at least forty, though in reality he was only thirty-one, would not have had the slightest compunction about having us executed or 'strung up'. Even the man's language, with its unmistakable Austrian accent, testified to his ruthlessness and vulgarity. He came, as I learned much later, from Salzburg where he had allegedly been employed as a motor mechanic.

After the sadistic threat with which he had opened the meeting, Höfle now dictated, in a businesslike manner, the text he had brought with him. It was entitled 'Information and Tasks for the Jews' Council'. He read it awkwardly and with some difficulty: evidently he had neither written this document nor edited it, and he was only cursorily acquainted with it. There was a strained silence in the room, made even more tense by the rattle of my typewriter, the clicking of the cameras of some SS officers, who kept taking pictures, and the gentle melody of 'The Blue Danube Waltz' wafting in from the street. Were the SS officers who were eagerly photographing the proceedings aware that they were recording a historic event?

From time to time Höfle looked at me to make sure I was keeping up. Yes, I was keeping up all right. I wrote down that 'all Jewish persons' resident in Warsaw, 'regardless of age or sex', were to be resettled in the east. What did the words 'resettled' mean? And what was meant by east? For what purpose were the Warsaw Jews to be taken there? Nothing was said about this in Höfle's 'Information and Tasks for the Jews' Council'. However, the text listed six categories of persons who would be exempt from resettlement – including all Jews capable of work, who would be accommodated in barracks, all persons employed by German authorities or enterprises or belonging to the staff of the Jews' Council and of Jewish hospitals. One sentence suddenly made me prick up my ears. The wives and children of such persons would likewise not be 'resettled'.

Outside, a new record had been put on. Softly, but quite clearly, I could hear the cheerful waltz which spoke of 'wine, women and song'. I thought to myself: life goes on, the life of the non-Jews. And I thought of the girl who was now busy drawing in the small flat. I thought of Tosia, who was not employed anywhere and, in consequence, was not exempted from 'resettlement'.

Höfle went on dictating. Now it was said that the 'resettlers' could take with them 15 kg of baggage, as well as 'all valuables, money, jewellery, gold, etc'. *Could* take with them, or *should*? I wondered. That very day, 22 July 1942, the Jewish Order Service, which had to carry out the resettlement programme under the supervision of the Jews' Council, was to bring 6,000 Jews to a location on the railway line, from where the trains would leave for the east. As yet no one knew where the transports were going, or what lay ahead for the 'resettlers'.

The final section of the 'Instructions and Tasks' set out the penalties for those who attempted 'to evade or disrupt the resettlement measures'. There was but one punishment, and it was repeated at the end of each sentence like a refrain: '... will be shot'. When Höfle had finished dictating, one of the members of the Jews' Council asked whether members of the Jewish Social Self-Help were also exempted from resettlement. Höfle quickly confirmed this. No one dared ask another question. Czerniaków sat there in resigned silence.

A few minutes later the SS leaders with their entourage left the building. They were no sooner outside than the deathly silence abruptly turned to noise and uproar. As yet, the many employees of the Jews' Council and the numerous applicants waiting outside did not know the new regulations. But it seemed as though they knew, or sensed, what had just occurred – that a sentence of death had been passed on the largest Jewish city in Europe.

I hurried back to my office because parts of the 'Information and Tasks' were to appear on posters throughout the ghetto within a few hours. I had to see to the Polish translation at once. As I slowly dictated the German text, my colleague Gustawa Jarecka typed it straight into Polish.

Was I a little in love with the Polish writer, Gustawa Jarecka? Yes, but it was an entirely different relationship from that with Tosia. I did not know much about Gustawa's past. She was one of those Polish Jews who had become totally alienated from their religion and, before the war, had had little to do with the Jewish world. She had come to the ghetto with her two children, a boy of eleven or twelve from an early and short-lived marriage, and a two-or three-year-old son, about whose father she never spoke. Czerniaków – this must be said to his credit – generously supported the many intellectuals in the ghetto who had no job. This meant that in most cases he employed them in some department of the Jews' Council. As Gustawa could type and knew German, she was assigned to my bureau.

I still see her before me – a slim woman with brown hair and blue eyes, in her early thirties, calm and self-controlled. She was quite young when her first book was published and, by the outbreak of war, had written three more books – realistic, socially critical novels, mostly set in a proletarian environment and revealing left-wing views. When I was able to read them, after 1945, they interested but did not exactly excite me. But she herself had profoundly impressed me from the moment I first saw her. What bound us together was, again, literature – not German literature, about which she was only scantily informed, nor Polish literature, of which I was largely ignorant. We talked mainly about French and Russian literature, about Flaubert and Proust, about Tolstoy. I owe a lot to those conversations.

One day I showed her three or four essays from my final years at school, of which, needless to say out of pure vanity, I had made beautiful typewritten copies while still in Berlin. She was impressed by these essays, probably to a much greater degree than they deserved. She asked me if I had read Saint-Exupéry's *Night Flight*. As I did not know this little book she translated it into Polish for me without my having asked her for it. Coming one year after Tosia's handwritten version of Kästner's *Lyrical Medicine Cabinet*, this was another unusual literary birthday present. At that point, if not before, I should have realized that her interest in me was even greater than my interest in her.

What was it that attracted me to her at a time when – or so it seemed to me – my life revolved around my friendship, my relationship, with Tosia? I did not know then, but I believe I do now. When Tosia and I had played the game of imagining that we might survive the war – improbable as it then seemed – and talked about a future together, I told her the plot of Wagner's *Meistersinger* quoting Hans Sachs's response to Eva's half-serious, half-joking wooing: '*Then I should have wife and child indeed.*'

167

To me, Gustawa was a contrasting figure. She was not only older than Tosia, she was also more mature and independent. Subconsciously I found in her that support which my mother could no longer offer me – and Tosia not yet. It almost seems to me as if Gustawa had loved me. On one occasion, when we were alone in our office because the other two employees who worked with us had gone home, I looked at her and put my hand on her shoulder. She said at once, with gentle determination: 'Stop that.' Then she added, as if wishing to cheer me up: 'Let's both stop that. You have Tosia – and that's great, and that's how it should remain.' I never again touched Gustawa – but I have never forgotten her.

Now here I was, on 22 July 1942, dictating to Gustawa Jarecka the death sentence which the SS had passed on the Jews of Warsaw. When I got to the part listing the groups of persons who were to be exempted from 'resettlement', with the provision that this regulation also applied to wives, Gustawa broke off typing the Polish text and, without looking up from her machine, said quickly and softly: 'You should marry Tosia this very day.'

The moment I had finished dictating the 'Information and Tasks', I sent a messenger to Tosia. I asked her to come over at once, bringing her birth certificate with her. She turned up immediately, rather overwrought because the panic in the streets was infectious. I asked her to come down to the basement with me, where, in the historical department of the Jews' Council, a theologian worked, with whom I had already made the necessary arrangements. When I told Tosia that we were now going to be married she was only moderately surprised and nodded agreement.

The theologian, who was entitled to perform the duties of a rabbi, made no difficulties and two officials working in the next room acted as witnesses. The ceremony was quite short, and soon we held in our hands a certificate according to which we had been married on 7 March. I cannot remember whether, in the haste and excitement, I even kissed Tosia. But I know very well the feeling that swept over us – fear. Fear of what would happen during the next few days. And I still remember the Shakespeare quotation which came into my mind then: '*Was ever woman in this humour woo'd?*'

The deportation of the Jews from Warsaw to Treblinka took place between 22 July and mid-September 1942, organized and supervised by Hermann Höfle. After the war he was arrested by the American authorities and interned. However, he succeeded in escaping. In 1961 he was rearrested in Salzburg where he was then employed at the waterworks. On 2 January 1962 the Hamburg district court summoned me as a witness in the investigation of Höfle. I was also to give evidence against him at the trial. But there was no trial. After his transfer to Vienna, Hermann Höfle committed suicide in his detention cell.

18

AN INTELLECTUAL,
A MARTYR, A HERO

Adam Czerniaków enquired of the SS whether it would be possible to permit the 'resettlers' to send back signs of life, such as postcards – if only to avoid panic in the ghetto. This proposal was rejected brusquely and, as always, without explanation. We were all horrified and helpless. Because even then, on the second day of the 'resettlement', 23 July, the suspicion arose that the persons deported were all being murdered. The ghetto's head man immediately realized what the Germans expected of him: he, Adam Czerniaków, was to be the executioner of the Warsaw Jews.

It certainly never occurred to him that he might go down in history as a tragic figure, let alone as a hero or martyr. Czerniaków, this bourgeois intellectual, had no interest in heroics, but he probably had no objection to the unusual role which had fallen to him – at least not until 22 July. A chemist by profession, he had studied in Poland and Germany (mainly in Dresden) before the First World War, and he attached importance to his academic title of Dipl.Ing. German culture, as emerged from various conversations I had with him, had exercised an important, probably a decisive, influence on him.

In the 1930s Czerniaków held a fairly high position in the Polish treasury department in Warsaw. This work, however, did not seem to satisfy his ambition. He became a member of the Warsaw City Council and later of the Senate of the Polish Republic; he was also a member of the board of the Jewish religious community of Warsaw – where, incidentally, he did not have an easy time because, coming from an assimilated Jewish family, he aroused the hostility of the orthodox Jews by the fact that he knew hardly any Yiddish.

When the Wehrmacht occupied Poland, most board members of the Jewish religious community fled towards the east. Czerniaków was one of those who remained at their posts. During the siege of Warsaw, the last president of the Polish capital still in office appointed him provisional chairman of the Jewish community. When the Germans arrived and ordered him to set up a council of twenty-four Jewish elders, he regarded this task as a historic mission. On several occasions he stressed the fact that he had been appointed to his office not by the German occupiers, but by the Poles.

Adam Czerniaków had thus become the head of the largest concentration of Jews in Europe and (after New York) the second largest in the world, in effect Lord Mayor of a huge Jewish city. He guided its self-administration, which had taken over the responsibilities of the religious community and, in addition, the duties of the Polish City Council. The Jews' Council was in charge of the usual municipal and state institutions, such as hospitals, public baths, post offices, assignment of accommodation, food supplies, urban transport, cemetery administration, various social institutions and finally, of its own militia. But the Jews' Council had yet another duty: it had to represent the Jews and implement the orders of the German authorities in all matters, without question.

Quite certainly Czerniaków was not up to such a dual role. It is equally certain that, with the best will in the world, no one person would have been able to discharge this – as it soon emerged – enormous and grisly task. Only a few people in the ghetto had any respect for him. Most disapproved of his activities; he was even reviled and hated. He was held partly responsible for the barbaric measures of the Germans, since few if any realized that virtually every day he endeavoured to mitigate the sufferings of the population – in most instances, though not in all, in vain.

Despite being repeatedly arrested and often humiliated, beaten and even tortured by his interlocutors, Czerniaków did not capitulate. Time and again he tried to extract at least small concessions from the authorities, which he visited ceaselessly. When an Italian institution offered to enable him and his wife to flee from occupied Poland, he declined because he considered it his duty to remain at his post. Only when his diary was published (the Hebrew translation in 1968, the

Polish original in 1972) were the sufferings and achievements of this chairman of the Jews' Council properly appreciated.

People were outraged by the fact that, among Czerniaków's circle, there were some exceedingly shady figures who were regarded as Gestapo agents. At first this was no more than a suspicion, but it proved justified. In consequence these people were, after Czerniaków's death, sentenced to death by the Jewish Fighting Organization and executed. However, these undoubted agents were Jewish liaison officers and therefore had to communicate with the Security Police and other German authorities. It was the Germans who compelled Czerniaków to collaborate with such individuals – but that, of course, was not realized in the ghetto.

Those who regarded him as a poor organizer were probably right; he was also a rather weak-willed and possibly even vain person. His somewhat annoying penchant for ostentation was bound to attract attention in the ghetto. He was fond of bombastic speeches, ceremonial openings and all kinds of festive events. When the children's playground had been opened a few weeks previously, Czerniaków had displayed an elegance unprecedented in the ghetto: he had worn a brilliantly white suit, a straw hat and white gloves, and had looked with contentment on what he had achieved for the children.

Czerniaków was fond of seeing himself in the role of a generous patron of the arts. People occasionally made fun of this, reluctant to believe that he had ordered decorative windows for his office in the building of the Jews' Council only in order to provide work for a few painters living in the ghetto. Nor was it generally known that he supported the Jewish Symphony Orchestra within the scope of his modest means.

Whenever he had an especially important document to dictate, or required help with a letter he needed to write in German, he would summon me. At sixty he seemed to me a dignified gentleman, a person demanding respect – but then I was only just over twenty. He would often ask me about the situation of the musicians in the ghetto. He was also interested in literature and I liked the fact that, in order to impress me a little, he would occasionally quote the Polish romantics or even the German classics, especially Schiller. Not until much later did it strike me that more than once he referred to a line from *The Bride of Messina*: '*Of all possessions life is not the highest.*'

One day we learned that Czerniaków used to write poetry and short stories before the war and that he had them published at his own expense. One of the women on his staff wished to give him special pleasure on some occasion or other: she ordered a decorated and splendidly illustrated copy of these (not particularly good) poems from Tosia. It was said that this present made him very happy. During the war, too, he was said to have secretly written poetry.

But nothing flattered his vanity more than the fact that he owned the only motor car in the ghetto. This scruffy vehicle was the most visible, the most striking, symbol of his power and dignity. It proved very useful not only for Czerniaków's almost daily visits to the German authorities. Twice he had been reviled in the street by desperate Jews and indeed threatened. Since then he was seen in the streets of the ghetto only in his car. If he had to leave it – for instance, at the cemetery where he gave frequent addresses – he was protected by several members of the Jewish militia.

Whatever Czerniaków was accused of, even his opponents would not dispute that, while perhaps a little naive, he was an honest, upright individual, a man of integrity. Although in the autumn of 1942 two militia commanders were executed as collaborators, following the death sentences passed on members of the resistance organization in the ghetto, no one ever accused him (or the twenty-four members of the Jews' Council) of collaboration.

The last time I saw Adam Czerniaków was on 22 July. I had come to his office to submit the Polish text of the notice which, as ordered by the Germans, was to inform the population of the 'resettlement' that had begun a few hours earlier. He was serious and self-controlled as ever. Having cast his eye over the document he did something entirely unusual: he corrected the signature. It had always been: 'The Chairman of the Jews' Council – Dipl.Ing. A. Czerniaków.' He crossed this out and instead wrote: 'The Jews' Council in Warsaw'. He did not want to bear the sole responsibility for the death sentences proclaimed on the poster.

Even on that first day of 'resettlement' it was clear to Czerniaków that there was literally nothing left for him to say or do. The following day his car was taken from him. Early in the afternoon it became obvious that the militia, no matter how hard it tried, was unable to muster the number of Jews demanded by the SS for that day's transportation. In consequence, heavily armed battle squads in SS uniform burst into the ghetto – not Germans, but Latvians, Lithuanians and Ukrainians. They promptly opened up with their machine-guns and, without making any distinction, rounded up all the inhabitants of the tenements nearest to the embarkation point. Henceforth these men in German uniform were known to be especially savage.

The fact that they could not care less about the documents of the Jews they were driving to their deaths did not surprise anyone. How could they, considering that they did not know a word of German? Hence what SS Sturmbannführer Höfle had dictated to me the day before was already null and void. All employment certificates, until then eagerly sought, proved to be useless scraps of paper. The document testifying that Tosia was my wife, and therefore exempt from 'resettlement', had become superfluous; it no longer had the slightest value. Nevertheless we carefully preserved it: even though our wedding on 22 July 1942 had been hasty and not especially solemn, and motivated initially by practical considerations, both of us took it very seriously – and do so still.

In the late afternoon of 23 July the 6,000 Jews demanded by the 'Operation Reinhard' staff for transportation had been reached thanks to the Latvians, Lithuanians and Ukrainians. Nevertheless, two officers turned up at the building of the Jews' Council shortly after 6 p.m. They demanded to speak to Czerniaków but he had already gone home. Disappointed, they beat the duty official of the Jews' Council with one of the riding crops they invariably carried. They demanded the immediate return of the chairman. Czerniaków presently arrived: for the first time he came to his office by rickshaw. It was also the last time.

The conversation with the two officers was quite short: it took only a few minutes. Its subject matter emerged from a note later found on Czerniaków's desk. The SS demanded of him that the number of Jews taken to the assembly point the following day be increased to 10,000 after which it would be 7,000 each day. These were not arbitrary figures but seemed to be based on the number of cattle trucks available: the trucks were to be filled to capacity.

Shortly after the two SS officers had left his office, Czerniaków called his servant and asked her to bring him a glass of water. A little later the cashier of the Jews' Council, who happened to be near

Czerniaków's office, heard his telephone ring repeatedly without being answered. On opening the door, he was horrified to see the dead body of the chairman of the Warsaw Jews' Council. On his desk was an empty bottle of potassium cyanide and a half-empty glass of water.

Two short notes were found on his desk. One, intended for Czerniaków's wife, read: '*They demand that I should, with my own hands, kill the children of my people. I have no other way out but to die.*' The other letter was addressed to the Jews' Council. It said: '*I have decided to resign. Don't regard this as an act of cowardice or an escape. I am powerless, my heart breaks with sadness and compassion, I cannot bear it any longer. My action will make everyone see the truth and perhaps guide them towards the right path to take...*'

The ghetto learned about Czerniaków's suicide in the early morning of the following day. Everyone was shocked, including his critics, his opponents and his enemies, even those who until the previous day had derided and despised him. His action was interpreted in the way he had intended it to be – as a signal that the situation of the Warsaw Jews was hopeless. It was understood as a desperate appeal for action. And many, especially in the circle of my friends, did not miss the fact that the man who had so often been accused of vanity had preserved his dignity at the decisive moment. The man who had been fond of grand and theatrical gestures had left a clear and plain message.

He had opted out quietly and simply. Unable to fight the Germans, he refused to be their cat's-paw. He was a man of principle, an intellectual who held lofty ideals. He had tried to remain loyal to those ideals even in an inhuman era and under scarcely imaginable circumstances. He had hoped that this might be possible even in the teeth of German barbarity. He was undoubtedly a martyr. Was he also a hero? When, in his office on 23 July 1942, he decided to put an end to his life he certainly acted in accordance with his ideals. Can one ask more of any human being?

When, shocked and bewildered, I heard of Adam Czerniaków's lonely death I thought of the poets whom he had not only loved and was fond of quoting, but whom he also took seriously. I thought of the great Polish romantics and the great German classics.

19

A BRAND-NEW RIDING CROP

The word 'honeymoon', the dictionary tells us, originally meant 'the first month after marriage' and now usually means a trip undertaken by newlyweds before settling down in their home. What about our honeymoon? Tosia and I certainly did not go on a wedding trip: we were spared a journey. After all, such a journey could have had only one destination – the gas chamber. But in the sense of 'the first month after marriage', we certainly lived through that. And it was one of the worst, the most terrible, months of our lives.

The murder of the overwhelming majority of the Warsaw Jews, which began in the morning of 22 July 1942 and continued until mid-September of that year, is referred to in historical accounts by terms which conceal the real state of affairs: 'Big Operation', or 'First Operation', or even, adopting the official German nomenclature, 'Resettlement'. The Jews were certainly deported and evacuated. But resettled? If so, where?

Hundreds of cattle trucks were loaded each day, with some six to seven thousand Jews on average. The largest number of persons deported on a single day, according to German records, was 13,596. The first victims were those who were a burden to society, especially to social welfare. The ghetto militia was under orders to empty the asylums for the homeless, the orphanages, the detention centres and other accommodation for the poorest and most wretched.

Most of the elderly and sick were taken not to the railway siding, but to the Jewish cemetery, and there they were immediately shot. Improbable as it may sound, some ghetto inmates believed that there might be a positive side to the fact that those incapable of work were executed on the spot: 'resettlement', they thought, need not invariably mean death; the Jews were possibly being deported because somewhere they were needed as labourers. The Germans, it was said, were planning a vast defensive system in the east, comparable to the Siegfried Line in the west. Maybe, it was thought, some hundreds of thousands of workers were needed to help build it.

In the long run, however, such rumours and speculations did not reassure anyone. It was understood that whoever rounded up people indiscriminately, forcing them – even women and children – into cattle trucks in such a barbaric manner, could have no intention of sending them to work for the Germans. Soon everybody, whether capable of work or not, was picked up in the street and taken to the assembly point. Instantly the streets were deserted. Those remaining in the residential blocks were ordered by loudspeaker to come down into the courtyard at once; anyone failing to comply was shot. Even so, many preferred hiding in cellars, in attics and elsewhere, to risk being shot on the spot, rather than 'resettlement'.

The Jewish militia had to help with this drive, in exchange for which the SS promised that they and their families would be allowed to remain in the ghetto, hence to stay alive. In spite of their fear of death, not all militiamen were prepared to carry out the German orders. Some who refused were instantly executed, others committed suicide. But most of them played a contemptible role during those days and weeks. Needless to say, the SS did not keep their word: at the end of the 'First Operation' nearly all the members of the Jewish militia were taken to the assembly point by the few of their own kind who were still allowed to remain behind.

The question of where the transports went was answered as early as the beginning of August. The Jewish sentries at the railway sidings had been noting down the numbers of the trucks: to their astonishment they found that the trains did not cover a great distance, that they certainly did not go to Minsk or Smolensk. The trucks were back in Warsaw within a few hours, four or five at the most.

It was soon learned that all transports went to a railway station north-east of Warsaw, little more than a hundred kilometres distant, the station of Treblinka, a small township in the vicinity. From there, a branch line of some four kilometres led to a densely wooded area, where the camp of Treblinka was situated. Was this really a camp? Before long it was discovered that there was no concentration camp there, let alone a labour camp. There was only a gas chamber – or, more accurately, one building with three gas chambers. What was being called the 'resettlement' of the Jews was only their evacuation from Warsaw. It had only one destination – Treblinka, one objective – death.

No one in the ghetto had any illusions. But what about hope? A new German term was beginning to gain currency – 'useful Jews'. These, it was assumed, were Jews who, within the meaning of the 'Information and Tasks', were exempted from 'resettlement'. But how was one to prove that one was doing something 'useful' when those who systematically searched the ghetto – mainly the Latvians, Lithuanians and Ukrainians – ignored the German work certificates and often threw them away or tore them up? It seemed safest not to move away from one's place of work. In most cases these were large German enterprises which, in the ghetto, manufactured all kinds of goods and whose German proprietors or managers had an interest in not allowing the deportation of the Jews employed by them – especially as these employees received either no pay at all or only minimal wages.

The staff of the Jews' Council, a workforce already greatly reduced, were likewise classified as 'useful' for the time being. That was why Tosia and I spent the whole day in my office. Unexpectedly, one of Tosia's relations turned up there, a businesslike and courageous woman who was living outside the ghetto as a non-Jew. She had come to take Tosia home with her, to save her. Admittedly, she said, she was unable to take me along as well. That would be pointless and dangerous. With my appearance, with my dark hair, I would be recognized and denounced as a Jew – and shot on the spot. That, she said, was now an everyday occurrence: she had herself witnessed a Jewess being discovered outside the ghetto and shot dead. Tosia, on the other hand – the aunt believed – could pass as an 'Aryan'. She had better think her offer over quickly and go along with her straight away, but of course she would have to part from me. That, too, was an everyday occurrence nowadays.

Tosia made her decision immediately, and without even consulting me. She said quite briefly that she would not leave me on my own.

And we remained together. For a woman to risk her life in order to save her friend, lover or husband – that was a theme I was familiar with from operas, ballads and short stories. I experienced it for the first time in reality in the Warsaw ghetto.

Two or three times in August there were surprise 'selections' at the offices of the Jews' Council. That was the term used for the procedure which served to drive a portion of those exempted – in disregard of their exemption – to the assembly point. A 'selection' worked like this: suddenly we all had to assemble in the yard, form ranks and then, one by one, march past an SS officer. As a rule this would be a young man of inferior rank, an Unterscharführer perhaps, holding a smart riding crop. One had to tell him where, and in what capacity, one was employed, whereupon he would indicate with his riding crop whether one was to go to the left or to the right.

On one side were those who were permitted to remain in the ghetto, on the other the ones who had to go to the railway siding and straight into the trucks. One side meant life, provisional life, the other meant death, instant death. Was the decision of the German with the rakish riding crop guided by any criteria? We had the impression that the more sturdy people, those capable of work, stood a better chance of ending up on the side of life. A good deal evidently also depended on what one looked like. Dirty, slovenly dressed and especially unshaven Jews were immediately assigned to the lines earmarked for the gas chambers. Anyone with dark hair such as myself then shaved twice a day. I have not been able to break this habit: even now I still shave twice a day.

Often, however, the SS Unterscharführer who was authorized to make decisions about our lives, was guided just by his whims. How else could one explain the fact that at times he would send twenty or thirty persons, including some who were young and smartly dressed, to the side of death with a nonchalant wave of his crop?

We, Tosia and myself, survived the August 'selections' in the courtyard of the Jews' Council building. My parents, too, whom I had accommodated there in a side building, were assigned to the side of life. Tosia's mother, however, who had found a hiding place in a textile firm, was one of those who, in August, were taken to the railway sidings. We never saw her again. When my mother heard that Tosia was now all alone, she immediately said: 'You're staying with us now.' We were grateful to my mother for regarding this as a matter of course.

There were unbelievable scenes in the streets of the ghetto during the 'Big Operation': long columns of people, not guarded or driven by anybody, moving towards the embarkation point with heavy luggage which, mostly before the day was out, proved totally super-fluous. They were acting in response to a notice by the Jewish militia which, referring to the German authorities, promised all those who volunteered for 'resettlement' an allocation of food – three kilograms of bread and one kilogram of jam per person. At that time there was as yet no certainty about what lay hidden behind the word 'resettlement'. Hundreds, and on some days thousands, of desperate and starving people believed that at the end of their terrible rail journey there would be a 'selection' and that at least some of the arrivals, chosen for work, would survive.

But what hope was there for those who did not volunteer for deportation, who did not commit suicide (which quite a few did every day) and who did not flee into the 'Aryan' part of Warsaw – which was particularly difficult and risky during the 'Big Operation'? A colleague of mine at the Jews' Council, an intelligent and witty person, whispered this sarcastic comment into my ear: 'All that will remain of us is a small delegation. More than that the dear Germans will not approve.' The man used to be regarded as a pessimist. But his prediction, if anything, was over-optimistic. Meanwhile, however, many wanted to believe that they would be part of the 'small delegation'.

Again there were rumours, this time about the allegedly impending end of 'resettlement'. The Germans no doubt intended to deport a certain number of Jews. Was the SS leadership aiming at one-third of the ghetto population, or at one-half, or even more? That the aim was the 'Final Solution' did not occur to anyone.

Some Jews believed that the outside world, which was informed by radio about what was happening in the Government-General, would protest against these monstrosities. It was thought possible, and secretly even confidently believed, that the SS would one day suspend the operation on orders from Berlin. During the final days of August and the first few days of September 1942 the atmosphere in the ghetto was in fact somewhat calmer. Some people believed that the worst was over.

On 5 September a new order was posted around the ghetto: all Jews still living in Warsaw were to report at 10 a.m. the following day for 'registration' in the streets of an accurately defined neighbourhood near the assembly point. They were to take with them food for two days and drinking vessels. Their flats must be left unlocked. What happened now was called the 'Big Selection': 35,000 Jews, that was fewer than ten per cent of the ghetto population before 'resettlement', were given yellow 'life numbers' to be worn on the chest. Those were predominantly the 'useful Jews' employed in German enterprises or in the Jews' Council. Thousands who did not receive any 'life numbers' disregarded the risk of the death penalty and hid out somewhere in the ghetto. The rest, some tens of thousands, were taken straight from 'registration', straight from the 'Big Selection', to the trains bound for Treblinka.

Some were conspicuous by their strange luggage. They were carrying musical instruments in their appropriate cases – violins, clarinets, trumpets, and even a cello. These were the musicians of the symphony orchestra. I spoke briefly to some of them while we were all waiting, for hours, for the final 'selection'. Nearly all of them gave the same answer to the question of why they were taking their instruments with them: 'Surely the Germans love music. Perhaps they won't send a person who makes music for them into the gas chamber.' Not one of the musicians deported to Treblinka returned.

And Marysia Ajzensztadt, the delicate, wonderful soprano whom the whole ghetto loved? Everyone was determined to help her, to protect her, including every militiaman. When she got to the embarkation point, a Jew who had some influence that day was able and willing to save her. But her parents were already in the truck and she did not want to be separated from them. She tried to tear herself away from the militiaman who was holding her. An SS man watching the scene shot her dead. According to other reports she was not killed at the railway siding, but had been forced into a truck by the SS man and gassed at Treblinka. No one who survived the ghetto ever forgot her.

As I was still needed as a translator, Tosia and I received the precious 'life numbers'. We were not at all sure that the Germans

would respect these numbers, but we would soon find out. One day
we were taken to the spot where today the Warsaw Ghetto Memorial,
erected in 1947, stands. There, as usual, was a bored young man with
an evidently brand-new riding crop. Once more those sent to the left
had to go to the embarkation point and hence to Treblinka; those
sent to the right would be allowed, for the time being, to remain
alive. The crop pointed to the right.

If only because of their age – my mother was fifty-eight and my
father sixty-two – my parents had received no 'life numbers' and they
lacked the strength and wish to hide out somewhere. I showed them
where they had to queue. My father looked at me helplessly, while
my mother was surprisingly calm. She had dressed carefully: she
wore a light-coloured raincoat which she had brought with her from
Berlin. I knew that I was seeing them for the last time. I still see
them: my helpless father and my mother in her smart trench-coat
from a department store near the Berlin Gedächtniskirche. The last
words Tosia heard from my mother were: 'Look after Marcel.'

As the group in which they were standing approached the man
with the riding crop he was evidently becoming impatient. He urged
these no longer young people to get a move on. He was about to use
his riding crop, but there was no need: my father and mother – I
saw it from a distance – began, in their fear, to run as fast as they
could, away from the smart German.

The following day I bumped into the commander of the Jewish
militia at the embarkation point, a brutal man I knew slightly because
for a few weeks he had been our neighbour in the ghetto. He told
me: 'I gave your parents a loaf of bread – more than that I couldn't
do for them. And then I helped them up into the truck.'

20

ORDER, HYGIENE, DISCIPLINE

Mila Street may not have had a very good reputation, but for a while it was extremely well known in many countries. The address 'Mila 18' was almost world-famous, even if those who came across it from time to time did not know what it concealed. It was a poor and ugly street in the northern part of Warsaw, which before the war was inhabited chiefly by Jews.

Its fame outside the Polish capital had to do with literature. The polish poet Władysław Broniewski made it the subject of one of his finest poems just before the Second World War. In it, he speaks of the bitter contrast between the friendly, almost lovingly tender name of the street ('Mila Street' means something like 'Lovely Street') and the appalling events which were taking place there every day. The poem begins with the words:

> *Lovely Street – it is not lovely.*
> *Lovely Street – do not walk there, my love.*

And it ends:

> *Even when I hurry to you*
> *I avoid Lovely Street,*
> *for who knows if I won't hang myself there.*

Admittedly the poet Władysław Broniewski, one of the most remarkable Polish poets of our century, is scarcely known outside

Poland – and the untranslatable poem 'Mila Street' is not known at all.

It was left to an American author of entertaining thrillers, Leon Uris, to gain international fame for 'Mila Street'. In 1961 he followed his sensational bestseller *Exodus* with a second novel, which likewise became a worldwide bestseller – *Mila 18*. In this building, more accurately in its spacious cellar, was the command post of the Jewish Fighting Organization, the centre of the Warsaw Ghetto Rising.

Immediately after the 'Big Selection' Tosia and I learned that our flat had been taken from us. While the 'selection' was going on, the boundaries of the ghetto had been rapidly reduced by the German authorities. The street where we had been living a few hours ago was now no longer part of the ghetto and we were not allowed to enter it. We could see from a distance that numerous trucks and huge furniture vans were standing there: the SS 'Collection of Valuables' unit was already busy removing the belongings of those who were by then en route to Treblinka. We now understood why, when we had to present ourselves for the 'Big Selection', we had been forbidden to lock our flats. Certainly, everything had been very well planned and organized.

Now we were standing in a long line, waiting to be assigned new accommodation, if possible a new flat. We were taken to Mila Street, I cannot remember the number. The flat we received consisted of one room, a kitchen and a minute bathroom. Within these walls some five, or at the most ten, hours previously, people had been living, probably a couple, who were now in an overcrowded cattle wagon going to Treblinka. No, more likely they had already arrived there and been driven out of the wagons by SS men. Perhaps a stern, calm officer was now explaining to them that they were in a transit camp and, before being sent to a labour camp, would have to undress – men and women separately, as was proper. Then they would have to shower thoroughly, because hygiene was the supreme law. Their clothes would also be disinfected. Money and valuables had to be handed over, but, needless to say, they would be returned to them after showering. There had to be order. Here there was strict discipline, German discipline.

Or were the two new arrivals from Warsaw already naked and in the 'tube', as the path was called which led to the gas chamber?

Perhaps they were standing close to my naked mother and my naked father, in the gas chamber which resembled a shower room with pipes fitted to the ceiling. There was no water issuing from the pipes but gas produced by a diesel engine. It took about thirty minutes before all those crowded into the gas chamber were asphyxiated. In their agony, in their final moments, the dying had not been able to control their bowels or their bladders. The corpses, mostly soiled with faeces and urine, were quickly removed, to make room for further truckloads of Jews from Warsaw.

Meanwhile we were in Mila Street, in the small flat which, that very morning, had evidently been abandoned by two people in a great hurry. Silently and uneasily we looked around. The bed had not been made, the kitchen table had not been cleared; on one plate, next to two half-empty glasses, was a half-eaten piece of bread, and the light was still on in the bathroom. A skirt had been flung over a chair, a blouse hung over its back. The clothes, the furniture, the two sofa cushions and the carpet – everything still seemed to breathe.

And the two people who had lived here, loved here and suffered here – whose beautifully framed photographs, along with other pictures, adorned the chest of drawers – were they still breathing? We dared not think about it. Did we have no scruples whatsoever, no misgivings about taking possession of the small flat on Mila Street? With great surprise and profound shame I admit: we had no scruples, we did not have to overcome any resistance. And those of our friends and colleagues who, having likewise escaped the gas chamber for the time being and now become our neighbours on Mila Street – they too were settling into the flats assigned to them, quickly and hastily, and, at least so it seemed, without misgivings.

Had the inhumanity we had witnessed made us inhuman too? Our compassion had certainly been dulled. We had had to watch our dear ones being driven to the trains for Treblinka, while we were spared. Except that we had no faith in our salvation. We were convinced that we had been allowed only a brief reprieve. The flats on Mila Street, we suspected, were but temporary accommodation for the final months, perhaps the final weeks, of the Warsaw ghetto.

By then, in the autumn of 1942, in addition to the 35,000 Jews with 'life numbers' living in what remained of the ghetto, there were roughly 25,000 who had somehow escaped deportation but had no 'life numbers'; they were called 'the wild ones'. We soon discovered that our lives were to be further restricted under the new conditions. We were no longer allowed to walk in the streets on our own; in the morning we had to march to our workplace in columns and in the evening return home in columns.

In the office of the Jews' Council I continued to be responsible for translations and for whatever correspondence was still being conducted with the German authorities. I had also found a place there for Tosia: she was engaged on small graphic tasks like making labels and inscriptions. She received no pay, but that was irrelevant, since the main thing was to have a place of work where one was more secure than in one's flat or out in the street.

The deportations were being run down, but they were not entirely at an end. Cattle trucks loaded with Jews whom the SS had picked up at some place or other were still leaving for Treblinka, though no longer every day. One day it happened that I was in my office without Tosia, who was to follow me later in another column. Suddenly I was informed that she was at the transhipment place. No one could know when the next train would leave. I had to act quickly. I sought out that brutal commander of the Jewish militia who had given my parents a loaf of bread for their journey to the gas chambers. I found him. It happened to be a quiet day, when no other SS men were present at the embarkation point. So he was able to release Tosia. She came to me, upset and in tears. How she had got to the railway siding, and what she had experienced there, she could not or would not tell me. I believe that the illness from which she suffered after the war, especially after 1950, must have begun that day. Whoever, sentenced to death, has at close quarters watched a train leaving for the gas chambers remains marked for the rest of their lives.

The atmosphere in the ghetto was always uncanny but the time we were about to face, in the autumn of 1942, differed from what had gone before. The streets of the small residual ghetto, once crowded, were empty during the day, everything was silent, even though the silence was tense, almost a kind of shrill silence. The silence of the graveyard? Yes, but above all the calm before the storm. No one seriously believed that the Germans had suddenly decided not to murder those Jews who were still alive, and no one believed the many rumours which claimed that everything would soon return to normal, that the SS would again permit religious services and maybe even theatrical performances and concerts. Did these rumours originate from German sources in order to mislead the Jewish population? one asked oneself. On the other hand, there were increasingly frequent rumours of an impending 'operation', of the next 'resettlement', the next deportations to Treblinka. Dates were being mentioned all the time, which got us into a state of extreme nervousness.

We all knew that the 'Second Operation' was bound to take place sooner or later, and that we must not on any account await developments passively. Some people were planning to flee from the ghetto into the 'Aryan' part of Warsaw. That was enormously risky. Anyone outside the ghetto who knew of the existence of a Jew and did not immediately denounce him, anyone who actually helped him or provided shelter for him, risked the death sentence, along with his family. Jews discovered in the 'Aryan' parts of the city – many had already escaped before the 'First Operation' or had not gone to the ghetto in the first place – were usually shot on the spot.

But even those who were afraid of fleeing were determined not to sit idly by and wait for the next measures by the Germans. The basements of many buildings were, with considerable effort and skill, converted into shelters and stocked with foodstuffs and water supplies, some were connected to the water mains, and sometimes also to the underground sewer system which could make it possible to escape from the ghetto. In the event of renewed deportations the most determined intended to hide out there and, hopefully, to survive.

Above all, it was decided to offer armed resistance to the next 'resettlement' – weapon in hand. The idea of such an unequal rebellion against the Germans had first been mooted by representatives of various Jewish organizations at a joint meeting on 22 July 1942 – the start of the deportation – but had been dismissed. As there were virtually no weapons in the ghetto, any resistance, it was then believed, would not even have symbolical significance. Now, in the autumn of 1942, the situation had changed: youth groups and political parties believed that the moment had come to unite and the Jewish Fighting Organization was set up. First of all, weapons had to be found, and these could most easily be obtained from Polish underground organizations. But everything had to be done quickly, because the next deportations were expected in December, or no later than January 1943.

In mid-January reassuring rumours began to emerge again, obviously originating from German sources and designed solely to encourage the Jews to relax their vigilance. On 18 January we were awakened shortly after six in the morning by a noise in the street. I ran to the window and, in spite of the darkness, saw hundreds, if not thousands, of Jews forming up as a marching column. From our staircase came rude words of command. I understood that anyone not immediately leaving their flats and coming down into the street would be shot on the spot. We dressed as fast as possible and ran outside. I immediately noticed two things: the column outside our building – we did not know where it began and where it ended – was guarded by a much greater number of gendarmes than before. The sentries were standing only ten to fifteen metres apart, their weapons at the ready. They wore German uniforms and, unlike in the past, they were not Latvians, Lithuanians or Ukrainians, but, as the language of their angry shouts revealed, either Austrians or Germans.

After a few moments we marched off. We had no doubt where our column was going. It was also clear that we would very soon arrive at the invariably overcrowded and filthy waiting area for the passengers destined for the gas chambers. I whispered into Tosia's ear: 'Think of the Dostoevsky anecdote.' She knew exactly what I meant.

In Stefan Zweig's *Sternstunden der Menschheit*, a book very popular both before and after the war, one of the 'historical miniatures' describes an unusual incident from Dostoevsky's life. Having been sentenced to death for political reasons in 1849, he had, according to Zweig, already had the shroud put on him at the place of execution, he had already been tied to a post and blindfolded, when suddenly a cry was heard: 'Stop!' At the last moment, the very last moment, an officer arrived with a document: the Tsar had converted the death sentence into a more lenient penalty.

This story about Dostoevsky, even though it is rather poor from a literary point of view, had, during my school days, much impressed me, along with other pieces from the same book. By reminding Tosia of the incident described, and largely invented, by Stefan Zweig, I wanted to implore her, in case we were separated, never to give up hope. Except that literary anecdotes were not much help now. As Mila Street was not far from the embarkation point, any attempt to escape from the column had to be now or never – especially as escape from the train to Treblinka was as good as impossible.

Anyone breaking out of the column was immediately fired on, and left dead by the side of the road, but this was a risk one had to take. I made a signal to Gustawa Jarecka, who was in our rank with her two children, that we intended to break out and that she should follow us. She nodded. I was on the point of running, afraid of the fatal shot, but I hesitated for a moment. Tosia pulled me out of the column and we ran into the doorway of a bombed-out building in our 'lovely' Mila Street. Gustawa Jarecka did not follow us; she and her two children perished in the cattle truck on the way to Treblinka.

Others from our column, who had broken away a little after us, told us that one of the gendarmes had tried to fire at us. Had he missed? Had his rifle seized up? Or had he, this German or Austrian, perhaps not wished to shoot us, had he perhaps ignored his orders and had misgivings about killing us?

From the doorway of the ruined house we jumped down into a basement which, to our surprise, was linked to other basements. Evidently some walls had been broken through here in order to build a shelter. Thus we reached the last basement, one at some distance from the street. There we no longer heard any shouts and no shots either, the silence was absolute. There we remained until evening. No one came looking for us.

After dark, it was possible to leave our hiding place. The following morning we hid, along with some of our friends, in an unoccupied building of the Jews' Council, where thousands of books and files from the archives of the old Jewish community of Warsaw were stored. Using countless ancient books we barricaded ourselves into the large room, which had only one entrance. There, behind this wall of books, we hoped to survive the 'Second Operation'.

This was only possible because the operation was suspended on the fourth day, 21 January 1943, after the 'resettlement' of some five or six thousand Jews. The German authorities decided not to continue with it, even though only half the trucks waiting at the railway siding for dispatch to Treblinka had in fact left, with the other half still available to the SS. The reason was that during this 'Second Oper-

ation' something occurred which the Germans had not expected –
the Jews were offering armed resistance. It was obvious, however,
that the further 'resettlement' had only been postponed and that the
SS, now ready for armed resistance, would murder the remaining
Jews and liquidate the ghetto.

If, after the January deportations, one wished to escape certain death,
one had to flee from the ghetto as quickly as possible. However, for
a Jew to have any chance of survival in the 'Aryan' part of the
city, three prerequisites were necessary. First, one needed money or
valuables to buy false papers, not to mention the likelihood of being
blackmailed. Second, one must not look Jewish or behave in a way
that might make the Poles suspect that one was Jewish. Third, one
needed non-Jewish friends and acquaintances outside the ghetto,
people prepared to help.

If a Jew who wished to flee into the 'Aryan' part of the city met
only two of these three prerequisites, his situation was already
dangerous; if he met only one of them, then his chances were minimal.
In my case, however, none of the three prerequisites applied, which
meant that it was pointless for me to try to escape. I had no money,
I had no friends outside the ghetto, and everyone – the Poles had a
surprising nose for this – would immediately recognize me as a Jew.
Things were not much better for Tosia. We thought she did not look
Jewish but soon had to convince ourselves that we could not rely on
that.

I was not a member of the Jewish Fighting Organization, but I
did participate in one of its resistance operations – almost by accident.
One evening, a few days after the end of the 'Second Operation', we
were sitting in a basement with two of our friends, reflecting what
could be done under these circumstances. We agreed that our situation
was hopeless – unless it was possible to get hold of some money in
a hurry. Wasn't it a scandal, I said casually, that the Jews' Council
still paid money to the Germans every week? Shouldn't one raid the
safe of the Jews' Council? I suggested, half in jest. But one of those
present, a young man whom I knew to belong to the Jewish Fighting
Organization, immediately showed interest in this adventurous idea.
He asked us not to talk about it to anyone for the time being.

The following day he told us that the plan would probably be carried out, only we would have to help. I was to supply the information necessary for the raid – about the model of the safe in the building of the Jews' Council, access to the room in which it was housed, and what kind of locks were on the doors. In conversation with the cashier, whom I knew quite well, I was to discover on what day the next handover of money to the German authorities would take place. I also had to steal some Jews' Council headed notepaper, on which Tosia would forge the signature of the chairman. We were not told why the organization needed this signed letter.

The operation was carried out during the night of 30/31 January 1943, but not in the way we had expected. No doors had to be broken open, nor had the safe to be forced. The Jewish Fighting Organization had found a better solution. Some of its members, disguised as Jewish militiamen, awoke the cashier in his flat at night and handed him a letter from the chairman of the Jews' Council, asking him to come at once and to bring the safe keys with him. The alarmed cashier was told that some Germans had suddenly turned up, demanding a larger sum. He was suspicious, but did as he was told.

When it became known the following morning that the Jewish Fighting Organization had succeeded in staging this raid and that they had seized the money intended for the Germans – over 100,000 Zloty – there was general rejoicing. The new chairman of the Jews' Council immediately reported the incident to the German authorities. They sent specialists over, who examined everything and discovered nothing. The friend who had arranged the contact with the Jewish Fighting Organization told us that it had been decided to use the major part of the money for the purchase of weapons. But as a reward for our idea, Tosia and I were to be given a bonus – we each received about five per cent of the confiscated sum. This was to make our escape from the ghetto easier.

Prior to the 'Second Operation' I did not seriously consider the possibility of fleeing into the 'Aryan' part of the city. I was aware of the continual danger of being identified as Jewish; I realized that every neighbour, every passer-by, even a child, could denounce me. The probability of meeting my death outside the ghetto was, I believed, 99 per cent. Inside the ghetto, on the other hand, there was a 100 per cent certainty of dying. So I had to seize this minimal chance – *we* had to seize it. On this point there was no difference of opinion between Tosia and myself.

A musician, an excellent violinist, gave us the address of a Polish working-class family who were badly off and prepared, for appropriate payment, to shelter Jews. As we were saying goodbye he looked at us sadly without saying a word. When we were already at the door, he picked up his violin from the chest of drawers and played, probably a little more slowly and in a more elegiac manner than usual, the first few bars of the Allegro molto from Beethoven's Quartet No. 3 in C Major op. 59. This musician was also intending to escape from the ghetto but perished in Treblinka.

How were we to cross the ghetto boundary? There were two possibilities. We could either join a column marching out to work early in the morning, in which case we had to break away from it outside the ghetto, quickly dispose of our Star of David armbands and make our escape. However, we could not take any luggage with us. The other possibility was that we might get out in the afternoon, some time between five and six o'clock, when the sentries were busy carrying out personal searches of those returning in the labour columns.

The second alternative had the advantage that we could take at least a small suitcase. Naturally the border sentries had to be bribed. This was arranged by the Jewish militiaman who organized our escape. He was given the bribe on the understanding that he would share it between the German gendarme and the Polish policeman. This is what he told me when we negotiated the amount. But he cheated me: he kept all the money himself. When his alleged accomplices, the German and the Pole, turned their backs on us at the floodlit border crossing, he called out to us: 'Walk on straight ahead now, quickly!' This is what we did. A bare twenty steps – and we were outside the ghetto. This was on 3 February 1943. What lay in store for us in the non-Jewish part of Warsaw we were to discover within the next two or three minutes.

21

STORIES FOR BOLEK

We had just crossed the boundary line dividing the two parts of Warsaw when, behind us, we heard the innocent yet alarming word, 'Halt!' Two officers of the Polish police, which was tolerated and made use of by the Germans, wished to see our papers. I said straight away that we had none, that we were Jews who had just come from the ghetto. In that case, they said, they would have to take us to the German gendarmerie.

We were alarmed but not immediately in despair. We knew, of course, that any German sentry could instantly shoot any Jew out of hand, but we also knew that the 'blue police', as the Polish police were called after the colour of their uniforms, while serving the German gendarmerie, liked patrolling near the ghetto entrances in order to exploit the escaping Jews.

Negotiations began immediately, following a pattern that is probably as old as the police itself. One man took a tough line and would not negotiate at all, while the other was quite chatty. He said that he himself would like to come to a quiet agreement with us but that his colleague, unfortunately, was very strict. Perhaps an appropriate sum would soften him up. The end of the incident was that we bribed the two police officers and they delivered us in a horse and cart to where we wanted to go. During our journey they remarked that, after all, we were all Poles.

Just as our life in the Warsaw ghetto had ended with bribery, so our life outside the ghetto started with bribery. In spite of the death penalty, quite a few Poles received Jews into their homes and hid them there, though mostly only for a very high remuneration. We stayed a few days with the working-class family the musician had recommended to us. There, too, we were harassed and had to move on as quickly as possible.

Extortion and escape – this was the pattern that was endlessly repeated. Thousands of Poles, often unemployed adolescents who had grown up without completing their education, and many of whose fathers were in captivity, spent their days suspiciously watching all passers-by. They were everywhere, especially near the ghetto boundary, looking for Jews, hunting down Jews. This pastime was their profession and probably also their passion. It was said that, even if there were no other signs, they were able to identify Jews by the sadness in their eyes.

Did these young ruffians, or 'Shmaltsovniks' as they were known in the Occupation jargon, really want to hand over their victims to the German authorities? No, they were not particularly interested in that. Instead they wanted to rob the Jews, relieve them of their money, jewellery and other valuables, or at least of a jacket or winter coat. If we showed ourselves in the street, even for only five minutes, we would immediately be in great danger. But somehow we had to get from one temporary hiding place to another – and this could not be done in the dark because of the curfew and because we had summer time. Then I had a simple but effective idea – I bought a *Völkischer Beobachter*, held it so that the front page with the swastika was visible and strode down the street briskly, with my head held high. The blackmailers and denouncers would, I hoped, take me for an eccentric German who had better not be importuned.

The rising in the Warsaw ghetto broke out on 19 April 1943 – a heroic and hopeless rebellion against inhumanity. After it had been finally crushed on 16 May by considerable German military effort, including tanks, some people succeeded in escaping from the ghetto, mainly through the sewers. This was a boom period for extortionists and denouncers. We too were affected, even though we were in hiding. Suddenly, with a great deal of noise, a young man appeared in our little room, a gaunt individual in shabby working clothes, who exclaimed dramatically, 'Hands up!' and demanded money. Having relieved us of our cash – which was not much – and my fountain pen, as well as some items of my clothing, he turned peaceable. Now he evidently felt like a chat. After a while he said, reassuringly, that he would not bother us again. As he lived in the same building as we did, he had most probably been brought in by the man who was hiding us. The two may have shared the booty.

It was obvious that we could not stay there any longer, that we had to move on – and, moreover, at once. But without money I did not know where to turn next. So, in resignation, we stayed put. The following day the door opened again, this time noiselessly. It was the same unpleasant neighbour, the gaunt young man who had robbed us. Now he was friendly, he wanted nothing more from me – or perhaps, yes, he wished to talk to me about the war, about its future course and about the probable fate of Poland. What I had to say seemed to please him. He was a precision mechanic by profession, unemployed at the time. His questions did not strike me as unintelligent.

The following day he came again. He had good news – of some alleged German defeats. Then he remarked casually: 'Yes, if you had money, something might be done for you. You could live in complete safety – with my brother.' His brother, he said, lived with his wife and two children in a small rented house on the edge of the city. 'Incidentally, he is a German or nearly German. No one would suspect him of hiding Jews.'

Tosia had meanwhile succeeded in obtaining 'Aryan' personal documents and had found a living-in job as a domestic servant. Was I to throw in my lot with a man who had exploited me – and certainly others as well – in the meanest possible way? That would have been reckless, even downright mad. But I was desperate, I could see no other way out. So I asked him to speak to his brother, the German. Even though I had no money left, I might manage to get hold of some. Was this request tantamount to suicide? I was afraid so.

Three hours later the precision mechanic, Antek, returned, clearly a little drunk. His brother, he said, had wanted to know all about me – whether he was talking about some door-to-door salesman or seedy street trader. No, Antek had replied, this was an educated person who spoke well and could tell a good story. The brother had said: 'All right, bring him here. I'll have a look at him.'

The suburb I had to go to was a long way off, on the opposite, or right, bank of the Vistula. One had to take the tram to its final stop and then walk a short distance from there. How was I to accomplish that without being discovered and denounced en route? Antek was streetwise. The trick with the *Völkischer Beobachter*, he said, would not protect me here. I should take the tram at about five o'clock in the afternoon, when it was packed – and, in order not to be immediately reported and taken to the police, I had to look quite different – no longer like a Jewish intellectual, but like a poor working-class Pole.

Antek transformed me into a miserable railwayman returning home from work. He got me an old railwayman's cap and an even older railwayman's jacket. The dark hair had to be got rid of, so my head was shaved bald. I also had to do without my glasses. My face was blackened with soot and I carried a large pair of rusty pliers. People would probably steer clear of such a grimy railwayman.

Thus disguised, I arrived at the terminus. There I was to follow Antek, who had travelled on the same tram and got off ahead of me, at a distance of twenty or thirty metres. Everything went well, except that to my horror he led me out of the suburban surroundings into a nearby forest, and then criss-crossed it. Surely he would not rob me again – he knew that I no longer had anything to take. Did he perhaps want to kill me? I would not have put it past him. But for what? Soon he again changed direction and, crossing meadows and fields, brought me back to civilization and to a small house standing alone. Only later did he explain that the long, and for me alarming, detour had been to ensure we were not being followed or observed.

The appearance of the man who was awaiting us with curiosity surprised me. Antek's elder brother, Bolek, a man somewhat short in stature, was an entirely different type. His features displayed nothing brutal or threatening. On the contrary, he made a solid and pleasant impression; he welcomed me politely and amicably. Then he offered me a small glass of vodka, which I could not very well refuse, even though I would have much preferred a piece of bread.

He was a typesetter by profession, his handwriting was beautiful, and – a rarity among simple people in Poland then – his spelling was perfect. Even though he had never read a book, he was an educated working-class man. That he was one of the countless unemployed during the German occupation was not surprising: printing firms were virtually no longer operating in the Government-General.

Bolek's wife, about the same age as him, was a rather brash, amply shaped redhead, who must have been good-looking in her younger days. Now in her late thirties, she clearly showed the effects of the ravages of time. To my surprise she was able to read fluently – but only romantic novels. She could not write at all and even had difficulty signing her name – again something not unusual in Poland then.

We had chatted for perhaps a quarter of an hour when Bolek surprised me with a simple statement, spoken with obvious sincerity. 'It would be nice if you could survive this terrible war here with us.' He said this in June 1943 – and this is what actually happened. In his primitive little house we survived the German occupation. It had neither a bathroom nor a toilet – one had to manage with the kitchen tap, which did not always function, and with an earth closet. Here our lives were saved – by Bolek, the typesetter, and by Genia, his wife.

Our lives? At first I was there on my own. But Tosia's career as a domestic servant was not a success. Her parents had taken great care over her education – she had learned all kinds of things, like playing the piano, English, French, and of course also German. But she had not learned how to iron or to peel potatoes or to clean vegetables. Small wonder that she was repeatedly dismissed from her jobs. In the end she found a position that seemed hopeful. One day, however, when she was alone in the flat of her new employer, she was unable to resist a temptation. She sat down at the piano and played a waltz by Chopin. The lady of the house, returning unexpectedly, may have had a weakness for Chopin, but she had yet to see a domestic servant who could play the piano. She had no doubt that her new servant was a Jewess, must be a Jewess. This meant the end of Tosia's professional career in occupied Warsaw. Her forged personal papers became useless. She did not hesitate a moment and, within hours, arrived at Bolek's house.

During the day we hid in the basement, in a hole in the ground, or in the attic; at night we worked for Bolek. Using the most primitive means we manufactured cigarettes – thousands and tens of thousands. He sold them, but made only a small profit. Thus Bolek and his family lived in poverty. But our condition was a lot worse: we were hungry. We actually believed that, in this respect at least, concentration camp inmates were better off than us, they received a bowl of soup every day, while we, if conditions were particularly bad, had to wait until the evening to get anything to eat – and then it was often only a couple of carrots. But worse than hunger was the fear of death, and worse than the fear of death was the continuous humiliation.

No matter how scarce money was, there always had to be enough for one purpose – Bolek could not live a single day without alcohol. Though I often saw him slightly intoxicated, I never saw him drunk. Never did we fear that he might let the cat out of the bag and endanger us, let alone suddenly throw us out. Genia, too, drank regularly, and even their two children, then aged six and eight, were given a little vodka from time to time – for 'training'.

Was Bolek, as his brother Antek had mysteriously hinted, really a German? The Germans, more accurately the ethnic Germans, were much better off in the Government-General than the Poles. They also benefited from vastly better food ration cards. However, Bolek, like nearly all Poles, spoke with great contempt of the ethnic Germans. These were people who, for the sake of food rations, had betrayed their country. We had to assume that the German nationality of the family was an invention of Antek's, to make himself seem important.

The Church and the priests were Bolek's particular bugbear: 'They booze, all of them, but they begrudge the vodka to us simple folk.' He had reached this conclusion while still a bachelor. When, shortly before his wedding, he had gone to confession, as was proper, he had been turned away by the priest for the not entirely improbable reason that he could not hear confession from someone who had been drinking. Bolek was deeply hurt and would tell anyone who wanted to hear it: 'They are all crooks – the Catholic priests and the Protestant ones too.' My objection that Protestant priests could not turn anyone away from confession – and why they could not do so – did not impress him. Even in the Bible, he claimed, it was said that these crooks publicly preached water and secretly drank vodka. 'But God created vodka for everyone, not only for the priests,' Bolek argued.

When he had drunk a little more than usual he would speak louder and more emphatically. Thus one day – we had not been with him long – he declared very slowly and solemnly: 'Adolf Hitler, the most powerful man in Europe, has decreed: these two people here shall die. And I, a small typesetter from Warsaw, have decided: they shall live. Now we shall see who wins.' We have often remembered this reckless pronouncement.

In spite of our totally isolated situation we were not too badly informed about the progress of the war. Bolek reported to us everything his neighbours and acquaintances told him. The numerous rumours circulating in Warsaw usually originated from those who risked possessing a radio and listening to broadcasts from London. The daily paper published in Polish in the Government-General was thin and useless. Much better was the German-language *Krakauer Zeitung* and its regional version, the *Warschauer Zeitung*. I made Bolek see that it was worth buying this paper because more could be discovered in its pages about the true situation of the war than from the Polish paper. I translated the most important articles for him – in a greatly simplified and slightly doctored form. That is to say: the news and articles I reported to him had to make it clear that the defeat of the Germans, and hence the end of our sufferings, was approaching by the day.

If my news was gloomy, Bolek threatened that he would no longer spend money on the German newspaper, he could not afford this luxury. I admitted that this paper's news coverage was poor and argued that it would be better if he changed to another German paper, such as *Das Reich*, which presented a truer picture of the war situation. He started buying *Das Reich* and I was soon one of its most attentive readers.

As a rule Bolek reacted sceptically to my over-optimistic reports. The Germans, he believed, would lose the war – but we would not live to see it. Because the Germans, the devil take them all, were still strong, and the Allies unfortunately were not in a great hurry: 'These gentlemen meet here and there, they have a cosy time: there is always plenty for them to eat in Teheran and enough vodka. And they certainly also keep warm. That's why the war is taking so long. Those gentlemen do not know that there's a typesetter named Bolek in Warsaw, who wants to get his friends through the war.'

In that house, which contained but a single book – unfortunately it was not the Bible, but a very clean, obviously unused, prayer book – I chiefly read the literary column in *Das Reich*. And, to be quite frank, with some enjoyment. But this was not my only reading matter. Incredible though it may seem, here, quite unexpectedly, I had a reunion with literature, moreover with German literature.

Although Bolek's house had electric light, this was frequently cut off throughout the whole suburb. We were then reduced to oil or carbide lamps, but made use of these only for work, that is for the manufacture of cigarettes. Poor as such lighting was, it was far from cheap. So we sat in the dark and talked about this and that, always listening out for anybody approaching the house.

One day Bolek's wife suggested that I should tell them a story, preferably a thrilling one. From that day onwards, as soon as it was dark, I would tell all kinds of stories to Bolek and Genia – for hours, for weeks, for months. These had but one aim – to entertain my hosts. The better they liked a story, the better we were rewarded – with a slice of bread, with a few carrots. I did not invent any stories, not a single one. Instead I told them whatever I could remember. In the gloom of that dingy kitchen I offered my grateful listeners dramatically heightened shortened versions of novels and novellas I had read, or of plays and operas, even films, I had seen: *Werther*, *William Tell*, *The Broken Jug*, *Immensee*, *Der Schimmelreiter*, *Effi Briest* and *Frau Jenny Treibel*, *Aida*, *Traviata* and *Rigoletto*. My stock of subjects and stories was clearly enormous; it was sufficient for many, many winter evenings.

It was an opportunity to discover what effect literary figures and themes have on simple people. To Bolek and Genia it was a matter of indifference who wrote the story of the old king who wished to divide his kingdom among his three daughters. They had never heard of Shakespeare. But they felt compassion for King Lear. Bolek, as he later confided to me, was thinking of himself and his children – even though he had literally nothing to leave them. Hamlet's reflections and conflicts, on the other hand, meant nothing to him.

Kabale und Liebe, however, Schiller's play of intrigue and love, got him seriously excited. 'D'you know, I knew that man Wurm, there was one exactly like him in our printing shop.' To my amazement, he was even more impressed by another play – perhaps because I related it with particular involvement and colourful detail. When I had finished, his comment was clear and determined:

'The devil take the Germans, all of them! But this Herr Hamburg, I like him! He is shit-scared of death – as we all are. He wants to live. He doesn't give a monkey's for honour and glory. Yes, I like that. I'm telling you: this German – the devil take the lot of them – is the bravest of them all. He is afraid, but he's not ashamed, he speaks up about his fear. Those who want to live let others live too. I believe this Herr Hamburg enjoys a little glass of vodka and doesn't begrudge one to others either. A pity he isn't the city commandant of Warsaw. This German – the devil take them all – wouldn't have anyone executed. Come on, let's drink to the health of this German Herr Hamburg.'

He poured a glass of vodka for each of us, exceptionally for Tosia and myself. Each time I am by the Kleiner Wannsee I think of Bolek, who sent all Germans to the devil and who drank to the health of the Prince of Homburg. I bow in spirit to the Prussian poet who ended his life here and to the Warsaw typesetter who risked his life to save mine.

While I was pleased that my stories interested my listeners, they made me feel depressed. I thought that the opportunity to make literature my profession had slipped from my grasp. The Jews have an expression for such regrets – *silken tsores.* Because we still had to fear for our lives each day and indeed each hour. There were days when Bolek was sick of it all and would have liked to be rid of us. Was he afraid that we might be discovered and he would be shot? Of course this was an important consideration, but, reckless as he was, he did not worry too much about this terrible threat. However, he was honest when he told us: 'It can't go on. You'll have to leave. We helped you for a while – now it's someone else's turn. Or else we'll all starve to death together.'

Whenever he wanted to turn us out Genia argued with him: 'Let them stay with us. We've held out together for so long, maybe we'll manage after all.' And whenever Genia lost patience, it was he who proclaimed: 'Damn it all. We'll manage all right – in spite of the Germans, the devil take them!' So we continued to be hidden by our protectors, we continued to produce thousands of cigarettes every night, and during the long evenings I continued to tell them stories of girls in love, young princes and old kings, winter's tales and midsummer night's dreams.

We continued to be terribly hungry, too, even when a relative of Tosia's sent us small sums of money by complicated roundabout routes. Sometimes the money was not enough even for the cheapest vodka. Suddenly Bolek had an original idea. There were no schools, but many parents had their children taught in private groups, known as 'conspiratorial courses'. Bolek suggested to his neighbours that he would do their children's school work. However, he was too nervous to do this in the presence of the children, he explained, and would therefore have to take their exercise books home with him. The homework was then done by us: Tosia was responsible for Polish grammar and essays, while I dealt with arithmetic. Bolek was not paid for this in money, but his neighbours frequently treated him to vodka – and that was what mattered to him. Moreover, his reputation within the settlement rapidly grew – and that was also important to him. He was grateful to us for our help, and we were glad to be useful.

In June 1944 Bolek suddenly told me that he had to talk to me about a very serious and dangerous matter. This sounded rather ominous, and I noticed that he was speaking to me in a different tone from usual. He sounded ashamed; the matter was evidently embarrassing to him. Eventually he came out with it. Shortly before we came to his house he had done something he had been meaning to tell us about, something he could no longer conceal. He had applied for recognition as an ethnic German – for himself, his wife and his two children. An uncle had persuaded him to do this, mainly for the sake of the improved food rations.

Bolek had signed the application form in a weak moment when he was drunk, he kept repeating as if by way of justification – and I considered this entirely plausible. He had never had anything to do with Germany in his life and, of course, he did not know a single word of German. Genia, however, had been a Protestant before her marriage, and that was sufficient grounds in the Government-General for being accepted as an ethnic German, especially in the final years of the war when no Pole wanted to make common cause with the Germans.

For many months the application had remained unanswered and Bolek had hoped that the whole business had been forgotten. Now he had suddenly been notified that his application had been successful. He was invited to collect his German papers and food ration cards at once. He did not know what to do. The Soviet army had already reached the territory of the former Polish state and it could be assumed that, in a few weeks' time, it would arrive on the banks of the Vistula. In a liberated Poland the traitors who had gone over to the enemy, lured by the Judas reward, would be hanged or, at least, interned. 'If, however' – Bolek tried to convince me – 'I throw this invitation down the toilet, the Germans, the devil take them, will smell a rat. Those Gestapo dogs will summon me and interrogate me and perhaps even order a house search – and that'd be the end of you.'

A house search? That seemed exaggerated to me, but it could not be ruled out. The situation was certainly tricky. Antek's statement that his brother was a German may not have been correct, but it was not entirely invented. My advice was simple. What had been done could not be undone. He would have to accept the German ethnicity awarded to him, but keep it strictly secret from friends and neighbours.

If we survived and a reconstituted Polish state were to question him about that damned German ethnicity, then I promised him that I would appear in court as a witness and declare on oath that he, Bolek, had applied for it at my request in order to protect us. In point of fact, it turned out to be a storm in a teacup. No one learned about Bolek's embarrassing indiscretion: his papers had evidently been destroyed during the Warsaw Rising of 1944. The perjury, which I would have committed without batting an eyelid, was not necessary.

Meanwhile we were following the advance of the Russians with growing impatience. Only the Soviet army could save our lives. The closer it came, the greater grew our fear of being discovered and murdered by the Germans at the last moment. An additional element of danger arose in August 1944: the Wehrmacht was establishing a new line of defence in the immediate vicinity of our hiding place. One house after another was being blown up: the Germans wanted a clear field of fire.

Our house, too, had been earmarked for destruction. This would have been a disaster for us. Where would the two of us, emaciated Jews clad in rags and not possessing a penny, find shelter? We would quite certainly have perished within weeks, or even days, of liberation. Incredibly, however, the house was not blown up in the end. Either this was no longer necessary or it was already too late.

By the beginning of September 1944 there was no doubt left that the German occupation had only a few more days to run. On the morning of 7 September, towards nine o'clock, we heard a huge noise – everything shook and our spirits rose by the minute. Never did I enjoy noise more – the louder the better. Because this was the Red Army, this was the expected, hoped-for and longed-for Russian offensive. Within a quarter of an hour our house was between the fronts. From the windows on its western side we saw German artillerymen, frighteningly close; on the eastern side – we could scarcely believe our eyes – we saw real Russian infantrymen. This exceedingly dangerous situation did not last long – perhaps half an hour. Then there was a vigorous hammering at the front door, probably with a rifle butt. Trembling but with his head held high, Bolek opened the door. Facing him was a kindly Russian soldier, asking in a loud voice: '*Nemtsov niet?*' – No Germans here? – when, only fifteen minutes previously, we had been fearing that someone might knock at the door and ask: 'No Jews here?' Whereas, only fifteen minutes previously, this question would have meant our death, the search was now not for Jews but for Germans.

Bolek said no and called me. He assumed that I would be better at communicating with the Russian soldier. The Russian looked at me sharply and asked: '*Amkhu?*' I had no idea that this was a word used in Russia – it means something like: 'Do you, too, belong to the people?' – by which a Jew assures himself that his interlocutor is also a Jew. Seeing me at a loss, he simplified his question: Was I a '*Yevrey*'? – the Russian word for 'a Hebrew', a Jew. I quickly replied: 'Yes, I Jew.' Laughing, he said: 'I Jew also. My name Fishman.' He squeezed my hand firmly and assured me that he would return, but meanwhile he was in a hurry: he had to get to Berlin urgently.

Were we therefore free? Bolek thought we should remain for the night: the Russians might withdraw their front line and the Germans, the devil take them, might temporarily return. The following morning we said goodbye: two weakened, starving, miserable people. Bolek muttered: 'We'll never see you again.' But he uttered these words with a friendly smile. Genia snapped at him: '*Don't talk rubbish!*'

We were about to leave when Bolek said: 'I have a drop of vodka here, let's drink a little glass.' I could sense that he had something else to say to us. He was speaking slowly and seriously: 'I implore you, don't tell anyone that you were with us. I know this nation. They would never forgive us for sheltering two Jews.' Genia remained silent. I deliberated for a long time as to whether I should quote this frightening remark here. But, on the other hand, we have never forgotten that it was two Poles to whom we owe our lives – Bolek and Genia.

We rose and said goodbye again. Did I imagine the tears in Bolek's and Genia's eyes? In Tosia's eyes and in mine? When, two or three months later, I was able to visit Bolek and Genia, I was in the army and wearing an officer's greatcoat. Bolek regarded me thoughtfully and said: 'So I've made the Polish army a present of an officer.'

We had promised Bolek and Genia that, if we survived in their house, we would, after the war, show our gratitude in an appropriate material form. We are to this day in touch with the only survivor of the family, their daughter. But is it possible to make adequate recompense for the risk that the two were running in order to save our lives? No, it was not the prospect of money that led Bolek and Genia to act the way they did. It was something entirely different – and I can describe it only with grand and hackneyed words: compassion, goodness, humanity.

PART THREE
1944–1958

22

MY FIRST SHOT,
MY LAST SHOT

We were free. How often had we longed for this moment, how often had we visualized it! Why were we not in a state of euphoria, as we had always imagined we would be? We had no time to reflect on this, we were still afraid. We feared that the Germans might return – for a day or two, certainly for long enough to discover us and murder us. We were free, but we were weak and miserable, filthy and lice-ridden, wrapped in dirty rags, we had no proper shoes. We were free, but very hungry – and there was nothing to eat anywhere. What were we to do, where were we to go? We had to do something so as not to collapse on the busy highway immediately after liberation, and possibly die there.

Soviet and Polish soldiers, trucks and horses, staff cars, handcarts and farm carts, cyclists and people on foot – all these were on the move. Everyone was going somewhere, everyone was hurrying in different directions. The victorious Red Army was in a deplorable state. The soldiers were exhausted and inadequately equipped. Their uniforms often looked pitiful. No soldier understood the English wording on the tins of meat they received, which came from the United States or Canada: it warned that this was intended not for human consumption but only for cattle. Cigarettes were handed out only to the officers; the ordinary soldiers received tobacco and made their smokes themselves from newspaper. Particularly suitable for this purpose was the paper on which *Pravda* was printed; that, it was said, accounted for the huge print run of this paper.

Fortunately no one was taking any notice of us. We were not conspicuous, because there were plenty of people who looked just as pitiful as we did. Everyone, whether in uniform or in civvies, was concerned only for himself. We had scarcely travelled two or three kilometres from Bolek's house when a Polish officer approached us. 'Halt!' he commanded. Then he asked: 'Are you Jews?' As we probably gave a start he said quickly: 'Don't be afraid. I'm a Jew myself.' Had we by any chance been in the Warsaw ghetto – and had we come across an Esther Rosenstein there? Like all Jews who had come back with the Soviet army he was searching for his relations. Unfortunately we were unable to give him any information about his sister.

We should get away from the front as fast as possible and make for Lublin. That, he informed us, was the provisional capital of the liberated part of Poland, there we would find help. But how were we to get there? He stopped an open army truck and ordered the driver to give us a lift. We asked shyly where we might get something to eat. He gave us a thick slice of bread each – with the remark: 'The great Soviet Union has nothing more to offer you at the moment.'

The truck was carrying all kinds of goods as well as several people in the same condition as ourselves. We were not exactly regarded with sympathy. But a well-dressed Pole spoke to me kindly. After a few minutes he asked me, the unshaven and dirty vagabond: 'You're a lawyer, aren't you?' Down at heel as I was, something had evidently remained to make him assume that I was a lawyer – my speech, perhaps, or my logical approach. He estimated my age at just under fifty. I was twenty-four at the time.

After spending the night in a barn, along with other refugees, we arrived in Lublin the following day. We spent the first night there in a seedy hostel for the homeless – until then I had known such places only from Gorky's *The Lowest Depths* – where we received a small one-off subsidy. It was just enough for a few cheap items of clothing which we bought in the market. Now we looked a little more like human beings. We took stock of each other and tried to smile. Tosia asked: 'Have we really survived?' I did something that was not then customary in the street. I kissed her. An elderly soldier walking past tapped his forehead at us.

A few days later we volunteered for military service with the Polish army. It was under Soviet supreme command, part of the Red Army. Today this decision may be difficult to understand. It certainly had nothing to do with heroics. But we considered it our duty, within the framework of our potential, to contribute something, even at this final moment, to the struggle against those who had murdered our people and tormented us. The fact that one received food in the armed forces as well as a uniform probably also played a part.

An army doctor examined us. We were turned down – on the grounds of being undernourished and emaciated, and much too weak. Nevertheless a surprised personnel officer asked us how we thought we might be useful to the army. I said that I had been thinking of a propaganda unit, more especially of a unit calling on German troops to surrender and, for that purpose, preparing leaflets and similar materials. That I was qualified for such work, having grown up in Berlin and lived there until the end of 1938, made sense to him. And Tosia, we suggested, might work in a graphics workshop – those, too, existed in the army. That made sense too.

We had achieved our purpose: we were enrolled in the Polish army. Once more we had to set out into the unknown. The unit we had been assigned to was in a miserable, isolated village in the eastern part of Poland. By a variety of military transport we at last arrived in the vicinity of that village. We had to walk the remaining four or five kilometres.

Happily we were not alone. Another civilian was bound for the same destination. I was struck by his beautiful, almost too beautiful, Polish. He was, as he hastened to inform us, a professional actor, commanded to join a theatre on the front line. Before long he set down his wooden suitcase – only officers had leather suitcases in the Polish army – on the narrow path we were following between fields and fallow arable land. In the warm afternoon sunshine he began to declaim – in a loud voice, bombastically and with grand gestures.

Clearly this man, who had long been unable to practise his profession, was happy to have found an audience of two as he suspected – not entirely uneducated people. The text he chose for his spontaneous open-air performance was a speech from *Uriel Acosta*, a historical play by the distinguished German author Karl Gutzkow. This play, successful in the nineteenth century, had also been occasionally staged in Poland before the Second World War, probably for the sake of Jewish audiences.

In this grand speech the central figure of the play, the philosopher Uriel Acosta, of Jewish origin but baptized as a child, turns away from Christianity and proudly and defiantly proclaims his Jewishness: '*Thus will I suffer with the sufferers – / You may accurse me. For I am a Jew!*' He had meant well, the actor, he wanted to please us. But we were feeling uneasy although we could not say exactly why at the time.

The German satirist Ludwig Börne once complained: '*It is like a miracle! It has happened to me a thousand times, and yet it remains ever new to me. One lot accuses me of being a Jew; the others forgive me for being a Jew; the third even praise me for it – but they all think of it.*' I am surprised that Börne regarded this as a 'miracle' and was unable to accept it. After all, his remark was made in 1832, when only a couple of decades had passed since the emancipation of the Jews. It seems to me a matter of course that, at that time and under those circumstances, he was denied the thing for which he longed – a normal existence as an equal citizen, that which the slightly older, Rahel Varnhagen, née Levin, called the '*most natural existence*', that which every peasant and every beggar enjoyed.

In the autumn of 1944 fighting was still continuing on every front, the German forces were still very strong, the Holocaust was by no means a thing of the past, Auschwitz had not yet been liberated. And we who were in a hurry to join the army, who were anxious to reach our destination before sunset, were a little disquieted by the fact that this provincial Polish actor, almost as soon as he had met us, thought it right to offer to us something Jewish.

Was this harmless show of sympathy a foretaste of what was in store for us over the coming decades and years? A Frankfurt taxi-driver once surprised me with the question: 'Do you know Mr Isaac Goldblum?' I said I do not, and he said 'You resemble him.' When I got into a taxi at Hamburg airport, the driver, a German, asked me (not unpleasantly): 'Do you come from Tel Aviv?'

When this question had been put to me repeatedly, I no longer contented myself with the answer that I came from Munich or from Stuttgart, from Vienna or Stockholm, but immediately added: 'But you are quite right – I am a Jew.' In the street in Wiesbaden a woman stopped me, asking for an autograph. She reassured herself: 'You are Mr Bubis, aren't you?' In a Salzburg restaurant I wanted to make a telephone call, only a local call. 'I thought' – I was told – 'you wanted to call Jerusalem.'

This sort of thing occurred infinitely more often twenty or thirty years ago. But quite recently I was asked what I thought about Israel maltreating the Palestinians. 'Every Jew is responsible for all Israel' – a Jewish journalist wrote before the First World War. Does this kind of thing only occur in Germany or Austria? For many years we spent our holidays in Switzerland. We tend to enjoy restaurants where a pianist entertains the guests. Hardly any of them fail to welcome us in a particular way. Nearly always it is the same world-famous hit which is assigned to us as a leitmotif – 'If I were a rich man' from the musical *Fiddler on the Roof*, which is set in an eastern Jewish village, a work which I neither love nor enjoy. But I give the pianist a friendly wave. After all, he means well – just like the Polish actor who recited Gutzkow's solemn monologue on the sandy field path. Are we being oversensitive? Certainly. Besides, as we probably suspected without fully realizing it: a person who was accidentally spared, while his dear ones were murdered, cannot live in peace with himself.

In the evening we eventually arrived at the village. The following day I reported to the local Commandant, where it soon emerged that the propaganda unit that I was looking for had not yet been set up. But its future head already existed, his name was Stanisław Jerzy Lec, he was a first lieutenant, which impressed me and which, as I already wore uniform, made me respectfully click my heels – only in spirit, of course. Lec, born in Lwów when it was still the Austrian Lemberg, was one of the best Polish satirical writers of the younger generation before the war. He was a poet and a jester, a master wearing a fool's cap. He was a fellow of infinite jest, of most excellent fancy – like the poor Yorrick, the King's jester, whose skull moved Hamlet to tears.

Lec, at thirty-five, seemed to me already a little corpulent. He held sway in a peasant's hovel. In his room there was a small table, a bed and just one chair, on which he sat in a brand-new uniform. He was engrossed in a manuscript and clearly annoyed at being disturbed. Without looking at me he asked with military curtness: 'D'you know German?' Then, without a pause, he asked me another question, as unexpected as it was incredible. In this pitiful hut surrounded by swamps and forests, First Lieutenant Stanisław Jerzy Lec of the Polish army wished to know: 'Do you know Brecht?' I said: 'Yes.' He evidently did not believe me, for he immediately asked: 'What?' I enumerated several titles. Now he looked up at me, his features lighting up. That somebody in this God-forsaken spot had heard of *Hauspostille* and of *Aufsterg und Fall der Stadt Mahagonny* [*Rise and Fall of the City of Mahagonny*] – that he had not expected. I am almost certain that the two of us, Lec and myself, were the only members of the Polish army who had ever heard the name of Brecht.

I was asked to sit down on the bed. Then this unusual first lieutenant, whose tone of command now became a little more civil, handed me a few sheets of paper on which a lengthy poem by Brecht had been typed. He would read to me a Polish translation he himself had made of this poem and I was to decide whether he had understood everything and correctly translated it. This was the first order I was given in the Polish army. Strange – wherever I went now, whether I wanted it or not, there was German literature – yesterday Gutzkow, today Brecht.

The translation was very good. But in order to prove to him that I was dealing with the matter conscientiously and that the subject was familiar to me, I drew his attention to two or three passages of the quite lengthy poem. They were superbly translated, I said, but perhaps there was still some room for improvement. Needless to say, these were just trifles. Lec's reaction disappointed me. He was not at all interested in my shy suggestions, he hardly listened to me. The audience was soon at an end. Not until much later did I realize that he did not want me to check his text, let alone correct it, he wanted me to praise and admire him. In 1944 I still had no experience of dealing with writers.

After the war, when we sometimes walked around in Warsaw together, and later, when Lec visited us in Hamburg, I noticed that our conversations always took the same course. As in that Polish village in October 1944, there was always only one subject for him – his poems, his aphorisms, his poetic translations. He never wished to know what was happening in my life, what I was concerned with. A vain and egocentric person? I have never known a writer who was not vain and egocentric – unless he was a particularly bad author.

Some conceal their vanity and hide their egocentricity while others ostentatiously admit to these weaknesses, with humour and without apology. When Lec flew from Warsaw to Vienna with a colleague, this man asked him on landing whether he was aware that throughout the entire flight he had only talked about himself. Lec replied with a short counter-question: 'You know a better subject?'

Nearly half a century ago Lec and I went for a long walk – from Warsaw's House of Literature, the headquarters of the Writers' Union, to the wonderful Lazienki Park and back. This is the finest chain of streets in the Polish capital. Lec was talking incessantly – and I, who have a reputation for not being exactly taciturn, listened in silence, only now and then providing a cue for him. Everything he told me interested and amused me – not least his improvised, and unfortunately unrecorded, plays on words. After an hour he said suddenly: 'This can't go on. We've been talking all the time about me. Now let's talk about you. Tell me, how did *you* like my last book?' I have related this remark to many colleagues, it has been quoted again and again and also attributed to other authors. This is how an international, and by now classic, anecdote was created.

In Germany in the 1960s and 1970s Lec was one of the few successful, indeed most famous, Polish authors. He owed his popularity not so much to his poetry, remarkable as it is, but to his aphorisms. His *Untidy Thoughts*, which linked up with a German tradition from Lichtenberg through Heine and Schopenhauer to Karl Kraus, circulated in hundreds of thousands of copies in an excellent translation by Karl Dedecius and were repeatedly reprinted in newspapers.

My contact with Lec reached its climax in 1964. I was by then enjoying his genuine sympathy: he perhaps actually regarded me as a friend, he esteemed me, indeed it is possible that he regarded me as an outstanding critic. This was due to but one reason: the newspaper *Die Zeit* had published my enthusiastic review of his *Untidy Thoughts*. It was, I believe, the first and last review by me which he read. This is an old story but it is ever new: an author's opinion of a critic depends on what that critic has said about him, especially about his most recent book. Is this another thing I learned from Lec?

He did not grow old. Suffering from cancer, he worked on his manuscripts almost to his final moment. When, at the beginning of May 1966 – he was then in a nursing home near Warsaw – he was brought the proofs of his latest book, he waved them away: 'I have more important things to do now. I am busy dying.' A little later he died. '*A pity that one travels to Paradise in a hearse,*' he said in his *Untidy Thoughts*. Also: '*The clock strikes – for all.*'

At his funeral a guard of honour was provided by outstanding writers and a military detail presented arms. Shots were fired, a young poet carried a velvet cushion on which lay the decorations of the deceased. A jester and a clown, Lec was buried like a hero. Yes, Poland is a strange and original country. Whether Stanisław Jerzy Lec really was a hero, I do not know. But I am certain that he was by far the most important European writer of aphorisms in the second half of our century.

Nothing came of my service in the propaganda unit that Lec was to have built up. A few days after my first conversation with him the project was cancelled, which I greatly regretted. Probably it would not have been to the liking of the Russians. However, Tosia and I were already enrolled in the army, so some use had to be found for us. The woman personnel officer – there were many women in the Polish army – noticed that we were more or less fluent in three foreign languages. So she sent us to military censorship, which was being organized in a nearby village.

We were by no means displeased. In his *Untidy Thoughts* Lec asked: '*You say words are superfluous? But where would one fit that which stands between the words?*' That was what we were supposed to find – that which stood between the words and was concealed between the lines. This branch of censorship was not responsible for books or newspapers. Our job was to discover the hidden content, find the false bottom, of letters and postcards. That seemed to us an exceedingly tempting task. Later I learned that several well-known authors had also been involved in field post censorship during wartime – Robert Musil in the Habsburg army and Ernst Jünger in the Wehrmacht.

But how, without appropriate training, were we to succeed in decoding what was hidden or enciphered? We would learn soon enough, we were told: our commanders were bound to be acquainted with subtle means of tracking down all those who were trying to use the army mails for their sinister machinations. Our work in military censorship, this much we realized, would require extreme acuity. Well, I consoled myself, we would manage somehow. It soon emerged that everything was a little different from what we, in our naiveté, had imagined. Over the next few days the soldiers assigned to the unit arrived in the village where the military censorship was stationed. We were soon nearly speechless with surprise at the simple minds of these young sons of peasants. During the five years of German occupation in Poland a whole generation of semi-literate people had grown up, a generation whose general education was minimal – which, of course, was precisely what the German authorities had intended.

How were these young sons of peasants to cope with such a delicate operation as censorship? Perhaps they were intended for sentry duty. But in point of fact – we soon discovered – these simple-minded soldiers were to operate as censors. The second surprise was that they were not at all bad at the job. This was because censorship work requires application and thoroughness even more than education and intelligence. The censors had to establish whether the letters – mostly from young servicemen writing home – betrayed any military secrets, such as data about weapons used or the location of units. Likewise, letters with mysterious or incomprehensible messages and allusions were not to be passed. Anything a censor considered questionable was to be submitted to a chief censor, who in turn, if he could not make a decision himself, would consult an inspector.

A completed secondary education was not expected even of officers in the Polish army under Soviet command. In consequence, even though we had no knowledge of censorship work, we were rapidly promoted – Tosia became a chief censor and I an inspector. At the head of the unit, as was then customary, were two officers delegated by the Soviet army, men in Polish uniform and able, at a pinch, to communicate in Polish. With the best of intentions one could not say that they were particularly intelligent officers.

As far as I remember, there was not a single case of a serious betrayal of secrets during the time that I was working in military censorship. But there were oddities all right. As Moscow was already planning a communist German state – under Walther Ulbricht who was to become first secretary of its Politburo, and as Stalin had coined the slogan that Hitlers came and went, whereas the German people would go on for ever, anti-German remarks during the war were not permitted in field post letters, not even the most harmless ones. Soldiers were not allowed to write: 'The devil take all Germans' or 'We are chasing the German bandits' but must say instead 'The devil take all Nazis (or perhaps all Hitlerites)' and 'We are chasing the Nazi (or Hitlerite) bandits'. Whenever a soldier used the word 'German' in a derogatory, let alone a hostile, sense, this had to be rendered illegible by the censor with the aid of a lot of ink. The intellectual level of the censorship, and its technical means, were about equal.

Dark formulations, calling for the censor, were found with particular frequency in the letters of female members of the army. For instance: '*My Red Indian isn't coming*' or, '*I am very worried because there is no sign of the Chinese*' or, '*All my efforts are in vain. Have you no idea how to get the thing moving?*' After much effort the mystery was solved: these letters always concerned a missed period. Anyone might have thought that the greatest secret of the Polish army was menstruation. What I learned then was that institutions surrounded by a halo of secrecy owe their reputation to the legends spread about them or to those which they themselves have launched. Once one comes to know them from the inside they are invariably disappointing. Ultimately matters are simpler than they seem. If the postal censorship of the Polish army demanded a sharp and experienced eye, then this was only required of the top people. I soon came to the conclusion that censorship work was not only stupid and boring but also totally unnecessary.

After a few days all persons employed in military censorship were made to sign a declaration to the effect that they would, without exception, keep secret anything to do with their work. This was a routine business without any significance. However, it was only from this duplicated sheet that I learned that I found myself in a unit which, while being part of the Polish army, actually came under the Ministry – then still called the Department – of Public Security. This did not worry me at all. I signed the declaration without hesitation – whether the censorship came under the supervision of one authority or another seemed a purely bureaucratic matter, of no concern to me. Yet this was to have consequences for my professional career over the next few years, consequences I never suspected and which proved exceedingly interesting.

In January 1945 I was eventually released from military censorship in that God-forsaken village and transferred to war censorship headquarters in Lublin, and somewhat later to recently liberated Katowice, where I had to organize the censorship. This I did so rapidly, to the delight of my superiors, that the service was ready to function even before any work arrived – because postal services were not yet operating. This earned me the reputation of a good organizer. As a result, almost as soon as I returned to Lublin I was ordered to take up a leading position in the foreign postal censorship in Warsaw, which had likewise only just been liberated.

Warsaw had been so badly destroyed that various Polish town planners and some famous foreign experts advised that the Polish capital should be rebuilt at a different location in the country. Needless to say, no one wanted to hear about that – neither the new authorities nor the population. The inhabitants, evacuated by the Germans, were returning to the city from all directions. They did not want to give up Warsaw, even though life there was intolerably hard. They settled in the flats which had, at least in part, survived, in basements and in huts. Uncertain and unclear though the future of Poland was, the people of Warsaw proved to be incorrigible optimists.

What about us? To begin with, Tosia and I were unable to find a flat, or even a room, in the wrecked city. We slept on a camp bed that we put up at night in my office. But we did not complain: there was a war on – and wartime conditions prevailed in Poland a lot later than May 1945. Besides, we too were optimists. The Allied armies were advancing, the early conclusion of the war was a matter of certainty. To our surprise, however, the expected joy at being alive still did not materialize, let alone a sense of happiness. After all, we had wanted to survive. And in order to survive we had suffered hardships we had regarded as unspeakable. We had borne affronts and humiliations. We had experienced hunger to a degree we would never forget. We had lived through a thousand fears – fear of death was an everyday experience for many years. As the end of the war approached, we, the liberated, were increasingly preoccupied with a simple question – why? Why were we, of all people, allowed to survive?

My brother Alexander had had a far better chance of surviving the German occupation than I had. He was, in many respects, a very different type from me. He was shorter, more finely built, and certainly also more timid and much inhibited. Above all, he was a very lovable person. He had a winning way with him, quite without arrogance or any form of aggression.

One might have thought that Alexander possessed that for which I had searched in vain all my life – the ring which Nathan the Wise said had the secret power of making anyone wearing it with confidence agreeable to God and men. Thus my brother who, unlike me, came to Warsaw only a short time before the war, had, even outside the ghetto, friends and acquaintances who would have helped him.

But he was afraid of fleeing from the ghetto – yet he could not remain there. At the 'Great Selection' in September 1942 he failed to receive a 'life number' because he was not employed by any institution. In November he was moved from the Warsaw ghetto to a camp near Lublin and, a few months later, to the prisoner-of-war and labour camp of Poniatowa, also in the Lublin district. There he had worked as a dentist and head of the camp clinic. On 4 November 1943 SS units drove all the prisoners out of their huts to ditches dug near the camp. There they were mown down by machine-guns. Altogether the SS murdered 15,000 prisoners at Poniatowa camp that day. Among them was my quiet, lovable brother Alexander Herbert Reich.

Exactly a year later, on 4 November 1944, I met a soldier in the Polish army, a non-Jew, who thought it right to tell me about what had happened to the Jews in Poniatowa. He had worked for a building firm near the camp, from where, if one needed medical assistance, one was given a pass to visit the clinic at Poniatowa. He had made use of this only twice, when he had toothache. I made him describe the dentist. He described him accurately – and there was no room for doubt. He also mentioned a rather large fair assistant. Again there was no doubt – this was the woman with whom my brother had been living in the ghetto.

Later the soldier had made enquiries about the dentist, who, he added, was so likeable. He was told that, along with his woman friend, he had been driven to the ditches. But I doubt if the Germans actually shot the two. Because they carried potassium cyanide on them. Why, I keep asking myself, did my brother have to die, why

was I allowed to survive? I know that there can only be one answer –
it was pure chance, nothing else. But I cannot stop asking that
question.

When, on 9 May 1945, news reached us in Warsaw that the
unconditional surrender of all German forces had been signed at the
Soviet headquarters in Berlin-Karlshorst, marking the conclusion of
the Second World War, a few happy and cheerful colleagues invited
us to walk out into the yard with them. The time had come, they
said, for a salute towards the sky. We released the safety-catches of
our pistols. Then my cheerful and exuberant colleagues simultaneously fired into the air. A moment later I too aimed my pistol
at the blue, sunny, pitiless and cruel sky, and pressed the trigger.
This was my first and last shot in the Second World War, the first
and last in my life.

Tosia was standing by my side. We looked at each other in silence.
We knew that we both felt the same emotions – not joy, but sadness,
not happiness, but wrath and anger. I looked up once more and saw
that a dark and menacing cloud had appeared in the sky. I felt that
this cloud above us would never disappear, it would stay there all
our lives.

23

FROM REICH TO RANICKI

If somebody had asked me in 1945 what profession I would like to follow and where I intended to live, I believe I would have tried to hide my indecision and would not have answered the question. I soon got tired of working in foreign censorship, which took up all my time. Although as yet there was very little evidence of peace, now that the war was over the postal censorship would sooner or later be dissolved. It was high time to consider my future.

To my surprise, however, I discovered that there was someone in Warsaw in 1945 who was already giving some thought to my future. In the Ministry of Public Security, under which censorship came, there was a major who had heard of me. He was interested in me, on behalf of the institution for which he worked – the Polish secret service, or more accurately, the foreign department of the intelligence service. This was not surprising. A search was then under way in the army for people, young intellectuals if possible, who spoke foreign languages and had travelled abroad, especially in Germany.

To have failed to respond to an invitation from the Polish authorities to work in the foreign intelligence service while the war was still continuing against National Socialist Germany – I would have regarded this as a stain on my character. I would feel ashamed to this day. Moreover, I was needed for a very particular task. I had been inactive for so long that the offer flattered me. It appealed to me even before I had any information about the work involved. I was attracted by an activity which was surrounded by a special aura, a sinister and dodgy activity, a sphere made into a myth by literature and the cinema. Naturally a wish for adventure played an important part in my decision. Except that very soon I did not have to make any decision at all.

Where, then, was I to be sent? If they had tried to lure me with Rome or Madrid, I might have had second thoughts. But the offer was Berlin. That decided the matter for me. To see Berlin again – who knows, I would probably have made a pact with the devil himself. The Polish secret service thus fulfilled my greatest desire. Germany, defeated and forced to her knees, fascinated me more than any other country on earth; yes, I wanted to go to Berlin at all costs. Would the destruction of the city where the whole disaster originated, fill me with satisfaction? Did I perhaps have a need to gloat over German hardships? By no means. It was not a thirst for vengeance that drove me to Berlin, but nostalgia – I wanted to see the city where I had grown up, the place that had moulded me.

The plan of foreign intelligence was simple. There was already a Polish military mission operating in Berlin. That was where I was to work, in the department for restitution and reparation. It was the task of this department to establish the whereabouts of machines and factory installations removed from Poland during the war and to demand their return. Simultaneously I was to work for the secret service.

As for my duties in the military mission, I would be instructed once I got there. But what was I to do for the secret service? The major acted very mysteriously. This was not something one could talk about now; he muttered something about numerous Nazis, about successor organizations whose activities extended to the areas now awarded to Poland. To begin with, I was to get a general impression of the state of things in Berlin, later I would receive the necessary instructions. By what channels? I would find out all right, the major said brusquely; then he added, a little more politely: in the secret service, patience was necessary. I understood that I was not to ask too many questions and so I prepared myself for the trip. Tosia could not accompany me, at least not straight away.

One evening in January 1946 I was driven into a totally dark, wrecked and desolate Berlin, along with three other employees of the military mission. I would have had every reason to gloat, indeed to feel deadly hatred. But there was no question of that. I was incapable of hatred – and this surprises me a little to this day. Does it need any justification? Hatred, in fact, is not an emotion I am familiar with. I can get very excited, heated and angry, I can lose my temper and blow my top. But to hate properly, for any length of time – no, that I could never do, that I still cannot do. I realize that this is not something to be proud of. But whatever has happened in my life, whatever wrong has been done to me, I have never rejected a person who wanted to be reconciled with me. The opposite, unfortunately, has happened quite often.

I had very little to do at the military mission and the secret service left me alone. No instructions whatever came to me – which, as time progressed, astonished me more and more and worried me less and less. Because there was something that fully occupied my ample free time – Berlin. I wanted to see it all – the houses I had lived in, the schools I had attended, the theatres I had loved. I was in search of my lost youth, that wonderful and terrible youth.

I stood in front of the building which I had once regarded as the most beautiful in the whole city, the building which had been the centre of my life – the ruined Theater am Gendarmenmarkt. It was a misty and rainy day. There was no one else standing outside the theatre. Suddenly I was all alone, and I felt my eyes becoming moist and tears running down my cheeks. But it was not the cutting wind blowing through the ruins that caused my tears. It was no doubt my youth which, in that cold and empty Berlin square, I shamefacedly lamented. I went on to the Friedrichstrasse railway station, slowly at first and then ever faster, as if to shake off my emotion.

I spent my evenings at the theatre – there were still performances in temporary halls – or at concerts of the Berlin Philharmonic, now headed by an almost unknown but excellent young conductor – Sergiu Celibidache. Of all theatrical performances, the one that left the strongest mark on my memory was Lessing's *Nathan the Wise*. In 1946 I saw this play, which was banned in the Third Reich, for the first time in my life. Paul Wegener, a famous actor before the war, was clearly anxious to avoid anything Jewish in his characterization of Nathan, either in diction or gesture. He evidently feared that this might have been misinterpreted as anti-Semitism.

What of the audience? I was interested to see how the Germans would react to the story of a Jew whose wife and seven sons had been burnt. But this was impossible to discover, because the auditorium was filled predominantly with officers in the uniforms of the four occupying powers – mainly Jews who spoke German surprisingly well. They were persons who had been expelled or who had fled and who were now gathered at a theatre not far from the Reich chancellery – to honour Lessing.

During the three months I stayed in Berlin I did not manage to make contact with any of my school friends, nor with any of my relations, who had either been expelled or sent to the gas chambers. In fact, I did not know anyone in the city of my youth. Thus it was a sad and lonely time, frightening but at times also happy. It made me more conscious of my homelessness than I had ever been in Poland, which had remained an alien country to me. I often ask myself what would have happened if, in 1946, I had been offered some cultural post by the Germans. Perhaps I would have remained in Berlin, in which case I would have certainly ended up as a critic, a literary critic, one way or another. But who was to offer me anything when no one knew me?

I had begun to think that I had been forgotten by the Warsaw headquarters of the secret service. But then, eventually, an instruction arrived – I was ordered back to base. I never knew why I had been sent to Berlin without having been given any job there. Probably the matter had not been sufficiently thought out: perhaps the Russians did not wish the Poles to gather any kind of information in Berlin.

Unlike the poet and officer Stanisław Jerzy Lec, the stern major with whom I had spoken before going to Berlin was unwilling to come clean with me. He considered it right to conceal from me the fact that the foreign intelligence service in the Security Ministry did not even exist at that time – it had yet to be set up. This was probably the reason why no one in Warsaw had bothered to contact me.

But even though I had done no work for the secret service in Berlin, the organization wished to continue employing me, not only in the Security Ministry but also in the Foreign Ministry. They promised me a post in the foreign service, moreover in a city which, since I had already spent some time in Berlin, now seemed to me the most desirable – London. There the only surviving member of my family was living – my elder sister Gerda Böhm, who had succeeded in escaping with her husband from Germany to England shortly before the outbreak of war.

I was to be trained in both ministries for my double duties in London – in the Security Ministry for intelligence work, in the Foreign Ministry for the consular service. In the secret service headquarters I had to work, for a short time, as a section head and a little later as a deputy departmental head. The place and time of the promised training, which I was eagerly awaiting, had already been announced. At last I would learn how the foreign intelligence service operated and should be organized; only now would I be made privy to the secrets of such work.

Three days before the appointed date I had to report to one of my superiors. Was I looking forward to the training, he asked cunningly. Without hesitation I said yes. Surely I realized, he said to my great surprise, that no one was going to train me. Instead it would be my task to train my colleagues.

I drew his attention to the fact that I had no idea of the subject matter. That did not surprise him, he commented with some irony, we were all beginners in that respect. Did I think that the Party members who had recently become ministers had been prepared for their tasks by anyone? In a pioneering age, one had to improvise. With a little intelligence this was quite feasible; he had full confidence in me. Besides, there was a Soviet adviser with whom I was to talk in a minute, he would help me. My superior smiled pleasantly.

Ten minutes later I was sitting in the office of the Soviet adviser. He was a friendly, courteous person and not without humour. He spoke some Polish. But instead of giving me the necessary advice, he wanted to hear from me how I visualized the planned training. Ignoring my evasive replies, he questioned me both persistently and pleasantly. I had no choice but to give in and tell him, at some length, what I knew about foreign intelligence and counter-espionage. Needless to say, all this came from the same source, one that was not invariably reliable – from novels, short stories and press reports.

The Soviet adviser was delighted and congratulated me. I was ideally suitable for this training, he said. Thus I became, for the time being, an instructor in the Polish secret service. I thought up a training course which, so I believed, was entertaining rather than useful. Once again I benefited greatly from German literature. My biggest success was the story of Colonel Redl and how he was unmasked as a spy, based on Egon Erwin Kisch.

Later too, whenever I asked any questions of the Soviet advisers, they reacted in the same way. They wanted me to discover the answer for myself, to suggest a solution. What I suggested was usually accepted as suitable. These advisers had not been sent to Warsaw to help us, but to seek information that might be of interest to the Soviet secret service – that at least was the case in the department in which I worked.

The most important task of the intelligence service was the gathering of information on Polish emigrés in the Western countries, about their attitudes, their intentions and their organizations. More accurately, the task was to discover in good time what steps the political emigrés intended to take against the new Polish state, what they were planning. For this task our service was scarcely equipped. Its absolute dilettantism was matched only by the primitiveness of its methods – no one had any relevant experience, and there were no technical aids at all. In the Foreign Ministry, where I worked during the last few months prior to my departure for London, the situation was totally different. There, in the department for consular matters, pre-war experts were employed. From them I was able to learn everything I needed. Incidentally, consular service is not particularly entertaining, let alone exciting.

Meanwhile I had joined the Communist Party of Poland (which then called itself the Polish Workers' Party). No one forced me to do so, no one even suggested it to me. Nor was it a spontaneous or hasty decision. But Tosia and I owed our lives to the Red Army. Had it not driven the Germans out of Poland, had it arrived in Warsaw only a little later, we should have been murdered just as my parents and my brother were, and just as was Tosia's mother.

Moreover, the ideas of communism had interested me at an early age. Now, shortly after 1945, they were exceedingly attractive, indeed, they had something captivating to offer me, as they had to many intellectuals, not only in Poland, but also in France, Italy and other West European countries. Certainly I was never one for marches, manifestations or demonstrations. But I was fascinated by the chance of participating in a worldwide, universal movement, a movement from which countless people expected the solution of the great problems of mankind. I believed that I had at last found what I had long needed: a refuge and – the word is difficult to avoid – safety.

227

There was, so it seemed to me, only one way to accomplish the long overdue reordering of society – communism. That was especially true for Poland. Most of the Polish intellectuals and artists, in particular the writers and journalists, were no supporters of the Soviet Union. However, after years of inactivity during the German occupation, they acted on the old English wisdom: if you can't beat them, join them. They realized that there was but one power which could protect Poland against chaos and organize the country's reconstruction – the Polish government established by the Soviet Union and recognized by the Allies.

Maybe German literature also played a small part in my decision to join the Communist Party of Poland. For, ever since my younger days, I had been impressed by a piece of classic nineteenth-century German prose notable for its grandeur, rhetoric and wealth of metaphors – the *Communist Manifesto* by Karl Marx and Friedrich Engels.

There is much to explain my decision in 1945, much also to make it understandable. Except that I do not wish to be misunderstood: in retrospect there is no doubt that it was a serious mistake. I realized this in the course of the 1950s. But as I knew even then, I owe certain experiences to my membership of the Communist Party, experiences which I would not want to have missed.

Another decision which dates back to 1945, which I also made without suspecting the consequences, has proved more durable. As my surname 'Reich' did not seem suitable for my work as a consul, it was decided that I was to work in London under another name. The concept of 'Reich', it was pointed out to me, was familiar to every Pole and every Englishman, even if they could not speak any German: it was too reminiscent of the 'Third Reich'. Was the name too German? Or was it too Jewish? It certainly was not Polish enough. Not wanting to delay matters I consented at once and, without giving it much thought, chose the name of 'Ranicki'. I thought this name-change would only be for the duration of my job in England. But it stuck to me – for the rest of my life.

Another reason why I wanted to move to London as soon as possible was that my work in Warsaw gave me little pleasure – mainly because I questioned its purpose and its usefulness. The reports and the information coming to headquarters did not greatly excite me. I considered most of the material pointless, if not indeed frivolous and misleading. The reports were passed on to various authorities of the state and, of course, to the Party. But one was never told – because of the perpetual secretiveness – whether anyone evaluated the information or even read it. My questions and doubts displeased my superiors. Everything, I was told, was still in its infancy, there was much talk of teething troubles. One had to be patient.

My patience was finally rewarded when I was transferred to London – not, as planned in 1947, but at the beginning of 1948. Our life there was pleasanter, more luxurious and also more free than in destroyed Warsaw. We had a very good time during the nearly two years we were in London. We had something that we did not even dream of in Warsaw – a well-equipped, spacious flat. We were also given a rather large American car.

Admittedly I did not have much time for literature. On the other hand, we went to the theatre frequently, as well as to the opera and to concerts. The two London experiences which remain strongest in my memory are Wilhelm Furtwängler, who, among other things, conducted Beethoven's Ninth Symphony, and Laurence Olivier, who acted many roles from Shakespeare to Anouilh. We travelled around England and Scotland, and occasionally spent a weekend in Paris. Once we spent our leave in Switzerland, on another occasion in Italy. We were privileged.

Do not run away with the idea that I just enjoyed my life and neglected my duties. The overwhelming part of my job – some 80 if not 90 per cent – was routine consular work, which fortunately was not very demanding. To begin with, I was vice-consul; later I was entrusted with directing the consulate-general, an office with some forty employees. At the age of twenty-eight, I was the youngest consul in London. The office functioned faultlessly, especially as I had two efficient deputies – lawyers who made my work easier.

And what about the secret service? Let me admit to what is probably a disappointing truth: I never wore either a false beard or a wig. I never used invisible ink, I had no weapon, no camera, no photocopier and no tape recorder. Admittedly I had a ball-point pen, an invention of capitalist industry which had not yet reached Poland. Of the forty employees at the consulate three or four, as well as myself, worked for the secret service. In addition, we had ten to fifteen collaborators outside the consulate, most of them unemployed or retired journalists. They supplied us regularly with information about the Polish emigrés, whose centre was London, the seat of the anti-Communist Polish government-in-exile. For modest fees they submitted extensive reports about mostly unimportant events of all kinds – the various political parties and trends within the refugee world, their internal squabbles, their ceaseless intrigues and, of course, about individual politicians.

A lot of this information came from meetings which, as a rule, were open to the public – but which embassy or consular staff could hardly attend themselves. These reports also contained a lot of gossip – and this was perhaps the most interesting part of them. Much of what those secret informers reported to us was gleaned from the Polish exile newspapers but, of course, they concealed the source of their information. We had no agents within the government-in-exile who might have sent us reports – not even in the guise of a secretary or doorman.

I myself had no contact with Poles living in exile, but I did have communications with English people and, most of all, with German emigrés. It was my task to evaluate the various pieces of intelligence and pass them on to Warsaw. I expect the material I sent every week was read only by junior staff and probably only cursorily because there was very little feedback and I rarely received requests or instructions from headquarters. To put it mildly, I was neither a zealous nor a talented organizer of this secret information service.

On one occasion, however, I scored a notable success. This concerned a topic that was beyond the scope of my responsibilities: British affairs were the business of the military attaché at the Polish embassy, with whom I was not permitted to have any contact and about whose work I knew nothing. There was a cousin of mine living in England, who had emigrated from Berlin shortly before the war. He worked in an English institution that was housed at Wilton Park, the former residence of the author and politician Benjamin Disraeli – about an hour's train journey from London. There, specially selected German prisoners of war were being re-educated by English and German intellectuals who were described as lecturers or professors.

These prisoners of war were supposed to return to their country as good democrats.

I decided to write a lengthy report about this institution. Warsaw headquarters showed great interest in the subject and in my information – and presumably passed some of it on to the Soviet advisers. My reputation rose considerably. This would doubtless not have been the case if I had mentioned the fact that what was happening at Wilton Park was common knowledge and that any journalist, including of course a Polish one, could have easily uncovered the whole project. However, secret services only appreciate the material they receive from their agents and from confidential sources. As a rule they are not interested in information that is generally accessible, or that can be read in any newspaper.

The advancement of my career, however, had little to do with the quality of my work and much to do with the political developments in the Eastern bloc. The conflict between the Soviet Union and Tito's Yugoslavia, that is the rupture between Moscow and Belgrade in the summer of 1948, was followed soon afterwards by the communist alignment of the Eastern bloc countries. The leader of the Polish communists, Władysław Gomulka, who was accused of seeking a 'Polish road to socialism', was overthrown. His succession was solved in Moscow in a manner that was both ingenious and surprising. Bolesław Bierut, a man about whose political past nothing was known – it was said that before the war he had been a trade union official – had been playing the role of a non-party president of Poland. Now he revealed himself as a long-standing Polish communist and overnight became not only a member of the Communist Party of Poland, but at the same time its First Secretary. Following the compulsory unification of the two great parties, the Communists and the Social Democrats, Bierut found himself, automatically, at the head of the 'United Polish Workers Party'. Thus the communists had now officially become the sole rulers of the country. The relatively liberal period of the immediate post-war years was followed by the era of Stalinism in Poland.

My position in London was becoming more and more untenable. The political show trials which were beginning in the capitals of several Eastern bloc countries were an alarming reminder of the Moscow 'purge trials' of the 1930s. Some of them, such as the trial of László Rajk in Budapest in 1949, had unmistakable echoes of anti-Semitism. What frightened us most was what was taking place in our immediate circle, however. In London we had made friends with Paula Born, a cultured and educated woman who held the position of First Secretary in the Polish embassy. During a visit to Warsaw in the summer of 1949 she disappeared. We soon learned that she had been arrested, under suspicion of having worked for the American intelligence service in Switzerland during the war. She remained in prison for several years – without trial, without justification.

We had every reason to be alarmed, the more so because I was soon labelled as a 'cosmopolitan'. 'Cosmopolitanism' was a term appearing with increasing frequency in the communist press, applied to intellectuals who were not considered sufficiently loyal to the Party line. I had not yet abandoned the cause of communism entirely, but my illusions had greatly diminished. On a visit to Warsaw I enquired at intelligence headquarters whether my activity in London was still desirable. I would be informed within a few weeks, I was told. I applied for dismissal instead of waiting to be dismissed. My superiors were happy with that.

During those years it was a fairly frequent occurrence for the diplomats of communist countries – including Polish diplomats – to refuse to return when recalled, or, if they were visiting the West on official business, to defect. They 'chose freedom' – that was the phrase. We too could have remained in England or flown to the United States or to Australia. The truth is that we never even considered such a possibility. We regarded it as a matter of honour to return to Poland.

Perhaps this had something to do with my Berlin youth, with my Prussian grammar school education. I had been taught that one had to be loyal under all circumstances and that no one was more despicable than a traitor. But a totally different factor could also have played a part: there was a very real possibility that a secret service agent who remained in the West could be pursued and perhaps tracked down – and that he might well meet with a deplorable fate.

Was it a mistake to return to Poland, to a country that had meanwhile clearly become a Stalinist state? It was certainly reckless. Anyway, in November the three of us arrived in Warsaw. Three of us? The third person was our son, born in London less than a year previously. That life would not be easy for me after my return seemed certain. But things turned out even worse than I had expected. Within a few weeks I was dismissed both from the Foreign Ministry and from the Security Ministry and I finished up in prison, where I was held in solitary confinement. But nothing happened to me there, I was not even interrogated. I just sat in my cell and waited, and I had plenty of time to think.

I had experienced a lot in my twenty-nine years, in fact my life had been a series of high and low points. My political career was definitely at an end – and for a good reason. What was I, who had never learned any trade, to do now? Not for the first time in my life I was faced with an uncertain future.

I was allowed one book in my cell, provided it was politically unobjectionable. I decided on a German novel, *The Seventh Cross* by Anna Seghers. Unfortunately the electric bulb in a wire cage on the ceiling was very weak. More light – that was my main concern at the time. I used all my energy to obtain a stronger bulb – and finally my request was granted.

While reading this book I realized more and more clearly that my career, on which I could now look back calmly, was based on a fatal misconception. I had believed that politics could become my profession. But as I read Anna Seghers's novel, which I love and admire to this day, I knew that literature interested me incomparably more than anything else. So I wondered, in my now well-lit cell, whether it might be possible for me to return to the long-neglected love of my youth – to literature.

Two weeks later I was a free person again. It had been decided not to put me on trial but merely to subject me to a Party proceeding. In a dramatic session, during which several of my former colleagues yelled at me rudely, I was expelled from the Communist Party. It was not until some time later that I realized the Party had been right in its judgement. It had identified my 'ideological alienation' sooner than I had done so myself.

At about the same time I was summoned to the Security Ministry, where I had to sign a declaration to the effect that I would never utter a single word about the Polish secret service or anything connected with it. Failure to comply – this was explained to me with great emphasis – would result in the most severe and most extreme consequences. I was well aware of what this meant. Even though the word 'death sentence' was not used, I had no doubt what my interlocutor was alluding to. I took the threat very seriously.

I never heard any more from the Polish foreign intelligence service. They no longer needed me and they left me alone – or so it seemed to me. In reality the Polish authorities were certainly searching for me after my departure from Poland. But this I only learned in 1994 from the German periodical *Der Spiegel*, which had obtained documentary material from the Gauck authority.

In October 1958 – by which time I was living in the Federal Republic – the Polish Ministry of the Interior, under which the security service now came, requested urgent official assistance from the GDR security authorities. The matter was evidently of particular importance because – as *Der Spiegel* reported – it was handled personally by Markus Wolf, then chief of the Stasi (secret police). A month later, however, the GDR Ministry for State Security had to inform the Ministry of the Interior of the Polish People's Republic: '*In spite of repeated investigations by the press office, the German Press Association, as well as by unofficial collaborators, it has not been possible to establish the whereabouts of the person in question.*' By now my articles and book reviews were appearing regularly in the Federal Republic – in *Frankfurter Allgemeine* and in *Die Welt*. Evidently the unofficial collaborators of the GDR Ministry for State Security did not read any newspapers. I for my part do not know whether this investigation had anything to do with 'the most severe and most extreme consequences' I had been threatened with. It is a fact, however, that for many years I was listed in the border search system of the Eastern bloc secret services.

I might add that in the autumn of 1960, when I had been living in the Federal Republic for more than two years, two officers of the Verfassungsschutz, the Federal German security service, visited me in Hamburg, where I was then based. One of the officials came from Bonn, the other was from Hamburg. They clearly did not take the Polish secret service of the immediate post-war period at all seriously. It had – they hinted somewhat patronizingly – been rather childish and ridiculous. I saw no reason to contradict them.

24

BRECHT, SEGHERS,
HUCHEL AND OTHERS

It was entirely possible in the early 1950s to live in Poland without being a member of the Communist Party. But someone who had been a Party member and been expelled for ideological or political reasons was in a difficult situation. And the situation of one who had not only been expelled but had also been imprisoned was even worse. I was an ostracized individual and I was made to feel this every day. When acquaintances caught sight of me in the street they suddenly crossed the road and preferred not to know me. They had good reason: they could not be sure I would not be arrested again. And people could be summoned and interrogated for having questionable contacts. However, not everybody was so careful: we had a number of friends who dared to stick by us.

The weeks and months after our return to Poland were even more exciting than I could have expected. It was suggested confidentially to Tosia that she should leave me and, moreover, get an official divorce from me. She rejected this suggestion by the Party without hesitation. Shortly afterwards she suffered a serious nervous breakdown. Was it a delayed reaction to what we had suffered during the German occupation? Or was it the result of what she had gone through after our return from London? The doctors felt sure that it was due to a combination of both. Although she was discharged from hospital after several weeks, Tosia had to have medical treatment for many years afterwards. Some time later she landed quite an interesting job as an editor for Polish Radio.

I was not unemployed either. It was customary to offer some form of work to persons expelled from the Party – to make sure they did not turn into enemies of the state or starve to death. I was asked what I would like to do. I said I would like to work in a publishing house, more particularly in one that published German literature. My interlocutor was at a loss for an answer. No one had ever asked for anything of the kind.

I was assigned to the publishing house of the Defence Ministry, a large enterprise that also published literature. It soon turned out, however, that it had no section for German literature. Anything German was ostracized in Poland after the war, including the German language – which was not surprising, considering what had happened there between 1939 and 1945. If I was heard speaking German, I was told to stop using the language of Hitler. I had no difficulty in tearing a strip off such people by pointing out that German was also the language of Marx and Engels – which always shut them up.

After some effort I managed to persuade the management of the Defence Ministry of the need to set up a German section – but only for the publication of books from the newly established German Democratic Republic. However, along with the works of GDR authors such as Willi Bredel and Bodo Uhse, I was permitted to publish some titles by Egon Erwin Kisch. One day, in early June 1951, a woman colleague, a good translator, asked me if by any chance I knew who Gerhart Hauptmann was. She had received a commission from Polish Radio for an appraisal of his work on the occasion of the fifth anniversary of Hauptmann's death and needed help. The next day I supplied her with several hurriedly written pages on Hauptmann's importance and weaknesses. She was delighted and asked me why I did not work as a critic.

I asked myself the same question. So I reviewed a German book which had just appeared in Polish and sent the manuscript to one of the foremost weeklies in the country, *Nowa Kultura*. To my surprise it was immediately published. Moreover, I was asked to supply regular reviews of German literature published in Poland. I wrote about Arnold Zweig, Hans Fallada and Bernhard Kellermann, about Anna Seghers, Johannes R. Becher and Friedrich Wolf, and also about authors of lesser importance.

The successful playwright Friedrich Wolf, the father of the film director Konrad Wolf and of the Stasi chief Markus Wolf, was then in Warsaw as the first GDR ambassador to Poland. I thought I would ask him to recommend some GDR authors who would go down well with Polish readers. His Excellency received me in a dignified manner, every inch the diplomat. As I already had some experience in dealing with authors I opened the interview with a brief comment on his plays. I assured him that both *Cyankali* and *The Sailors of Cattaro* were unforgettable experiences for me. I praised *Professor Mamlock* as the 'play of the century' – admittedly an exaggeration. Wolf poured out some cognac for me and ordered coffee from his secretary.

Now we were getting down to business. As for translations into Polish – the ambassador told me – one of his novels would be particularly suitable, and possibly also another. Gratefully I made a note of the titles, but before I could ask about other authors he mentioned a collection of his short stories written in exile. He would also like to draw my attention to a comprehensive documentary, as well as a novella – everything, needless to say, written by himself. I then tried to steer the conversation to younger GDR writers. Certainly, the ambassador replied, he would deal with them in a moment, but first he had an idea that might interest me. Surely one could publish a volume of his selected plays in Polish translation. He had numerous articles as well, and as these were very topical in their subject matter, I should not fail to read them.

I nodded. We drank another cognac, the mood was steadily improving. After about an hour I drove back to my office, generously loaded with presents. In my briefcase I had seven finely bound books, all of them by Friedrich Wolf. On my list I had nine titles strongly recommended to me for translation, all of them by Friedrich Wolf. This pleasant ambassador, I thought to myself, had a talent for self-promotion as well as writing.

Ultimately the success of my efforts in persuading the publishing house where I worked to bring out more German literature was modest. Nevertheless, my superiors were satisfied with my work. I was not satisfied, but of course I kept quiet about this. The emphasis of the publishing house was on political and current affairs and military history, which was why I welcomed a job offer from one of the two leading Polish publishing houses for fiction, Czytatel. I was to be in charge of a department which included a fairly large German section. No sooner had I given notice to the Defence Ministry than

I was informed that certain members of the Central Committee had raised objections to my employment by Czytatel. A person expelled from the Party for 'ideological alienation' could not be permitted to hold a leading post in publishing.

Because I could no longer withdraw my notice, I suddenly found myself without a job. But the fact that by then I had already published a number of reviews turned out to be fortunate for me. I had no choice but to turn what had been a sideline into my main activity. I continued writing reviews for several Polish newspapers and periodicals, but I did not change my general subject – this would always be German literature. Almost overnight I had become what I had dreamed of in my youth – a critic.

Could this really work? Would I be able to make a living as a freelance author? To begin with, everything went reasonably well. My articles were well received and published. In addition I built up a good relationship with three or four publishing houses, for which I wrote reports on German books. I tried to persuade them to have some of the most memorable German works of the past translated into Polish, books which were still largely unknown in Poland – both by writers of our own century, such as Hermann Hesse and Heinrich Mann, Arthur Schnitzler and Leonhard Frank, and of the nineteenth century, such as Fontane, Storm and Raabe – names which then were known only to German scholars in Poland. Whenever such Polish editions materialized I furnished them with extensive prefaces or postscripts.

Soon I had built up a reputation for being a reliable and readable expert on German literature. That it pleased me, goes without saying – but at the same time it was my misfortune. A somewhat older friend, a communist of long standing and an expert on the practices of the Party, warned me: 'The Central Committee did not stop your rise in publishing merely so that you could make a career as a critic. One of these days the comrades will wake up to this and regard it as a provocation. You must apply for readmission to the Party. Most probably nothing will come of it, but it may just make the committee a little more friendly.'

That seemed to make sense. Thus, in order not to jeopardize my work as a critic, I requested that my expulsion from the Party be re-examined and quashed. I never received a reply. But my work was not interfered with, at least for the time being. However, it always remained in the shadow of anti-German attitudes which, in spite of official Polish propaganda, scarcely abated.

When the working-class writer Willi Bredel visited Warsaw, I invited him to lunch. Unlike many GDR authors, Bredel was both a worker and a writer, moreover one whose books had scored some success in Polish translation. I pointed out to our housekeeper that our guest admittedly was a German, but a decent fellow, who had fought not for, but against, Hitler. She was to make a special effort and produce a good meal. She nodded. Oh yes, the meal would be good, but she would have liked to know whether our guest was not by any chance that German who had killed her husband in the concentration camp.

None of the German writers who visited Poland in the early and mid 1950s could be suspected of having sympathized with the Nazis – they were nearly all of them former emigrés. Nevertheless they were mostly ignored or at best given a cool reception. That was also true of Anna Seghers, who visited Warsaw in December 1952. I was keen to meet her, the more so as her Polish publishers wanted me to write a monograph about her work.

I knew everything Seghers had published and, as well as *The Seventh Cross*, I admired her novel *Transit Visa* and several of her stories, in particular *The Outing of the Dead Girls*. I therefore knew that methodical thought was not one of the strong suits of this widely educated author. Anna Seghers was not greatly interested in discursive prose; it was probably a little strange to her. Nor am I certain whether Marxism – as has often been said – really did help to shape her personality. That it did not exert any marked influence on her thought processes is clear from her widely differing articles and speeches. Most of these – especially the more important ones – consist of loosely connected fragments or, more accurately, of observations, impressions and fleeting images, of fractured memories, reflections and narrative passages.

When we met in Warsaw, Seghers gave me a lot of her time – perhaps because she had been asked to do so by her publisher. She was simply dressed, and her manner was similarly without affectation. But she made a conflicting impression in me: there was something ingratiating about her – and, at the same time, something uncanny.

This was due to her facial expression, her features and gestures. One moment she smiled amicably – and the next she regarded me seriously and sadly – one moment she was cheerful, the next seemingly resigned and melancholic. One moment she would be listening to me attentively and indeed with concentration – the next moment I suspected her of being absent-minded. These changes came about quite suddenly and unexpectedly.

Our talk lasted about two hours. I had prepared a great many questions, to all of which, whether they were acceptable to her or not, she tried to reply conscientiously. But the longer the conversation lasted the more I feared that it would yield nothing for my study of Anna Seghers. I asked precise questions – and received imprecise and vague answers. They were more like emotional remarks which might, at a pinch, be regarded as poetic or fairy-tale-like.

Eventually we got round to *The Seventh Cross*. I commended the composition of the novel with absolute sincerity. Anna Seghers waved this aside. What I was commending, she said, was not her work at all: she had borrowed the plot from Manzoni's novel *I promessi sposi*. She urged me to read this book. I followed her advice that very week – and discovered no appreciable analogies. The composition of *I promessi sposi* may have profoundly impressed her, but if it provided a model for her own novel, then this was discernible only to herself.

Her reference to Manzoni was the only specific thing that emerged in our talk about *The Seventh Cross*. The rest were trivialities and some meaningless phrases. A thought flashed through my mind. This modest and pleasant person chatting about her characters in a broad Mainz dialect, this worthy and likeable woman, did not understand *The Seventh Cross* at all. She had no inkling of the sophistication of the artistic devices used in her novel, or of the virtuosity of its composition. A moment later another thought was troubling me. There were hundreds of thousands, perhaps millions, of people who had not only read this novel, published as it was in twenty or thirty languages, but also correctly understood it; there were numerous critics who had intelligently and cleverly elucidated and interpreted it. But there was only one person who had written it, who had composed it. As we parted I did something that was no longer customary in Germany: bowing deeply I kissed Anna Seghers's hand.

In the 1960s the critic Ernst Bloch told me of an occasion when, in November 1911, he had been invited to dinner at Richard Strauss's home in Garmisch. Strauss had struck him as an ordinary busy person, a man who simply enjoyed life. The talk was about *Elektra*, but apparently it was young Bloch who did all the talking, while Strauss, who was eating dumplings and drinking beer, remained silent. Only now and again would he grunt something that Bloch took for agreement. It had been, Bloch said, a 'horrible' evening. Suddenly an awful thought had occurred to him: this man Strauss, this Bavarian beer-drinker, did not understand anything at all of the subtle, refined, delicate and wonderful music of *Elektra*. As Bloch was telling me this he laughed happily, probably at himself.

What did I learn from my conversation with Anna Seghers? That most writers understand no more about literature than birds do about ornithology. And that they are the last people to judge their own work. Although as a rule they know approximately what they had intended to demonstrate, elucidate, and accomplish, this knowledge clouds their view of what they have actually achieved and created. It is up to the critic to examine – as carefully and thoroughly as possible – what the author has written. Whatever the author might additionally say about his work should not be ignored, but neither should it be taken too seriously.

However, I learned something else on that occasion. There can be literature without criticism, but no criticism without literature. In other words, in Brecht's words, '*First comes the grub and then morality.*' First comes poetry and only then comes theory; first comes literature and only afterwards comes criticism. For this reason we should be careful not to underrate, let alone forget, what we owe to those writers who really have made a contribution to our literature.

I recall two further lots of visitors from East Berlin. First, in February 1952, came Bertolt Brecht and Helene Weigel; in August 1956 came Peter Huchel. I talked to Huchel repeatedly in Warsaw and also accompanied him to Kazimierz, a particularly beautiful and interesting town on the Vistula. Basically Huchel was a non-political person – one felt that at once – and also a non-political poet. He was by no means indifferent to social issues, they played an important part in his work. But he viewed them predominantly in emotional terms, perhaps even naively. He was the bogey of the East German

Socialist Unity Party, which compelled him in his later years to write a few political poems.

I remember collecting Huchel from the Hotel Bristol, the Warsaw hotel for foreigners. He was waiting for me at the entrance. I said straight away: 'Herr Huchel, I'm afraid I have sad news. I've just heard on the radio that Brecht has died.' Huchel's reply came immediately, as if shot from a gun: 'For heaven's sake – what's to become of *Sinn und Form*?' I had to hide my shock: he was not moved by the death of the greatest German poet of our age, a poet who was scarcely fifty-eight, but by the death of the patron and supporter of the periodical *Sinn und Form* [*Meaning and Form*] which Huchel edited.

We met again on several occasions, more especially in the 1970s when he was living in the Federal Republic. In July 1977, when I visited him at Staufen in the Breisgau, his state of health was still quite good. On one of our long walks, he showed me a wonderful ancient Jewish cemetery. His conversation was restricted to two topics – himself and the periodical *Sinn und Form*. Two topics? In reality this was one and the same topic. He was also planning to write a book which was, simultaneously, to be an autobiography and a history of the periodical which to him invariably was the centre of the world. I do not suppose that much of the German literature of our era will survive. But a few poems by Peter Huchel will.

Not only was Huchel virtually unknown in Poland at the time, so too was Brecht. Not a single book by him appeared in a Polish translation; only one of his plays had ever been staged, and this without appreciable success – his *Dreigroschenoper* [*Threepenny Opera*] in Warsaw in 1929. What induced Brecht to visit Warsaw in 1952 was not any particular interest in communist Poland or in its still ruined capital but an urgent wish to acquaint the Polish public with his work and also with his productions for the Berliner Ensemble.

On the day of his arrival a lunch was given in honour of Brecht, Helene Weigel and the GDR writer Hans Marschwitza who had arrived at the same time but in whom there was little interest. The luncheon party was small, the disappointment great. Because Frau Weigel, immediately on arrival, informed us – a handful of critics and translators – that Brecht was not feeling well and that he sent his apologies for his absence.

After lunch Helene Weigel took me to one side for a private word. To welcome Brecht I had written a short article for one of the main Warsaw dailies, the German translation of which, as I now learned, had immediately been handed to Brecht at the railway station by a representative of the GDR embassy. He had, Helene Weigel said, liked the article a lot. Small wonder, I thought to myself, as I had generously praised and lauded the visitor. Unfortunately, she went on, he could not receive anyone. But he would make an exception for me. Would I report to Room 93 at the Hotel Bristol at 5 p.m.? There I would be granted the interview I had asked for.

This was fine by me and I turned up on the dot. To my surprise I found an acquaintance of mine outside the door to Brecht's hotel room, a man who worked as a translator from German. I looked around and saw another acquaintance, a publisher, likewise waiting to be admitted. And somebody was already with Brecht – a theatrical producer. No doubt every one of us had been told that he alone would be received – and now we were queuing up. Eventually my turn came.

I stepped into the room and was amazed by what I saw. Brecht was sitting behind a table on which stood a large bowl – and in that bowl were things that simply did not exist in Warsaw in 1952 - oranges, bananas and grapes. Brecht had either brought the fruit with him from Berlin or the GDR embassy had arranged for it to be put there. He did not offer any of this fruit to his visitors.

These coveted delicacies, however, created a distance, a gulf, between him and his guests. Had he, in expectation of his visitors, deliberately left that bowl of fruit standing on the table of his hotel room? No, it was probably a coincidence. Yet the fact that it even occurred to me that he might have used the bananas and oranges as useful stage props was typical of the atmosphere that Brecht, deliberately or otherwise, invariably created. I had the impression that he was always acting.

His apparel also contributed to that impression. In Warsaw he wore the seemingly proletarian, strikingly simple dark-grey jacket that, it was rumoured, had been tailor-made for him from the best English cloth. Did he want to dress up? Did he need such nonsense? Of course he did not. But he would not do without his bit of fun.

Why, one would be entitled to wonder, do so many writers, painters

243

and composers attach so much importance to creating an often expensive and usually slightly ridiculous image? Nor is this something that is only indulged in by mediocre or unsuccessful artists. Even Richard Wagner had a weakness for dressing up in costume and for a colourful stylization of his surroundings. I have always liked the remark of Thomas Mann's Kröger: '*Would you like me to be running around in a torn velvet jacket or a red silk waistcoat? As an artist I'm already enough of an adventurer in my inner life. So far as outward appearances are concerned one should dress decently, damn it, and behave like a respectable citizen...*'

Brecht received me pleasantly and patiently answered all my questions. We first talked about Shakespeare's *Coriolanus* which he was then preparing for production by the Berliner Ensemble in a new translation. Then he told me about an as yet unfinished play of his, based on a political activist famous in the GDR, a stove-fitter. Was this going to be a didactic play, I asked, or – and here I let a silly question slip out – something in the style of the *Dreigroschenoper*? Pained, Brecht turned away: 'I haven't been writing like that for a long time.' I realized I had committed a *faux pas*, but quickly regained my composure: 'Herr Brecht, I can understand very well that you don't wish to hear about the *Dreigroschenoper*. Goethe similarly couldn't bear people talking to him about Werther all his life.' The comparison was intended by me as a joke, but Brecht took it seriously and was clearly gratified. To him, the parallel seemed entirely appropriate.

It was not until much later that I learned that, when the first edition of his *Collected Works* was published during his years in exile, Brecht was unsure whether to call himself 'Bert' or 'Bertolt'. The writer Ruth Berlau then argued for 'Bertolt' on the grounds that 'Will instead of William would not have been right either at the time.' The use of Shakespeare as an argument instantly persuaded Brecht in favour of Bertolt.

When I turned the talk to Kurt Weill, Brecht became monosyllabic. Whether the music for one of his plays was written by Weill or by Eisler or by Dessau was of no great importance, he observed. He himself usually had a more or less clear idea of the music needed for his texts: the composer only provided a little help.

Brecht then asked me if there was anything special being staged in

Warsaw at the time. I mentioned an excellent performance, except that it was a play that would probably not be to his taste – Bernard Shaw's *Mrs Warren's Profession*. Indeed he did not wish to know about Shaw, but I tried to persuade him to see the play none the less – because of the lead character, the famous Polish actress Irena Eichlerówna.

As he did not quite know what to do with his evening – there was little taste in Poland then for social contact with German guests – he yielded. And when I spoke to him the next day he was most enthusiastic about Eichlerówna. What an exceptional actress, he would bring her to Berlin, she would be perfect for the main role in his play *Die Gewehre der Frau Carrar* [*Señora Carrar's Rifles*]. That was a wonderful idea, I said, except that Eichlerówna did not know a single word of German. For a moment Brecht was silent, then he said: 'That doesn't matter! All the others will speak German and she'll speak Polish. That will be real alienation.' Needless to say, nothing came of it.

Brecht was not in the least interested in Poland and he did not care for sightseeing. His life revolved around a single subject – his work, his theatre. There was but one question for him: how best could he arrange for his writings to be translated into Polish, published and, most especially, staged? He only wanted to talk to people who could bring this about – to theatre directors, producers and actors, to publishers, translators and journalists.

Everyone who met him reported having experienced Brecht as a hard-headed businessman determined to sell his wares, as an efficient impresario of the poet Bertolt Brecht. As for the charisma that was supposed to emanate from him – admittedly this was said more often by women – I certainly do not remember having been aware of it during those days. Brecht neither fascinated nor charmed me. However, though this may sound like a contradiction, he profoundly impressed me. Beyond his stage-managed image, beyond the play-acting element, there lurked a purposeful, sovereign and well-focused energy. Behind his relaxed manner there was an almost uncanny will-power.

Thus his person was surrounded by a special aura. This has frequently been described but, as often in such cases, it is not something that can be put into words. In his early diary there is an entry dating back to 1921, an entry one would have scarcely expected of him: '*Where there is no mystery there is no truth.*' Maybe Brecht's characteristic aura really had its origin in a mystery that could not be elucidated or defined – the mystery of the genius.

It is possible that even then I realized, or at least surmised, that Brecht did not make the theatre his life's work because of his commitment to the class struggle, but that he concerned himself with the class struggle because he needed it as an impulse and as a theme for his work. It was not the world reformer Brecht who needed the theatre and poetry, but the theatre man and poet Brecht who needed world reform, or Marxism, as an ideological foundation and a goal.

25

JOSEF K., STALIN
QUOTATIONS AND
HEINRICH BÖLL

I was skating on very thin ice that could crack beneath me at any moment. How long would the Party tolerate a person expelled on 'ideological' grounds publishing reviews, moreover without working for an institution or belonging to the Polish Writers' Union or the Journalists' Union? I therefore, a little hesitantly and timidly, applied for admission to the Writers' Union. To my great surprise I was instantly admitted. Even though I had been expelled from the Party? Or perhaps – as experts on the Polish writers' scene suspected – just because I had been expelled from the Party? At any rate, I now felt a little more secure.

At the beginning of 1953, however, difficulties arose. One paper did not wish to accept an article by me: they were sufficiently well supplied with manuscripts at the moment. Another editorial office informed me that my article was not sufficiently topical. Elsewhere I was told that they could not publish so much about German literature. Eventually someone had the courage to tell me the truth: an elderly woman editor of a monthly journal explained to me why a review of mine that had been with them for several weeks would never appear – because nothing written by me was now allowed to be published. She would leave it to me to lodge a protest if I chose. To whom was I to protest? She had no answer to that.

Who had instructed the newspapers and publishing houses not to publish my articles irrespective of their quality? The censorship? In contrast to other communist countries the censorship in Poland was not a secret institution: the address and telephone number of the 'Office for the Supervision of the Press, Public Performances and

Publications' was to be found in the Warsaw telephone directory. But there was no point in protesting to the censorship because it was merely an executive organ. It was clear to me that I would have to appeal to the authority by which I had been condemned as an ideological alien and expelled from the Party – the Central Committee. The Central Committee resided in a huge building that one could not enter without a special pass. I did not know anyone in the building who would have been prepared to apply for a pass for me. In consequence I could intervene only by telephone. But to which department?

I turned first to the Department for Art and Literature. I was told that they knew nothing about a ban on my publications. Perhaps I should try the Department for Publications and Publishing. The comrades in this department similarly knew nothing about my case. As I had been expelled from the Party, I was told by them, I would have to approach the Central Control Commission. The Bureau of that Commission informed me that it concerned itself only with questions of Party membership and not with professional activity.

I was accused, but I could not discover what I was accused of. I was sentenced, but I did not know who had sentenced me. I never dreamed that I might find myself in a situation reminiscent of Joseph K. in Kafka's *Trial*. And just like the geodesist K., who wanted to report to the castle but could not get near it, I continued to be denied access to the headquarters of the Central Committee. I remained dependent on the telephone, on women secretaries who invariably refused to connect me to the person I wished to speak to under some pretext or other.

Eventually the Central Control Commission referred me back to the head of the Department for Art and Literature, where I had started my efforts. I phoned him again. This time he confirmed that it was quite true that a publication ban had been issued against me – by the Politburo. But why? My publications, I was told, could not be tolerated on ideological grounds. Would this apply all my life? His answer was: 'Yes.' And why? For that I should turn to the Central Control Commission. His reference to the Politburo made it clear to me that any interventions with heads of departments in the Central Committee were pointless, because a higher level of the Party, the highest, had ruled on the matter. At least now I knew that.

For the moment I was still a member of the Polish Writers' Union. I asked its president, the novelist and dramatist Leon Kruczkowski, whose principal works were then being translated into German, if I could have a word with him. His reply sounded encouraging: 'Of course, if you wish this very day.' Certainly, he told me, it was unacceptable that a member of the Writers' Union was prohibited from practising his profession. He would immediately intervene at the highest level, with the Politburo. A week later he was disappointed to have to inform me that his efforts had not been successful.

The publication ban remained in force for roughly another eighteen months. However, this was immaterial to the Writers' Union. Although I was not permitted to publish my work, I remained a fully-fledged member. Maybe this was a covert demonstration that they were not prepared to countenance such interference by the Party. Certainly I was grateful to the Writers' Union – and continue to be grateful. Because this was a ray of light at a time that was particularly dark for me.

In the summer of 1953 a small brochure of mine appeared despite the ban. This was a curious affair. Shortly before the publication ban a publishing house had prepared a popular lecture of mine for publication in a large print run, with the lengthy title 'Progressive German Literature during the Time of Nazi Darkness'. The publishers now had to abandon this publication, which was not at all to their liking. After prolonged and persistent efforts, my inoffensive pamphlet was eventually authorized – with the stipulation that my name must not appear on it. As I refused to use a pseudonym – this would have been tantamount to an admission of guilt – a compromise was reached. Instead of my name, my initials, M.R., were printed on the cover and on the title page.

In material terms we were badly off, because Tosia's salary was very modest. We were living in a two-room flat: one room was our son's, the other served as our dining and bedroom and also as my study. Soon our cleaning woman refused to work for us: she could not work in a household where the wife went out to work every day, while the man sat at home reading novels.

From time to time my sister, who was not well-off either, sent us parcels from London. That was the normal thing. Nearly all our friends received parcels from relations in the West, mainly of clothes, because no clothes of a decent quality were available in Poland. Those who had no relatives or friends in the capitalist world were badly off.

In this difficult situation I was helped by a coincidence. Alfred Kantorowicz, an East Berlin journalist and a professor at Humboldt University, was visiting Warsaw. The German programme of Polish Radio wanted to broadcast a conversation with him. I was asked if I would be prepared to talk to him. I said I would be glad to do so, but I had to draw their attention to the fact that there was a ban on publishing my work. They were aware of this, of course, but had already obtained special permission, admittedly on two conditions: my name must not be mentioned and on no account was I to be allowed to take part in a live broadcast. Evidently they were afraid that I might come out with something derogatory about the government or communism.

For the first time in my life I was in a broadcasting studio and for the first time ever I saw a tape recorder. The editor said: 'When the red light comes on you begin and after exactly five minutes you finish.' This was the only instruction I received, but my chat with Kantorowicz must have been to their liking, because they invited me to do regular radio chats with German visitors. Thus I repeatedly interviewed authors and journalists, musicians, theatrical people and publishers. As a rule these came from the GDR. Mostly they assured their listeners that they admired Warsaw and, needless to say, loved the Poles.

The visitors I remember included the conductor Heinz Bongartz, the head of the Dresden Philharmonic. I conceived the idea of not only recording a chat with him but also an excerpt from his rehearsal with the Warsaw Philharmonic Orchestra. The programme included Schubert's great Symphony No. 9 in C Major. After the famous horn passage in the first movement Bongartz tapped his desk, dissatisfied: 'No, gentlemen, this won't do. What the horns sing here – that is the German Romantic feeling for nature. Would you please play this wonderful passage more vigorously and more intensely, with more emotion, gentlemen. It must sound fuller and also mightier. Here, at this point, one must see the German forest.' The leader of the orchestra, who functioned as interpreter, stood up, turned to the wind instruments and exclaimed in Polish: 'Horns louder!' As Bongartz was busy making a note in his full score he evidently did not notice that the Polish translation of his request was astonishingly brief. He had the passage played again – and again tapped his desk: 'Gentlemen of the horns, that was magnificent, that was exactly what I wanted.' Whenever in later years I heard orchestra players complaining about conductors talking too much I was reminded of Heinz Bongartz and of the Polish leader of the orchestra who proved a master of concise summary: 'Horns louder.'

This broadcasting work, which was not without interest and not difficult either, enabled us, during the time when I was prohibited from publishing, to live more or less adequately – together with Tosia's salary, of course. But the ban continued, and the acquaintances I met in the street or at the theatre continued to behave in an unpredictable manner. Some, whom I knew only cursorily, now greeted me very cordially, while others – and they were the majority – did not wish to run any risks and even tried to avoid telephone conversations with me. I just had to keep my nerve. I could not let the matter rest, I had to do something. Again I wrote to the Central Committee, this time only about the publication ban. And again I received no reply.

In 1954, however, about a year after Stalin's death, there appeared the first signs of a protest movement by the Polish intellectuals against the regime. This began seemingly harmlessly: at a meeting of the Writers' Union a new guide to the history of Polish literature was criticized. The talk was about the textbook, but what was implied was the entire cultural policy of the Party. Soon there was talk of the 'Thaw', the title of a novel by Ilya Ehrenburg, an important work even though of no great literary significance.

I too benefited from the more liberal climate. In the autumn of that year I phoned the Control Commission of the Party and innocently asked whether anything had changed in the matter of my publication ban. Some comrade or other obligingly told me that he would look into the matter that very day. A little later I was informed that I should report to Comrade Z., an influential official, the following day. Evidently my case was looking up.

On this occasion I was admitted at once. True, the man did not speak to me in his office, but standing outside in the corridor. Z was an elderly, gaunt, and probably rather melancholy man who, as I

251

heard later, had spent several years in Soviet camps. He had examined my dossier, he said gruffly, and could not find any reason for a ban on my professional work. I could publish again, as of now. He reacted to my questions by shrugging his shoulders: 'That was a mistake, a misunderstanding.' Beyond that, he could not, or would not, give me any explanation. I never discovered why the ban was imposed on me in the first place or why, after more than eighteen months, it was lifted again. Other people, who had spent years in prison, had the same experience. That was the way of things in Poland during the Stalinist era.

However, the period of Stalinism was by no means over. There was progress, but it was very slow: the steps forward were dogged by all kinds of reverses. The old cultural functionaries were still firmly in the saddle, as I was soon to discover. A publishing house had commissioned a popular account of recent German literature from me. In the book, I was to deal only with authors and titles published in Polish translation since 1945, in other words, not with people like Kafka or Musil. The task did not greatly attract me, but it was reasonably well paid – and I needed the money.

A large part of the manuscript was already finished when the publication ban compelled me to drop the whole project, so I was quickly able to complete the job once it had been lifted. Although the publisher's reader, a pretty, dark-haired young girl, was satisfied, she observed with a roguish smile that I had failed to make a single reference to Stalin. This oversight would have to be remedied. It was, she said, continuing to smile, a condition imposed by the censorship.

No newspaper or periodical had demanded anything of the kind of me, even in Stalin's lifetime. That was quite possible, the charming young reader observed, but that had been before my publication ban. So I asked her: how often should Stalin be mentioned? No doubt this question was a familiar one because her answer came off pat: at least once in every one hundred pages, in other words four times in all. I soon met this request. I quoted a trivial observation of Stalin's about the dialectical method in communism and a bombastic telegram to Pieck and Ulbricht, I referred to a short story by Anna Seghers in which Stalin figured. The pretty reader did not think this was enough: she demanded, softly and gently, another passage in which I should – that was obligatory – not only quote Stalin but unambiguously identify myself with the quote. I should bring her that quotation, along with my comments the following day. We arranged to meet – as was not unusual in Warsaw then – in a café.

From Stalin's writings I chose that famous remark of 1942, to the effect that the German people must not be identified with the Nazis, that Hitlers came and went, but the German people endured. This slogan, disseminated by Soviet propaganda for years, and which probably saved the lives of countless German soldiers in Soviet captivity, still seems to me appropriate and highly important.

My friendly reader also liked the quotation I had chosen. We smiled at each other, then we drank some vodka, then I stroked her arm, and then we understood each other. She asked, with unmistakable irony, if I wanted to see her library – or perhaps her stamp collection? Yes, I said, I was exceedingly interested – but did not specify in what. There was no more talk of postage stamps or a library. But the couch of my political mentor was very wide and I was certainly not disappointed. '*But what her face was like I know no longer / I only know: I kissed it on that day.*' I think back with pleasure to the publisher's reader who extracted from me those Stalin quotations with charm and honour.

My book was published in 1955. Its awkward title was *From the History of German Literature 1871–1954*. It began with Fontane and Hauptmann, followed by Thomas and Heinrich Mann, Feuchtwanger, Arnold Zweig, Brecht and Anna Seghers. I have not the slightest reason to be proud of this opus. Even though one or two chapters, the occasional passage, seem passable to me now, I frequently blush when I turn its pages.

All in all it is a rather slapdash piece of work which, like many of my articles prior to 1955, clearly reveals the devastating effect which socialist realism had on me. Yes indeed, my literary criticism was influenced by Marxist, and certainly also vulgar Marxist, literary theory until then. Perhaps I should mention that this was the theory which later, around 1968, was discovered and celebrated by the Left in the Federal Republic.

But is this surprising? Between 1951 and 1955, I was a beginner and, moreover, as a critic I was self-taught. I had never taken part in a seminar, there was no one who could have advised or warned me, let alone helped me. Like every beginner I needed models. Where was I to find them? In Polish literary criticism, of course, except that this too was greatly influenced by socialist realism. This was even more true of criticism in the GDR, which was of a much lower calibre than in Poland.

Besides, when I started to write in 1951, Poland was totally cut off from the Western world. Today no one has any conception of the practical consequences which the Iron Curtain had for intellectual life in the countries of East Europe. Books, newspapers or periodicals in German were obtainable only if published in the GDR. My frequent attempts to get hold of books which were then published only in the West – for instance, the works of Kafka or Musil, or of contemporary Western authors – were always unsuccessful. I was unaware of the existence of the weekly newspaper *Die Zeit* and if anyone had then asked me about the leading critics or the major literary publishing houses in the Federal Republic, I would not have been able to come up with a single name.

Not until 1956, as part of the discussion of Stalinism, did the Iron Curtain become more permeable. I was again permitted to travel, though initially only within the Eastern bloc. In the summer of 1956 Tosia and I were able to take part in a 'study trip' to the Soviet Union, organized by the Polish Writers' Union. However, we were faced with unexpected difficulties. The relevant authority refused to grant Tosia a passport because we had no proof of having been married at a register office. We only had the certificate issued by the theologian in 1942, the document that saved Tosia's life. It was useless to point out that there had been no other forms of marriage in the Warsaw ghetto, and that this certificate had until then been recognized everywhere.

But we were reassured that the necessary authorization by a court was quite simple and would take only three months. But the trip to Moscow and Leningrad was to start in two weeks' time. So I hit on what seemed to me a highly practical solution. If it was really true – I said to the official – that my wife was not my wife at all, then surely I could marry my wife. Yes, he answered, no problem, provided we produced both our birth certificates.

The following day we were married – once again. The business was swiftly performed by the official, a young man with a sense of humour. He wished us the best of luck as we took our leave. Out in the street we looked at each other helplessly and also worriedly. No, we were not cheerful – probably because we were both thinking of that 22 July 1942, when the murder of the Warsaw Jews began and when we were married the first time. We took a few steps in silence, uncertain where to go or what to do. Then I pulled myself together and kissed Tosia. She looked at me sadly and said softly: 'Let's find a café.'

Two weeks later we travelled by rail to Moscow. Our luggage contained, among other things, two rolls of toilet paper. Friends laughed at Tosia: surely we would be put up in a luxury hotel for foreigners and there would be no shortage of anything. As soon as we moved into our room – an exceptionally large and splendidly equipped room – Tosia inspected the bathroom. She found there a great quantity of cotton wool but no toilet paper. That was how things were in the summer of 1956.

We spent a few days each in Moscow and Leningrad and visited everything that tourists were recommended to see. Some things certainly impressed us, but we felt relieved when we were able to board a Polish ship in Leningrad, which was to take us to Gdynia. I asked myself why the land whose novels were among my greatest literary experiences seemed so alien to me. I found no answer to this question. Well over forty years have passed since then, during which we have repeatedly visited London and Paris, Rome and Stockholm, and New York. But we have never returned to Moscow or to that undoubtedly wonderful city which is once again called St Petersburg.

Two other trips abroad, which I was able to make in 1956 thanks to the opening up of the Polish frontiers, left me with quite different memories. Both were to the GDR, especially to East Berlin, where I had not been since 1949. I visited Arnold Zweig, Stefan Hermlin and a number of other writers in their villas, their spacious apartments and their attractive summer cottages; I looked at the choice of consumer goods in the shops and bought a few things for Tosia and our son, things not available in Poland, especially clothes. The standard of life in East Berlin was incomparably higher than in Warsaw.

Then – there was no Wall yet – I risked the displeasure of the GDR comrades and went to West Berlin. Everything that was available there made what I had only just admired in East Berlin seem poor and shoddy. Warsaw, East Berlin and West Berlin – these, in 1956, enjoyed a standard of living on three different levels. A Polish colleague whom I happened to meet on Kurfürstendamm told me: 'We Poles won the war, but the Germans, damn them, won the peace.'

It was to the greater permeability of the Iron Curtain that I owed my acquaintance with a West German writer, incidentally the first who had visited communist Poland – an acquaintanceship which never blossomed into friendship but remained a difficult and sometimes complicated relationship. It was to endure for many years and at times to take an almost dramatic course.

On a misty and rainy Sunday morning towards the end of 1956 I was standing on a platform at Warsaw Central Station, a former goods station which was still in its desolate wartime state, impatiently waiting for the train from Berlin which, as usual, was late. Finally the two authors arrived whom I was to welcome on behalf of the Polish Writers' Union – Heinrich Böll, about whom little was known in Warsaw, and his friend, the journalist and satirist Ernst-Adolf Kunz, who used the pseudonym Philipp Wiebe, about whom nothing was known at all.

I took the two gentlemen to the hotel and, over breakfast, told them that the Polish Writers' Union would make every effort to render their short stay in Warsaw and Kracow as pleasant as possible and to meet all their wishes. At that point Böll had only one wish, admittedly an urgent one – he wanted to know whether there was a Catholic church near the hotel. All the most beautiful churches in Warsaw and those most worth seeing – I informed him – were in the immediate neighbourhood of our hotel. However, Böll was not interested in sightseeing. Instead he wished to attend Mass at once. I was a little surprised, probably for no good reason.

Wherever he went, in Warsaw and in Kracow, he was treated with great courtesy. The Poles are a hospitable nation. Böll was surprised, even touched. Admittedly he had no idea of what was going on behind the scenes: his visit was a major headache for the Writers' Union. A reception had been planned in his honour in the elegant House of Literature. Some fifty writers had been invited. But they all declined. Worse still, they refused point-blank, not bothering with excuses. Some of them asked about the guest's recent past. Had he been an emigré or a deserter, had he been imprisoned or in a concentration camp, or in a 'punishment' battalion? When they were told that throughout the war he had been an ordinary German soldier, no more and no less, they turned down the invitation. Even eleven years after the Second World War Polish writers felt no desire to welcome a German. To spare their guest the affront, the reception, which had already been announced, was swiftly moved from the assembly room to a smaller room in the House of Literature. There it was not quite so obvious that only six or seven people had turned up – exclusively translators and publishers' readers.

We wanted Böll to tell us about recent West German literature. His account was businesslike and modest. What he told us was informative, but did not strike us as particularly interesting. Nevertheless we were profoundly moved by his words, and indeed alarmed: here was a writer from the Federal Republic, regarded in Poland as a revanchist, who spoke of German literature and German guilt practically in the same breath – and every one of his rather simple and at times awkward sentences was convincing. Instantly this unceremonious guest gained for himself the sympathy of the people he was addressing: he did not try to fool anyone. We felt that this German writer, who had worn the uniform of the Wehrmacht for six years, had the gift of grace – the gift of a charisma which, as so often in such cases, defied description.

The few participants at this meeting left the House of Literature in silence, impressed but also rather confused. Soon Böll himself was impressed and confused – admittedly for entirely different reasons. As I walked with him through the city, I showed him, needless to say at his own request, the destruction in Warsaw, which was still visible at every step; I showed him the rebuilding that was taking place. My comments were as dry as possible and he said little by way of reply. I believe he suffered a lot during those hours.

Böll had a generosity which is by no means common among artists and writers: he was always ready to help. In the spring of 1957 I wished to visit the Federal Republic for the first time. However, I could not obtain an entry visa. Böll immediately intervened in Bonn, with the Foreign Office and with other authorities; the daily *Die Welt* published a short article in protest, the Secretary of the SPD group in the Bundestag intervened with the Federal Minister of the Interior.

Three months later I received the visa, but I never discovered why it had been denied me in the first place. Apparently it was just a matter of an inadequately completed questionnaire. Eventually in December 1957, my long-planned trip to the Federal Republic materialized.

When, in 1958, I decided to leave Poland and, if possible, to live in Germany, I had to apply for a new passport since a Polish exit passport was always only valid for one trip and had to be surrendered after a person's return. This new passport, in the official formulation, was to entitle me to a 'study trip' in the Federal Republic for a period of no more than three months.

Again there were difficulties, this time not from the German side. Since no foreign currency was ever authorized for such trips, the Polish authorities demanded that I provide an affidavit by a well-known citizen of the Federal Republic, who would undertake, if necessary, to finance my stay in the West. Again I turned to Böll, who was then on holiday in Switzerland. He sent me the necessary document by return. In the meantime the Polish passport regulations had once again been changed and I no longer needed his affidavit. Later, when I was living in the Federal Republic, he never reminded me of this guarantee. Probably he had long forgotten about it. But I still have Heinrich Böll's letter of 8 May 1958 with the official authorization of his signature.

We had not long been living in the Federal Republic when Böll came to Frankfurt to visit us in the shabby furnished room we then occupied. He brought with him a bouquet of flowers. Tosia said to me later: 'He is the first German who's given me flowers.' I thought to myself: Perhaps he is the first German altogether.

Böll asked us immediately if we needed money or whether he could do anything for us. I did not need any money. We were not exactly well off, but it would be an exaggeration to claim that we were penniless. My articles were being published, even if such work was then poorly paid; my work for the radio was broadcast and paid better. When Böll heard this he looked at me sharply and said: 'Over the next few weeks you'll have a lot to do with the authorities, like any new arrival. German authorities frequently ask for statements by witnesses. Don't ever forget: I am a very good witness and I'm always at your disposal.' And he smiled roguishly.

He never spoke about the fact that he often and willingly helped others – that was something he kept to himself. But once he did discuss with me a somewhat reckless rescue operation. He wanted to bring a Czech woman, who had long been trying in vain to get an exit permit, out of the country illegally. We discussed several possibilities. A few days later Böll drove to Prague and brought the woman across the Czechoslovakian frontier, initially to Yugoslavia, with a fake Federal German passport. From there he sent me a postcard: 'Just a quick line to inform you that the matter I talked to you about has gone well ... Details in due course. One thing is certain: we live in a strange world!'

I have written a lot about Böll – first in 1957 in Poland and then, after 1958, in the Federal Republic. I have commended and praised him but I have also been critical of some of his books. Too often, too severely? I cannot answer this question, but I know that I only hurt him when I believed that I had to do so. And that in doing so I was hurting myself. I continue to admire some of his satires and short stories, especially *Doktor Murkes gesammeltes Schweigen* [*Dr Murke's Collected Silences*]. But I do not think very highly of his principal works, his novels. I always felt closer to the prose of Wolfgang Koeppen or Max Frisch.

I gave my book on Böll the title *More than a Poet*. This, some of my colleagues thought, need not be taken as a compliment. Böll himself was not at all pleased when he was described as a moralist, he preferred to be seen as an artist. On one occasion, when in a telephone conversation I commended his views in some new work, he said rather angrily: 'There's no charge for proper attitudes.' In 1972 I was asked by the Royal Academy in Stockholm who I thought should receive the Nobel Prize for Literature. Without hesitation I named Heinrich Böll, that German preacher with clownish features, that clown with priestly dignity, the man who, almost overnight, had become a *Praeceptor Germaniae*, a teacher such as Germany had never had before. But I do not overrate my influence: if I had not proposed him I believe he would have received the prize anyway. My candidates on subsequent occasions were Graham Greene, John Updike, Max Frisch and Friedrich Dürrenmatt. None of them was awarded the Nobel Prize.

I particularly disliked Böll's novel of 1979, *The Safety Net*. My review in *Frankfurter Allgemeine* began with the words: '*No, nothing*

259

can shake my admiration for Heinrich Böll. Not even the novel The Safety Net.' It was these opening sentences that particularly annoyed him; he replied to me angrily on television. During the next few years we repeatedly corresponded with one another but we did not meet again until October 1983, at a reception in a hotel on the Rhine. Böll, already clearly marked by his serious illness, nevertheless agreed to give a *laudatio* for a Polish woman translator.

As soon as he caught sight of me he made straight for me and asked, half threateningly and half innocently: 'Do we still shake hands?' I replied, 'Yes, of course.' But he did not extend his hand to me, not yet. Instead he moved closer. I was not sure what he intended. I waited, a little nervously, for what would happen next. At all costs I wished to avoid a scandal. But Böll merely whispered a single word in my ear, one that had always been a particular favourite with the German people: 'Arsehole!' Then he said aloud, laughingly: 'Now everything's all right again.' And he embraced me.

I learned a lot from Böll – including the simple realization that goodwill, or even friendship, between an author and a critic is possible only when the critic never discusses the books of this author and when the author reconciles himself to that fact once and for all.

And there is something entirely different that I would like to mention here. Although I have known two German writers who frequently and emphatically proclaimed their Christianity, only one of them convinced me of the seriousness and sincerity of his faith – Heinrich Böll.

26

A STUDY TRIP
WITH ALL SORTS OF
CONSEQUENCES

In October 1956 an exciting political change took place in Poland: Gomulka, who had been accused of 'Titoism' and 'Nationalism', and imprisoned for a number of years, was once again at the head of the Communist Party. To the delight of writers and journalists, who had significantly contributed to his victory, he immediately promised freedom for the press and for literature. Admittedly, censorship continued to exist and all texts had to be submitted for approval. However, as the censors had received no new directives from the Central Committee of the Party they did not know what they were required to object to, and so editorial offices and publishing houses received the texts back unchanged. Censorship had clearly become superfluous and it was said that it would soon be abolished.

If this department was due for the *coup de grâce* anyway, then – many of the censors believed – it would be wiser to commit public suicide and thereby, up to a point rehabilitate itself. A meeting of the Party organization in the censorship department therefore resolved to request the Central Committee to disband the department. The letter containing this request was to be published in the press. However, a paradoxical and absurd situation arose: the censorship department desired to be dissolved, but at the same time prohibited publication of the letter which made this desire public. This was probably the oddest ban in the history of the Polish press.

The demands of the censors were not met and soon they were again doing their duty. The new Party leadership, under Gomulka, did not live up to its many promises. Soon there was every reason to talk about gradual, but perceptible, 're-Stalinization'. Another new line? Certainly, but it had very little effect on cultural life. Polish publishing houses were at last able to publish the work of West German authors and the irritating rule that newspapers and journals could review only books that were available in translation was dropped.

From 1956, therefore, I was able to steep myself in Western literature. I wrote not only about the authors of the older generation, but also about the representatives of post-war literature, most of whom were still unknown in Poland – such as Frisch and Koeppen, Böll and Andersch, Martin Walser and Siegfried Lenz. For the first time in my life I also worked as a translator. Together with my friend, the Polish critic Andrzej Wirth, who was later to teach at American universities and who, in 1982, founded an Institute for Applied Theatre Studies at the University of Giessen, which he headed until 1992, I translated Kafka's *Castle* in Max Brod's stage adaptation and Dürrenmatt's *Der Besuch der alten Dame* [*The Visit*].

In consequence my financial situation improved and I no longer felt I was being discriminated against. My expulsion from the Party was rescinded at the beginning of 1957, though I did not discover this for some time because no one thought to tell me. But I could sense that I was no longer ostracized: like other citizens I was able to profit from the new freedom of movement and travel abroad – now no longer just within the Eastern bloc. In 1957 I visited Austria and subsequently the Federal Republic.

However, the atmosphere in Poland was becoming increasingly tense, especially for Jews. Small though their number was by comparison with before the war, they had been playing a major role in the public life of communist Poland. Now that the Party – largely also under Soviet pressure – was anxious to contain the followers and protagonists of the 'Thaw', scapegoats were needed. The Jews, who were anyway unpopular – to put it mildly – more especially Jewish intellectuals, were, as always, predestined for that role. The Jews could not fail to notice that, as greater freedoms were granted to the populace, violent anti-Semitic prejudices and resentments were re-emerging. Worse still, these resentments were being ruthlessly fanned by many an official at the top of the Party and, to say the least, not opposed by others. Jews were faced with a new situation – they were able to emigrate, especially to Israel. But would they be permitted, or perhaps even encouraged, to do so by the Polish authorities?

I too was greatly unsettled, and made nervous, by these anti-Semitic attitudes and occasional excesses. I asked myself what I was really doing in this country, the country where I was born but to which I had not returned of my own free will. I never forgot for a moment to whom I owed my survival in the Second World War. But something I had felt on my first post-war visit to Berlin was now, ten years on, even stronger. Much as I had published in Polish – though invariably about German literature – Poland, ultimately had remained an alien country to me. Had it ever been my home? As for communism, I had long ceased to believe in it. Was there any point therefore in living here?

What I had written about German books in Poland in 1957 and 1958 made me doubt, not for the first time, whether I had addressed the right readership. I had published a major study of Hermann Hesse, but who in Poland wanted detailed information about his development and his work? Today I realize what I was not fully aware of at the time: that my articles, albeit written in Polish, were really aimed at German readers.

The Jews, Heine said, *'knew very well what they were doing when, at the fire of the Second Temple, they abandoned the gold and silver ceremonial vessels, the candelabra and the lamps, saving only the Bible to take it with them into exile. Holy Writ became their "portable fatherland".'* Perhaps I only realized in the late 1950s that I too had a 'portable fatherland' – German literature.

The question as to whether or not I should leave Poland and go to Germany was soon eclipsed by another, which engaged all my attention – the practical question of how to manage it. Emigrate to Israel and from there return to Germany? That was very risky. I had to allow for the possibility that the Polish authorities would reject my application and not permit me to emigrate. The consequences of this were predictable: I would very probably have another publication ban imposed on me. Tosia, who now had a job at the Polish Institute of International Affairs, would inevitably be dismissed. It would therefore be very reckless to apply for emigration.

There was only one other way of leaving communist Poland. I could apply for a visitor's permit for the Federal Republic, a 'study visit' – from which I would not return to Warsaw. However, it was unthinkable that the Polish authorities would authorize such a trip for me, along with my wife and our son. My plan therefore was to send Tosia and nine-year-old Andrew Alexander to my sister in London. I would then travel to Frankfurt by myself. This road to the West had one serious drawback: we would not be able to take our furniture, our books or the rest of our possessions – probably not even our winter clothes because this would give rise to suspicion. The whole thing would therefore probably only be feasible in the spring or summer of 1958. We would have to give up everything we owned in our flat. But we were determined to pay this price. And if, despite all the many difficulties, we succeeded in getting to the West – what were we to live on there?

In December 1957 I visited the Federal Republic for the first time. I spent ten days in Hamburg, Cologne, Frankfurt and Munich. I spoke to a lot of writers and journalists. But I did not mention, or even hint, to any of them what I was thinking about every day and every hour that I was in the Federal Republic – my firm determination to turn my back, along with my family, on the communist world as soon as possible and to settle in a West German city. As I was chatting with those friendly and exceedingly obliging gentlemen, I found myself wondering how they – the wealthy publisher, the well-known leader-writer, the famous novelist – would behave towards me if next year I called on them, no longer as the guest from Warsaw, the influential critic of German books in Poland, but as a refugee needing help, as a penniless writer looking for work.

My journey of reconnaissance began in Hamburg. Someone had suggested to Norddeutscher Rundfunk that it might be a good idea to do an extensive interview with me. That suited me down to the ground because the hard-currency allowance Warsaw had authorized for me would not stretch beyond cheap hotel accommodation. Outside the radio building, where I had been asked to wait, I was approached by a very young man, fair-haired and rather shy. He would interview me the following day. Would such a beginner make a good job of it? He soon proved to be experienced and extremely competent. My fee was substantial.

After our recorded conversation he mentioned, casually and, as it seemed to me, confidentially, that he had written two or three 'little

books' not entirely without critical acclaim. That his third book was
a veritable bestseller – this, the reticent young man failed to mention.
Nor could either of us then suspect that only a few years later he
was to write one of the most successful novels since 1945, *German
Lesson*. Disregarding the chilly weather we walked along Rothen-
baumchaussee, after which Siegfried Lenz invited me to lunch at his
home the following day. The food was very good and our conversation
very lively. We spoke about Kafka. I was too busy listening to notice
what I was eating. With the dessert it occurred to me that good
manners demanded that I should praise my hostess for the quality
of the meal. So I said: 'The schnitzel was superb.' That was an
embarrassing mistake. A silence immediately descended on the table.
Because what I had eaten was not a schnitzel, but a steak or a cutlet.
Most embarrassing indeed.

I was to be reminded often of my *faux pas* – for years to come.
But whenever I was mocked for mistaking a steak for a schnitzel (or
the other way round) Lenz, a tolerant man, would defend me. He
would point out that the error was all the more excusable because
such an important topic was being discussed. But Lenz is unaware,
to this day, that he too was mistaken: while I was sitting at his table,
eating and talking, I was not thinking of Kafka at all. I was thinking
of my future in Germany. I asked myself how this young man would
treat me if, in a few weeks' time, I were to turn up on his doorstep
as a suppliant. While talking – not to say, lecturing – about Kafka's
sufferings from his Jewishness I answered my own question. This
fair-haired and somewhat shy young man would lead me to all
the potential employers in Hamburg, to publishers, editors and
broadcasting people. He would urge them to commission work from
me. He would, on my behalf, write letters to colleagues in Cologne
and Frankfurt, in Munich and Baden-Baden. He would advise me in
every respect, he would offer me money, as much as I wanted, without
any fuss. So long as people like Siegfried Lenz were living in this
country I could risk arriving without a penny. I would not go under
here. Whence came my trust in him, considering that I had only met
him the day before? I do not know. But I do know that I was not
mistaken, that everything happened exactly as I had suspected and
hoped. I shall never forget it.

I also know that I hurt Siegfried Lenz and that this hurt remained with him for a long time. In my book *German Literature in West and East*, published in 1963, I naturally devoted a chapter to his work. This contained favourable and respectful comment, but also expressed some doubts. But I could not have acted otherwise; I felt I must not allow myself to be corrupted by friendship. Thus the chapter on Lenz revolves around the thesis that he is a narrator whose talent emerges much more often in the short story and in the novella than in the novel. He was a born sprinter, I said, who was determined to prove himself also as a long-distance runner.

No novelist likes this kind of comment – in spite of references to outstanding examples from the past: Chekhov, Maupassant and Hemingway were also stronger in small epic forms than they were in the novel. Nor did it help that I referred to other contemporary authors of whom the same was true, such as Marie Luise Kaschnitz or Heinrich Böll.

In my chapter on Lenz, should I have concealed my true opinions which, as I believe, are not refuted even by his popular and famous novel *German Lesson*? Over the years and decades I have willingly, on all kinds of occasions, written or spoken about Lenz, but I have been careful never again to discuss his work in any of my literary criticism. Siegfried Lenz understands what lies behind my restraint and I am grateful to him for that.

From Hamburg I travelled to Cologne, where Heinrich Böll welcomed me on the platform like an old friend. He asked me what I wished to see in his native city. To begin with, I said, I wanted to see the cathedral. He was a little disappointed to find that I wanted to do the same as every other tourist. In Cologne, he said, the smaller Catholic churches were more beautiful and more important. After Lenz, Böll was the second person whose existence made me view my future in the Federal Republic with greater optimism.

In Frankfurt I met a rather robust publishing house employee, Siegfried Unseld, who seemed to me a little gauche and unsure of himself, yet at the same time efficient and ambitious. Someone had told me that he was Peter Suhrkamp's rising star and possibly had a great future ahead of him. His visiting card revealed that he had a doctorate. I asked him what his doctoral subject had been. This is always a useful topic of conversation among scholars because it has a liberating effect upon the person questioned and lightens the atmosphere. Peter Suhrkamp's vigorous young protégé told me his subject – Hermann Hesse. We were immediately engrossed in lively conversation.

Everything went swimmingly until I, tempted by the Devil, observed that in political matters Hesse surely displayed a sometimes irritating and even disarming naiveté. His apocryphal story of *Demian* was published in 1919, when there was no such thing as the Nazi Party, but even so it contained important motives that might be understood, or misunderstood, as Nazi. Needless to say, Unseld would have none of this; he protested with growing vehemence.

There were two things of which I was as yet unaware. First, that Unseld owed his contact with Suhrkamp, and thus his post in Suhrkamp's firm, to Hesse. Second, that Unseld even then divided all the world's writers into two categories – Suhrkamp authors and the rest. Certainly, in his conversation with me he did not let a single opportunity pass for promoting the publishing house which would one day be his.

Sometimes I have the impression that Unseld is not an easy person to deal with. Understanding between us may have been hampered by the fact that our interests were similar, yet they were different. My passion was literature, his was the book. He was probably the greatest publisher of German literature in the twentieth century. But great and successful publishers are not necessarily lovable figures; perhaps they cannot be. I do not retract the sentence with which, in 1984, I concluded an article marking Unseld's sixtieth birthday. It was a quotation from Kleist: '*Such a fellow ... I never saw in my whole life.*'

The following day I was at Hessischer Rundfunk, where I met Joachim Kaiser in his small, sparsely furnished office. Our conversation was far from mundane: he instantly understood me and I understood him. After scarcely ten minutes we talked as if we had known one another for years – in those quick shorthand sentences that one had best avoid in public because they usually give rise to misinterpretation. Even then Kaiser had a bad reputation. I had been warned by a colleague that he was exceptionally vain, extremely arrogant and a terrible know-all. He was not yet thirty, but he had already learned that success arouses envy and fame generates doubt. Over the years Kaiser attracted an increasing amount of envy and disfavour. But he also earned a lot of recognition: he is the most frequently plagiarized music critic in Central Europe.

In the late 1970s Alfred Brendel invited me to dinner in London. We started with soup. But before I could take the first mouthful my host remarked with assurance: 'That man Kaiser is a bad critic, isn't he?' How – I asked with gentle irony – had he reviewed Brendel's last concert in Munich? Not too favourably, it appeared.

The evening dragged on, we talked a lot about music, but my host mentioned no other German music critic. A few years later I saw Brendel in Frankfurt. It was again a long evening and Brendel, who had given another concert in Munich recently, mentioned only one German critic in the course of our conversation – Joachim Kaiser, this time very respectfully.

From Frankfurt I went on to Munich. There I met two extraordinary people – a great writer who wished to know nothing about literary life, Wolfgang Koeppen, and a minor writer who was in love with literary life, Hans Werner Richter. In the train returning to Warsaw shortly before Christmas 1957 I knew one thing for certain: I had to do everything in my power to escape from Poland and the communist world.

27

A YOUNG MAN WITH
A MASSIVE MOUSTACHE

My final months in Poland, in early 1958, were a strange and exciting time. Many of our Jewish friends were preparing to emigrate – most of them to Israel. There was a sense of departure in the air, a melancholy atmosphere. These people, who had little or nothing in common with Judaism, all regarded themselves as Poles. And they had all placed great hopes in communism. They had been convinced that, once the many initial difficulties were overcome, a just state would emerge in Poland, a society in which there would be room also for Jews.

They were to be bitterly disappointed. During the first few post-war years the Jews had been urgently needed, but now the authorities would be relieved to see them leave Poland. As yet they had not been expelled – this did not happen for another decade, until 1968, when Jews, among them many Party members and old communists, were described as enemies of the new Poland and pilloried as 'Zionists'. They were fortunate in that there was a country which was prepared to receive them at any time – Israel.

During these months we were frequent visitors to one of the platforms of the depressing Warsaw central station to bid farewell to friends and acquaintances. Some asked us when we would meet again. Even non-Jews, who had no intention of emigrating themselves, were sometimes a little surprised to find that we were making no preparations of any kind to leave Poland – but they did not question us outright. We were careful not to say or do anything that might give rise to the suspicion that we too intended to make a new life for ourselves in the West. If our plan was to succeed, then it must be kept absolutely secret. Not a single person, none of our friends and not even our nine-year-old son, must suspect, let alone know, that we intended not to return from our simultaneous trips as visitors to England and to Germany.

Our intended secret move – even with so little luggage – required a lot of decisions. There was one worry that we did not have, one matter that required no decision – the question of what to do with our money. We had none, we were continually living hand to mouth, always waiting for the next salary cheque, the next fee. This was not pleasant, but we did not let it get us down because most of our friends were in a similar situation.

But how were we going to live outside Poland – even modestly? As a start I wrote a few articles on theatre and literature in Warsaw for *Die Welt* and got them to pay my fees into an account in the Federal Republic. That would be enough to tide us over for two or at best three weeks. But this was not a job I could count on once I was in Germany. Would the West German papers be prepared to print my reviews? I had tried to work a little as a critic in the GDR: the periodical *Neue Deutsche Literatur* was clearly happy to publish some of my articles in 1956 and 1957 and these even produced some feedback. But no one in the West read the *NDL* and standards there were certain to be higher. If I did not succeed in finding work as a critic – a possibility that could not be ruled out – then perhaps I could work as a translator from Polish.

I therefore thought it advisable to acquire a large German–Polish and Polish–German dictionary. Only one was worth considering, a four-volume dictionary published in Vienna in 1904 and long out of print. I bought two of these volumes for a lot of money in a second-hand bookshop in Warsaw, but the other two could not be found anywhere. In the spring of 1958 Tosia spent a short holiday with our son in the Riesengebirge in southwest Poland. The writer Carl Hauptmann, Gerhart Hauptmann's elder brother, had a house in Schreiberhau that was open to the public. On a shelf there Tosia spotted the two volumes I so desperately wanted. Shamelessly she stole them for me, for our future in Germany. I have never needed these dictionaries, but I still have them.

I also endeavoured, during those last few months in Poland, to learn all I could about literary criticism in the Federal Republic.

The daily newspaper *Frankfurter Allgemeine* now had a regular correspondent in Warsaw – Hansjakob Stehle. We were useful to one another: I helped him to find his way about in Polish cultural life and he helped me to understand what was happening in the Federal Republic. From time to time he provided me with West German newspapers, especially with *Frankfurter Allgemeine.*

In that paper I read the arts section and, with particular attention, the book reviews. I thought them beautifully and often even elegantly written – but was it really necessary or appropriate to serve up such simple observations so solemnly and elaborately? With a little luck, I thought to myself, I could probably match those reviewers. This paper did not offer a lot of information on contemporary German literature. I was therefore glad that an opportunity soon arose from a far from ordinary encounter.

In May 1958 I had a telephone call from my friend Andrzej Wirth. He had a problem and he asked for my help. He was expecting a young man from the Federal Republic of Germany who knew nobody else in Warsaw. Something had to be done for the poor chap and he, Wirth, could not manage it on his own. Would I, as a special favour, spend an afternoon with him? I asked suspiciously whether the man was a writer. That – Wirth replied – only time would tell. So far the man had written two plays, one of which had already been a failure and the other might well be before long. My friend did not believe that the young man would ever manage to produce a successful play. Nevertheless he seemed to be talented, though it was too early to say where that talent lay.

The following day towards 3 p.m. I went to the Hotel Bristol, where the German guest was to wait for me. At that time the lounge was empty: there was no sign of a German writer anywhere. Only a single armchair was occupied – but by a person who somehow did not seem to fit in. The Bristol was then the only luxury hotel in Warsaw, occupied almost exclusively by foreigners whose clothes alone set them apart from the Poles. The man in the armchair was, to put it mildly, carelessly dressed and also unshaven. He seemed to be doing something that was not customary in an elegant hotel lounge. He was asleep.

Suddenly he pulled himself together and strode towards me. I was alarmed. It was not so much his massive moustache that frightened me but his glassy-eyed, almost wild stare. Here was a man, I thought, whom I would not like to meet in a dark street: no doubt he had, if not a revolver, at least a knife in his trouser pocket. While I was still engaged in my internal monologue, the young man very politely introduced himself. His glassy gaze was later explained by his admission that he had drunk a whole bottle of vodka with his solitary lunch.

I suggested we went for a walk. He agreed and we set out. Despite his huge consumption of alcohol he was in no way unsteady but strutted bravely along with me. But his response to the many churches and palaces I pointed out to him was tepid. He was evidently concerned mainly with himself and disinclined to make conversation. I thought perhaps I should change the subject and decided to seek his views on the literature now being written in the Federal Republic. As he continued to be monosyllabic and tetchy I tentatively named a few names. Wolfgang Koeppen? Stubborn silence. I believe he had not read a single line of his. Heinrich Böll? A mocking but undoubtedly gentle smile. Max Frisch? Frisch's novels were much too precious for him, my guest. Alfred Andersch? At this name my companion revived. Andersch's then very successful novel *Zanzibar* was something that did not please his writer colleagues. The fleeing Jewess in *Zanzibar*, the young man said, was pretty and elegant. But suppose she had been ugly, with pimples? Would she then have been less deserving of pity? I commended the novel: my guest, it seemed, did not approve of that.

I next tried him on the authors of the previous generation – from Thomas Mann by way of Hermann Hesse to Robert Musil. I got the impression that the young man had little interest in the subject. Admittedly I was not then aware that his excessive intake of alcohol had made him drowsy. How did one make a writer, or someone who aspired to being a writer, come to life? There is a question that loosens the tongue of even the most obdurate candidate. It is: 'What are you working on now, my young friend?' Then he was off. He was writing a novel. This did not surprise me at all: I have come across very few writers in my life who were not in the middle of writing a novel. Would he like to tell me something of the plot? He would. He was writing the story of a man: it started in the 1930s and went on almost to the present day. Who was that man? A dwarf.

Oh. The last time I had read about a dwarf was in my childhood – a fairy-tale by Wilhelm Hauff. What next? I asked, with no great curiosity. This dwarf, he explained, was also a hunchback. What? A dwarf and a hunchback – was that not a little too much? The hunchback dwarf, the young man continued, was an inmate in a lunatic asylum.

That was enough for me; I really did not wish to know any more about the planned novel. And I was beginning to worry about the guest in my charge. His gaze was still staring and wild. One thing seemed certain to me: nothing would come of that novel. Gradually I had lost my taste for talking to this not overly polite West German. I saw him back to the hotel. We parted coolly and probably both privately agreed that this had been a boring and unnecessary afternoon.

No, it was not unnecessary, at least not for me. At the end of October 1958 I saw the young man again. At a meeting of Group 47 at Grossholzleute in the Allgäu he, Günter Grass, read two chapters from *The Tin Drum*, then still a work in progress. According to Hans Werner Richter's recollection I had taken a lot of notes during the readings, but stopped writing after the first few sentences of Grass's prose. That was quite true. I liked those two chapters, I was almost enthusiastic about them; I said as much in a report on the meeting which I wrote for the Munich weekly *Die Kultur*. In fact, I liked them a great deal better than I did the novel as a whole, published the following year, about which I expressed my doubts. One thing I learned at Grossholzleute was that there is no point in listening to what an author tells you about the plot of a novel he is writing. Such accounts, as a rule, are totally useless. Because the boldest and most original ideas as a rule spawn pitiful books, while seemingly absurd motifs can result in magnificent novels.

Later in that same October evening, while we were enjoying some wine, somebody asked me to tell them a little about my experiences in Warsaw during the German occupation. So as not to spoil the mood of those present – after all, they had all been German soldiers during the war, some presumably also in Poland – I chose some innocent episodes. I told them how, during that gloomy period, I became a narrator of stories all of which I had gleaned from world literature. Afterwards Grass asked me if I intended to write about this. When I said I did not, he asked my permission to use some of these motifs. It was not until many years later, in 1972, that he published his *Diary of a Snail* in which I discovered my experiences. He had attributed them to a teacher nicknamed Zweifel, or Doubt.

When we met again on some occasion I remarked casually that I should have a share in his royalties from the *Diary of a Snail*. Grass turned pale and lit a cigarette with a trembling hand. To reassure him, I put a proposition to him: I would renounce all my rights for ever if in return he made me a present of one of his sketches. I could almost hear a load being lifted off his chest. He agreed; I was to chose the drawing myself. To this end he invited Tosia and me to his house at Wewelsfleh in Schleswig-Holstein. He would, with his own hand, prepare a meal for us. I accepted, despite my memory of a soup made by Grass, which I had recklessly eaten in the summer of 1965, on the occasion of the wedding of the Berlin German scholar Walter Höllerer. It had tasted disgusting. I expected the worst. But then a critic must have courage.

On 27 May 1973 we set out for Wewelsfleh. It was not an easy journey: to reach the village one had to cross a river over which there were no bridges. We had to entrust ourselves to a ferryman. Eventually we got there and I was able to choose a sketch. I politely asked Grass for a dedication. He thought for a moment and then wrote: '*For my friend (Doubt) Marcel Reich-Ranicki.*' Almost a play on words.

Then he served us fish. Now I hate and fear fishbones. And I did not realize that there existed any fish with quite so many bones – though I cannot rule out that over the years their number has grown in my recollection. Anyway, it was both a torture and a delight. Undistinguished as he may have been as a producer of soup, he was magnificent with fish. The meal was risky but tasty – and it had no ill-effects whatsoever either for Tosia or myself. Yet it had some consequences: what was left of the fish, mainly its numerous bones, was sketched by Grass the following day. And very soon this fish was at the centre of a novel by him. It was a flounder.

I do not remember whether, in Wewelsfleh, we exchanged reminiscences of our meeting in Warsaw. Fifteen years had passed since then and our lives, our roles and situations had become totally transformed. The unknown and poor young Grass had become a world-famous and, as is quite proper, wealthy author. And I had long become a citizen of the Federal Republic of Germany and, for nearly fourteen years, had been the only regular literary critic of the most reputable German weekly, *Die Zeit*. Moreover, I had – though I was not able to tell this to Grass – just signed a contract for a new post, the most interesting one in the literary world of the Federal Republic – that of Literary Editor of *Frankfurter Allgemeine*.

After my unproductive and yet important and instructive initial meeting with Grass in Warsaw in May 1958 I remained there for only a few more weeks. My mood was far from cheerful, it was rather nostalgic. I have never thought of myself as Polish, not even as half Polish, as I said to Grass in Grossholzleute. So what is it that, to this day, binds me to Poland? It is the language, of which I still have a command; it is the Polish poetry, which I love, the great poetry of the Romantic age and the wonderful poetry of the twentieth century. And, of course, Chopin.

However, it was not my parting with Poland that I found difficult, but my parting with Warsaw. For nearly twenty years I had experienced and suffered a lot there, and also loved. Loved? Yes, there was a long and serious relationship, a friendship with a young woman psychologist. She had meant a great deal to me. The gratitude which I feel, when thinking back to this love affair, is to two women – the other is the one who put up with it. And my marriage? Perhaps it is the real test of a marriage if one partner, aware that the other is involved in an affair, while of course suffering, rejects the idea that it could really endanger their marriage. Tosia and I have both had occasion to test our marriage in this way.

While our parting with Warsaw was sentimental, our sadness was eclipsed by fear – that our travel plans would, at the last moment, go awry. And also by fear about the future. Yet I never doubted for a moment that my decision to leave Poland was the right one. And we were firmly resolved not to be separated on any account. Tosia flew to London with our son only after I had received my exit passport for the Federal Republic. Up to the very last moment we were afraid our passports might be withdrawn. As I watched the plane for Amsterdam, where the two had a stopover, disappear in the distance I asked myself if we would ever see each other again. As soon as Tosia called me from London to confirm their arrival I got in touch with a friend in whom I had full confidence. Even so it was only on the day before my departure that I disclosed my intention to him not to return. I gave him the keys to our flat, where everything that I owned had to be left behind – including my by then quite considerable library.

My passport was for a once-only trip to the Federal Republic and for a stay there of no more than ninety-one days. The German 'Notice of entry' was limited to ninety days. The luggage I dared to take with me consisted of a medium-sized case of clothes, a fairly heavy briefcase with various papers (including all the articles I had published in Poland), a few books including the four-volume Polish–German dictionary, and a rickety old typewriter. *Omnia mea mecum porto.* Yes, I now possessed absolutely nothing beyond this sparse baggage. Of course, I still had 500 Zloty in cash, but no bank in the Federal Republic would accept Polish currency. It was worthless. In addition I had about twenty marks. More than that the foreign-currency department of the Polish National Bank was not permitted to authorize me.

The Polish customs control passed without problems. Only my typewriter was viewed with suspicion and entered in my passport ('Make: *Triumph*'). But when all the checks were done and the officials gone, the train did not move off. There were only a few passengers in the carriages, the platform was totally empty, the silence was eerie. I was afraid. Would I be taken off the train and perhaps even arrested? Fifteen minutes passed, nothing happened; the silence – it seemed to me – was becoming unbearable. But then, quite unexpectedly, without any word of command or other sound being heard, the train started to move. I could hardly believe my eyes. It really was pulling out, quite slowly and quite gently, in a westerly direction.

A few minutes later my luggage was examined once more – this time by two unsmiling GDR officials. I might have said to them what Heine said to the Prussian *douaniers*:

> *Ye fools, so closely to search my trunk!*
> *Ye will find in it really nothing:*
> *My contraband goods I carry about*
> *In my head, not hid in my clothing.*

Once again I had nothing, nothing at all – except this invisible luggage, German literature.

PART FOUR

1958–1973

28

RECOGNIZED AS GERMANS

When, on 21 July 1958, I stepped off the train at Frankfurt central station, I knew that a new chapter of my life was beginning. But I did not know where, or on what, I was to live in West Germany; I had no idea what lay ahead of me. I had decided on Frankfurt as my first port of call because of its central position and also because my mother's youngest brother, a lawyer and horse-racing enthusiast who during the war had served in the Foreign Legion, was living there. He would put me up for the time being.

First of all I had to find a livelihood. I had to go out looking for work. What was I to do? I had no hesitation – I wanted to try to work as a literary critic in Germany, as I had been doing in Poland. Would I succeed? I was by no means certain. I had no choice but to knock at a lot of doors. I had to expect direct or indirect refusals and rejections. But it had to be tried and, if necessary, tried repeatedly. Financial reasons compelled me to act at once – there and then, in Frankfurt.

Was it a humiliating situation? Certainly, but I did not see it that way. To me it was more like a challenge. I was determined not to act as a fugitive or as an emigré in need of help, as a suppliant. I read the literary pages of the principal newspapers and thought: these writers are not all that special. I said to myself: I am going to show them. And, naturally, I had to start at the top. I had no sooner arrived in Frankfurt than I went to the offices of *Frankfurter Allgemeine*. I asked to see the Arts Editor, Hans Schwab-Felisch. He was amicable and helpful. The fact that we had both been at school in Berlin made our conversation easier.

Had I by any chance brought a manuscript along, he asked. I produced one from my pocket. It was an article on the occasion of a new book by Jarosław Iwaszkiewicz, an author highly regarded in Poland. Schwab-Felisch started to read, slowly and carefully – and when he had finished the conversation started afresh. Quite coolly and casually he said: 'Yes, that's OK. We'll publish it this week.' I asked: 'Are you going to cut it?' He replied briefly: 'No.' I told him that in Poland I had always used the pseudonym Ranicki, but that my real name was Reich. How was I to sign my contributions now? His answer was prompt: 'Why don't you do as I have done – adopt a double-barrelled name, but certainly starting with the monosyllabic one – if only for rhythmical reasons.' This made sense to me, and without hesitation I said: 'I agree, put down Marcel Reich-Ranicki.'

He, Schwab-Felisch, was not the man responsible for book reviews; for that I should see the Literary Editor of *Frankfurter Allgemeine*, Professor Friedrich Sieburg. He uttered that name with an ambiguous and ironical smile – or so it seemed to me. Sieburg was then regarded as the most original and most powerful literary critic in Germany – and also, as invariably happens in this business, by far the most controversial. A conservative writer and journalist, he emphatically opposed, if not indeed despised, the more recent German literature, especially if it revealed any left-wing influence.

Sieburg had many readers and many admirers, but he also had no shortage of opponents and bitter enemies. He enjoyed the reputation of an excellent stylist. His writing was melodic and, at the same time, invariably succinct; he had an unusual liking for the informal, but also, on the other hand, for a dignified, slightly archaic manner of expression – which merely intensified the ingratiating effect of his diction. There were all kinds of rumours about his past in the Third Reich. One thing was certain: he had been very well off then. During most of the war he had been in the diplomatic service. I had every reason to mistrust him. It was clear to me that he would be neither a patron nor a friend to me.

Living in Württemberg, Sieburg discharged his duties at *Frankfurter Allgemeine* by post or telephone. As a rule he would only turn up at the editorial office in Frankfurt every other week, always on a Tuesday. Schwab-Felisch had briefed him about me. My talk with Sieburg took place the following Tuesday afternoon. He was wearing an elegant tweed suit; on his hand I caught sight of a beautiful, perhaps too beautiful, ring. He was evidently in a great hurry, almost to the point of discourtesy. It was as if he had come from London that morning, with a meeting to attend in Lisbon that evening and lunch in Istanbul the following day.

He therefore got down to business at once. What, he asked, did I wish to write about for *Frankfurter Allgemeine*? I had noticed, I said, that the books of writers from the GDR – I do not remember if I really uttered these three letters or referred to the 'Zone' – were not reviewed at all in his section. Sieburg was baffled; his amazement could not have been greater if I had accused *Frankfurter Allgemeine* of ignoring Mongolian poetry or Bulgarian drama.

He asked, not without a trace of mockery, what author from the 'Zone' I had in mind. Quite recently, I said, a new novel by Arnold Zweig had been published there. Sieburg's face lit up: Yes, that was certainly 'a literary topic'. It was obvious what he meant: even though published in East Berlin, a work by that author was certainly literature. He nodded encouragingly and asked me to give his secretary the precise title of that particular book and the name of its publisher. When I did so, naming Aufbau-Verlag, I was asked for its address. The people at *Frankfurter Allgemeine* had never even heard of the best and most important publishing house in the GDR. My review of Arnold Zweig's *Time is Ripe* appeared at the head of the Frankfurt Book Fair Supplement of *Frankfurter Allgemeine* in September 1958. Over the next few months I wrote eight more book reviews for that paper; they were all immediately published, uncut.

After my visit to *Frankfurter Allgemeine* I went on to Hamburg to test out my chances there. At the editorial office of *Die Welt*, then probably the most important West German daily, after *Frankfurter Allgemeine* I spoke to the Arts Editor, Georg Ramseger, a slim, wiry man who was clearly anxious to be recognized as an ex-officer. He had been a reserve officer. I remember him chiefly as a braggart. He listened to what I had to say, then stood up, adopting a military posture. After a smart about-turn he opened the bookcase behind him with a theatrical gesture and at random – or so it seemed – picked four or five books. These were novels, all by East European authors. Surely this cannot have been an accident. He handed them to me with a touch of solemnity. Then he said in a rasping voice, in a manner suggesting the officers' mess: 'Write about these books. If your reviews are good, we'll print them. If they are bad, we won't. That's all I can do for you.' I had not expected anything more. For the next three years I wrote book reviews, notes and occasional general literary articles for *Die Welt*.

During my brief stay in Hamburg I received a lot of advice from experts on the literary life of the Federal Republic. Needless to say, all that advice was well-intentioned. Some told me: 'You want to establish yourself here as a reviewer of Slav literatures. Eventually you should become the Pope for East European matters.' Others warned me: 'Don't on any account allow yourself to be pushed into a Polish or Slav corner. Because then you'd hardly earn enough to keep alive.'

A totally different piece of advice was given me by the journalist Heinz Liepman, a former emigré now settled in Hamburg. He told me: 'I've read two of your articles and I can reassure you. You'll make a career all right in this country – but on one condition. You may take it from me, I'm an old hand here. I worked for *Frankfurter Zeitung* before Hitler. This is what it's about: you must change your name immediately. With the name Reich-Ranicki you're lost here. To begin with, nobody can remember it, and secondly nobody will know how to pronounce it. I implore you – do change your name, and do so today.'

I thanked him warmly for his advice and said I would think about it. Three years later – Liepman had by then moved to Switzerland – I met him again in Zurich. We walked along the lake, chatting. Abruptly he stopped and asked: 'Do you remember? When you visited me in Hamburg I advised you to change your name at once – or else you'd be lost as a critic. Do you remember my advice?' 'Yes,' I said, 'of course I do.' And Heinz Liepman said pensively: 'It just goes to show how wrong one can be.'

Siegfried Lenz also gave me some advice – and his was the most important. By writing reviews for *Die Welt* and *Frankfurter Allgemeine*, Lenz argued, I would make a name for myself, but I would not be able to live on those meagre fees, and certainly not able to support Tosia and Andrew, who were shortly to arrive in Frankfurt from London. I should work for the radio, where the pay was infinitely better. He took me from one departmental head to another in Norddeutscher Rundfunk, he telephoned the heads of the evening chat-shows and cultural programmes. He tried to smooth my way everywhere – and in most cases he succeeded.

I had no lack of commissions, so I could actually afford to return some money sent me by my sister, who was not too well off herself, by return of post. Also I no longer had to live with my uncle. Hansjakob Stehle, the Warsaw correspondent of *Frankfurter Allgemeine*, was just beginning his annual home leave in Frankfurt. As soon as he heard that I had decided to stay in the West, without being greatly surprised, he reacted spontaneously – not with words but with deeds. To my astonishment he produced a leather case from his trouser pocket, put it down on the little table between us and slid it across to me: 'Here are the keys to my Frankfurt flat.' I made use of his offer, gratefully, for a few weeks. Often in my life – unfortunately – I have been reminded of the old saying that a friend in need is a friend indeed. My few friends always were, and are, good friends. Hansjakob Stehle is one of them.

A thing that worried me, however, was my residence permit. The German entry stamp in my passport expired in October 1958 and was not renewable because my Polish passport was no longer valid. I could have applied for political asylum. No doubt the official formalities would have been settled quickly and smoothly. But my case would inevitably get into the newspapers here and I would be expected, if indeed not obliged, to write incriminating accounts of life in communist Poland.

However, I had no wish to take part in the Cold War. I had ended my working life in Poland with literary criticism and that was how I hoped to make a living in Germany. I therefore turned to the military mission in West Berlin – there were no Polish consulates as yet in the Federal Republic – where I had once worked myself. Having decided to extend my stay in Germany for professional reasons, I requested an extension of my passport. It is not difficult to guess the outcome – I received no reply at all to this communication. What was I to do next?

Just as Molière's Monsieur Jordain did not realize he was speaking prose, so I too had failed to see the obvious solution – to apply for German citizenship. Having graduated from a German school and having been expelled and deported from Germany during the Third

Reich, I had, as it turned out, sufficient prerequisites for German citizenship. I was entitled to be recognized as a German. It was merely necessary to establish whether I belonged to the German 'cultural sphere'. That was to be established by two officials from a ministry in Wiesbaden, who involved me in a protracted conversation – not about *Faust* or Schiller's ballads, but about Pasternak's *Doctor Zhivago*. This Russian novel, which had just been published in German, was the talk of the day then.

All went well and we, Tosia and I, were recognized as Germans. A few friends of ours offered us their condolences. They could not understand why it meant so much to us to have passports which, at long last, safeguarded our livelihood and which, provided we could afford the fares, entitled us to travel abroad. The critic Willy Haas, who had once been the editor and publisher of *Literarische Welt* and who had returned from exile a few years previously, asked me worriedly what it was that I liked so much about the Federal Republic. I replied: 'First of all, that one can leave it at any time.' Haas was speechless. He had never lived in a country which treated its citizens like prisoners.

With our new passports in our pockets we hurried to the nearest travel agency. We wanted to find out the cheapest way of getting to London as soon as possible, to see our son Andrew, who by then was ten years old. No sooner had we been reunited than he challenged me with a serious complaint: surely I could have let him into our plan to leave Poland. He would not have revealed to anyone that we intended to remain in the West. What difference would it have made to him? I asked. He would, he said sadly, have brought something with him from Warsaw. What was that? His answer perplexed me: in Warsaw he had just been reading Henryk Sienkiewicz's novel *Quo Vadis* and he would have liked to have brought it along with him to finish it. It was not a toy that the ten-year-old mourned, but a book. I bought him a copy of *Quo Vadis* that same day.

29

GROUP 47 AND
ITS FIRST LADY

At the annual general meeting of Group 47 at Grossholzleute in the Allgäu in the autumn of 1958 no one took any notice of me. Most of the participants had not seen each other for a year and were busy talking among themselves. A visitor from Warsaw was of little interest to anyone. However, the German short-story writer and poet Wolfgang Weyrauch sought me out, and not without good reason. When I was in Hamburg at the end of 1957 he had asked me if I could help him. Polish Radio had broadcast a play of his but did not wish to send him his fee in hard currency. I intervened in Warsaw and he received a reasonably generous payment in Western currency. Now he thanked me profusely for my help. We had an animated chat but when I told him that I was not returning to Poland, Weyrauch looked confused, suddenly said he had to see to something, turned away and disappeared. I never saw him again. Other authors, too, especially those reputed to be on the political Left, carefully avoided me as soon as they heard that I intended to stay in the West.

Even before accepting Hans Werner Richter's invitation and coming to Grossholzleute I knew that Group 47 was an exceedingly strange organization. It had no statutes and no board, it was neither an association, nor a union, nor a club, nor a society. There was no membership list. Inquisitive questioners were told by Richter: 'I'm the only one who knows who is a member, and I'm not saying.'

That writers are difficult people, with marked individual and frequently anarchist leanings, I had, of course, long realized. Most of the time there is no point in even trying to group them into a single category. There is nothing they detest more than colleagues publicly reading from their own work. But with Group 47 everything was different: its organization followed no set form, its meetings followed no tradition. However, it was immediately obvious that the proceedings were highly disciplined, that order ruled here, German order. Everyone stuck to a precisely defined, though unwritten, ritual.

The reading of a piece of prose or, less often, of a few poems was followed by spontaneous oral criticism. Anyone attending was allowed to participate in this – with the exception of the author, who was not allowed to contribute a single word. Some found this practice cruel despite the fact that no one was obliged to expose himself to such criticism. Any judgement, as soon as it was made, was questioned by the other participants, especially by the professional critics, and amended, supplemented or revised. General thoughts on literature or even on specific authors were not asked for. One had to stick closely to the text. The atmosphere was serious and tense and only very rarely did it become rowdy.

Most importantly, everyone accepted that Group 47 was headed by a man whom no one had elected but who nevertheless exercised unrestricted power – Hans Werner Richter. He was the group's founder. When I came across Group 47 in 1958 he was fifty – some ten or twenty years older than most participants. He was acknowledged to be a cheerful organizer, a discerning arbitrator, a benevolent yet severe manager, and ultimately a despot. He decided who was to be invited to a meeting and who was permitted to read a manuscript. He, Richter, had the right to interrupt any reading without giving a reason; he decided who could speak in the discussion, when and for how long, and he determined whether or not the Group 47 prize was awarded.

Everybody obeyed him, even long-established and famous authors. Anyone not willing to do so could always just stay away from the meetings. When, at a meeting in Sigtuna in Sweden, in 1964, Richter announced at about lunchtime that they had, for the moment, come to the end of the readings, some of those present rose from their seats. Richter thereupon called out: 'Stop, I didn't say we'd take a break here.' Like obedient schoolchildren everyone sat down again – Enzensberger and Erich Fried, Hans Magnus Heisenbuttel and Hubert Fichte, Alexander Kluge and Jürgen Becker. Richter watched this with obvious satisfaction and briefly announced: 'Break.' This is how he ruled – briskly and with humour, unceremoniously and informally.

What was the basis of his authority? He came from a simple background: his father was a fisherman who evidently was little concerned about his son's education. As Richter himself claimed, he had learned nothing through studying, most things had just come to him naturally. His education, including his literary education, was and always remained scanty. A journalist rather than a writer, he was more interested in politics than in literature. Richter's novels – they have long been forgotten – are all weak. He had no idea at all of contemporary literature. But he was shrewd enough to get good advisers and nearly always followed their recommendations and heeded their warnings. In discussions he would avoid making literary judgements. I never quite escaped the suspicion that the readings, to Richter, were only a necessary evil. Yet it was true that this enthusiastic dilettante loved the whole literary scene, though in a very critical manner, and that time and again he was driven by his enthusiasm for club life. What he needed was not literature but authors: he enjoyed flattering them and handling them with diplomacy.

Was he taken at all seriously as an intellectual by the members of Group 47? Probably not, by most of them. But he was greatly respected – as a chief. Just because Richter did not see himself as an artist, because he could not write well and always remained unsuccessful as an author, he had the time and inclination to organize Group 47, to direct it and keep it alive for many years. He certainly owed his popularity, his importance among the literary public, not to his books or his increasingly infrequent newspaper articles, but to his role as the central and dominant figure of Group 47.

It was probably due to Richter's mentality and attitude that there never was such a thing as a literature of Group 47. The many misunderstandings which the name triggered were due to the simple word 'Group', which suggested a literary movement, a school or a trend. It would have been better if another name, such as 'Forum 47' or 'Studio 47' or 'Arena 47', had been chosen. This Group 47 was not a phenomenon of literature, but an exceedingly important phenomenon of literary life in Western Germany after the Second World War. It was nothing other than a gathering point, a centre of

German literature functioning for three days of the year, yet it was an indispensable testing ground and an annual parade of talent.

The procedure of the meetings was unusual. One did not get a single glimpse of the manuscript to be judged: one had to comment on a literary work that one had merely heard read aloud. I thought this questionable and alarming. But I soon realized that, for such writers' meetings to be able to take place at all, this ritual was acceptable and even necessary.

The listeners followed the text that was being read out – whether good or indifferent – with close attention. Many took notes. I too jotted down key words and individual formulations and soon ventured to ask for the floor. Richter let me speak, and it seemed to me that what I had to say was received with interest and approval.

The next meeting of Group 47 was in October 1959, no longer in a modest tavern but at a castle in the Karwendelgebirge in the Austrian Tyrol. Richter's invitation, that invitation so coveted in literary circles, arrived well in advance. The contents of his letter surprised me: I must be sure to come, he could no longer do without me as a critic. I had introduced a new tone into the discussion, a tone the group desperately needed.

The letter impressed me and almost made me happy. Was Richter trying to flatter me? Not only that. During the months prior to my departure from Poland I had read some of the work of the laureates of the group – Ingeborg Bachmann, Ilse Aichinger, Heinrich Böll, Günter Eich and Martin Walser. I was familiar with the names of many of the authors present at Grossholzleute, such as Hans Magnus Enzensberger and Wolfgang Hildesheimer, not to mention Günter Grass. On the whole I felt comfortable in this group of writers, and certainly not an outsider. And now I had learned from Richter that Group 47 had accepted me. That was how I understood his letter. I had been resident in Germany again for less than a year, but already I knew where I belonged. I thought I had found a kind of refuge. However, with the benefit of hindsight, I had mistaken my situation. Many years later I was forced to accept the fact that this had been a case of wishful thinking.

In his memoirs, published in 1974, Richter thought it necessary to point out that at the 1958 meeting, though this was the first I had attended, I had straight away taken notes. This he commented on in a disapproving manner: '*So acclimatization is that fast!*' He had evidently disliked the fact that I had not behaved like other foreign guests of Group 47 who generally confined themselves to the role of silent observers.

Yet, at the same time, Richter had recommended me to the weekly *Die Kultur* as a reporter of the Grossholzleute meeting in 1958 – no doubt mainly because he expected from me (with justification) a favourable account of the then still very controversial Group 47. In my article I called Richter a dictator, jokingly of course, immediately adding: '*Although we oppose any kind of dictatorship, this is one we gladly accept.*'

This was a remark he could not forget. Twenty-eight years later Richter brought it up in his book *In the Establishment of Butterflies*. He took umbrage, because of a single word in my report for *Kultur* – but it was not the word 'dictator' which annoyed him. He objected to my use of the word 'we': '*Reich-Rancki wrote "we", as if he already belonged, even though I had indicated nothing along those lines.*'

Not until I read this in 1986 did I realize the magnitude of my mistake, my misunderstanding, in 1958. I had been convinced that the Group 47 people saw me as a critic moulded by German literature, one whose exclusive field was German literature. Whether or not I deserved to be a member of Group 47 I did not know. Certainly I could not claim it by right. Nevertheless I believed that I was entitled to a place – albeit the most modest place – in the literary life of post-war Germany.

Shamefacedly I had to admit the embarrassing truth: I had really believed that I belonged in the group 'as a matter of course'. That was the meaning of the word 'we' that I had so recklessly used. '*I invited him again and again*' – Hans Werner Richter recalled – '*and yet he somehow remained an outsider, one who belonged and yet did not belong fully. I cannot explain why this should have been so or why I felt that.*'

Could he really not explain it? Or did he not wish to? In his book Richter mentions that I escaped the Holocaust, but not once does he say that I am a Jew. The book contains three more essays about Jews who were in Group 47 – Peter Weiss, Wolfgang Hildesheimer and Hans Mayer. But in their case, too, one would look in vain for the word 'Jew' or any term alluding to Judaism. Yet these are authors whose personality and literary oeuvre are most definitely marked by their belonging to the Jewish minority and by their expulsion from Germany.

Nothing could be further from my mind than to accuse Richter of even the slightest anti-Semitic sentiments. But he thought it right and necessary to remain silent about the Jewishness of the writers portrayed by him. His attitude to Jews was inhibited and tense even forty years after the end of the Second World War. This, I believe, makes him a typical figure of his time.

During the 1960s the importance of Group 47 steadily increased and its public role became more visible. This was due to two related reasons – on the one hand, the success of many authors who were identified with the group and, on the other, the undeniable circumstance that the group, believed to be on the political Left, was being continually attacked and reviled, most frequently by the CDU, the Christian Democratic Union.

In January 1963 a CDU politician went so far as to describe it as a 'secret *Reichsschrifttumkammer*', the Nazi 'chamber of literature', outside which no writer could work or publish. That was the ultimate public insult. This analogy, which was quoted again and again, and which even led to a court action, helped to popularize Group 47 just because it was so absurd. More than that – it established its myth. This myth, and the enormous success of the group, was further enhanced by Richter's stubborn refusal to let himself be tied down to any kind of theses or postulates, let alone to a programme. Outsiders found it hard to understand that a man who had been politically active for many years, did not see the group as a political organization and consistently opposed any such attempts. When Martin Walser, in the early 1960s, tried to transform it into a Social Democrat shock troop, he triggered immediate and serious conflict with Richter. The outcome was that Walser had to retreat.

Firmly though Richter held the reins, very occasionally he relaxed his grip. Now and again deviations occurred from the unwritten rules. Why did Richter permit them? To loosen up the system occasionally? Possibly. But another reason may have simply been that he always acted just as he pleased and that he enjoyed a little arbitrariness because Group 47 was his personal toy. Thus, to quote only one example, Ingeborg Bachmann was allowed to play a part that was diametrically opposed to everything that was customary in the group, something that was not compatible with its style, something that was conceded to her alone.

I first saw Ingeborg Bachmann at the meeting at Castle Elmau in 1959. She had long been famous: she had, in 1953 at the age of twenty-seven, received the prize of Group 47. Did one realize at the time that she was perhaps the most important German lyrical poet of our century? At any rate, in the group she was treated with special respect. It is also a fact that she fascinated many people, especially intellectuals of various ages. Some newspapers called her the 'First Lady of Group 47'.

At Castle Elmau she read her prose piece 'Everything'. She gave the impression of being nervous and confused. Before she started reading, part of her manuscript dropped to the ground. Three gentlemen rushed forward and quickly picked up the sheets and carefully placed them on her table. There was complete silence in the hall: some feared that the incident had left her speechless. In the end her voice was audible.

But one had to strain one's ears to catch her words. Ingeborg Bachmann read very softly, at times she merely whispered, shyly and diffidently. She was evidently inhibited, helpless and a little confused. Did she find it difficult to speak louder or did she want, by whispering, to compel the attention of those present and to enforce absolute silence? Was she what quite a few people, mainly women, suspected – an actress? This seems to me too strong a term. In spite of her success she was a very unsure and, in some respects, a threatened person, an unhappy person seeking protection in pretence. In the very respectful discussion which followed, three critics (Walter Jens, Hans Mayer and myself) interpreted the parable of *Everything* – each in a different way. Some time later Ingeborg Bachmann gave lectures and ran seminars within the framework of a newly established guest professorship for poetics at Frankfurt University. At one of these events she was asked which of the three interpretations of her story *Everything* had been most to her liking. Her answer, breathed softly, was: 'None.' That was all she would say on this subject.

Ingeborg Bachmann's next reading to Group 47 was in October 1961, at the Göhrde hunting lodge on Lüneburg Heath in northwest Germany. Although once again she was in the throes of a crisis that made it almost impossible for her to work, she was on the way to becoming the *Primadonna assoluta* of contemporary German poetry. Richter therefore set great store by her participation. She alone was to read on Sunday morning, at the concluding session. However, she had only brought with her one rather short poem. That did not prevent Richter from organizing Ingeborg Bachmann's performance. It became, even more so than at Castle Elmau, a votive hour, though a particularly embarrassing one.

She read the poem *You Words*: this has thirty-seven lines and begins '*You words, arise, follow me!*' It is, I believe, an unsuccessful poem, a bad poem. The reading only took a few minutes and was followed by a strange silence. Did this suggest reverence? Or perhaps disappointment? Richter broke the silence by saying: 'I propose that Ingeborg reads her poem once more.' Everyone silently agreed but wondered what would happen next. After the second reading Richter surprised those present with a remark that amounted to an instruction, one that I had never before heard at a meeting of Group 47. 'I propose', he declared, 'that we do not criticize this poem.' But why not? Because of its overwhelming quality? If anyone believed that, then it could only have been the poet herself.

Or were we to abstain from criticism because of the questionable nature of the text? Richter had no intention of justifying his unusual decision. No one objected; neither did I. The silence seemed endless. Eventually the participants got up and left the hall. It now occurred to me that I should have said that surely the poem was not so bad that it should be exempt from criticism. But it was just as well that I said nothing. Because the exemption of the awkward poem from criticism was ultimately not an act of respect – as Richter wished his decision to be understood – but a secret act of pity.

I next met Ingeborg Bachmann in Berlin in 1965. She was rather cool towards me: evidently she did not particularly like what I had written about her and her work in my recently published book *German Literature in West and East*. But even so she made me a present of the libretto of Hans Werner Henze's opera *The Young Lord* which had just been premièred. I asked for a dedication. She thought this a little silly, but if I insisted she would do what she usually did in such cases – open any page of the libretto and, without looking, touch a line with her ball-pen. But when she read the line thus found she looked at me astonished and confused. Clearly the words intended for me did not seem quite right to her. They came from the second act of the opera and ran: '*May the good spirit continue to favour you...*' Ingeborg Bachmann only hesitated for a moment and then wrote: '*May the good spirit continue to favour him...*'

In December 1968 I met her in Rome. I was giving a lecture at the German Cultural Institute on what was then a very popular topic: 'The Role of the Writer in a Divided Germany'. To my surprise Ingeborg Bachmann turned up at the reception given at the German embassy after my lecture. Before long we agreed to leave the party as quickly as possible. We spent a few hours at various bars in the city centre. Strangely enough I cannot recall what we talked about, but I do remember her appearance. Over the three years since we last met she had changed a great deal. Ingeborg Bachmann had visibly aged. Her face seemed to be marked by illness. She was wearing a light, somewhat extravagant, and apparently very expensive dress, which struck me as being too short. She talked pensively and entirely rationally. But her self-control was slightly affected. I never saw her again.

But I had another experience of her, albeit of a very different kind. In March 1971 I was teaching at Stockholm University, but without suspending my work for *Die Zeit*. I was in the middle of reviewing Ingeborg Bachmann's first novel, *Malina*, which had just been published after a gap of ten years. Such dramatic intervals between publications, though usually unreported, are invariably registered by the literary public – nervously by some, sensation-hungrily by others, curiously by all. Because most writers are either in the middle of a crisis or have just overcome a crisis or are afraid of a crisis. That is why they enjoy the crisis of a colleague almost lustfully.

I read the novel as a poetic medical report, as a case history of serious suffering. I read *Malina* as a book about Ingeborg Bachmann. The novel's first-person-singular narrator acknowledges: '*I am ... unable to make intelligent use of the world.*' She speaks of the '*monstrosity of my misfortune*'. I therefore related these confessions of the novel's heroine to the author herself. And, also during the month of March 1971, I saw Ingeborg Bachmann on the screen in my lonely Stockholm hotel room. She was visibly trying not to duck the questions of her polite interviewer. She talked about the 'sickness of men'. She said: 'Because men are incurably sick ... All of them.' In the novel *Malina* I read: *'It's coming over me, I am losing my mind, I am beyond consolation, I am going mad.'*

I was deeply moved. I felt, I suspected, that something terrible lay ahead for Ingeborg Bachmann, perhaps a frightful end, perhaps very soon. A line from an old verse came into my head and would not go away. It tormented me ceaselessly, it became an obsession – the words *'And I desire not to be guilty of it.'*

Although my review of *Malina* was then half-written, I did not feel able to complete it. I would have to tell the editorial office that I had failed in the face of that novel. Dieter E. Zimmer, who was then in charge of the literary section of *Die Zeit*, seemed to understand my decision.

When Ingeborg Bachmann died on 16 October 1973, under circumstances never quite explained, I was asked to write her obituary. It concluded with the confession that I regarded a few poems from her volumes *Deferred Time* and *Invocation of the Great Bear* among the most beautiful written in the German language this century. I asked myself, guiltily, why I had never said this to Ingeborg Bachmann.

30

WALTER JENS, OR
THE FRIENDSHIP

The reason why I felt that I was part of Hans Werner Richter's circle, why I was reckless enough to regard Group 47 as a second home, was because of one of the participants whom I met for the first time at the autumn 1959 meeting. It so happened that he was sitting not far from me. Even before we had exchanged a single word we communicated with one another about the texts that were being read. Time and again our eyes met. During the break we got into conversation. And we remained in conversation for the next thirty years. I am talking about Walter Jens.

His personality, and hence also his work, was moulded by an illness he had been suffering from since childhood – asthma. The consequence of this was that, as he once said, he had to fight for air every day. I do not believe I am exaggerating when I say that this perpetual shortage of breath is perceptible not only in every one of his books, regardless of their degree of importance, but, in a deeper sense, in everything he had achieved. His mother, a teacher, was a modest but also exceedingly ambitious woman who, as I was told, had been determined to transfer her ambition to her son. She was reported to have repeatedly told the sick boy: 'You are a cripple; therefore you must become an intellectual giant.' The need for recognition – which is part of every writer's nature and character – was systematically developed and consistently encouraged in Jens from a very early age.

It was probably this need that shaped Jens's attitude to scholarship and literature, to politics and the Church, and quite possibly to his entire life. The fact that, to the astonishment of his colleagues, he never needed to be asked more than once to take on some honorary post or other, was possibly also due to this recognition mania. It was his good and his bad fortune at one and the same time. Jens soon began to question his decision to study classical philology, made during the war, realizing that this subject could not provide him with the public forum he so desperately longed for and needed. This was perhaps the reason why, as early as 1950, he approached Richter with the request to take part in a meeting of Group 47.

He was invited but he did not fit into that circle. He was the only civilian amidst former Wehrmacht soldiers. Jens belonged to the same generation, but, as an asthma sufferer, had only seen and experienced the war from a distance. *'And this distance'* – Hans Werner Richter recalled – *'made him different from us.'* Moreover, Jens was an academic among all those self-taught persons, an assistant professor of the University of Tübingen.

Richter believed that Jens must have felt like a *'foreign body'* in Group 47. But Richter, normally a good judge of people, was mistaken. Jens was nearly always interested in other people. Inside Group 47, however, as indeed later also in other literary circles or surroundings, his self-absorption was such that he only dimly perceived his relations with the outside world and, because of this, often indulged in illusions. In juries debating the quality of his work, it often struck me that it was the judges Jens considered his devoted friends who most vigorously argued against him. Not infrequently he believed he was being esteemed by persons whose judgement of him was not favourable at all.

Jens simply disregarded the fact that he was isolated within Group 47 and therefore did not suffer from it. Even so he may have welcomed the fact that a newcomer had appeared in the Group who was not only solitary and lonely, but also did not fit into the framework. Here was a stranger holding forth on German literature, whose situation, while not comparable to that of Walter Jens, was nevertheless fairly close. Regardless of all obvious differences, Richter's judgement about me – *'he somehow remained an outsider, one who belonged and yet did not fully belong'* – applied to Jens as well.

Before long a friendship developed between us which, within a few years, we were convinced was indestructible. Whenever we talked critically about Hans Werner Richter Jens would always remind me that the two of us owed him a great debt of gratitude, for without him we would not have met, or at least not for a good many years. On one occasion I suggested to Walter Jens that whichever of the two of us survived the other should write his obituary. Jens immediately accepted this proposal and later, when our paths had long diverged, publicly confirmed it.

It was a highly unusual friendship – not only by far the most enduring and important of my life, but also quite certainly the strangest. We would meet at Group 47 events and later at the Klagenfurt competition for the Ingeborg Bachmann Prize; we appeared together in television chat shows, chiefly in Berlin; now and again I would go to Tübingen to give lectures, and now and again Jens, mostly for professional reasons, would come to Hamburg or Frankfurt; we would jointly, along with our wives, attend the Salzburg or Bayreuth festivals. But all this would only amount to a handful of meetings each year. The real substance of our relationship was of an entirely different nature – long before sex by telephone had been invented, we two practised friendship by telephone.

At first we would call each other once a week, then more often, and eventually, if the occasion arose, sometimes several times a day. Our conversations lasted twenty or thirty minutes, sometimes for a whole hour or even longer. This dialogue, which extended over decades, had a serious purpose: both of us, Jens and myself, were dependent on this exchange of information and views, on this discussion – albeit for different reasons, associated with our individual needs and circumstances.

In Hamburg, where we lived from 1959 until 1973, I was condemned to a solitary working life. Reading was followed by writing, writing was followed by reading. Social contact, which I almost totally lacked, advice from colleagues, which I frequently wanted to hear, friendly warnings and also encouragement, which I urgently needed – all these I found in my telephone conversations with Walter Jens. And what was his position? He was working in Tübingen, among a large number of colleagues, where he was by no means isolated. And yet I suspected that even there, just as in Group 47, he was rather lonely.

Perhaps the most important remark about Jens was made by himself. In an interview published in 1998 he confessed that he was *'a man with fragmented experience'*. He said: *'I cannot do justice to life in its variety. I lack a sense of reality in the broadest sense.'* This statement confirms what his novels, stories and dramatic pieces lack, no matter whether written for the stage, for television or for radio – life in its variety.

He loves toying with themes and theses, with questions and formulas, with ideas, with tradition. But it is not the toying of an artist, but of an intellectual. Jens, rather like me, is a coffee-house writer without a coffee-house. Our coffee-house was the telephone. His element is not the sensual, but the discursive. That is why his epic and dramatic attempts are nothing more and nothing less than illustrations of theses. His most important writings are speeches, essays and tracts.

It is no accident, but logical and revealing, that eroticism is nowhere to be found in his voluminous work: *'I was never really tempted to represent this. No, I didn't want to write about the erotic.'* His adversaries maintain that he could not tell a Bach fugue from the 'Blue Danube'. That is a wild exaggeration. But whenever we came to talk about Wagner – a subject on which Jens was very intelligent and knowledgeable – I always had the impression that he boldly interpreted Wagner's work without bothering about the music: he probably regarded it as a rather distracting, or at least an unnecessary, element.

Jens described his main characteristic as curiosity. That he should be lacking a sense of reality and yet feel a powerful, unconcealed and never-satisfied curiosity, might at first appear to be a contradiction. In reality, however, the one stems from the other and constitutes the basic trait of his being. And it was this basic trait that made him a unique partner in dialogue. Whatever I spoke to him about, he would pose questions that proved that he had listened attentively and that he was genuinely interested in the subject. Only once did he angrily interrupt me: I had asked him if it was raining as heavily in Tübingen as it was then in Hamburg. That he could not tolerate: 'Have you gone totally mad? Are we to discuss the weather like my mother-in-law?' Yet there were areas on which, if I remember rightly, he never questioned me, which remained untouched – my life in the Warsaw ghetto, my experiences in the Polish Communist Party and in the foreign service.

Literature and literary life – these were the topics of our conversations. There were no greetings, no solicitous enquiries (such as how the other person was), we came straight to the point. For instance: 'That article by Böll is not at all bad, but not sufficiently edited.' Or: 'That thing by Andersch is too superficial, he could have saved himself the trouble of writing it.' Or: 'Surely the review of the Bachmann stories is rather mendacious.' There was no need to specify which articles we were referring to in these brief remarks. We each knew what papers the other read.

We often talked about our next books. Jens at one time was planning a monograph on Lessing. It was a fascinating project. Unfortunately he never wrote that book. In another conversation he said to me: 'The time has come for a new book on Schiller. I think I'll do that book.' At once he sketched out its main argument and outline. You can take it from me: it was a wonderful book. Regrettably, however, it never materialized. One of Jens's favourite projects, recurring like a refrain, was about an author both of us admired, each in his own way – Fontane. He spoke about this project passionately and brilliantly. Needless to say, the project never took off.

He took great interest in my plans, occasionally encouraging me to take on projects he had himself abandoned. Such as: 'Perhaps you should write the long overdue book about Fontane.' Whenever I was looking for a title or a striking formulation for a thesis, he invariably took great trouble to advise me. His advice was nearly always good, often brilliant. At a time when we had long quarrelled Jens once said: 'We owe a great deal to each other.' These things are not susceptible to measurement, but I cannot avoid the feeling that I owe him more than he does me.

His curiosity was always focused on people who did not fit into a framework, who had problems with themselves, and on those who suffered and needed help. Alcoholics, pill-poppers and drug addicts, neurotics, depressives, melancholics both interested and irritated him, as did homosexuals, lesbians and men who were impotent. He wished to be accurately informed about their difficulties and complexes. Whatever I was able to tell him about these subjects he gratefully acknowledged. Anyone in trouble could be sure of his compassion. Except that I believe he preferred not to be directly in touch with such people; he was content, as a rule, with second-hand information. Occasionally in our telephone conversations I quoted to him Mephisto's advice: '*My friend, all theory is grey, and green / The golden tree of life.*'

Often he broached a subject that would not leave him alone. He knew that there were men who, despite being married, chose sometimes to sleep with other women. Needless to say, he disapproved of anything like that and abhorred it. In his remarks about such practices, which to him were ultimately incomprehensible, two words invariably appeared: 'disgusting' and 'unhygienic'. If Jens were ever to stray into a brothel – obviously just as a curious tourist – he would, when asked what he would have to drink, probably answer: 'Camomile tea.'

Once, when a Jewish theologian came to Tübingen, Jens invited him to dinner. Such a guest must of course be given kosher food. But what was kosher? Jens immediately phoned an Old Testament scholar at Tübingen University and asked his advice. The man promptly obliged and instructed his colleague about the numerous prohibitions that had to be observed. Jens pedantically noted down all the rules. In conclusion the helpful Old Testament scholar remarked: 'What I've just told you, my dear colleague, was of course the state of affairs some two thousand years ago. But don't you worry. Because nothing has changed for the Jews in the meantime, at least not in this respect.'

Inevitably, during those thirty years of our friendship, there were occasional crises. But we never forgot what we meant to each other. There were certainly periods when my telephone conversations with Walter Jens were the high points of my life. When our relationship was in serious jeopardy in the autumn of 1990, he wrote to me: 'Have a look at the dedication, read my speech about you again – that alone matters …' The dedication he was referring to read: '*For Marcel, in friendship that, never mind turbulences, is indestructible. Walter.*'

But Jens was mistaken, totally mistaken. Our friendship proved destructible after all and let those who so cruelly contributed to its destruction square this with their consciences. And yet Jens's words are not entirely wrong. What has remained indestructible is the memory of the years and decades of this friendship. In his book *Montauk*, Max Frisch had this to say about his relationship with Ingeborg Bachmann: '*We didn't pass the final test too well, either of us.*'

31

LITERATURE AS
AWARENESS OF LIFE

We had no furniture and no curtains, no bedlinen, no towels, no crockery, no radio and, worst of all, no library. The only books we possessed were the four volumes of that large German–Polish dictionary, which turned out to be entirely superfluous. The clothes we had brought with us from Poland were insufficient, the more so as we had had to leave our winter clothes behind in Warsaw. We lived in a single small room in Frankfurt, as lodgers. This was our living room, bedroom and study. There was no desk to write at. Some people later suggested that we had been welcomed in the Federal Republic with a red carpet. That was not so, nor did we expect it. I am still astonished that we did not in the least mind our – to put it mildly – confined living conditions during the first few years in the West.

Instead we were in good spirits, which continued to improve. Contrary to my misgivings I had no problem finding work. The articles commissioned from me were written effortlessly and I kept receiving new briefs. *'Of his application'* – Lessing says in his *Hamburger Dramaturgie – 'every man is entitled to boast.'* So here goes: Over the first six months in the Federal Republic I wrote thirty-eight articles – fifteen for *Die Welt* and *Frankfurter Allgemeine*, the rest for various radio stations.

The dailies, as mentioned earlier, paid exceedingly modest fees for reviews and similar contributions, while the radio paid much better. Nevertheless my published articles were of a markedly higher standard than my broadcast texts. I found it difficult to formulate reviews which would merely be listened to by the public with the same care as those intended for the top papers in the country. In other words: there was only one reason why I worked for the radio – to make the money I urgently needed.

At the beginning of 1959 I proposed to *Die Welt* a series of 'profiles' of the better-known authors from the GDR. As my articles for *Die Welt* – I subsequently learned – were being widely read, the editor agreed to this, then almost outrageous, suggestion – even though such a series was basically thought to be unnecessary. The details were soon agreed. The only difficulty was the title of the series. 'Writers from the GDR' was unacceptable to *Die Welt*, while I disliked the paper's counter-suggestion of 'Writers from the Soviet Zone'. We eventually agreed on a compromise: 'German Writers from beyond the Elbe'.

By June 1959 fourteen profiles had appeared – of Arnold Zweig and Anna Seghers, Ludwig Renn and Willi Bredel, of Peter Huchel and Stephan Hermlin, Erwin Strittmatter and Franz Führmann. My introductory article developed the thesis that a picture of contemporary German literature emerged from the work of those authors who practised their profession east of the Elbe. This banal idea was then regarded as rather bold. A compromise title also had to be found for the anthology which was published in 1960 on the basis of this series of articles, and the chosen one did not seem very appropriate to me: '*There, too, Germany has something to say. Prose from "over there"*.'

This was the first anthology of GDR literature published in the West. Even the Norddeutscher Rundfunk, which enjoyed the reputation of being liberal, would not hear of those three initials. The series of broadcasts which I regularly wrote for the NDR for something like three years had to be called *Literature in Central Germany*.

Of course I tried to be fair to these authors, most of whom were completely unknown in the West, and this may explain why, at the time of East–West confrontation, some commentators described me as a kind of pioneer of a détente policy in the Federal Republic. However, no sooner had my series of articles on GDR authors been published in *Die Welt* than *Frankfurter Allgemeine* gave me notice of termination of our collaboration. I was emphatically assured that this had nothing to do with the quality of my contributions. Was it the slant of my series in *Die Welt* that they did not like in Frankfurt? That too was denied, albeit less strongly.

It was the doing of Friedrich Sieburg, who had anyway tolerated rather than supported me and who had usually refused to let me review the more important books that I wished to write about. He had, I was told, disliked the fact that my work had been appearing, with increasing frequency, in *Die Welt* and been broadcast over the radio. He was afraid – I could hardly believe this – that the competition was trying to build up the new arrival into a counter-figure. He was reported to have told his assistant: 'Don't you worry about him. His type have elbows. He's going to force us against the wall.' His type – what could he have meant? But Sieburg, whom I did not like from the start, was probably right: I did not fit into *Frankfurter Allgemeine* the way it then was. I did not care at all for the paper's pointedly conservative and stuffily dignified attitude.

My style, too, made me an outsider. In a letter to Walter Hasen-clever in 1935, the poet Kurt Tucholsky commends an article in *Basler Nationalzeitung* but describes it as 'written too elaborately (as if from Sieburg's kitchen: where others use oil, they use mayonnaise)'. That is precisely how most texts in *Frankfurter Allgemeine* were then being written – very elegantly, a little ponderously and often over-elaborately. I wrote no better – of course not – but I wrote without mayonnaise.

One thing was clear: *Frankfurter Allgemeine* was not the place for me. So why should we stay in Frankfurt? Hamburg appealed to me more and that was where the bulk of my work increasingly was. That was where *Die Welt* and Norddeutscher Rundfunk were located. Moreover, it was in Hamburg that a paper was published that could claim to be the intellectual forum of the Federal Republic and, simultaneously, the organ of German post-war literature – *Die Zeit*.

This paper, unlike *Frankfurter Allgemeine*, published the work of former emigrés, such as Theodor W. Adorno and Golo Mann, Hermann Kesten, Ludwig Marcuse, Robert Neumann and many others who are by now forgotten. And this was important to me. That was, I believed, where I belonged, that was where sooner or later I hoped I would end up. Meanwhile, the prospects did not look very bright. I did not know anyone on *Die Zeit* and no one on that paper showed any interest in me.

In the summer of 1959 we moved to Hamburg and, without having to wait long, had a small flat assigned to us. We had to make do with two-and-a-half rooms for the three of us (our son had meanwhile rejoined us), including my study. It was certainly a tight squeeze, but we were content. We were better off by the month, especially as my broadcasting fees enabled us to buy some basic furniture. In the autumn of 1959 *Die Welt* surprised me with a commission which I regarded as an honour: I was asked to review a new novel by Heinrich Böll, who by then was the most popular post-war German author.

A few weeks later, what I had wished and hoped for actually came about: *Die Zeit* approached me with the offer of regular work. I was asked to review the most successful first novel of the year, Günter Grass's *Tin Drum*, which had already been enthusiastically acclaimed elsewhere. I supplied a very one-sided review, giving incomparably more space to the young author's brashness and braggadocio, to the weaknesses, inadequacies and flaws of the novel, than to the (by me then certainly underrated) excellence of his prose. My review appeared at once, uncut.

After my articles on the writings of Böll and Grass I was accepted as a critic – not necessarily by the authors, but by the editors, my employers. From then on I wrote simultaneously for the daily *Die Welt* and the weekly *Die Zeit*, not only book reviews but also major critical articles and many glosses. By 1960, though I had only been in the West for two years, *Die Zeit* in a survey listed me among the 'leading book reviewers' in the German-speaking world. From October 1960, my reviews were published under a special by-line: '*Marcel Reich-Ranicki discusses...*' After seven articles had appeared with this by-line, it was abandoned again. Other reviewers, understandably, had felt disadvantaged.

At about the same time *Die Ziet* established a special column for my glosses and shorter commentaries; this was called 'Over here and over there' and appeared in every issue. These pieces produced such a powerful audience response that the Third Programme of Norddeutscher Rundfunk wished to broadcast them every Saturday evening, after they had appeared in *Die Zeit*. In correspondence between Rudolf Walter Leonhardt, the literary editor of *Die Zeit*, and Rolf Liebermann and Ernst Schnabel, the respective editors of the Third Programme of NDR and of *Sender Freies Berlin*, it was agreed in December 1962 that my column 'Over here and over there' would be continued as a 'joint enterprise' of the two institutions. If I am correctly informed, this collaboration between a newspaper and a radio station was the first of its kind.

A little earlier, at the end of 1961, I had handed in my notice to *Die Welt*. At the beginning of 1963 my hopes were fulfilled: I became a regular employee of *Die Zeit*. This meant that I not only received a fixed monthly salary, but also the customary retirement pension and health insurance. My work remained unchanged. I continued to have to deliver articles, but I had no editorial duties. It was said that I was the only person in the Federal Republic at this time who was employed solely as a critic. The year 1963 also saw the publication of my first book in the West, *German Literature in West and East*.

The publicity it generated greatly exceeded both my hopes and my fears. There was a lot of reaction, friendly and unfriendly, enthusiastic and crushing. It was not so much the scale of the response that surprised me as the fact that the proportion of negative, or at least sceptical, judgements was far greater than I had expected.

At the beginning of 1964 I initiated a broadcast series, *Literary Coffee-House*, that was transmitted simultaneously by several radio stations; some of the programmes were also televised. As a rule, these were live broadcasts from the no longer existing Wine House Wolf in Hanover, a place repeatedly mentioned by Gottfried Benn. These took the form of extended conversations with only three participants: Hans Mayer and I were the permanent hosts, the third being a guest, usually a well-known writer or occasionally a literary historian. The discussion was about literature and literary life, but sometimes also about totally different topics, mostly current affairs.

The guests included Theodor W. Adorno, Rudolf Augstein, Ernst Bloch, Heinrich Böll, Friedrich Dürrenmatt, Hans Magnus Enzensberger, Max Frisch, Günter Grass, Hans Werner Henze, Walter Jens, Wolfgang Koeppen, Siegfried Lenz, Hilde Spiel and Martin Walser – an impressive list, as anyone would admit. Each transmission ended with the words from Brecht's *Der gute Mensch von Sezuan* [*The Good Person of Szechwan*]: '*It is a curious way of coping. / To close the play, leaving the issue open.*' When ZDF, the Second German Television, created the *Literary Quartet* in the late

1980s, I linked this up with the *Literary Coffee-House* of the 1960s and kept the Brecht quote as a conclusion.

A final example: a Hamburg secondary school teacher asked me to recommend a few short stories to her that would be suitable for the written school-leaving examination. They should preferably be by contemporary authors. I met her request, but it occurred to me that she was probably not the only teacher who needed such texts. So I compiled an anthology, entitled *Invented Truth*, that remained on the bestseller list for several months. This eventually developed into a five-volume collection of twentieth-century German short stories, the most comprehensive ever.

Am I saying, then, that one success followed upon another? Did I, during my first few years in Germany, move from triumph to triumph? That would be a great exaggeration. Certainly there was nothing triumphant about our everyday life in Hamburg. We continued to live in those two-and-a-half rooms for which I was indebted to the social-welfare housing scheme. My income was still insufficient to subsidize a bigger flat. I still had to work on the seventh day of the week. Even after several years in Hamburg we still felt rather lonely, or, more accurately, isolated.

There was therefore no euphoria – especially as Tosia's health left a lot to be desired. There were serious and prolonged crises. Was I ungrateful? Of course I realized that I had achieved a success such as I could scarcely have expected. The great dream of my young years – to work in Germany as a critic of German literature – was fulfilled. How had I managed to accomplish this in such a short time? I have often been asked this irritating question and have usually avoided answering it. After all, comment on one's own achievements, or even self-praise, is always risky and often disastrous. Heine was quite right when, in his *Confessions*, he said: '*I would be a vain dandy if I boldly emphasized the good things I might say about myself.*' To duck this delicate question entirely would, on the other hand, be a sign of cowardice.

My rapid success – or as some, be it benevolently or snidely, said: my astonishing success – was due to the particular character of my criticism. Consciously or unconsciously I adopted a tradition that was officially outlawed in the Third Reich, a tradition which my colleagues abandoned after the Second World War. Admittedly there was no particular model I tried to emulate. But I learned a great deal from the great German critics of the past, from Heine and Fontane, from Kerr and Polgar, from Jacobsohn and Tucholsky. I am still learning from them, and even more so from the splendid critics of the German Romantic age. I render them my thanks by referring to them and quoting them time and again.

They all worked for newspapers, and that moulded their style. They had the same target audience in sight – the public. This is by no means a matter of course, least of all in Germany, where the discussion of literature is often enough in the hands of scholars and literary people – to which I have no objection. Except that these scholars are writing for scholars and the literary men for literary readers. The public tends to be overlooked. Even without Heine, without Fontane and the rest of them, I would have written predominantly for the readers and not for my own circle. My temperament alone would have ensured that.

The most important thing – Fontane once said – is to be, at least, understood. Anxious to make my sentences comprehensible I often consulted a dictionary of foreign terms – searching for German equivalents that I might use instead of the foreign terms that forced themselves on me. In order to make what I wished to say understandable, I frequently took the liberty of exaggerating and oversimplifying. I am convinced that good critics have always simplified things for the sake of greater clarity, that they have always brought arguments to the edge or the point of the knife, to make them transparent and clear. Whatever I may be accused of, it will not be a reluctance to say 'yes' or 'no'. Many readers were grateful that they could effortlessly tell from my reviews whether I recommended or rejected some new publication.

The great critics of the past therefore stimulated and encouraged me; they influenced me, both with regard to my views on the role and task of the literary critic and to my day-to-day practice. Around 1970 I decided to write a book of profiles of important German literary critics from Lessing to the present day. I wanted to allow myself plenty of time for this project. I originally budgeted for about fifteen articles, which would take some ten years to write. Eventually there were twenty-three essays and they took me a quarter of a century to complete. My book *Advocates of Literature* was not published until 1994.

Somebody suggested that, while this volume may contain twenty-three profiles, concealed within them was a profile of the critic who, consciously or otherwise, had produced a self-portrait and a confession – the image of the author. I enjoyed reading that. If you write about other people you cannot avoid writing about yourself at the same time. This is undoubtedly doubly true of the critic who, writing about other critics, nearly always reveals what he thinks of his colleagues – and hence also of himself – what he expects and demands.

But there is an entirely different factor that may have contributed to my success as a critic. At the risk of being accused of arrogance I must say here what I profoundly believe: literature is my awareness of life. That, I believe, emerges from all my views and judgements on writers and books, perhaps even from mistaken and erroneous ones. Ultimately it is this love of literature, this occasionally monstrous passion, that enables the critic to practise his profession, to discharge his duty. And sometimes it may well be just this love that makes the persona of the critic bearable, and in exceptional cases even attractive, to others. It cannot be repeated too often: without love of literature there can be no criticism.

32

CANETTI, ADORNO, BERNHARD AND OTHERS

My situation was good. Some of my colleagues even thought it enviable since I was employed by *Die Zeit* but allowed to enjoy all the privileges of a freelance author. In point of fact, I was not required to go to the office or to attend conferences. I did not have to judge or edit manuscripts, I did not have to read proofs. I was only expected to write – nothing else. And it was entirely up to me how much or how little I wrote: I received my salary regardless.

These were indeed privileges. I owed them entirely to Rudolf Walter Leonhardt, the Arts Editor of *Die Zeit*, who had not allowed his passion for literature to rob him of his common sense. He was an enthusiast with a tiptoe approach. I was supported by Leonhardt because he liked my kind of literary criticism and also because the editorial office soon discovered that my articles were pushing up the paper's circulation.

I worked not only as a book reviewer on *Die Zeit*; now and again I was also allowed to review plays. I chiefly discussed the premières of works by German playwrights, such as Peter Weiss, Günter Grass, Martin Walser and Tankred Dorst. And when I felt like commenting on a new Shakespeare production or a Chekhov première, the Theatre Editor of *Die Zeit* was always generous: he, Hellmuth Karasek, frequently passed on to me attractive tasks he had intended to take on himself. Occasionally I also wrote about operas, mainly about Wagner and Richard Strauss.

However, my domain was, and remained, literary criticism. Even though I might write about the Russians from Isaac Babel to Alexander Solzhenitsyn or, far more often, about the Americans from Ernest Hemingway to Philip Roth, literature in the German language was always at the centre and in the foreground. It was agreed with *Die Zeit* that I could have the pick of books by German authors and only afterwards would the remaining titles be assigned to other reviewers. I have no complaints: the editorial office strictly observed this agreement.

Only once, in 1969, was another reviewer given a book I had wanted to write about – moreover without my being consulted. This annoyed me, and although I was not particularly interested in this relatively unimportant book (it was Reinhard Letta's slim prose volume *Enemies*), I immediately reviewed it elsewhere – in *Der Spiegel*. This was intended as a warning to *Die Zeit*. I freely admit it: I was not easy to work with.

I was therefore free to write about whom I chose. I wrote about the contemporary authors of what was then the older generation, the ones born before the First World War – Anna Seghers and Marie Luise Kaschnitz, Arnold Zweig, Elias Canetti, Herman Kesten, Friedrich Torberg, Wolfgang Koeppen, Max Frisch, Hans Erich Nossack and Peter Huchel. I analysed the works of authors of the middle generation – such as Heinrich Böll, Günter Grass, Friedrich Dürrenmatt, Arno Schmidt, Günter Eich, Peter Weiss, Alfred Andersch, Wolfdietrich Schnurre, Erich Fried and Wolfgang Hildesheimer. But I venture to point out, in all modesty, though with a hint of satisfaction, that I never devoted a single article to a famous, frequently admired and highly praised German prose writer. I am referring to Ernst Jünger. His work is alien to me. I feel entitled to keep silent.

I also remained silent on another, totally different, occasion. I never wrote anything about Nelly Sachs and her poetry. But I visited her in Stockholm in February 1965. I had been warned by friends at the Goethe Institute that our conversation would be difficult and not very productive. Her mental state, they said, was alarming and her soundness of mind rather limited. I was not put off. Nelly Sachs was still living in a working-class neighbourhood of Stockholm, in the small flat on the third floor of a tenement block that had been assigned to her after her escape from Germany in 1940. Even after receiving the Nobel Prize in 1966 she remained in that shabby flat – until her death in 1970. The small, delicate and graceful lady could have been my mother. She welcomed me cordially and unaffectedly, as cordially as if we had known each other for years.

Asked about her health, she answered me immediately and at great length. It would not be too bad, except that she was being persecuted and terrorized by an illegal German Nazi organization in Stockholm. Those Nazis, meanwhile, were being watched by the Swedish police so that she, Nelly Sachs, was no longer in immediate danger. However, the Nazi organization was continually disturbing her sleep by means of radio waves, at times making it totally impossible. And there was nothing the police could do about that. Insomnia was her most terrible torment and she would have to suffer it to her dying day – she was sure of that.

She told me all this quite calmly. I was at a complete loss for words. I do not know whether she had been informed that I had grown up in Berlin or about my subsequent experiences. But she asked not a single question; she did not wish to know anything about me. Nelly Sachs was concerned only with herself. As soon as she moved away from the subject of her persecution to some other topic she spoke simply and rationally. When I took my leave after about an hour she gave me one of her books, writing into it two lines of verse of hers which, during our conversation, I had quoted: '*In place of a homeland / we hold the transformations of the world*'. I had originally planned to write a short account of my visit to Nelly Sachs for *Die Zeit*. But I was no longer capable of it, I capitulated.

I also capitulated in the face of the first two prose works by Thomas Bernhard. I read his 1963 novel *Frost* with mixed feelings: I was fascinated and impressed, but I was confused. A major talent? I was not quite sure. A critic who cannot make up his mind – I thought – must come to terms with his uncertainty and should not confront the public until he was able to commit himself one way or the other. With Bernhard's next book, *Amras*, I was faced with the same dilemma. When I now reflect what it was that stopped me from writing about him, a single word comes to mind – fear. I was afraid that I might not be able to do justice to his prose. Just as I had hesitated for many years before writing about Kafka, so, for the time being, I withdrew from Thomas Bernhard's books.

But when I had read his story 'The Carpenter' in *Neue Rundschau* in 1965, my conflicting attitude to the young Austrian writer was

314

finally overcome. This work of fiction, as well as another that was published soon afterwards under the title 'The Coin', gripped me more than Bernhard's earlier books. Next to appear was the novel *Distress* and the small but weighty collection *Prose*. Was I no longer afraid of Bernhard? Was I now up to writing about his work? It is doubtful if one can be up to it at all. Goethe said to Eckermann in 1827: *'The more incommensurable and ungraspable to the mind a poetical production is, the better.'* I do not like this remark. Did Goethe mean this to be taken literally? Or did he merely wish to suggest that the incommensurable and ungraspable might well benefit the author and his imaginative writing?

Thomas Bernhard felt, and knew, incomparably more than he was able to put into words. That was why he was able to express that which is in his books. But his work is marked by stark and haughty imperfection. No doubt he would have rejected as an absurd or arrogant expectation the idea that it was his task to deliver something perfect. His business was the fragmentary – and an 'exaggerated fanaticism'. His prose is oppressive even when he narrates with seeming lightness and cheerfulness. The more I thought I understood it, the more it disquieted me.

My conversations with Bernhard, however, were neither oppressive nor disquieting; they were usually relaxed and pleasant chats. I met him repeatedly – in Berlin, in Frankfurt, in Salzburg and, once, in August 1982, in Ohlsdorf in Upper Austria. On that occasion he was exceedingly friendly. You can guess the reason: I had written enthusiastic reviews of his autobiographical books, *The Cause*, *The Cellar* and *The Breath*. We talked for several hours but we did not once mention what either of us was then working on. I did not wish to know anything about his current work and he asked me no questions concerning literature or criticism. Bernhard was one of those many writers who created literature – magnificent literature at that – but had no particular interest in it.

We talked a lot about music, which Bernhard loved without – as I believe – having any deep attachment to it. His musical taste was quite good, his often apodictic judgements seemed to me original and quaint. I noticed, however, that various – by no means obscure – composers were unknown to him. During that part of our talk I had my tape recorder running, which did not worry him in the least.

What Bernhard said to me was amusing, but not, I believed, suitable for publication. I have wiped that tape.

In his house in Ohlsdorf the walls were distempered brilliant white, while the windows and doors were surrounded by jet-black bands. His home was uncanny. Anyone so disposed can also find this harsh colour contrast in his writings. They presented a polarized tension, especially between melancholia and humour. Bernhard was a laughing melancholic, a frightening jester. He was a merry poet of distraction and destruction, of decline and fall, of dissolution and extinction.

About the time when I began to write about Thomas Bernhard, during the 1960s, I often concerned myself in *Die Zeit* with the books of younger authors, of writers still almost or totally unknown – for instance Reinhard Baumgart, Jurek Becker, Peter Bichsel, Wolf Biermann, Rolf Dieter Brinkmann, Hubert Fichte, Alexander Kluge, Adolf Muschg, Ulrich Plenzdorf, Gabriele Wohmann and Wolf Wondratschek. These were nearly all benevolent, commendatory articles.

Even so I soon enjoyed the reputation of a wild man hitting out in all directions. In these circumstances it was perhaps not a very good idea to bring out a collection of my negative reviews under the title *Nothing but Drubbings*. By the way, these were never about books by beginners, but by unquestionably established authors. The book concluded with the sharpest and most radical condemnation of my own work – written by Peter Handke. The whole thing was meant to be understood as a contribution to the debate on German literature and criticism during those years and as a plea for that negation which conceals nothing other than emphatic affirmation.

The book was very successful; it appeared in four different editions and in many reprints. But it achieved something I had not wished: instead of abolishing prejudices, it hardened them. Henceforth, when my name was mentioned in papers or periodicals the title *Nothing but Drubbings* was added in brackets. Gradually, even though I had published several other works that seemed more weighty to me, this book became my trademark, not a very friendly one. Even though I had written a great many positive reviews and even though, while reading those old reviews, I often asked myself whether I had not too often praised books that hardly deserved it, I continued to be regarded as a specialist of damning reviews. A sketch by

Friedrich Dürrenmatt shows me, armed with an outsize pen, crouching on many heads, presumably those of my victims. It is titled 'Ossiary'.

But I am not complaining about this – if only because I have myself often characterized writers with formulas. They too were not exactly pleased to be given labels by me. Not surprisingly I felt a need to supplement my book *Nothing but Drubbings* by a counter-volume: *Nothing but Praises* appeared in 1985. In addition to some birthday articles it mainly contains addresses given by me on the occasion of prize-givings and various anniversaries. It ranges from Ricarda Huch to Hermann Burger. However, despite this book, I am still regarded as a literary executioner.

As I have written many books and edited an even greater number I have often had occasion to read criticism of my own work. This has included – not unexpectedly – a great many damning reviews which – again not unexpectedly – left nothing to be desired in terms of sharpness and aggressiveness. I am all too aware of the pain and the suffering which can be caused by critical reviews, and I must therefore be prepared to accept acts of revenge and outbursts of hatred from aggrieved authors. Except that some of these seem to me to have gone beyond the bounds of human behaviour. Perhaps they are worth mentioning as occupational hazards.

In 1965 I hailed the young author Rolf Dieter Brinkmann in *Die Zeit* as a new talent in German prose writing. In 1968 I enthusiastically praised his first novel *No One Knows Any Longer*, also in *Die Zeit*. In November 1968 the two of us, Brinkmann and I, were sitting together on the platform of the Academy of Fine Arts in Berlin. I had met him for the first time immediately prior to this event. To my surprise he glared at me furiously. I had no inkling that he was planning to cause a scandal. Our discussion had not been going on for long when, without any obvious cause, he screamed at me: 'I ought not to be talking to you at all, I should have a machine-gun here and shoot you down.' The audience was outraged and angrily left the hall. Brinkmann had achieved the scandal he had obviously intended. His publisher's editor tried to pacify me: 'Surely you are a father figure to him, and that includes patricide – you should understand that.' I did not.

Another writer who wished me dead, or at least would not be

sorry if I were, was Peter Handke. In his book *The Lesson of Sainte-Victoire*, published in 1980, he portrays me as a barking and slobbering *'leader of the pack'* in whom *'there was something damned'* and whose *'killer lust'* had been further enhanced by the ghetto. The very remarkable lyrical poet Christa Reinig similarly longed for and pictured my death – moreover in elaborate detail. Let me make it quite clear: I have never said a single word against her, but quite a few in her favour. In Reinig's *The Woman in the Well*, published in 1984, her friend complains that he cannot go on writing because at every sentence he finds himself wondering how I would judge his book. He was supposed to finish it in a year. He is being reassured: *'I'm telling you, by then Reich-Ranicki will long be dead ... Maybe some hidden illness is gnawing at him. A cancerous tumour, a heart attack, some mental disease. All that can erupt next month and then you'll be free to write as you please. He laughs at my naiveté. No, all this is quite out of the question. I say: In that case he'll have a road accident, he'll be run over or crushed by someone overtaking on the inside.'*

The history of literary criticism, and not only of German literary criticism, shows that those who frequently damn the work of others are themselves very often attacked and damned. Some might view this as a profound kind of justice. Certainly the literary business has always been perilous. Anyone who practises it seriously is in great danger and he who sows the wind must expect to reap the whirlwind. I am therefore not complaining. But I will not conceal the fact that I have been shocked by the brutality of some of the observations directed against me.

Was the brutality of those writers due to their sensitivity, to their vanity? Thomas Mann had the self-centredness of a child, the touchiness of a prima donna and the vanity of a tenor. But he believed that egocentricity was the prerequisite of his productivity: only the man who took himself seriously would torment himself. He had no hesitation in claiming that everything that *'seems good and noble, spirit, art, morality'* stemmed from *'a human being taking himself seriously'*. Because writers experience everything more strongly and intensely than other people, they must torment themselves more than others. Their need for continual self-confirmation derives from this. This makes sense to me – but I find it surprising that an author's

318

success, even worldwide success, does not in the least lessen that need.

Goethe's relative failures – from *Iphigenia* to *Elective Kinships* – evidently hurt him more than his truly international triumphs delighted him. Thomas Mann was hungry for praise, thirsting for recognition. He insisted that his publisher, his secretaries and his family concealed from him any critical statements about his work. He regarded the slightest criticism as a personal insult and indeed a monstrous affront.

What do writers hope for from those who comment on their work in public? When, in 1955, I published something about Arnold Zweig and quite needlessly also sent it to him, he thanked me with an anecdote: '*Heinrich Mann, Arthur Schnitzler and Hugo von Hofmannsthal are walking together by the Starnberg Lake, talking about literary criticism. Hofmannsthal, asked what he thought of book reviews, gave the classic reply in his Viennese accent: "Praise is what we want, praise is what we want, praise is what we want."*' Georg Lukács devoted an extensive essay to the subject, 'Writer and Critic'. After some subtle and often highly involved reflections he surprises his readers with this discovery: '*A "good" review for an author is usually one that praises him or damns his rivals, a "bad" one is one that criticizes him or promotes his rivals.*'

Martin Walser, one of the most intelligent essayists of contemporary German literature, and also one of the most stimulating and eccentric of intellectuals, Germany's cleverest chatterbox, knew very well what he was talking about when he bluntly declared that the prototype of the author was the Egyptian shepherd Psaphon who had taught the birds to sing his praises. Touchiness, vanity and self-importance – I have observed all these weaknesses in poets such as Erich Fried and Wolf Biermann, whose talent was surpassed only by their egocentricity. Nor are they easily overlooked in an author as unusual as Elias Canetti.

I made Canetti's acquaintance in Frankfurt in 1964: we agreed to have an extensive conversation in London, where he had been living for many years. Shortly afterwards I came to London and immediately telephoned him. He seemed pleased and was exceedingly polite, but first of all wanted to know how long I would be staying. When he learned that I would be in town for a whole week he was even more pleased. The point was, he explained, that although he was in London at the moment, he had just withdrawn to a secret hiding-place. He would therefore be grateful if I would be good enough to phone again in five days' time, between 6 and 7 p.m., because only then did he pick up the receiver.

My phone call, Canetti requested, had to be done in a particular manner. Having dialled his number I was to let his instrument ring five times and then put down my receiver. Then I was to dial his number again. After the fifth ring of this second call he would answer. This was his arrangement with his friends. Other calls he would leave unanswered. I confirmed that I would do as he requested. But I wanted to know how it happened that, though I had just called at a different time of the day, he had answered after the very first ring. I do not recollect his reply.

When I visited him in his modest and far from spacious flat in Hampstead, Canetti immediately impressed me. He was condescending and courteous and above all talkative. What struck me most forcibly was his charisma. I have occasionally encountered a similar aura with actors, but only rarely with writers. But actors need a role, their lines, to exercise their charisma. In everyday conversation it soon disappears. Canetti was a conversational type. No sooner had he begun to talk and to lecture than I was enchanted by his personality. This short, portly, but by no means ponderous gentleman proved an excellent *causeur*. His sovereignty was authentic, yet a touch of decent play-acting was unmistakable. A factor in this may have been that his German was marked by the most attractive Austrian accent. To exaggerate a little: regardless of what Canetti was saying, it was a pleasure to listen to him.

Needless to say, we talked about literature. He had read scarcely any of the contemporary writers. He admitted his ignorance with a touch of defiance and haughtiness. Of the great German-language authors of the first half of the twentieth century he acknowledged only a few – but about those, especially Kafka and Karl Kraus, he talked most stimulatingly. Polite though Canetti was, it soon became clear that listening was not his strong suit – perhaps because he had so much to say and because, contrary to the impression he was trying to convey, he did not have all that many people to talk to in London. As soon as he started to talk about his work and his life, as soon as he focused on his own person, sketching it for his visitor, a certain solemnity became perceptible. No one had as yet read large portions of his diaries and various notes written years ago, he explained; and for reasons of security, to block access to importunate journalists and critics, and to other inquisitive persons, they were written in a secret script.

I asked myself whether anyone was really all that interested in those notes or whether, as with his drill for telephone callers, this was not – to put it disrespectfully – merely pomposity. In his personal profile there were elements that, at first sight, seemed incompatible – a smugness he was unable to conceal and an air of loneliness in which he had evidently taken refuge.

When we first met, in December 1964, he was still an outsider among outsiders in Germany. Only a few of his books had been published and they had not found many readers. Those numerous German and Austrian prizes and titles with which he was honoured – not to mention the Nobel Prize – were still in the future. The role of a temporal seer, which he subsequently acted with such charisma, was not yet his, nor did anyone in Germany realize that this author's work and personality would attract a cult following.

We parted very cordially. No doubt Canetti was hoping to have found a new member of his but slowly growing congregation and I had undeniably succumbed to his charisma at our first meeting. However, this initially strong effect markedly faded over the next few years, and not without reason. We met a few more times, but our relationship never developed into friendship.

In 1967 I was preparing an anthology of the judgements and commentaries of many writers, philosophers and journalists on Heinrich Böll. As always in such cases, there were refusals as well as acceptances. Jaspers and Heidegger were unable to participate, but many others did – from Adorno and Rudolf Augstein by way of Lukács and Ludwig Marcuse to Martin Walser and Zuckmayer.

I also asked Canetti to contribute a few words about Böll, however brief. Jaspers had written to me that he had not read a single line of Böll and that 'in order to do anything at all one has to confine oneself to what is important to one personally'. A similar reply, though rather different in tone, came from Canetti. In his letter he said: 'I am in the embarrassing situation of an ignoramus who has not sufficiently concerned himself with Böll's work. Strictly speaking, I should feel ashamed before his seven million readers who know him better than I do.' The irony was unmistakable: Canetti was hinting that I had made a demand that was not quite worthy of him.

Following the almost euphoric initial meeting our relations noticeably cooled, especially as Canetti was not happy with my first review of one of his books, the small and attractive volume of poetical prose *The Voices of Marrakesh*. I had, he said, praised a secondary piece of writing of his at the expense of his principal works – which was quite true. More than six years had elapsed since my unsuccessful attempt to enlist him as a contributor to the Böll anthology; I had meanwhile taken over the literary section of *Frankfurter Allgemeine*. The one-hundredth anniversary of the birth of Hugo von Hofmannsthal was approaching and I was hoping to observe it in the paper in a suitable manner. In spite of his rejection in 1967 I ventured once more to involve Canetti, hoping that Hofmannsthal, unlike Böll, was a subject that met his demands. I wrote him – if I remember correctly – an obsequious letter. I admit that I was surprised by his prompt reply. He had, he said, just returned to London from his 'rural hideout' and found my letter: 'I was more than a little astonished by it. I thought you realized that I do not write for newspapers ... I can write only what I have to write from inner necessity and cannot accept suggestions from outside on what to write. The idea that I would write something in connection with some one hundredth anniversary makes me laugh ... Least of all about Hofmannsthal, who never meant anything to me and who, on the contrary, I believe is boundlessly overrated!'

I was tempted to remind Canetti that Heine and Fontane had very effectively and very often worked for newspapers, as had Döblin and Musil. But in the end I thought it wiser to forgo a correspondence about this subject and about Hofmannsthal's work. Instead I reviewed two volumes of Canetti's spaciously conceived autobiography, *The Tongue Set Free*, dating from 1977, and *The Torch in the Ear*, dating from 1980. Of course I said in those reviews that, thanks to its literary culture and human maturity, Canetti's autobiography far outstripped most, or nearly all, books then published in the German language.

What caused me misgivings was the fact that Canetti evidently did not in the least resist the need to stylize his own past or to create his own mythology. Nor could I help wondering whether the calm which disturbed me and the composure which irritated me had not been bought by a deliberate rejection of all that concerns and alarms us today. Was it due to his self-love and his vanity, to that 'taking oneself seriously' to which Thomas Mann attributed such fructifying significance? I felt perplexed by a sentence that struck me in Canetti's memoirs, one that could scarcely be surpassed in its honesty. Most of the poets he had come across, he wrote, had displeased him. This might be due to the fact – Canetti admits – *that perhaps one would like to be the only one*.

Accusations of self-love, vanity and self-importance – to an exceptional degree – have also been levelled at a man who, despite a number of obvious differences, might well be compared to Canetti – Theodor W. Adorno. The two were much the same age (Canetti was born in 1905, Adorno in 1903), both were Jews and emigrés, both were personalities of extraordinary breadth and stature, and both had their widest audience in the Federal Republic. Adorno died unexpectedly at the age of sixty-five.

Why did he die so young? A silly question, but justified in this case. Whether he was one of the most important thinkers of our era I cannot judge. But there is no doubt that he was one of the most successful German philosophers and cultural critics. The enormous impact made by his writings made him happy. At the same time he suffered a lot, especially in the final years of his life. The more famous he became, the more often he was attacked and occasionally derided, the more he had to suffer from the envy and malice of many of his contemporaries.

The last major attack on him occurred in 1963. A young man, who was apparently unable to understand Adorno's ideas, let alone discuss them, was out to compromise him. He sought and eventually found what he needed: a review published by Adorno in 1934 in the *Official Bulletin of the Reich Youth Leadership*, in which the critic commended choral settings of poems by Baldur von Schirach and also, again positively, quoted a formulation by Goebbels. The denunciation hit home. Now all those who envied Adorno gloated and jeered – those who believed that he had wronged them, those who felt that he had ignored them, those who had long wanted their revenge. It was the hour of the disregarded, the failures, the resentful. Of course that 1934 article was not admirable, but anything that needed saying about it had already been said by its author himself.

Worse than the two or three objectionable sentences, according to Adorno's detractors, was the triumph of repulsive malicious pleasure, of naked infamy and – how could it be otherwise – of plain anti-Semitism. One was reminded of a verse by Hoffmann von Fall-ersleben, words that cannot be quoted too often in Germany: '*The greatest scoundrel in the land / is and remains the informer.*' The attacks on Adorno abated little over the next few years. Every effort was made to make his life difficult. But no matter how vulnerable he was, he refused to be put off, he continued his work – to the benefit of us all.

I saw Adorno repeatedly – in Hamburg, in Vienna and, above all, in Frankfurt. Every conversation, even a casual one, was remarkable, though our first encounter left the deepest mark on me. This was on 6 July 1966 in the Hessischer Rundfunk. He took part, as a guest, in a broadcast of the *Literary Coffee House*. The recording – this was his condition, which we accepted – had to take place in Frankfurt, at 10 a.m. Adorno arrived punctually and was most polite, perhaps too polite. But he surprised Hans Mayer and me with the sad news that he was scarcely up to a discussion that day. The previous day had been exceedingly tiring for him: in order to last through the seminars and examinations he had taken a stimulant. Now he was totally exhausted and therefore begged us to be good enough to do all the talking; he would confine himself to a few cues and occasional observations. This sounded like the announcement of a famous singer that, at the dress rehearsal, he would unfortunately only be able to 'mark' Lohengrin.

Hans Mayer and I were firmly resolved to oblige and help the scholar in his trouble. I therefore put a simple question to him, one that he must have welcomed. Even a person who had never read any of his writings was surely acquainted with his (usually misquoted) remark that to write poems after Auschwitz was barbaric. I wanted to know what he had meant by that. Adorno replied promptly and not at all curtly. The longer he spoke the better I liked his explanations. I understood everything – and this was a sensation that I could not always claim when reading his writings.

I do not remember the further course of the conversation. One thing was certain: Mayer and I, who are not exactly known for our reticence, hardly said a word: our guest had evidently forgotten that he was tired out. Adorno would not be slowed down or interrupted.

No sooner was the recording over than he hastened to ask us ingenuously: 'Was I good?' Yes, in fact very good. Vain as a tenor? Certainly. But I have, over the years and decades, encountered any number of vain authors whose achievements were merely indifferent. Why should one deny a little vanity to a great man in whose debt we all are?

There was a marked difference between the vanity of Adorno and that of Canetti. Canetti's was linked to his ambition to act as a categorical accuser and sole judge of the world. Of course the symbolical role that he was aspiring to, and perhaps already trying to furnish with sacerdotal and majestic dignity, escaped more accurate definition – being located in the no-man's-land between literature and philosophy, art and religion, between severe criticism of the epoch and exalted life. Canetti did not mind at all being praised as an almost archaic and mythical figure, as the 'prophet from Ruse'.

That was not the case with Adorno. He too wanted to be celebrated – but primarily as an intellectual and scholarly authority. He too wished to have followers. One was not to follow him blindly, however, but with critical admiration for his critical thought. Canetti's self-love sometimes turned to transfiguration. Adorno was not interested in that. His element was not the sacral, but the peacock nature which he made no attempt to conceal. His participation in the *Literary Coffee House* was a demonstration of that self-satisfaction. Adorno's vanity resembled that of a singer or an actor. What he wanted was not silent adoration but tumultuous applause. Enormous though his need to please was, it contained something disarming, something that made his vanity more comprehensible and also more attractive than Canetti's – helplessness. In his need for approval, in his constant search for praise, there was something touching, something childlike.

Shortly after our *Coffee House* recording Adorno asked me whether I had read his latest book. I replied, truthfully, that unfortunately I had not as yet had an opportunity to do so. Adorno was visibly disappointed – and I regret to this day that I did not tell him that it was a unique masterpiece. Who can tell whether, without that childlike vanity, Adorno would have succeeded in creating his works?

Perhaps we sometimes lack understanding of the foibles of great men. People are fond of quoting the two short lines with which Brecht's poem *To Those Born Later* ends: '*Look back on us / with indulgence.*' Sometimes it seems to me that these words are addressed to us by all who have made a contribution to literature.

33

A TAVERN AND A
CALCULATING MACHINE

On 25 August 1964, I testified as a witness in the criminal proceedings against the former SS *Obergruppenführer* Karl Wolff at the Court of Assizes in the Munich Palace of Justice. I had initially enquired from the public prosecutor's office that had summoned me whether there had perhaps been a mistake – because I had never met Wolff, the Chief of Staff of the Reichsführer-SS Himmler, nor had I heard anything about his activities. This was taken note of, but they wanted to question me all the same. I was to give evidence about the conditions in the Warsaw ghetto. Had it been possible to drive regularly through the streets of the Jewish Residential Area without being aware of what was happening there every day?

Various papers carried accounts of my testimony. The result was that I was approached for an interview about the ghetto by a woman editor of Norddeutscher Rundfunk. We met at the Café Funkeck in Hamburg, diagonally opposite the radio building. The journalist, no more than thirty, was not particularly pretty, but not without charm. This charm probably stemmed from an obvious seriousness that seemed to contrast with her youth. She wanted to record a thirty-minute conversation. Her questions were exact and intelligent, they revolved around a central problem: How could it have happened? We did not interrupt the recording once.

When it was over I discovered to my surprise that we had been talking for nearly fifty minutes. Why did she need to know so much? She answered, a little embarrassed, that she had asked partly out of personal interest – I was not to blame her for her eagerness to know. I wanted to find out something about her. But she was suddenly in a hurry. I looked at her and could see tears in her eyes. I asked quickly: 'Forgive me, but did I catch your name correctly – Meienberg?' 'No, Meinhof, Ulrike Meinhof.'

When I heard in 1968 that Ulrike Meinhof, by then a well-known journalist, had, along with Andreas Baader, founded a terrorist group, that she had been wanted by the police and eventually arrested, and when in 1976 she committed suicide in her prison cell, time and again I thought back to our conversation at the Café Funeck. Why had Ulrike Meinhof, whose future I could not have suspected, impressed herself so deeply on my memory? Could it have been because she was the first person in the Federal Republic who genuinely and seriously wished to hear about my experiences in the Warsaw ghetto? And was it conceivable that there was a link between her burning interest in the German past and the road that led her to terrorism and crime?

About the middle of the 1960s the political climate in the Federal Republic underwent a marked change. The 'Grand Coalition' of 1966 had created an entirely new situation. The socialist and Marxist forces, and, in a wider sense, the young generation, did not feel represented by the Opposition in the Bundestag; they felt disillusioned and let down. Two new concepts appeared in public discussions: 'extra-parliamentary opposition' and 'student movement'.

I could not remain indifferent to what was happening. Of course I sided with those who called for radical university reform, operating with the effective slogan *'Under the gowns the mildew of a thousand years'*. No matter how frivolous and frequently ugly some of the demonstrations of the often muddle-headed political movement associated with 1968 may have been, it had the historical merit of having brought about and accelerated the long overdue, and until then foot-dragging, confrontation with the Third Reich, more particularly with the Nazis, in the public life of the Federal Republic. That was true of politics, of the judiciary, and especially of the universities – more particularly in German studies, medicine, art history and musicology.

Nevertheless my sympathies for this noisy and chaotic revolt were kept within bounds and my mistrust was steadily growing. I certainly did not take part in any 'sit-in', 'go-in' or 'teach-in', I never experienced any 'happening', I never attended a single meeting or demonstration, I never joined any march. I witnessed quite a lot of these events, but only on the television screen. The shouting agitators, the slogans chanted in chorus, the columns moving in formation – I had seen it all before and I abhorred it since my youth.

That the theoreticians and leaders of the revolt were pursuing political aims was quite obvious. But the endlessly repeated and often rhymed slogans could not conceal a rather alarming state of affairs: the movement had a predominantly, though not exclusively, emotional and perhaps intuitive origin. Those participating in it protested against conditions in the Federal Republic, but for most of them it was an entirely vague protest against what, with some revulsion, was called the 'Establishment', in other words the world of their fathers. What the rebellion was against was therefore clear; what it was hoping to achieve was a lot less clear; and how it hoped to achieve it was totally unclear.

Scions of the affluent society, constantly referring to Marx and Engels, had evidently chosen the revolution as a spare-time hobby with minimal risk. Words like 'bourgeois' and 'proletarian', 'capitalism' and 'exploitation' were used with increasing frequency and often mindlessly declaimed. Terms like 'utopia' and 'dialectics' became magic formulas, much as jokers are in card games. Very soon a crass disproportion emerged – between the grand objectives and the limited possibilities, between great words and even greater helplessness.

What concerned and astonished me most was the role of the writers in this revolt. Many had no hesitation in joining a political and social movement whose attitude to art and literature was essentially one of contempt. No longer were writers expected to speak on behalf of the individual, defending the individual against the institutions and the powers that used and misused him for their own purposes. Instead, literature was to mobilize the individual politically. It was to serve as the tool of ideology, it was to play its part in changing the world. Paradoxically, those who demanded this most noisily were those who should have been most interested in the autonomy of literature – the writers. All this seemed very familiar to me. I had experienced it before, and not so long ago – in Poland. Very soon I was to be taught a surprising lesson about these latest trends of the Zeitgeist in the Federal Republic – a lesson that was both amusing and sad.

In October 1967 a meeting of Group 47 was held at the Pulvermühle tavern, idyllically situated between Nuremberg and Bayreuth. As usual, writers were reading from work in progress – among others Günter Eich, Günter Grass, Siegfried Lenz, Jürgen Becker, Horst Bienek. But a lot of other writers were present – such as Dorst, Hildesheimer, Schnurre, Heissenbüttel, Wohmann, Kluge, Ruhmkorf and Härtling – most of them taking part in the criticism of the texts presented. Although the meeting followed the customary format, there was something unusual about the event. The texts read were nearly all non-political and the critical discussion was focused not so much on content as on form and language. The many, often heated, debates during the breaks were unusual, too: these clearly turned on political issues.

About lunchtime the participants in the meeting, who were listening attentively to a piece of prose about the anarchist Bakunin by the Swedish writer Lars Gustafsson, were startled to hear noisily chanted slogans through the closed windows. Two slogans were being continually repeated: 'Group 47 is a paper tiger' and 'Poet, poet!' In between the jeering some toy balloons were evidently being made to burst. A young man dressed as a clown broke into the meeting, carrying a poster announcing: *This is a meeting of the Nice Guys*. He was quickly ejected from the room. Hans Werner Richter declared a break.

Everyone went outside where a large crowd had gathered, mostly of young people, brandishing streamers with slogans, placards and loudhailers. They were students from the nearby University of Erlangen who had come specially for this demonstration ('demo' was the term then in use). Some wore carnival costume. The spectacle had also attracted people from the adjoining village, including quite a few women and children.

Many of the Group 47 participants were amused by the whole business, but some writers, especially those with declared left-wing sympathies, such as Martin Walser, Erich Fried and Reinhard Lettau, urgently demanded a dialogue with those who, on their posters, ridiculed them as 'writer oldies'. They hastened to assure the youthful demonstrators of their warmest sympathies and of their readiness to engage with them in honest, and indeed brotherly, talk. The brief addresses of these authors all contained as a refrain an almost imploring assurance: 'Friends, colleagues, mates, comrades – surely

we are all in the same boat, surely we are all pulling in the same
direction.' To this, the students reacted in chorus: 'We want discussion.'

But no dialogue ensued – perhaps because it was impossible to
discover from the students what they actually wished to discuss. One
thing only was certain: they regarded Group 47 as insufficiently left-
wing and demanded from it more vigorous political engagement –
especially, as their leaflets stated, against the *disciplining tendencies
in the overall process of late-capitalist society*. Instead of a discussion
with the writers there was a small book-burning: the demonstrators
set fire to *Bild-Zeitung* and other publications.

I immediately wrote a short account of the Group 47 meeting for
Die Zeit and the paper carried a considerably more extensive article
a week later. Both articles, as in past years, were concerned with the
readings and the criticism of the texts read. Not until much later did
I realize that I had committed a grave mistake: I had not, by as
much as a single word, mentioned the student demonstration. I had
ignored it in my articles because I had not taken the events in front
of the Pulvermühle at all seriously. I had thought them laughable
and some aspects even repulsive. I had no wish to deflect from what
I considered far more important – the state of contemporary German
literature in 1967, which had just been so strikingly illuminated by
this meeting of Group 47.

Ridiculous as this unexpected confrontation may have been, one
should not overlook its symptomatic character. Similar spectacles
were staged towards the end of the 1960s and in the early 1970s.
Time and again they showed up the insecurity and helplessness of
many intellectuals who, afraid of having got into a blind alley,
overreacted to the pleas of the opposition students and those who
thought like them. Some writers went straight out to look for a
barricade. Were they neglecting literature in order to devote themselves to politics more strongly than before? Or did they perhaps
seek refuge in politics only because they were having problems with
their writing?

Certainly I was not impressed by the literature that was then being
produced. But I had no intention of turning my back on it. I merely
decided to concern myself more often than previously with the
German literature of yesterday, the literature produced between the

end of the nineteenth century and the Second World War.

What about the editorial office of *Die Zeit*? I continued to be treated impeccably. My numerous wishes regarding reviews were invariably met. I could write as much and whatever I wanted about the great German writers of the recent past. I therefore wrote about Fontane and Thomas Mann, about Hofmannsthal and Schnitzler, about Döblin, Hermann Hesse and Arnold Zweig, about Horváth, Tucholsky and Joseph Roth. These reviews gave rise to what I had always intended, my book *Re-examination*, published in 1977.

Likewise, I received the major new books by contemporary authors for review – Frisch, Dürrenmatt, Böll, Grass, Eich, Andersch, Johnson, Handke, Christa Wolf and Franz Fühmann. When, without a topical reason, I handed in an over-long article about Arno Schmidt, the editor responsible for literature, Dieter E. Zimmer, uttered a groan but published it without a cut.

When I felt like tackling Anglo-Saxon prose, I promptly received what I wanted – new books by Hemingway and Graham Greene, Bellow and Malamud, John Updike and Philip Roth. But what about poetry, especially German poetry? In a nocturnal telephone discussion lasting nearly two hours – this was in 1967 – Rudolf Walter Leonhardt assured me that he valued and admired me, more especially my reviews of novels, stories and essays. I did not like that: I immediately suspected some hidden criticism. And I was right: Leonhardt hinted that the delicate vibrations of fine German poetry were not perhaps quite my line. This I would not accept.

The following morning I asked Dieter E. Zimmer to let me review a volume of poetry. I wrote about Günter Grass's recently published book *Questioned*. No sooner was this very extensive and very laudatory article published than Erich Fried telephoned me: surely that was going too far, my article amounted to a 'personality cult'. No doubt he could now expect his own poetry to be discussed by me at equal length. Two other poets also got in touch: they had no intention of commenting on the quality or lack of quality of Grass's poems or of my exegesis, but, like Fried, they called for a similarly extensive tribute to their poetry.

Did I have a wonderful time on *Die Zeit*? Yes and no. As before, there was no need for me to work at the office. As before, this was represented to me as a very special bonus for which I should be suitably grateful. I was to be spared the tedious and often boring day-to-day work at the paper's office, in order that – as I was repeatedly assured – I could devote myself exclusively to my writings, which were so important to *Die Zeit*. But even if I had chosen to visit the office, would I be welcome there? I sent in my manuscripts by post. If there was any particular urgency I delivered them in person, which was easy enough. Soon, however, I was told not to trouble myself about delivery: a messenger would collect my manuscripts. And this was what happened. There were two editorial conferences each week at *Die Zeit* – a small one at which the column editors prepared the next issue and a main conference attended also by trainees and sitters-in. I was never invited to either and I did not wish to intrude. Thus over my fourteen years of *Die Zeit* I never once attended a conference.

I had found what I had longed for: a place that was home – but only for my work, not for my person. I felt I was being excluded – and the more successfully I wrote for *Die Zeit*, the stronger this feeling grew. During the 1960s and 1970s I sat in our small flat in the Hamburg suburb of Niendorf, isolated and alone, producing one article after another. The bulk of my books published in these decades thus came into being – *Literature of Small Steps: German Writers Today*, *Nothing But Drubbings*, *Disturbers of the Peace: Jews in German Literature*, *On Literature in the GDR*. Because my contact with the world rarely went beyond telephone conversations, I was happy to be invited, from time to time, to give lectures – in the Federal Republic and in other countries. These mitigated the solitary nature of my existence, at least temporarily.

In 1968 I taught German literature for one semester at Washington University in St Louis. My not very onerous obligations included lectures and seminars. As I had never taken part in one, I asked a colleague with a good many years' experience of academic life what a seminar actually was. He responded with a counter-question: how did I imagine a seminar? I told him, earnestly but awkwardly. That, he replied, was precisely how a seminar should be run. How strange. Once again I was to teach others without having learned anything myself.

The readers of *Die Zeit* were not aware of my absence because, even though in St Louis, I supplied the office with articles, mainly about young German writers – from Hubert Fichte to Rolf Dieter Brinkmann. On my return I discovered that nothing had changed for me and nothing was going to change: there was no place for me in the office.

'*Will you permit me to tell you a story?*' Nathan the Wise asks Sultan Saladin. Very well, I too will permit myself a story here. In Poland many years ago there lived a man, a Jew by the name of Chaim Selig Słonimski. He was born in 1810 in Białystok and died in 1904 in Warsaw. Having in his youth studied nothing but the Talmud and rabbinical literature, he later devoted himself to mathematical and astronomical studies. About 1840 he succeeded in constructing a calculating machine. News of the extraordinary invention reached Tsar Nicholas I. He wished to see the machine. Słonimski was therefore invited to St Petersburg for an audience with the Tsar. But before being admitted he was firmly instructed that he must only answer His Majesty's questions and otherwise remain absolutely silent. The audience went well until the Tsar asked how he could convince himself that the machine really calculated correctly. Let His Majesty set him an arithmetical task, the mathematician submissively suggested. His Majesty might then be graciously pleased to work it out in the conventional manner, with pencil and paper, while he would attempt it with the new machine. His Majesty might then compare the results. This made sense to the Tsar. No sooner had the two unequal gentlemen started calculating than the happy inventor of the machine exclaimed: 'I've got it!' The Tsar looked up angrily: someone had dared to speak in his presence without being asked. There was an icy atmosphere in the audience chamber. The disgruntled Tsar silently turned back to his evidently very demanding arithmetical problem. At last the two results were compared – and His Majesty announced, curtly and clearly: 'Machine good, Jew bad.' Incidentally, in 1844 Słonimski received an important Russian prize for the invention of this calculating machine. A little later he was made an honorary citizen of St Petersburg.

This story was related to me in London in 1948 by the excellent Polish poet and essayist Antoni Słonimski, a direct descendant of the nineteenth-century mathematician. I have never forgotten it and I was often compelled to think about it. Was what I experienced at *Die Zeit* something similar to what happened to Chaim Selig Słonimski? Did the Tsar's words, suitably amended, also apply to me: Manuscripts good, Jew bad? In short, anti-Semitism?

Like the members of other minorities, many Jews are sometimes too quick to ascribe any difficulties encountered by them in their lives to the dislike or hostility of the non-Jewish world around them. That is regrettable, but maybe one should not blame the Jews too much for this mixture of mistrust and oversensitivity. After all, over-reactions always have their justification, and here this is obvious: centuries and millennia of chicanery and persecution.

I was firmly resolved to resist the suspicion that now and again I was confronted by anti-Semitic resentment. Yet I could hardly be unaware of the fact that, having now lived in the Federal Republic for more than twelve years, the newspapers, publishing houses and broadcasting stations there – all of which were happy to make use of my work – never offered me a post, not even the humblest. Editors of *Die Zeit*, on the other hand, even those at the top, were being offered various posts in other institutions over those years. I also noticed that the staff of the arts department of *Die Zeit* was being repeatedly enlarged – but I was never invited to join it.

In a letter from the young Friedrich Schlegel to his brother August Wilhelm, dating from 1792, I found the following sentences: '*I have long noticed what impression I nearly always make. People find me interesting and avoid me ... They like viewing me from afar, like some dangerous rarity.*' Which applied to me? Was my case reminiscent of the situation of the Jewish mathematician or of the great German critic who complained that, though he was not a Jew, he was being avoided and kept at a distance, that he was quite simply unpopular? I had no doubt: my case was like Friedrich Schlegel's and had absolutely nothing to do with my being Jewish.

In 1996 I was given a book of unmistakably official character. It was a *Festschrift* entitled *Time and 'Die Zeit' – 50 Years of a Weekly*. In this book I was puzzled by a brief, matter-of-fact piece of information. While I was working on *Die Zeit* – it said – there had been frequent discussions on whether I should be employed in the editorial office. However – and I only learned this in 1996 – the editors of the arts department had entertained '*grave misgivings*' as to '*whether they could stand such a power-conscious, quibbling indi-vidual*'. I was shocked. The German word used, *rabulistisch*, does

335

not have a pleasant ring. It means something like a hair-splitter, pettifogger or quibbler and is rarely used nowadays. But it is often found in the militant Nazi press, especially in the articles of Joseph Goebbels. He almost invariably used this term with an adjective – either '*Jewish quibbling*' or '*Jewish-Marxist quibbling*'. I confess that I was no longer quite so sure that my situation resembled that of the great German critic Friedrich Schlegel. Perhaps, after all, it was closer to that of the Jewish inventor of the calculating machine, Chaim Selig Słonimski.

My collaboration with *Die Zeit* remained flawless. But as I had not the slightest hope of a post inside the editorial office I knew I had to leave the paper. Where would I go? In no circumstances would I lobby for a job. On the other hand, I could not delay much longer because I was over fifty now. An invitation from Sweden was therefore most welcome. From 1971 to 1975, first for a few months, then for several weeks each year, I acted as permanent visiting professor of New German Literature at the universities of Stockholm and Uppsala.

In 1972 I received the first honour of my life – an honorary doctorate of the University of Uppsala. The ceremony was exceedingly solemn: the bells of the ancient cathedral of Uppsala were rung, cannons were fired from a tree that Linnaeus was reported to have personally planted in the neighbourhood of the university. I was moved – although there was some irony in the fact that for my contribution to West German literature (that was the official citation) I was being honoured not by a German but by a Swedish university.

In 1973 I completed the farthest-reaching lecture tour of my life – to Australia and New Zealand. By then I had handed in my notice to *Die Zeit* and – what no one was yet supposed to know – had signed a contract for a new job. Before the year was out I was to assume the directorship of the literary section of *Frankfurter Allgemeine*.

PART FIVE

1973-1999

34

THE SINISTER GUEST
OF HONOUR

It was in 1966 that I met Joachim Fest at the house of hospitable mutual friends who lived in a suburb of Hamburg. He was then working in Norddeutscher Rundfunk, where he was responsible for the television magazine *Panorama*. After that we would occasionally meet, go to the theatre together, and eventually we visited each other. Gradually a somewhat unusual relationship developed between us, a temporary friendship that, if it really was friendship, revealed two things on Fest's side: genuine cordiality, albeit combined with reserve, with a certain formality. I believe he was a little proud of that formality and he only slowly, or perhaps never, quite overcame it with regard to me – either because he was unable to do so or because he did not wish to.

Some time later we unexpectedly met at a hotel near Baden-Baden. We had both gone there for the same reason – not so much for recuperation as for a short break. We needed to interrupt our daily routines, as least for a brief period. So we would recline on the spacious hotel terrace, enjoying the comfortable loungers and the dimly visible French landscape in the distance. Our talk soon got round to the cunningly constructed recliners on which a young, exceedingly literate engineer was in the habit of resting in a sanatorium in Davos – Hans Castorp from Hamburg.

This state of affairs continued for a long time, for a good many years. Our conversations often started with Thomas Mann and, after many detours, usually via Goethe, Heine and Fontane, via Mozart, Schubert and Wagner, returned to Thomas Mann. Fest's quick comprehension facilitated our communication; his knowledge,

339

especially of the arts, was stimulating and made our talks entertaining, wherever and whenever they took place. I learned a lot from him and maybe he also learned something from me.

I certainly admired his erudition. Admittedly it had astonishing limitations. In twentieth-century literature he did not acknowledge more than three or four geniuses, and, with a very few exceptions, he did not wish to know about the music of this period. But then this applies to many of us. Except that Fest defended such gaps in his education with a defiance that surprised me and struck me as arrogant. The poets and composers whose work he did not know only had themselves to blame, and what they had achieved seemed to him unimportant, if not indeed contemptible. This worried me a little. I wondered if these resolute rejections, this at times imperious obduracy, did not harbour a serious danger. However, I was happy to have found such a splendid conversation partner and therefore, for the time being, attached no importance to these slight misgivings.

Back in Hamburg we met ever more frequently and our telephone conversations grew ever longer, especially in the evenings, when, exhausted by intensive and solitary writing, we longed not so much for rest as for a relaxed exchange of views about the issues that had occupied us during the day. I was then working on a small book, *Disturbers of the Peace: Jews in German Literature*, while Fest was writing a major and important work entitled *Hitler: A Biography*.

Even before that monograph of his was completed, let alone published, Fest was invited to assume responsibility, as a co-publisher, of the cultural section of *Frankfurter Allgemeine*. That was a prestigious offer, if not perhaps a particularly attractive one. The point is that *Frankfurter Allgemeine* does not have an editor-in-chief, nor a deputy editor-in-chief, but six – or lately five – 'publishers'. And outstanding soloists do not as a rule content themselves with playing in a sextet or a quintet.

Nevertheless Fest had reasons, a variety of reasons, for accepting this offer. He informed me of it and, at the same time, asked if I would be willing to go to *Frankfurter Allgemeine* with him and there assume the direction of the literary department. This was entirely unexpected, but I did not hesitate for one moment before saying yes to him. *Frankfurter Allgemeine* was not too happy to accept Fest's condition, but did so largely because the publishers of the paper had no illusions about this department. They realized that the literary section, at one time headed by Friedrich Sieburg, had long lost its former quality. What worried them most was that it was run without regard to the readership.

Towards the end of April 1973 I had a meeting in Frankfurt with the manager and with the chairman of the board of publishers of *Frankfurter Allgemeine*. Our meeting was not at the paper's office but, for reasons of secrecy – no one was yet to know that I would be joining *Frankfurter Allgemeine* – at a hotel near the airport. I instantly agreed to the conditions and terms proposed to me, except that I wanted the contract to state specifically that 'the areas of literature and literary life' were my concern and that I was 'directly answerable to the publishers'. This was important to me: on no account did I wish to come under some Arts Editor. With my arrival, therefore, culture was to be divided into two spheres under heads of equal standing – general arts, directed by Günther Rühle, and literature. My request was met.

Fest was satisfied and I was more than satisfied. Some fifteen years after my return to Germany I at last had a post in literary life – possibly the most important one. The literary section of the paper, I hoped, would develop into a forum and an instrument of the highest quality – assuming that my collaboration with Fest was not impaired by any problems. There was nothing to suggest – at least not for the time being – that there would be problems.

Fest's book on Hitler was published at the beginning of September 1973. To mark the occasion the publisher, Wolf Jobst Siedler, gave a big reception at his house in Berlin-Dahlem. Tosia and I were invited, no doubt at Fest's suggestion. We were in excellent spirits until, from the hall of the spacious and elegant villa, we glanced through the open door into an adjoining room and there saw something that took our breath away. A few people were talking animatedly with a gentleman in a dark suit, an impressive gentleman probably in his late sixties, who seemed to be at the centre of the group. Our host was attending to him with the utmost courtesy, if not respect. It appeared that Fest was not the guest of honour that evening, but the well-built, pleasant-looking gentleman.

Tosia turned pale. I too suddenly did not feel very well. One thing was obvious: we had two possible courses of action – we could remain in spite of the guest of honour or we could leave the splendid villa at once, which of course would have created a bombshell. I rapidly considered the options, but before I could do anything, the matter was decided for me: Siedler approached us and led us, politely but energetically, to the guest of honour, who was now taking two or three steps towards us. He greeted us like old friends – yes, he greeted us with real cordiality.

This well-dressed gentleman was a criminal – one of the worst war criminals in the history of Germany. He had caused the deaths of countless human beings. Not so long ago he had been one of the closest collaborators and intimates of Adolf Hitler. He had been sentenced to twenty years' imprisonment by the Nuremberg International Tribunal. I am talking of Albert Speer.

I do not recollect what the conversation was about. But whatever I said, Speer pleasantly nodded agreement, as if to say: the Jewish fellow citizen is right, the Jewish fellow citizen is welcome. On a little table, if I am not mistaken on a velvet cloth, lay the book that was being festively launched that evening – a volume of 1,200 pages.

Its black jacket showed the book's title in large white letters: *Hitler*. There was no mistaking what this typography was intended to suggest, what it was resolutely claiming – grandeur and monumentality. Speer looked at the solemnly displayed book with a roguish smile and said slowly and emphatically: '*He* would have been content with this, *he* would have liked it.'

Was I rigid with horror? Did I shout at the mass murderer who stood there respectfully joking about his Führer, did I call him to order? No, I did not do anything of the kind. I kept silent, horrified. But I wondered what kind of person our host, the publisher and journalist Wolf Jobst Siedler, must be if he thought it possible to invite Albert Speer and us to the same gathering; if it had not occurred to him that he should warn us whom we would meet at his house.

However, what did I care about Siedler, who never was my friend and never would be? But what about Fest, who quite certainly had known that Speer would be one of the guests at this reception? Why had he not warned, or at least informed, me? I think I know the answer. It probably never occurred to him that I might – to put it mildly – have misgivings about shaking hands with one of the top Nazis or sitting at the same table with him.

And why did it not occur to him? Perhaps because Fest is someone whose egocentricity, at times amounting to hard-heartedness, often manifests itself in a lack of interest in other people. His person is surrounded by a cool aura, by a protective cloak on which he evidently depends and of which he is inordinately proud. Does this have anything to do with cynicism? I never asked Fest if he thought of himself as a cynic. But I suspect that, of all the accusations that might be levelled at him, he would be happiest with this one.

The evening with Speer was not a particularly good omen for my future collaboration with Fest. More than that: it foreshadowed the dramatic controversy that would break out between us many years later; it already contained the nucleus of that conflict. I realized none of this in the autumn of 1973; or, at best, I surmised it and repressed it. I had no interest whatever in quarrelling with Fest, especially at that point in time, so I avoided any conversation with him about this sinister encounter.

On 2 December 1973 Tosia and I were travelling by train from Hamburg to Frankfurt. We were not alone. In the same compartment was the newly appointed publisher responsible for the cultural section of *Frankfurter Allgemeine*. Like myself, he was to take up his post the following day.

35

MAKE WAY FOR POETRY!

My first day at the office of *Frankfurter Allgemeine* was neither friendly nor pleasant. Few of the editors or women secretaries of the arts department made the slightest effort to make me feel welcome. And it was surely no coincidence that the room assigned to me looked neglected, its furniture in a deplorable state. However, I was not greatly surprised or discouraged by any of this, it in fact scarcely bothered me. The undisguised hostility actually spurred me on. I was in good spirits and they improved by the day.

I immediately got down to work, dictating letters, editing manuscripts and, above all, telephoning – first of all to the few members of the staff whom I wished to keep on. The first person I called was Günter Blöcker. I also telephoned writers and critics whom I was hoping to take on. Perusal of the not too numerous manuscripts my predecessor had left me confirmed what I had already guessed: most of them were ponderously and awkwardly written, some by reviewers who obviously did not care whether or not they were understood by their readers.

I had to find new contributors as soon as possible. Where was I to look for them? I thought first of well-known authors. As reviewers, they might greatly enhance the attractiveness of a paper's literary section, and not only because their names were familiar to the readers. More importantly, their individual style would make the literary section more colourful and lively. However, those who write a book review only once or twice a year, who are, if the expression is permitted, 'Sunday drivers of criticism', are far more willing than professional reviewers to risk their reputation, when writing reviews as a favour. After all, the reputation of such authors does not depend on their journalistic work, but on their novels or volumes of poetry.

Even so, I did not hesitate to invite a number of well-known authors to work for me on an occasional basis. My efforts were not in vain. Wolfgang Koeppen, Heinrich Böll, Golo Mann, Siegfried Lenz, Hermann Burger, Hans J. Fröhlich, Karl Krolow, Peter Rühmkorf and Günter Kunert all went along with my request. In spite of some reviews written as a favour – which I was unable to prevent – I never regretted my approach. It was these authors who rapidly lent some glamour to the literary section of *Frankfurter Allgemeine*.

What about university professors? Many German academics then wrote in a jargon they considered scholarly, though in fact it suggested pseudo-scholarship. Their writing, larded with foreign words and technical terms, mostly for no good reason, was incomprehensible to most readers. Their manuscripts at times had the pervasive smell of classroom chalk. There was a clear need for some discreet and patient editorial guidance on my part. Gradually at least fifteen German-literature academics, who until then had never, or only rarely, written for the press, developed into good and even excellent critics.

The question arises whether this educational role was perhaps a way of compensating myself for the fact that my road to the university had been blocked. That is quite possible – although this would have had no discernible effect either on the paper or on the German scholars concerned. And it is equally possible that bridging the traditional gulf between academic German scholarship and literary criticism, especially criticism in the press, was the most important achievement of my fifteen years on *Frankfurter Allgemeine*.

That this gulf does not exist in the Anglo-Saxon countries was instantly apparent in the manuscripts of the scholars of German or Austrian origin who had lived and taught there for many years. They did not need convincing that literary criticism in the press, while making great demands on its readers, and rightly so, should at the same time be comprehensible and easily readable. I was particularly impressed by contributions from such German academics as Heinz Politzer, Peter Demetz, Gerhard Schulz, Wolfgang Leppmann and, later, Ruth Klüger.

Soon unsolicited submissions started arriving, almost daily, from professors in a variety of disciplines in Germany, Austria and Switzerland. Most of these proved unusable – not necessarily because of their quality. These texts, which were often quite useful, had been conceived as lectures or as prefaces to books, and for that reason were not suitable for a daily paper. Nevertheless one such contribution, a postscript, drew my attention to an extraordinary scholar.

The 150th anniversary of Goethe's death was in March 1982. To mark the occasion, publishing houses in the German-speaking countries had flooded the market with books by and about Goethe. While it was impossible to review them all, it would be unthinkable to ignore them. I therefore decided to write a collective article with recommendations, suggestions and criticisms. No more than ten selected titles would be discussed.

Among the many new publications there was a hefty volume with the title *Goethe Tells a Story* and the somewhat unusual subtitle *Stories, Novellas, Accounts, Adventures and Confessions*. I began to read the postscript. Its first paragraph stated that this was '*a book for light-hearted readers*', intended '*for the curious, the adaptable, those willing to expose themselves for once to a raconteur's voice regardless of current ideas about this classic.*'

After reading the first page, or perhaps the first paragraph, I asked my secretary to find out more about the editor of this book from the publisher, Artemis Verlag in Zurich, and where he could be contacted. Even before I had finished reading the postscript, which I liked better with every page, I received the answer I needed: the editor of this Goethe volume, Peter von Matt, was Ordinary Professor of New German Literature at the University of Zürich. I had not expected that. Professors do not as a rule write for '*light-hearted readers*', let alone for those not concerned with '*current ideas about this classic*'. I was immediately sure that I had found a new and excellent collaborator. I was not mistaken.

A particular concern of mine was the reviewing of poetry. Reviews of volumes of poetry in *Frankfurter Allgemeine* and in other papers were often thorough and learned, and possibly also fair. But they frequently had one fatal flaw: they were, to put it bluntly, rather boring – and some are still, to this day. This was not only the reviewers' fault; part of the problem was the subject matter. Of course it is possible to write about new poetry seriously and, at the same time, amusingly, but it is extremely difficult. Without quoting examples – a lot of them – the discussion of poetry is meaningless. On the other hand, it is often the quotations that impair the readability of the reviews.

Bad Times for Poetry is the title of a poem by Brecht. He was writing about the 1930s, but virtually nothing has changed in this respect. Something, therefore, had to be done for poetry – not once or twice, but continually. I therefore conceived the idea of extending the existing poetry reviews by introducing a regular weekly column. This would not present volumes of poetry however, but individual poems from all periods of German poetry. Writers, scholars of literature, poets and critics would then discuss these. I repeatedly requested, though not always successfully, that these comments be written as personally as possible. Thus the *Frankfurt Anthology* was born.

The editorial office at first showed little interest in my project, but neither was it opposed. One of the paper's publishers, an experienced and sceptical editor, observed: 'If he's so keen on it, let him do the column. It's not going to cost us much space because he won't manage more than three or four pieces.' The first contribution – on Goethe's poem *Um Mitternacht* [*At Midnight*] – was published in *Frankfurter Allgemeine* on 15 June 1974. My introductory article had the title *Make Way for Poetry!*

To date, nearly 1,300 contributions have appeared in this *Anthology*, by some 350 authors, discussed by some 280 critics. Many of these – ranging alphabetically from Rudolf Augstein to Dieter E. Zimmer – worked on other newspapers, mainly on *Die Zeit, Der Spiegel, Süddeutsche Zeitung* and *Neue Zürcher Zeitung*. I was hoping that this *Frankfurt Anthology*, initiated and published by *Frankfurter Allgemeine*, would come to be regarded as a German-language institution: and, indeed, anyone who had anything to say about German poetry was to take part in it, regardless of everyday rivalries.

A lot of readers protested against the selection of the poems – in letters and sometimes even in telegrams. We should stop printing the incomprehensible verses of contemporary poets and instead have more of Hölderlin, Eichendorff and Mörike. But there were also complaints from those who were tired of always finding verses by Hölderlin, Eichendorff and Mörike in the *Anthology*; they wanted

347

more modern poets. These letters convinced me that I was on the right track. Because that was precisely what I wanted: the admirers of the older poetry to be acquainted with the work of contemporary authors and the lovers of modern poetry to be reminded of the German poetry of the past. But there were other complaints too. When a telegram asked: 'Why so much Goethe?', I replied, also by telegram: 'Because local Frankfurt boy.' Gradually the *Frankfurt Anthology*, which appeared simultaneously in book form – so far there are twenty-two volumes – grew into a small library.

Within a very short period *Frankfurter Allgemeine* had thus become a major forum for literature – mainly for criticism, but also for poetry, which was published not only in the weekend supplement but also in the daily arts pages, as well as for novels and short stories, which appeared as to-be-continued serials, and for reports and commentaries on literary life. Eulogies have occasionally suggested that my efforts were aiming at '*the magnificent if utopian endeavour to make literature a public affair*' and that I had given back to German literary criticism the rank of an institution. In confidence: this is a vast exaggeration. I have no illusions on this point. But such tributes do in fact hint at what I had been striving for in spite of their lofty tone, so I always welcome them.

The fact that literature was being so widely promoted on the pages of *Frankfurter Allgemeine* did not, by any means, meet with approval only among the literary public – many colleagues on the paper applauded it, too. With increasing frequency I was being called a 'Super-Critic' or even a 'Pope of Literature', but it was not certain if these were respectful and amicable appellations or malicious sneers. The ironical, derogatory and mocking flavour of this labelling was not lost on me: I could not avoid the suspicion that anything I was commended for was, at the same time, an accusation.

The greater my success, the more often did I come up against envy and jealousy, and sometimes undisguised hatred. This was quite often hurtful. But I consoled myself with Heine's splendid remark that the hatred of his enemies was an assurance that he was not doing his job too badly. Within a few years it was openly and clearly stated that I had grabbed too much power for myself. A lengthy television documentary about me even opened with the bold assertion that the literary section of *Frankfurter Allgemeine*, under my direction, was the greatest centre of power that had ever existed in the history of German literature.

The word 'power' does not have happy connotations; it suggests – not without justification – its misuse and arbitrariness. Sympathies therefore tend not to be on the side of those wielding power, but on that of the victims. It is quite true that I have tried to concentrate as much power in my hands as I thought necessary – and this is true not only of my work on the paper. My participation in literary life during those years went far beyond *Frankfurter Allgemeine*. I was a member of many juries; in 1977 I was a co-initiator of the Klagenfurt competition for the Ingeborg Bachmann Prize and until 1986 I was the spokesman of the jury for that competition.

But permit me to ask: was this a good thing or a bad thing for literature? For whose benefit did I, for fifteen years, run this big department of *Frankfurter Allgemeine*? I imagined, and I still believe, that it was to the advantage of literature.

I worked from early morning till late at night – partly at the newspaper's office and partly at home. I practically never had a free weekend; I only reluctantly, and then not in full, took the leave I was entitled to. I worked hard, enormously hard. Why did I? No one expected me to, let alone asked me to. Much of what I was doing I did not have to do myself; I could have delegated it. So why this great effort, this ceaseless hard work? For the sake of literature? Yes, certainly. Was it my ambition to continue the tradition of Jews in the history of German literary criticism in a leading post before the eyes of the public? Certainly. Did my passion have anything to do with my longing for a home, the home that I lacked and that I believed I had found in German literature? Yes – and perhaps to a greater degree than I realized.

All these answers are correct, yet none of them quite hits the spot. If I am being honest, I must also admit that behind my workaholism, because that is what it was, there was nothing but the pleasure which my work on *Frankfurter Allgemeine* gave me from day to day. My hobby and my job, my passion and my profession, coincided completely.

The many series then published in *Frankfurter Allgemeine* all sprang from more or less personal motivations. I will confine myself to two examples. How was what had happened in Germany, and on behalf of Germans, between 1933 and 1945 reflected in the lives of those who were then children or juveniles? Because I myself was among them, my interest in this question never abated. The result was a series *My School Days in the Third Reich: Reminiscences of German Writers*, which, in book form, is still being used in many schools.

Another example: How good are the novels of the first half of the twentieth century, that I had read in my youth? As I was unable in many instances to re-evaluate my impressions and recollections, I got numerous writers, journalists, critics and scholars to answer that question. The result was the series *Novels of Yesterday – Read Today*. This submitted 125 German novels to re-examination, ranging from Heinrich Mann's *Im Schlaraffenland* (1900) to Hermann Broch's *The Death of Virgil* (1945). Thus emerged a far from usual guide to the novel, running in book form to three volumes.

What about the promotion on the discovery of new talent? This is a laborious and mostly unsuccessful business. But it amused me nevertheless. One occasion at least has engraved itself on my memory. At the beginning of August 1979 I took part in a television discussion in Vienna. The topic was women's literature, though it was not quite clear whether the organizers were thinking of literature by, for, or about women.

When I got to the studio, four ladies were already present, clearly keen to do battle. As I had a reputation of being an opponent of female emancipation, even an enemy of the female sex, they doubtless intended to maul me in front of the live camera. But I too was ready for the fray. Except that my interest in the impending debate suddenly vanished when I saw that one of my partners was an outstandingly attractive woman. She was both tempting and seductive, lovely and lovable and I was so enchanted by her that I scarcely noticed the others. I liked her even better during the discussion: she spoke very intelligently and had the additional attraction of agreeing with everything I said. What was supposed to be an argument turned into a secret erotic dialogue. Anything I said was intended only for her and whatever she said, so it seemed to me, was addressed to me. She had to return to her hotel immediately after the transmission but parted from me with the meaningful words: 'You'll hear from me soon.' Indeed, after a few days I received a letter with an invitation and then another. I sent her one of my books but did not answer her two letters. To explain the reason for my reticence would be inappropriate. I certainly never saw her again. But I would like to record her name: Lilli Palmer.

After her hasty departure I got into conversation with another participant. She was a young German academic, by profession literary editor of Radio Bremen. I do not recall what we talked about, probably our conversation was not very productive. No doubt, I asked ironically, she had a novel in her desk drawer. 'No,' she replied cheekily, 'but now and again I write poetry.' The devil must have prompted me, because I said to her: 'Why don't you send me some?' No sooner had the words been uttered than I wanted to retract them. To my regret she took my invitation seriously. A short time later I received four poems from Bremen. Long experience told me that they would be bad or awful. The covering letter, briefly referring to our talk in Vienna, was strikingly short.

I immediately read the poems. I was delighted and moved by them. This had never before happened in my work on *Frankfurter Allgemeine* – a young woman who had not yet published anything had sent me not only printable poems, but poems which proved that even today German poetry may be and can be beautiful. I was determined to publish the verses of the unknown author in *Frankfurter Allgemeine*. I summoned Ulrich Greiner, who was then working in the literary department – he was later to spend a few years as Arts Editor on *Die Zeit* – and, without giving him a hint of my enthusiasm, asked him to read the manuscripts. When he returned them to me he was almost as excited as I was. His verdict was: 'Publish the lot at once!' He wanted to know the name of the author, which was not on the manuscript. I had mislaid her letter. But I found a crumpled envelope in my wastepaper basket. The name was just about decipherable: Ulla Hahn.

I was never bored on *Frankfurter Allgemeine*, except perhaps – and that quite frequently – at the conferences which were held every fortnight. Were they really necessary? One of the publishers explained to me in confidence that for tactical reasons it was advisable to give the editors an opportunity now and again to let off steam. Admittedly, most of them did not take up this opportunity and preferred to keep silent. Even worse: one of the publishers enjoyed dismissing the criticisms of the editors (which were rare enough and invariably carefully worded) with silly jokes. The other publishers tolerated this in silence.

I attended those conferences regularly and frequently spoke at them, needless to say critically and often a little rebelliously. I was told my remarks helped to enliven the often somnolent atmosphere. But while my colleagues liked my observations, the publishers did not, so I accomplished virtually nothing. In the end I got fed up and, as an experiment, stayed away from the conferences. I felt sure that this would not be permitted in the long run, but once again I was mistaken. Only my colleagues wanted me back; the publishers, on the other hand, were glad not to have to answer my questions. They had got rid of a disturber of the peace.

Within my own sphere, of course, I could do what I liked. Not a single article, not a single poem, not a single announcement – nothing that I believed should be published remained unpublished during those fifteen years. I had arranged with Fest that any author who contributed to contemporary German literature, regardless of his political views, could be published in *Frankfurter Allgemeine*. The decision on who contributed to contemporary literature was left to me. Fest kept his word – and, if I recollect rightly, I never had to remind him of this arrangement.

More and more often I authorized the publication of the work of left-wing authors, including, of course, Communists. Whether this was to the liking of the publishers I do not know. But no one dared to complain. In May 1976 I published in the *Frankfurt Anthology* a poem written by Peter Paul Zahl, sentenced as a terrorist to fifteen years' imprisonment. I asked Erich Fried to comment on it. Someone said: 'It's about as far left as one can go.' No one on *Frankfurter Allgemeine* objected.

My freedom as director of the literary section was therefore unlimited, and this freedom enabled me to accept a few things I did not like about the paper. To be honest, I rarely read more than the arts section every day and only exceptionally the leading article. This saved me a lot of time – and a lot of annoyance.

At the risk of repeating myself: I was well aware and never forgot to whom I owed that freedom of which I made such ample use. It was Joachim Fest.

36

ONE IS A GENIUS ONLY
DURING WORKING HOURS

If I were asked who my most important and most original collaborator was over those fifteen years in the literary department of *Frankfurter Allgemeine*, the one whose critical prose left the strongest impression on me, I would unhesitatingly name Wolfgang Koeppen. During that period, I must add, he gave me the greatest pleasure and the greatest satisfaction – but also the worst headaches.

Koeppen's novel *Death in Rome* did not reach Poland until 1956, two years after the West German edition. I was able to get hold of it because it had also been published in the GDR. I did what I could to get it translated into Polish – and towards the end of 1957, when the Polish edition became available, I wrote an extensive and enthusiastic review of it. What particularly fascinated me was the tremendously suggestive rhythm of its prose, its new tone. So long as there was an author like Koeppen, I declared, one need not worry about the future of German post-war literature.

When I was in Munich in December 1957 I was most anxious to meet Koeppen. In my youth I was puzzled by many a paradoxical statement in Oscar Wilde's *The Picture of Dorian Gray*, a novel I loved, such as this one: '*Good artists only live in their works and are therefore totally uninteresting as personalities.*' I was even more baffled by what I found in Plutarch: '*Revere the arts and despise the artists!*' So when a school friend in Berlin once invited me to visit the flat of his temporarily absent uncle whose flowers he had to water, I jumped at the offer. That uncle was a real writer – the Silesian poet and story-teller Friedrich Bischoff. Even though I did not meet him I felt happy to be in his flat and to be able to look around in it. Inevitably my curiosity about famous writers, my need to make the acquaintance of the authors of books I admired, has diminished over time.

In December 1957, however, I was sitting in a Munich restaurant, looking forward to talking to the author of the novel *Death in Rome*. I expected him to be like his poetic prose – severe and sharp, possibly rather aggressive. But the gentleman who cautiously approached my table made a totally different impression.

Koeppen might have been a respectable senior schoolmaster teaching Greek and history, loved by his students of both sexes and engaged, in his free time, in writing a book about Pericles. Aggressive was the last thing the writer with whom I spent the evening was; he was not even self-assured, but somewhat shy, if not inhibited, very friendly and obliging, strikingly soft-spoken and unfailingly polite. Koeppen answered my questions courteously, perhaps too courteously. I posed one question after another – not because I wished to learn much about him but because I was afraid that our conversation would otherwise dry up. I was reluctant to admit to myself that our talk, on which I had set such store, had turned out to be disappointing.

Things were much the same later on. We would meet not infrequently, in Munich or in Frankfurt, but I cannot recall a single revealing or stimulating conversation. During his time in Berlin, before the war, Koeppen had known many writers, journalists and actors, some of whom I was interested in and asked him to tell me about. He did so very obligingly – but whereas even the shortest book review or the most hasty letter revealed Koeppen the writer, nearly everything I heard him say was rather pale and colourless. Koeppen was not a raconteur. Nor could one credit him with charisma. Could Oscar Wilde have been right?

In Heinrich Mann, whom, incidentally, Koeppen esteemed more highly than I did – which may have been a generation problem – I found the astonishing observation: '*There is no genius outside business hours. The most solemn giants of the past used to laugh with their friends and talk nonsense. One should stick to one's hours.*' In point of fact, Koeppen had a beautiful style, but only when he was at his desk with his typewriter in front of him – in other words: during working hours.

When we parted on that first evening he gave me a copy of his novel *Death in Rome*. This pleased me, but I asked, as was only polite, for a dedication. Koeppen seemed surprised. Yes, certainly, but this could not be done quickly, he would have to think about it. With an embarrassed smile he said he would take the book home with him and bring it back the following day with a dedication. I was somewhat taken aback, but of course agreed. Twenty-four hours later Koeppen handed me his novel for the second time. However, I dared not read what he had written in his presence. Not until I was back in my hotel room, still in my overcoat, did I curiously open the book. The dedication ran: 'For Mr Marcel Ranicki in friendly dedication.' Signature. Date. That was all.

In his short story *Tristan* Thomas Mann says of the writer Detlev Spinell that this oddball, writing a letter, *'was making miserably slow progress'*. He continues: *'No one could have watched him without reaching the conclusion that a writer is a man to whom writing comes harder than to anyone else.'* As I read Koeppen's dedication I fully realized what a strange and unusual writer he was.

He was not an author one could rely on. He never kept delivery dates and it never worried him if, in his gentle but determined manner, he offended or simply let a client down. Blessed as he was with a unique talent, he suffered at the same time from a weakness of will, from a powerful tendency towards inertia and lethargy. It seems scarcely credible, but Koeppen, whose almost lifelong profession was that of a freelance writer, wrote rarely and very reluctantly. Unreliability and a sense of responsibility coexisted in Koeppen; collaboration with him required a lot of patience and at times was a torment. Publishers, editors and broadcasting people who acknowledged his talent were ceaselessly chasing and reminding him, beseeching and warning him. In their desperation they often threatened or flattered him – and now and again they were even successful. But on no account could he be persuaded to part with a manuscript before he thought it was ready.

Of course I realized all this when I started work on *Frankfurter Allgemeine*. But I was not put off. On the contrary, I regarded it as one of my most urgent tasks to gain Koeppen as a contributor on the literary section. I lured him not only with high fees, the highest paid by *Frankfurter Allgemeine* at the time, but also with subjects that would motivate him.

I asked him for articles on Kleist, Kafka and Karl Kraus, on Thomas Mann and Robert Musil, on Arnold Döblin and Robert Walser, and on many others. They could even be quite short, I would tell him, in order to get him to write at all. All this in a daily paper? Of course, one had to find the right occasion, but that was not difficult. New editions or illustrated volumes, and especially anniversaries, provided suitable pretexts. Only rarely, as I have said, did Koeppen send his manuscripts in on time. Even at the beginning of our collaboration I found this astonishing request in a letter from him: '*Please urge me, press me, but not too much.*' This I had to do frequently; mostly I had to extract the manuscripts with panic telegrams or telephone calls. In the end they arrived, by telephone at the last moment, because fax machines did not then exist.

However, Koeppen was not one of those irritating contributor who, as soon as their text had arrived at the paper's office, would phone in to delete two words or add three. He never changed a single word – nor would it have been necessary. And when I read what he had written about Grimmelshausen, Shelley, Flaubert or Hemingway I felt that it had been worth waiting for. However, before long I began to fear that, in this new situation, Koeppen would no longer write the novel which he had repeatedly spoken about over the past few years. Now he talked about it less and less frequently; more often he mentioned a short book of prose with the title *Youth*. But whenever I asked him about that book, he referred to the literary criticism that was now taking up so much of his time.

I had no choice therefore but to cut down on the number of current commissions from him. But this I could justify only if I provided him with other, if possible regular, sources of income, so that he would be free from financial worries. I turned to four writers whose books were then achieving particularly large print runs, asking them for help. They were Max Frisch, Heinrich Böll, Günter Grass and Siegfried Lenz. Each of them contributed what he thought an appropriate (and in two cases very generous) sum to a bank account codenamed 'Reference Grass Pigeon'. However, it would have been reckless to hand the sum over to Koeppen: handling money sensibly was not his thing. So an amount was sent to him from this account each month – not enough for his keep, but a sufficient basis for his livelihood. He asked me where the money was coming from, but I had the impression that he did not really wish to know. He certainly was never told.

This discreet rescue operation was successful. Even though the widely expected novel did not materialize, at least a book by Koeppen appeared after a break of fifteen years – the poetic, autobiographical *Youth*. It is a fragment of fragments. That it is an entity is nevertheless due to its style – both in terms of its language and its atmosphere. I admire this book as much as I do his principal work, the novel *Pigeons in the Grass*.

Koeppen was close to me for reasons beyond the extraordinary, to me undeniable, quality of his prose. To questions by interviewers he invariably replied: 'I have no home.' Indeed, he was not at home anywhere, he was a stranger everywhere. But he was not wholly lonely. He was always living in the realm of literature, which was a permanent part of his existence. In it time and again he sought protection and refuge, in it he found what he needed – asylum, albeit temporarily. But nothing, the French say, is more permanent than the temporary. Koeppen's love was for loners, outsiders, the affronted, the persecuted and the ostracized. He was the poetical agent of all minorities – from Jews to homosexuals.

This quiet, reserved and never brash man, though born in Greifswald and brought up in East Prussia, was close to me because he was nevertheless moulded by Berlin. There was something of Berlin in the rhythm of his language and its tempo, the precision of his expression, his never fully satisfied hunger for news, his – as one might put it – newspaper mania. Perhaps this is also true of Koeppen's enthusiasm, always moderated by scepticism – that enthusiasm without which one cannot concern oneself with literature in the long run.

He believed in nothing but literature. He loved poets and artists, he felt obliged to them, he considered himself their debtor. He knew no other gods beside them. His veneration was indestructible, his gratitude touching and, even in high old age, almost youthful.

When on 21 March 1996 I followed Wolfgang Koeppen's coffin at Munich's Nordfriedhof I knew that a major section of my life was at an end.

357

37

THE MAGICIAN'S FAMILY

It happened on 13 August 1955 in the coastal resort of Ustka, which until recently had been called Stolpmünde. The sun was shining magnificently; the sky could not have been bluer. The Baltic was calm, one might say majestic. I was sitting in a wicker beach chair, reading Goethe. I was doing so voluntarily, yet at the same time on the instruction of an employer. Yes, I was being paid for it, albeit not very generously. I had to prepare a selection of Goethe's poems for a Warsaw publisher. I was thinking to myself: the older I get (I was then thirty-five), the more Goethe's poetry delights me – whereas in my childhood and early youth it had been Schiller's ballads that aroused my love of German poetry.

For an instant I interrupted my reading. As I looked up I saw a fair-haired girl, of perhaps sixteen or seventeen, pretty and full of charm, approaching my wicker chair – light-footed and in joyful mood. The girl brought me two envelopes and was smiling happily, as if sure that they could only contain good news. Then she made a coquettish curtsey and quickly ran away. Her light-blue skirt, thin and wide, fluttered up.

One of the two envelopes contained a letter posted in Switzerland. It opened with the words: '*On the instruction of my husband, who unfortunately is ill in the local hospital – happily he is better again – I am answering your kind letter of 9 July.*' The letter was signed: '*With kind regards, yours Katia Mann.*' The other envelope contained a telegram from Polish Radio in Warsaw. It ran: '*Thomas Mann died yesterday. Stop. Request obituary fifteen minutes if possible today.*' Was I shocked? Did I have tears in my eyes? Or was I still thinking of the pretty girl in the blue skirt? I do not recollect. But I am certain that I felt alone. I realized that Thomas Mann had impressed and influenced me, perhaps even moulded me, more than any other German writer of our century. Since Heine, I knew that there had been no writer to whom I was indebted to such an extent and so profoundly. I felt somewhat helpless in my wicker beach chair.

I had long ago been taught in a Prussian grammar school that good form demanded that anything womanish and effeminate, anything elegiac, be manfully resisted. If, however, the feminine and the sentimental was getting the upper hand, then one should unconditionally and immediately remember one's duty. I therefore walked quickly to the holiday home where I was staying, taking with me the letter from Zurich, the telegram and the volume of Goethe. The obituary that was expected of me had to be written at once. The weather had abruptly turned, a rough wind was blowing off the sea. It seemed to me that it had suddenly gone chilly.

I was not to meet Katia Mann until April 1967. I had gone with Hans Mayer to Zürich, to the home of the Mann family at Kilchberg, right on the city boundary of Zürich, in order to record a conversation with Erika Mann for the *Literary Coffee House* series. A name-plate at the entrance said: '*Dr Thomas Mann*'. Yes, actually Doctor Thomas Mann. In the hall hung various framed diplomas recording his Nobel Prize and other awards, as well as several honorary degrees. I should like to think that these were displayed only after Thomas Mann's death. We were led into a living room whose large window offered a magnificent view of Lake Zürich.

A few moments later Katia Mann appeared. She wore an ankle-length dark grey dress. She looked like a severe *Domina*, like an impressive abbess. Hans Mayer was clutching a large bouquet of flowers which Frau Mann made no attempt to take from him. She snapped at him rather sharply: 'You wrote that my husband's late work was crumbling.' Mayer, still holding the flowers and looking like an embarrassed schoolboy, stammered helplessly: 'But, gnädige Frau, I ask you, I most humbly ask you to consider ...' Katia Mann immediately cut him short: 'Don't contradict me, Herr Mayer; you wrote that Thomas Mann's late style represented a crumbling. I'll have you know that more doctoral theses about my husband are submitted and printed every year throughout the world than about that man, about that Kafka.'

Mayer was spared a reply because the door opened and in came Thomas Mann's daughter – his 'bold and wonderful child', her father had called her, echoing Wotan's words about Brünhilde. Erika Mann, the former actress, wore long black trousers of silk or possibly brocade. She supported herself on metal crutches. Since 1958 she had suffered several fractures of her feet and hips; her entrance was therefore a little laborious, but at the same time proud and vigorous. Here was a self-confident woman, determined not to hide or ignore her disability, but to emphasize it and employ it for additional effect. From the first moment one was aware of an unusual personality. That Erika Mann, now a little over sixty, had once been beautiful and imperious like an Amazon queen was instantly obvious. There they stood facing me – two female representatives of this family, unequalled in our century. What the Windsors are to the British, I was thinking, the Manns are to the Germans, at least to the intellectuals.

Together with Erika Mann we moved to another room, where the microphones and the books which she intended to mention were already in place. It was not long before we discovered that Erika, who since 1947 had been helping her father as an excellent editor of his late works, was as acute and quick-witted as ever in conversation about literature, invariably spirited and argumentative. With unmistakably vicious satisfaction she told us that she had taken legal action against two German papers which had referred to allegedly intimate relations between her brother Klaus and herself, that she had won those law suits and been awarded substantial damages. At times one might think that Erika Mann, the Amazon queen, had in her later years become a Fury. But one also realized that she, who had the gift of loving passionately and, probably more often, of hating, had only rarely had the good fortune of loving truly – and that she was by no means popular, not even within her own family.

In the autumn of 1983 the Third Programme of German television broadcast an in-depth documentary on Klaus Mann. After I had respectfully and benevolently reviewed this film in *Frankfurter Allgemeine* I received a confused letter from Monika Mann, Erika's sister, born in 1910. One thing in it was clear: Monika reviled Erika as a 'witch' and asserted that she had contributed to Klaus's death. More than that: she had probably been responsible for her brother's suicide. A few months later Monika sent me a short contribution about conditions in the Mann household, intended for *Frankfurter Allgemeine*. The article was again aimed chiefly against her sister Erika, and in it she referred to: '*her obsession-nurtured closeness to her father, degenerating into jealousy.*' Publication of this article, with its unmistakably libellous content, was out of the question.

Disagreeable too, though for different reasons, was my contact with Thomas Mann's youngest son Michael, born in 1919. He had had some success as a violinist and viola player, but at about the age of forty he turned to German studies which he taught at the University of California in Berkeley. In 1974 I conceived the idea – as it soon turned out, not exactly a happy one – of asking him for a book review for *Frankfurter Allgemeine*. He wished to review the newly published German edition of the poems of W. H. Auden. I agreed, but no sooner had his manuscript arrived than Michael Mann telephoned from San Francisco to withdraw it. A little later we received a new version of the short article. It was thin on content and stylistically poor but we published it after a thorough reworking of the text. Simultaneously I asked Michael Mann – very cautiously, needless to say – whether he would prefer to write his contributions for *Frankfurter Allgemeine* in English. He did not accept this suggestion and I did not follow up his proposal to review further books.

In October 1974 I met him in Frankfurt. He gave me the impression of a seriously disturbed person. He greeted me, as well as some other people who were present, with an unusually low bow – so low that the upper part of his body was in a horizontal position. In the last letter I received from him, in the autumn of 1976, he was looking forward to meeting me in the winter. This meeting did not materialize. During the night of 31 December 1976 and 1 January 1977 Michael Mann died in Berkeley. The laconic announcement contained no details. I immediately contacted his brother Golo Mann, who confirmed the news, mentioned heart failure as the cause of death, and asked me to dispense with an obituary or even with an announcement. He was not prepared to explain this request. In point of fact, no German paper reported his death – except *Frankfurter Allgemeine*.

In my brief obituary I referred chiefly to Michael Mann's German studies publications.

Only later did the circumstances of his death become known. On behalf of the family, he had been preparing for publication Thomas Mann's diaries from the years 1918 to 1921. This work had been completed towards the end of December 1976 and was to be celebrated with friends on New Year's Eve. Michael Mann was already in his dinner jacket and people were ready to set off. At that point he decided to have a short rest first. He told the other members of the party to go on ahead and that he would follow shortly.

But instead he remained at his home near San Francisco, where he was found the following morning. He was lying in his bedroom, still wearing his dinner jacket, covered with a light rug and surrounded by flowers. The lights had been turned down. He was no longer alive. The post mortem revealed that a combination of alcohol and barbiturates had led to his death. He had previously made a number of unsuccessful attempts at suicide. The brief obituary in the *San Francisco Chronicle* concluded with the words: '*There will be no interment.*'

Just as with his brother Klaus Mann, who had committed suicide in 1949, Michael Mann's death was in part blamed on his father by friends, contemporaries and literary historians. There is no doubt that Michael suffered from his father's extreme coldness of temperament – right from his childhood. Thomas Mann's story *Early Sorrow*, written in 1925, painted an angry, almost vicious, portrait of the then six-year-old Michael. Although I only knew him slightly, he left a firm mark on my memory – perhaps because his misfortune was so great and its causes were so obvious.

The grave and terrible fate of being a son of Thomas Mann was a source of suffering also to Golo Mann. But he was the only one of the three sons who succeeded in taking to heart his father's maxim that man shall let death have no sovereignty over his thoughts – that one should resist the temptation of determining the hour of one's death oneself. Golo Mann died in 1994 at the age of eighty-five. His *German History of the 19th and 20th Centuries* and his truly monumental biography of Wallenstein made him the most successful German historian of the century, acknowledged and esteemed by colleagues and admired by countless readers, even those who normally give a wide berth to historical works. Nevertheless he was a melancholic loner who for many years regarded himself as ostracized and rejected. In his old age he was famous and wealthy, but when, in a questionnaire by *F.A.Z.-Magazin*, he was asked: 'Who would you wish to be?', he replied succinctly: 'Someone happier than myself.'

I first made Golo Mann's acquaintance in Hamburg in 1970. Closer and more continuous contact did not develop until 1974, when I began to pester him with letters requesting reviews – something I indefatigably and stubbornly continued to do until the end of the 1980s. I was as anxious to gain his collaboration as I had been to gain that of Wolfgang Koeppen, though for different reasons. Golo Mann was in many respects an ideal author for the literary section of *Frankfurter Allgemeine*, not only because of his exceptionally wide knowledge and genuine erudition. I considered it one of my most important tasks to run a literary section that would be read not only by colleagues and experts but, ideally, by anyone interested in literature. Unlike many another contributor, I never needed to remind Golo Mann who the target audience of his articles should be. His ideal was Saint Augustine, who, he said, made even the most difficult ideas easy for the reader.

He wrote all his articles in a pleasantly natural *parlando* which achieved a maximum of clarity, transparency and descriptiveness – a style that seemed to have nothing in common with that of his father. But the reality was probably different: Golo Mann's language had probably developed in conscious or subconscious opposition to Thomas Mann's exceedingly contrived diction – just as, at an early age, he had decided on a life in opposition to his father. In a telephone conversation, which touched on his relationship with his father, he told me: 'I wished him dead.' I was shocked and, somewhat upset, asked him: 'Do you know what you've just said?' Golo replied: 'Yes, that's how it was. I wished him dead. It was unavoidable.' Apart from the monograph on Friedrich von Gentz, he had not been able to write his books until after the death of his father – by which time he was forty-six.

We met in Hamburg and Dusseldorf, Frankfurt and Zürich, but not very often. On the other hand we frequently exchanged letters and had telephone conversations. Two topics were at the centre of these communications – literature and the Mann family. Golo Mann commended my articles and books, and now and again expressed reservations. But where my articles about the members of his family were concerned, he had a fundamental objection which he voiced on various occasions. In connection with an essay on Klaus Mann he said that all my judgements were correct; what was missing was 'sympathy'. And commenting on my articles on the individual volumes of Thomas Mann's *Diaries*, Golo repeated his general criticism: too little sympathy, too little love.

Whenever critics discussed books by his father he was irritated and considered writing a letter of protest – which he usually failed to do. Yet he himself enjoyed bad-mouthing individual works of Thomas Mann. He did not think very much of *Tonio Kröger*: nothing was right in the dialogue with Lisaweta, he said, it was 'nonsense'. Which of Thomas Mann's two stories – *Tonio Kröger* and *Early Sorrow* – was the worst, he asked me with a sneer. I did not take any of this seriously. 'If one listens to you talking about Thomas Mann's books,' I said to him, 'one is bound to conclude that you regard him as a particularly poor and untalented author.' Golo Mann contradicted me immediately. One could not say that – after all, the 'Joseph' novels, as far as format and quality were concerned, were something like the *Iliad* or the *Odyssey*. Well, I said to myself, we are back home again – and I could sleep peacefully.

Golo Mann was fond of relating anecdotes about his father, mostly the kind that were not flattering. I for my part told him an anecdote that, as it turned out, he had not heard. *The Magic Mountain* had appeared in the autumn of 1924 and within a few weeks there was a lot of trouble – among others with Gerhart Hauptmann, who was offended and angry about being parodied and caricatured in the novel as Mynheer Peeperkorn.

At that time Thomas Mann, who was on a brief visit to Zürich, looked in on an elegant gentlemen's outfitters on Bahnhofstrasse, where he had long been a customer. It was early in the morning. He was greeted by the proprietor with appropriate devotion. However, the man seemed a little nervous, quickly excused himself and walked up the stairs to the first floor of the store. After a few minutes he returned and informed Thomas Mann that he had another customer upstairs, the Herr Doktor Hauptmann. Did the Herr Doktor Mann wish to see his colleague, Gerhart Hauptmann? Thomas Mann instantly replied: 'No, it's a little too early in the day.' The proprietor bowed politely and said: 'The Herr Doktor Hauptmann is of the same opinion.'

Golo Mann was delighted: 'A delightful anecdote indeed. Except that it is an invention from start to finish. If it had really happened T.M. would have plagued us with this story countless times.' But Golo Mann was mistaken. The near-encounter in a Zürich gentlemen's outfitters did take place, though not until 1937.

In one of our extensive telephone conversations – this was in December 1975 – we discussed Thomas Mann's sexuality. Homosexual feelings and thoughts, Golo said, had not been unfamiliar to Thomas Mann, as was well known. But he had never been a practising homosexual. The idea that he had had contacts with boy prostitutes was absurd. His homosexual activities, according to Golo, had 'never gone below the belt'. Ultimately his homosexuality had kept within adolescent limits. One might say, Golo suggested, that Thomas Mann's sex life had been similar to that of a Prussian general. Vis-à-vis women he had been timid and reserved. That was why he had occasionally resorted to the services of prostitutes.

Asked about allegedly intimate letters from Thomas Mann to Klaus Mann, whose publication had apparently been prevented by the family, Golo Mann declared that such rumours proved total ignorance of the real father–son relationship. How could such letters exist when there had never been any closeness between Thomas and Klaus Mann? The father had 'abhorred' the homosexuality of his son Klaus. The subject had never been discussed between them. In his family, Golo informed me, there had been two kinds of homosexuality – a Mann kind and a Pringsheim kind. The Mann kind had been reserved and full of inhibitions and complexes; the Pringsheim kind, on the other hand, had been cheerful and life-asserting. Klaus had belonged to the Pringsheim tradition of his mother's family, while he himself belonged far more to the dark and complicated Mann tradition.

On one occasion we were walking near Kilchberg, not far from Zürich. As I was aware that Golo knew innumerable poems by heart I asked him to recite some for me. He began with Latin verses, by Horace and Ovid, and went on to Heine, Eichendorff and, repeatedly, Goethe. I asked him what Goethe meant to him. Goethe was as important to him as the air we breathe, as the light without which we cannot live, he responded, or something along these lines. He repeatedly used the word 'gratitude'.

When I went on to ask about his relationship with Thomas Mann, Golo did not duck the question, but answered monosyllabically. Now I was hearing different words – fear, revulsion, bitterness, probably also hate. As we were passing the Kilchberg cemetery he suggested we visited the grave of Conrad Ferdinand Meyer. There was no mention of the fact that Thomas and Katia Mann were buried in the same cemetery. When Golo Mann died in 1994 he too was buried in the Kilchberg cemetery – but, at his express wish, as far away as possible from the grave of his parents. In point of fact, his grave is close to the cemetery wall.

On my way back to Zürich I reflected that I had never in my whole life, encountered a person who had suffered so much from his father, or who owed so much to poetry, as Golo Mann, that hapless son of a genius and that happy admirer and noble enthusiast of literature.

38

MAX FRISCH, OR
EUROPEAN LITERATURE
PERSONIFIED

I well remember my first meeting with Max Frisch. It was in October 1964 at the Hotel Luisenhof in Hanover. It was his turn to be our guest at the *Literary Coffee House*. I was looking forward to making his acquaintance because I had a weakness not so much for his plays (except for his didactic *The Fire Raisers*) as for his novels and diaries.

As soon as I had settled in at the hotel I went downstairs, hoping to find one or the other of the two participants. From a gallery on the first floor I saw a gentleman walking up and down the lobby, slowly and perhaps a little bored. This was Max Frisch. I remained there for a while, watching him. This jovial, almost dignified, gentleman, I thought to myself, is the man who has written *I'm Not Stiller* and *Homo Faber* and to whom we owe those wonderful *Diaries*. World literature personified? No, a different term occurred to me, one at first glance more modest – European literature personified.

I had no hesitation about walking up to him and introducing myself. I felt certain that nothing could go wrong. No sooner did Frisch hear my name than his face lit up. He firmly and cordially shook my hand; perhaps, who knows, the famous man was about to embrace me. At any rate he said, not without solemnity and with some emotion: 'I thank you.' Although I had expected a friendly greeting I looked at him silently and expectantly. He quickly added: 'I thank you for your plea.' Now we were both moved – until one of us – I believe it was him – uttered the welcome (if not original) words: 'Let's go to the bar.'

The background of this business is simple enough. A few weeks before our meeting Frisch's five-hundred-page novel *Gantenbein* had appeared. He had worked on it for years and, understandably, there was nothing on earth then that he was more keenly interested in than its critical acclaim. This came soon enough.

Die Zeit carried a detailed essay about *Gantenbein*, written by my former colleague Hans Mayer. This considerable scholar had a lot to say about it, important and illuminating things. But he absolutely refused to answer his own question whether it was a good or a bad novel. Any reader, even one who had been bottom of his class, was bound to realize the implication: much as the reviewer had been able to say about *Gantenbein*, there was but little he had gained from the novel; he virtually rejected it.

Frisch had been not only disappointed but offended and hurt. For, in the 1960s, the influence and authority of *Die Zeit* were especially great in the field of literary criticism. However, a mere two weeks later, the same paper published a second, likewise very extensive, review of *Gantenbein*. This had been written by me. I declared myself for the novel. In this 'Plea for Max Frisch' I had vigorously argued against Hans Mayer.

Hence the author of *Gantenbein* was doubly content: I had praised his novel and cast doubt on all of Mayer's counter-arguments. It was my review that was the reason for Frisch's extremely cordial greeting in the lobby of the Luisenhof. I had been practising my trade long enough to have no illusions: I realized that an author's relations with a critic nearly always depended on just one thing – how that critic had assessed the author, more particularly his latest book.

After my plea for *Gantenbein* Frisch naturally remained favourably disposed to me. The more so as, in 1972, I warmly reviewed his new prose volume, his *Diary 1966–1971*. I declared Frisch '*a classic of the present*'. I was even more enthusiastic in my 1975 review of his book *Montauk*. I cannot rule out that by then he regarded me as a good critic.

Nevertheless our relationship was neither quite free from friction nor entirely harmonious. The principal reason for this was that I was anxious to gain him at least as an occasional contributor to the literary section of *Frankfurter Allgemeine*. I wrote to him, I phoned him, I occasionally met him. I always suggested subjects that I assumed would be especially tempting to him. He would reply promptly and amicably, but there were always excuses. I certainly received no manuscript from him. I was annoyed by this, I even regarded it as a defeat.

Yet in 1977 Frisch surprised me with a present. He sent me a wonderful etching – his portrait, drawn by Otto Dix. This was intended, as he later informed me, to make up for the many disappointments he had caused me. The point was that various political aspects of *Frankfurter Allgemeine* were unacceptable to him. That was why he did not wish to write for this paper, and nor would he do so in future.

Writers, however, whether famous or not, are not necessarily reliable people when it comes to saying yes and no. Thus Frisch after all surprised me with a contribution. At the beginning of 1978, a manuscript arrived – in defiance of his earlier disappointing announcement. It was an excerpt from his play *Triptych*, which by then had neither been published nor staged. I was overjoyed – but not for long. There was not a single scene in the whole of *Triptych* that would be suitable for pre-performance publication in *Frankfurter Allgemeine*. This shocked and alarmed me. It soon turned out that no theatre in the Federal Republic was prepared to stage the play. This has not changed to this day.

I also disliked Frisch's next book, *Man in the Holocene*. It was immediately clear to me that I must withhold comment. Much though the subject interested me, I found the story alien and laboriously contrived. Did I lack the sensory equipment for its tone or its style? I do not regret having thought it proper to remain silent about some books; on the contrary, I regret not having remained silent about others. My decision not to write about *Man in the Holocene* did not jeopardize the somewhat distant but correct relationship between Frisch and myself – at least not for the moment.

I think back with pleasure to visiting him in May 1980 in his small Zürich flat on Stockergasse. My next visit, however, had more important consequences – this was to his new, exceptionally light and spacious, apartment, again in the centre of Zürich, on Stadelhoferstrasse. He had chosen it, he said, because everything he needed was close by – at the top of his list he mentioned a pharmacy. The apartment was very pleasant, but the construction of an S-Bahn, a city railway, line in its immediate proximity worried him. The noise was unbearable. Nevertheless he had taken it, seeing that it was difficult for him to find suitable accommodation – mainly because of his reputation. Why?

Many Zürich citizens, Frisch maintained, did not wish to have anything to do with him because they regarded him as a militant left-winger. He reviled and attacked Switzerland cheerfully and vigorously. The only thing still tying him to the country was his passport. I did not believe a word of it. Why, in that case, did he live in Zürich? Surely he could live wherever he wished – and, as everybody knew, he had tried living in Berlin, New York and Rome. Yet Zürich had remained the centre of his existence. He was quite simply, I told him with a laugh, too many things at the same time – an urban European author, a Swiss regional poet, and an indigenous cosmopolitan. Frisch did not contradict me.

Whatever I said, he was and remained in excellent spirits. I soon discovered the reason: he was working on a new story and was convinced he had found an excellent subject. It was not just politeness that made me give free rein to my uncontrollable curiosity: I really wanted to know about it. I did not have to wait for long. Frisch uncorked a bottle of champagne and began to talk with verve.

An unusual criminal trial had recently taken place in Zürich. He had attended it each day. What he told me about the course and the details of the proceedings, about the defendants, the witnesses and the jurors – it was all magnificent. I could not think of any more exciting or more interesting story for Frisch. Here a great and experienced raconteur had an appropriate, indeed ideal, subject. I was quite sure of that. I congratulated him and thought to myself: this hour – because his account had taken at least that – would long remain in my memory.

Impatiently I awaited the book. It was published in the spring of 1982 under the title *Bluebeard*. It did not just disappoint me, it horrified me. It appeared that Frisch's attitude to his subject had changed. Did he no longer believe in the suggestive power of the persons and motives he had encountered in the Zürich courtroom? Or was his self-assurance shaken? Whichever – he had stripped an unusual and exciting story, one that spoke for itself, of its immediacy and vividness by all kinds of modifications and alienating touches. I did not believe – as I had after reading his *Holocene* story – that this could be my fault. That was why I did not want to back away. I wrote frankly what I thought of the new book, trying to mitigate the bitter taste by means of loving turns of phrase, to sweeten the pill of condemnation – something that invariably is in vain. Not for the first time I was reminded of Goethe's words in *Iphigenie*, words that apply also to criticism: '*Refusal wastes its breath in eloquence / The only word the other hears is no.*'

Over the following years we occasionally exchanged letters, but I did not see Frisch again until April 1986. He was in Frankfurt, where, following the showing of a very long film about him, *Conversations in Old Age*, he was to answer questions from journalists. Many had been invited, few had turned up. I was then working on a review of Günter Grass's novel *The Rat* and was anxious to complete it for the next literary page of *Frankfurter Allgemeine* so I too did not take part in the event.

However, there was another reason for this. Such performances are nearly always insincere and embarrassing. Heiner Müller steadfastly refused to go to première parties, saying: 'I don't want to lie.' Admittedly Müller was very much present at the party following the première of his production of *Tristan* in Bayreuth in 1993. Those who refuse to oblige their praise-hungry colleagues with friendly lies often have no inhibitions about accepting their flatterers' lies at face value.

The evening after the showing of *Conversations in Old Age* I met Max Frisch at the home of the publisher Siegfried Unseld. He greeted me very differently from that time at the Luisenhof in Hanover – coolly, indeed frostily. Had my absence from the press conference annoyed him? Perhaps, but he soon began to talk about *Bluebeard* and my review of it. I expected the worst and that was how it turned out. Frisch was undisguisedly irritated, called me 'impertinent', and became rude and aggressive.

He then declared that it was all his fault: he had made a mistake and should never have revealed the contents of his book to me. That was the chief reason for my unfavourable – and, as he thought, one-sided, unjust and cruel – review. But I was, and still am, convinced that my judgement of that story, even if I had known nothing about its subject, would scarcely have been any more positive. Once more I had to reconcile myself to the fact that an author's attitude to a critic depends on what that critic has said about his latest book.

371

I never saw Frisch again. In the winter of 1991, when my book with the more important articles I had written about him was in preparation, Frisch himself, at the publisher's request, selected the photographs for it. He received a copy about two weeks before his death and cordially thanked me for it: he was happy, he said, that the crisis between us over the *Bluebeard* review had now blown over and that I, as he put it, was loyally on his side.

The atmosphere on that last evening, in April 1976, had made it impossible for me to tell Max Frisch something that, despite all my enthusiasm, had perhaps not sufficiently emerged from my reviews. I wished to tell him that I owed him a great deal, that some of his books were an inseparable part of my life, indeed that I loved them – *I'm Not Stiller* and *Homo Faber*, *Gantenbein* and *Montauk*, and not least the two *Diaries*. More than that: that his writings meant more to me than those of Dürrenmatt or Böll, of Grass or Uwe Johnson. Does this mean that Frisch was the better writer? No, this is not a comparison of qualities.

Whether this speaks for him or against him, it is a fact: unlike Dürrenmatt or Böll, unlike Grass or Uwe Johnson, Frisch wrote about the complexes and conflicts of the intellectual. Time and again he addressed us, the intellectuals from the educated bourgeoisie. More than anyone else, Frisch understood our mentality and recognized our hunger for life and our capacity for love, our weakness and our helplessness. That which over many years we sensed, surmised, thought, hoped and feared without being able to express it – he articulated it and dramatized it. He was the poet of his and our world without ever poeticizing it. He has, time and again, made us and everyone else aware of his and our – the word can no longer be avoided – identity.

Thus we were, and are, able to find in his work, in the work of the great European writer Max Frisch, what we all seek in literature – our sufferings. And, also, ourselves. That was what I would have liked to have said to him then.

39

YEHUDI MENUHIN
AND OUR QUARTET

The first time I heard the name Menuhin – I was still a child and had only been living in Berlin a short time – the word 'divine' was used. Someone – it must have been around 1930 – told us in our sitting room about a concert by the thirteen-year-old with the Berlin Philharmonic, quoting Albert Einstein's judgement about his playing: '*Now I know that there is a God in heaven.*' From the very start the reputation of the violinist Yehudi Menuhin preceded him. That is how it remained: year by year the fame of the prophet with the violin grew, the fame of the virtuoso who offered the public balm for the ear and for the soul. Hidden behind the bombast of reference to supernatural beings was, as in most such cases, nothing other than the helplessness of those who attempted to capture this art in words.

About ten years later, when Tosia and I were vegetating in the Warsaw ghetto, a young man sent us word through mutual acquaintances that we would be welcome at his place towards 5 p.m. the following day: a few gramophone records would be played. In the small room where our host, scarcely older than ourselves but already married, lived with his wife of about the same age, seven or eight people were sitting on the floor. We listened to Berlioz and Debussy. After that, something happened that left me feeling stunned: what so affected me was a violin concerto (more precisely the first movement of a violin concerto) which at the time I did not know – Mozart's Concerto No. 3 in G Major, played by Menuhin. I was speechless. I love that movement to this day and I believe that no one played it more beautifully than the youthful Menuhin.

On our way back through the overcrowded and filthy streets of

373

the ghetto we talked about our obliging hosts. We envied them. They not only owned the record of Mozart's Violin Concerto in G Major, but also had what we could only dream about – a room of their own, scantily furnished, to be sure, but with a bed. We were both thinking the same. And if I remember correctly, I quoted, in defiance of the strident and ceaseless shouts of the street traders and beggars, Shakespeare's lines about music being the food of love.

I first saw Menuhin in Warsaw in 1956. The 'Thaw' was making it possible, at least temporarily, for great Western musicians and actors to appear in Poland. They all came – from Leonard Bernstein and Arthur Rubinstein to Gérard Philipe and Laurence Olivier, and indeed also Menuhin. His concert was crowded; in the corridors of the Warsaw Philharmonic, only recently rebuilt, there was a throng of men and women students from the College of Music who had the cheapest tickets for standing room only. The huge podium, which had space enough for a symphony orchestra plus an even larger choir, was totally empty. There was not even a piano because the programme consisted entirely of solo sonatas by Bach and Bartók.

Menuhin walked briskly on to the podium. After the storm of applause which greeted him, an uncanny silence fell. Expectantly we waited for his legendary tone, which we only knew from the gramophone record: in a moment we would actually hear it. But Menuhin lowered his violin again. No one understood why he was not beginning to play or what his friendly beckoning of the bow signified: he was inviting those standing along the walls and in the corridors to come up on to the podium and sit on the floor. They all obeyed – hesitantly at first, then faster and faster. This image has stayed with me ever since: hundreds of young people sitting on the floor, and in the middle of them a slender young man at whom they were all gazing.

My first conversation with Yehudi Menuhin was, rather surprisingly, at the beginning of 1960. I was travelling by train from Cologne to Hamburg and went to the restaurant car. As there were no empty tables, the waiter put me at one already occupied by three people. After a cursory glance at the menu I looked up at my neighbours and froze with shock – so much so that, rather impolitely, I asked: 'Who are you?' My neighbour replied quite calmly: 'Yehudi Menuhin. And this is my sister Hephzibah.' There was no side to him, he was speaking quite naturally, without any pretension.

I recollect two questions I put to Menuhin during that train journey. I wanted to know whom he regarded as the greatest living violinist. His answer came at once: David Oistrach. Then he added: 'There's something of a gypsy fiddler in him' – meaning, of course, Oistrach's temperament, his joyous and primeval manner of playing. Lest I misunderstood him, Menuhin added, laughing, that in every great violinist there was a small gypsy. Then we spoke about the monotony of a virtuoso's life. He was travelling from one town to another, appearing every evening to perform a Beethoven or Brahms sonata with his sister. Was this not, I asked, very strenuous in the long run, if it went on for weeks. And did it not – this was what particularly interested me – also get boring? Menuhin reflected for a moment and then gave me an answer of great simplicity, if not banality – an answer I have never forgotten. He said: 'If one makes a real effort every evening, it never gets boring.'

In the autumn of 1979 I was on a lecture tour of China which took me to Peking, Nanking, Canton and Shanghai. In Nanking I was recommended to visit the zoo. It was a dull day, yet there were thousands of people thronging the avenues and standing in front of the animal cages, adults as well as children. Suddenly they seemed to become restless, turned away from the cages, called out to each other and communicated by signs. No doubt something sensational had occurred. But it was not a lion or a giraffe or a rhino. I was the sensation. I was competing with the hippopotami and the giant snakes. I was followed, I was surrounded, I was shamelessly stared at. The crowd accompanied me in amazement, without dignifying the tiger or the camels by so much as a single glance. They held their children up for a better look: evidently they were being instructed about this strange creature from a distant land. The sensation would have been even greater if the white-skinned stranger had had fair hair.

What I experienced at the Nanking zoo would not have happened in Peking or Shanghai, where a lot of Europeans could be seen at that time. In Peking, along with the interpreter assigned to me, who never left me alone for a moment, I went to a special shop selling articles available only against Western currencies, such as whisky or Coca-Cola. Likewise accompanied by a Chinese, no doubt an interpreter, a familiar figure stood before me. It was Yehudi Menuhin. This accidental meeting in a strange city surprised us both: again I was speechless.

I asked him what he was doing there. He answered briefly: 'Beethoven and Brahms with the local orchestra.' And what was I doing? 'I'm giving lectures on Goethe and Thomas Mann.' Menuhin was silent, but not for long: 'Ah well, we're Jews of course.' After a moment he added: 'That we travel from country to country, spreading German music and German literature, and interpreting it – that's good and how it should be.' We regarded each other thoughtfully, and perhaps a little wistfully. Two or three days later I heard Menuhin play the Beethoven concerto in Hong Kong. Critics said that he was past his peak, that he no longer played as perfectly as in the past. This may be true. But perfection was never his thing – more 'the divine' that Einstein spoke of.

On 22 April 1986 Menuhin had his seventieth birthday. Shortly afterwards it was celebrated by a splendid event at the Redoute in Bad Godesberg. Musicians had come from all over the world, as also had leading German politicians. I had been asked to give a short address. I chose the subject that had occupied Menuhin's life – 'Music and Morality'. Music, I said, was a goddess, moreover the most wonderful we know. But unfortunately, over the centuries and millennia, she had been at the service of all those who wished to make use of her – rulers and politicians, ideologists and, of course, priests. Hard though it was for us to reconcile ourselves to the idea, music was a whore, though perhaps the most delightful one that ever existed. Music had been used to create fear of God, to arouse patriotic sentiments and to drive human beings into battle and to their deaths. Songs had been sung by slaves and also by slavemasters, by concentration camp inmates and also by their guards. The young people who, along with us in a small room in the Warsaw ghetto, had listened to Mozart's Violin Concerto No. 3 in G Major, played by Yehudi Menuhin, had all died in the gas chamber. Any causal connection between music and morality was just a piece of fine wishful thinking, a frivolous conceit.

What about Menuhin? In every situation and with unassailable consistency he had understood art and life, music and morality as a unity – or, more correctly, he had firmly wanted to understand them as a unity. Time and again he had proclaimed and demanded that synthesis; for well over half a century he had lived that synthesis before our eyes. He had endeavoured to make the violin a weapon against injustice and hardship on this earth. As a child – he would often recall – he had been convinced that with Bach's Chaconne or with Beethoven's violin concerto one could make people if not good, then at least better human beings. I suspect that secretly he believed that until his death on 12 March 1999.

But those generous and truly noble efforts of Yehudi Menuhin – were they quite free from quixotic traits? Was it possible that this artist of our century was naive despite his genius? Fontane says about Old Stechlin that he was *the best that we can be – a man and a child*. What did he ultimately accomplish?

When Thomas Mann, on some occasion or other, was besieged by journalists, he answered their questions patiently in an extensive letter, in which one sentence struck me: *Your last question as to the "real purpose" of my work is the most difficult to answer. I would simply say: Joy.* Maybe this also tells us what Menuhin provided for us – joy, pleasure and happiness. Nothing more, nothing less. That is what we have to thank him for – in admiration and reverence.

And what did Mozart or Schubert accomplish? Did they succeed in changing the world? Yes, certainly, but only to the extent that they added their work to the world as it existed. One consolation is left to us: we only know what music has failed to prevent. What our world would be like without music – that we do not know. Is not the same true of poetry? Did I ever hope that literature could educate people or change the world?

No one with even the most cursory knowledge of literary history is likely to fall for such illusions. Have Shakespeare's tragedies and histories prevented a single murder? Did Lessing's *Nathan the Wise* at least curb the steadily growing anti-Semitism in the eighteenth century? Did Goethe's *Iphigenie* make human beings any more human? Did even one individual, after reading Goethe's poems, become noble, generous and good? Did Gogol's *Government Inspector* reduce corruption in Tsarist Russia? Did Strindberg succeed in improving the marital life of Swedish citizens?

Millions of spectators in innumerable countries have watched Bertolt Brecht's plays. But Max Frisch doubted whether a single one

377

had, as a result, changed his political views or even re-examined them. He even doubted whether Brecht himself believed in the educational effect of his work. During rehearsals he, Frisch, had had the impression that not even proof positive that his plays could contribute nothing to the transformation of society would have affected Brecht's need for theatre.

No, I have never seriously believed in any appreciable pedagogical function of literature, but I do believe in the need for commitment. In other words, even though writers cannot change anything, they should strive for change – for the sake of the quality of their work. In the late 1950s and even more so in the early 1960s, by which time I was living and writing in the Federal Republic, this postulate more or less clearly emerged from my articles, with the words 'social criticism' now and again cropping up.

In 1968, however, and in the following years a militant and gloomy hostility to art was gaining ground in the literary life of the Federal Republic – and the demand for the kind of commitment that was to be the foundation of new novels and plays, along with the then fashionable term 'utopia', disappeared from my articles. When Thomas Mann wrote *Buddenbrooks*, or Proust his *Remembrance of Things Past*, or Kafka *The Trial*, they could not have been further away from thinking that their prose could improve society – yet they created works which remained unsurpassed in our century. I expected nothing from a literature which aimed to change the world; I could no longer imagine it. Unless, of course, one was prepared to forgo quality and to use the literary form solely as a vehicle for political or ideological theses and visions. But naturally there was no question of that.

Like every critic, I wished to educate – but not the writers. A writer who lets himself be educated is not worth educating. I was aiming at the public, at the readers. To put it bluntly: I wanted to explain to them why the books I considered good and beautiful actually were good and beautiful; I wanted to get them to read those books. I cannot complain. My reviews – at least most of the time – had the desired effect on the public. Nevertheless, this effect did not seem to me sufficient: surely one should not content oneself with the fact that an important, if perhaps difficult, book was taken notice of only by a minority.

In the summer of 1987 I was visited by two erudite gentlemen from ZDF, the Second German Television – Dieter Schwarzenau, who is still working there, and Johannes Willms, who has for some time been Arts Editor of *Süddeutsche Zeitung*. The gentleman drank tea and schnapps and were in high spirits. It took some time before, possibly encouraged by alcohol, they came to the point. Would I like to do a regular literary slot for ZDF? I firmly declined. But the gentlemen carefully ignored my answer. Instead they wanted to know how I might envisage such a programme. I thought to myself: I will make all kinds of conditions until my visitors despair and give up.

Each transmission, I said provocatively, should run for at least sixty minutes, better still for seventy-five. There should be no more than four persons, including myself. I would perform two functions: I would simultaneously be the moderator and one of the four persons debating. The two gentlemen were not to be ruffled; they nodded agreement.

If I wanted to end this useless conversation I would have to bring in the heavy guns. In the programme, I said, there must be no fading-in of pictures or film clips, no songs or *chansons*, no scenes from novels, no authors reading from their works or, walking in a park, obligingly explaining their work. The screen was to show nothing but those four persons talking about books and, as was to be expected, arguing about them. Only someone who knows anything about television can realize the pain this caused the two gentlemen. After all, the continual domination of the visual is the sacred law of television. And I had dared to rebel against that law. Surely my polite visitors would never swallow that. I waited tensely for their reaction. Would they go pale or perhaps even faint? But things turned out differently. Messrs Schwarzenau and Willms inhaled deeply through their noses, downed another schnapps, and softly declared: 'Agreed.'

In the early days of television the press occasionally discussed the 'eternal conflict' between the screen and the book: television, it was claimed, was 'the sworn enemy of the book'. I often objected to this thesis, and in 1961 I disputed this conflict in *Die Welt*. Instead I demanded an alliance that I felt sure would benefit both sides. In the course of the conversation with the two gentlemen from ZDF I asked myself whether their surprising offer, unlikely though it seemed, might perhaps provide an opportunity to do something for literature, more precisely for its wider dissemination. The attempt seemed worth while: there was nothing to be lost and who knows, quite a lot to be gained.

The new programme was first transmitted on 25 March 1988 – *Literarisches Quartett* [*Literary Quartet*]. Sigrid Löffler and Hellmuth Karasek were part of it from the start. Reviewers were disappointed and ungracious, to put it mildly. One of my famous colleagues observed briefly that the thing was dead already, that the *Quartet* was stillborn.

What did I hope to achieve with the *Literary Quartet*? Basically the same as with my printed criticism; the *Quartet* was to be a mediator between writers and readers, between art and society, between literature and life. But even though this *Quartet* had the same aims as reviews in newspapers and journals, it was using different means. And it was addressing, at least in part, a different audience. I have always considered clarity the main aim of criticism, and I believed this to be even more true for television. One had to speak here with even greater clarity, formulate accurately and comprehensibly because so many things could distract from the spoken word – Sigrid Löffler's hairdo, Hellmuth Karasek's jacket or my tie. I also insisted that in our discussions of books there must be no readings and no prompt notes.

Was I aiming at an entertaining programme about literature? No, I was not – but neither was it to be avoided. If the *Quartet* was found to be entertaining by many viewers, I am happy. Of course, we also wished to entertain – in line with the tradition of German literary criticism from Lessing to Heine and Fontane, and on to Kerr and Polgar. It was not our aim to discuss books *because* they were being talked about. But we were happy when the books we discussed began to be talked about. We did not follow the bestseller lists. But we were pleased if the books we discussed ended up there.

In addition to readers or aficionados of literature, our audience also included people who did not wish to know anything about it. But now and again they would watch the programme because they enjoyed our conversation, and perhaps also our arguments. And it appeared that these viewers, perhaps surprised by their own sudden interest, would get hold of one or other of the books we had been talking about. I make no secret of the fact that I had a particular interest in those very viewers. The *Quartet* is being blamed for a lot of things. The most frequent complaint is that the programme is banal, at times populist and always superficial, that nothing was being appropriately justified, that everything was being simplified. Such complaints, and many others, are entirely fair – and I am the one responsible for these shortcomings.

As five books are discussed in every programme, an average of fourteen to fifteen minutes is available for each of them – this means about three-and-a-half minutes per title for each of the four participants. During these three-and-a-half minutes something needs to be said about the individuality of the author, about the subject and the problems of his new book, about its motives and characters, about the artistic means applied, and sometimes also something about certain topical, chiefly political, aspects. In short: are there any proper analyses of literary works in *Quartet*? No, never. Are things being simplified? Invariably. Is the result superficial? Yes, even very super-ficial. We can do no more than hint at the impression the books have made on us personally and state briefly what we think is good or bad about them. Beyond that – and this is true of the three permanent members of the *Quartet* as well as of any guests – we have to forget our literary-criticism ambitions, not entirely but in part.

Is it worth while? We are told that there has been no series in the history of German television that has had such an immediate and powerful effect as *Quartet* on the sale of literary works, including, and especially, demanding works. But is such an effect one of the tasks, or even duties, of criticism? Yes, certainly, and today more than ever. What matters today is holding on to the public. In other words: we should see to it that the public does not run away – to other, and not necessarily less honourable, leisure pursuits.

I would regard it as a great wrong if my professional achievements were judged solely on the strength of the *Literary Quartet*. What I had to say, and what I have said, on literature can be found in my articles for newspapers and periodicals, and in my books. However, the one thing which I had hoped, but never quite managed, to accomplish during my long life as a critic – making a broad impact on the public – has been made possible solely through the medium of television.

40

JOACHIM FEST, MARTIN WALSER AND 'THE END OF THE CLOSE SEASON'

Am I to write about the German historians' dispute? Is there any point in doing so? Thirteen years have since passed and some of the principal participants in the argument are no longer alive. The latest edition of the Brockhaus Encyclopaedia lists the dispute – *Historikerstreit* – as a keyword, but adds that it was unproductive for scholarship. Evidently what once excited the German intellectual world had itself become history. But it has not yet been forgotten, that unfortunate dispute.

Let political historians and sociologists discuss it – I do not belong to that circle. I played no part in the controversy, so I do not need to comment on the affair. Now, after the passage of thirteen years, I am entitled to remain silent.

But whether I like it or not, I suffered from this historians' dispute. I felt ashamed because it originated with *Frankfurter Allgemeine* and because the paper did not play a creditable role in it. I felt ashamed because it had been inspired by Joachim Fest and because of his role in the dispute. I cannot imagine my life without either – the historians' dispute or Joachim Fest.

In the autumn of 1985 a film by the film-maker and dramatist Rainer Werner Fassbinder was to be premièred at the Kammerspiele; its title was *Refuse, the Town and Death*. It was repeatedly criticized for its aggressive anti-Semitism. The planned première could not take place because members of the Jewish community in Frankfurt were occupying the stage in protest. I was sitting in the auditorium, alarmed and dismayed. I did not know what to do, any more than anybody else present, chiefly critics, reporters and journalists.

Eventually, slim though my chances were, I decided to intervene. I walked up on the stage and spoke to Ignatz Bubis, the chairman of the Jewish community. The representatives of the community, I told him, had achieved their goal by keeping the stage occupied for several hours. They had prevented the film being shown and, at the same time, demonstrated a new Jewish self-assurance. But now it would be right to leave the stage, to enable the reporters, who had come from all over Germany as well as from abroad, to see the performance. Bubis answered that the demonstrators – mainly elderly people, survivors of concentration camps – were bound by a resolution of the council of the community. My intervention was therefore fruitless and pointless.

Fassbinder's film is of no literary merit – a sloppy and distasteful piece of work. Even so I regard it as typical of its time: however awkwardly and brutally, it explores a Federal German problem – the German attitude to the Jews. The phrase then coined for this trend was 'the end of the close season' – suggesting that the time had come to speak openly and honestly, indeed ruthlessly, about the Jews and their role in this country.

At first it might be thought that Fassbinder and his followers have little or nothing in common with the historians' dispute. Yet that dispute was directed against the same Federal German taboo. The lecture of the Berlin historian Ernst Nolte, which opened the debate and also concerned itself with German attitudes towards the Jews, reflected the same trend. The historians' dispute thus continued the discussion provoked by Fassbinder's film, though of course through an entirely different medium and on a different level.

Nolte's lecture was published in *Frankfurter Allgemeine* on 6 June 1986 – under the heading: 'A past that will not go away. A speech that was written but could not be delivered.' According to an editorial lead-in, this address was to be given at the Frankfurt *Römerberggespräche*, except that the speaker's invitation had been revoked 'for reasons unknown'. What the title and the lead-in claimed was not true: Nolte was certainly not prevented from giving his address and no one had withdrawn his invitation. Even the formula 'for reasons unknown' suggests that the paper was being economical with the truth. A simple telephone call to the Frankfurt city administration, the organizer of the *Römerberggespräche*, would have helped to clarify the state of affairs as set out in the correspondence with Nolte.

Nolte's unwieldy article, often couched in pseudo-scientific jargon, contained two simple ideas. First: the German murder of the Jews was by no means unique, but was comparable with other mass murders in our century. Second: the Holocaust was the consequence, if not a repetition, of the Bolshevik rule of terror, a kind of German protective measure and hence, as Nolte suggested, an understandable reaction. He was thus trying to defend National Socialism, to minimize the German crimes and, if possible, blame them on others, especially the Soviets. The anti-Semitic tone of his article may have been more or less camouflaged, but it could hardly be missed. It evidently did not occur to Fest, or he did not think it opportune, to do what fairness should have demanded after our long years of collaboration – show me Nolte's article before publishing it.

Some of the editors at *Frankfurter Allgemeine* were irritated, others appalled. Such things had never before appeared in the pages of the newspaper. It was assumed that Fest had only allowed the provocative article to be printed in order to publish a convincing and effective rejoinder that was ready and waiting in his desk drawer. The matter was of some importance as Nolte's theses were astonishingly close to the slogans of the right-wing radicals, not to mention the frequently anti-Semitic tone of the beer-cellar politicians. However, there was no rejoinder. The contributions sent to *Frankfurter Allgemeine*, protesting against the scandalous article, were all rejected by Fest without explanation. Some of my colleagues believed that I myself should reply to Nolte's confused and irresponsible arguments. But this I would do only if Fest asked me to do so. And there was no question of that.

Not until five weeks later was there a polemical reply to Nolte and a few other historians who championed a similar revision of historiography. This reply was by Jürgen Habermas, and it appeared not in *Frankfurter Allgemeine* but in *Die Zeit*. *Frankfurter Allgemeine* merely published a few 'letters to the editor' and it was only after twelve weeks, and repeated demands, that a response to Nolte's theses appeared in that paper. This was written by Fest himself. We could not believe our eyes: Fest emphatically defended Nolte, he declared himself in agreement with nearly all his arguments, and only hesitantly and with great reluctance uttered the few reservations that he felt he had to make. From that moment onwards the German as well as the foreign press increasingly often bracketed Fest's name with Nolte's. *'It's always worried me / to see you keep such company!'* says Goethe's Gretchen.

It was Eberhard Jäckel in *Die Zeit* who demonstrated the absurdity of Nolte's ideas and the disastrous nature of Fest's eventual rejoinder. One could breathe again. A lot of other articles followed – mainly in *Die Zeit* but also in publications such as *Der Spiegel* and *Merkur*, *Frankfurter Rundschau* and *Neue Zürcher Zeitung*. A journalistic and moral triumph had dropped into the lap of *Die Zeit*. An unprecedented situation had come about: the debate triggered by *Frankfurter Allgemeine* was taking place everywhere except in *Frankfurter Allgemeine*. Serious damage had been done to the reputation of the features section of the paper that had prided itself (not without justification) on its tolerance and liberal attitudes – and it had undoubtedly been done by Joachim Fest. Many people believed that *Frankfurter Allgemeine* had been compromised and that Fest had reached the low point of his career.

A fuller account of the historians' dispute does not belong here. But it is to the credit of the majority of German contemporary historians that the rewriting of the historical picture aimed at by Nolte and his supporters did not take place. Nolte himself never changed his views; on the contrary, to the delight of the right-wing radicals, he confronted the public with increasingly unpleasant and hair-raising assertions. Thus he declared that Hitler had been justified in interning and deporting all German Jews. He did not flinch from comparing them to vermin. As for the question, posed by himself, whether the Nazis had ever treated the Jews cruelly, Nolte denied this. After all, they had been killed *'without cruel intention, the way one wants to get rid of vermin to which one similarly does not wish to cause pain'*.

As late as December 1998 Nolte praised the Waffen-SS as the *'ultimate in warriordom'* and hoped that its history would be written *'with blood from the heart'*, *'even though, and just because, one knows that their great feats of arms plumbed the depths of unchivalrous behaviour, to wit the killing of defenceless persons, especially of "inferior" persons and Jews.'* The gassing of Jews therefore, according to Nolte, was no more than unchivalrous behaviour.

Are those who doubt this scholar's soundness of mind wrong to do so? In 1994, by which time Fest was no longer a publisher of *Frankfurter Allgemeine*, the paper finally distanced itself from Nolte. He reflected, it was said, *'the whole delusion of the period researched by him'*. It is a delusion that at times comes very close to insanity. *'But though this be madness, yet there is method in't'* – as Polonius says in an 'aside' during his conversation with Hamlet.

It may seem surprising that I am devoting so much attention to a minor, and indeed a contemptible, figure of modern German history. But this chapter is not about Ernst Nolte; it is about Joachim Fest. Over the years of our, in many respects, happy and fruitful collaboration we had countless talks – particularly about the Third Reich and everything connected with it. If I remember correctly, Fest never tried to justify the Nazi crimes nor did he attempt to minimize them. But he frequently tried to relativize them. He was fond of pointing to the mass murders committed by other dictators and would often remark that 'Stalin was as great a murderer as Hitler'.

Did Fest want to offset German guilt against the crimes of others? In theory and in principle he was, of course, against this. Yet such comparisons cropped up repeatedly, not only in his verbal observations but also in the article in which he defended Nolte. Nothing characterizes his attitude more clearly than the fact that he arranged for this article on German mass murder to be illustrated with a photograph showing a gigantic mound of skulls. The caption below the picture read: *'Genocide exposed in Cambodia but unacknowledged by the rest of the world.'*

Time and again, in our almost daily conversations, I emphatically protested against such opinions, but evidently not strongly enough. Certainly I did not achieve anything: even Nolte's vilest assertions failed to bring Fest to his senses. Eventually, in 1987, Nolte declared that the *'Final Solution of the Jewish question'* had not been the work of the Germans, but *'the collective work of European fascism and anti-Semitism'*. He declared this even though neither Italian nor French fascism were responsible for the persecution of the Jews. Was Nolte's thesis due to ignorance, or are we dealing here with the deliberate dissemination of untruth?

On this point, too, Fest remained silent. I could no longer bear this and was resolved to bring matters to a head. I went to his office and asked him if he regarded Nolte's statement as acceptable. No, he replied after some reflection, Nolte had gone a little over the top. Would Fest be prepared to protest against this patent untruth, which was tantamount to a falsification of history? Yes, he replied; not straight away, as this might be misunderstood, but in six months' time. This, Fest promised me, he would certainly do. When the six months had elapsed he informed me that he would on no account distance himself from Nolte's views. I was not given the assurance I asked for. After that, Fest and I no longer spoke to each other. The political and moral consensus which had existed between us regarding the Third Reich and its consequences, the consensus that was fundamental to my work on *Frankfurter Allgemeine*, and indeed my whole existence in the Federal Republic – that consensus was needlessly, indeed wantonly, destroyed by Joachim Fest.

A friendship that had meant a great deal to me was at an end. The fact that Fest had, at the same time, damaged his own reputation, which he largely owed to his monumental book about Hitler, was no consolation to me. I have questioned the reason for his sinister role in the historians' dispute. Did he really believe the German people were being wronged in connection with the Nazi crimes? Was the cause therefore to be found in his patriotism, in a national pride that had clouded his vision? There is nothing wrong with patriotism as such – yet it often makes me mistrustful. Because only one step separates it from nationalism, and from there it is just one more step to chauvinism. I like Nietzsche's dictum that one should neither love nations nor hate them.

Or were Fest's attitude and tactics the result of a single inconsidered decision, one he had possibly taken without having carefully examined Nolte's manuscript, a decision his pride would not allow him to renounce or revise – even though there would have been time enough to do so? Could he have believed that I would accept what he had done in this matter? Could he have assumed that I would remain silent when the paper on which I was employed denied that the Holocaust had been the work of Germans? No, this seems to me out of the question. But it was clearly unimportant to him.

Why is it that some writers, journalists or historians may secretly realize the mistakes they have made, but will not publicly admit them?

Presumably this reluctance has something to do with a weakness of which they are ashamed, a lack of authority and self-assurance which they wish to conceal at all costs, or with a vanity that impairs their self-control.

Could this be true also of Fest? I would be dishonest if I were to avoid this question. But there is another question that troubles me more. Is it conceivable that Joachim Fest was totally unaware of what he had done to me? That he is still unaware of it? The man to whom I owe the most gratitude also inflicted the most pain on me. I cannot stop questioning it, I cannot forget it – neither the one nor the other.

Even though the discussion yielded virtually nothing for scholarship, the German historians' dispute was evidence, at least partially, of the spirit of the time. It met the need – by no means only of the right-wing radicals – to revise attitudes towards National Socialism. The strength of this need emerged in the autumn of 1998, when Martin Walser made a speech in the Paulskirche in Frankfurt, a speech that re-opened 'the end of the close season' debate more than a decade after the Fassbinder film and the historians' dispute.

Walser also dealt with the question of the crime of the century, the German crime (although he carefully avoided the words 'crime' and 'guilt'). He was troubled by the question of what had happened in the past and how we should deal with it in the present.

Did Walser in his speech, which was the subject of furious discussion for months, recommend turning one's back on the German past? Did he advocate closing the notorious chapter of Auschwitz? He has disputed this. But the fact that many contemporaries put such an interpretation on his speech, a speech that teemed with vague formulations and malicious allusions to unidentified individuals – could this fact really have surprised Walser? One thing is certain: he did nothing to prevent the predictable misunderstandings, if indeed such they were. On the contrary: his defiant avowal in favour of looking the other way proved a call to follow his behaviour whether he intended it to or not.

Walser gave vent to the most dangerous German resentments, he repeated what could be heard at tables in beer cellars – and he supplied new arguments and new formulas for those beer drinkers, for the extreme right wing and for all those who, for whatever reasons, do not like Jews. His speech had the effect of drawing a line between those Germans who, as he claims, felt it to have 'liberated' them and those German citizens who are represented by his principal interlocutor, Ignatz Bubis, the President of the Central Council of Jews in Germany.

It cannot be denied that Walser's speech deeply affected and wounded me – mainly because it was delivered by a writer whose work I had been commenting on ever since 1957. But there was also a positive side to the fact that it was written and delivered. Because, like the Fassbinder film and the historians' dispute, this speech reminded us of the moral and political climate in the Federal Republic a decade later.

Walser's remarks in his speech about the memorial being built in Berlin to the murdered Jews of Europe were typical of that climate. He was, and is, against that memorial. I was not, and am not, against it, but neither am I for it. I do not need it; my father, my mother, my brother and the many other members of my family who were murdered by the Nazis need it even less. I have not uttered a single word on this matter.

Once the memorial has been erected I shall go to see it. Whether I shall feel any strong emotion there, I do not know. Certainly not as much as I did in December 1970 when I saw a picture that made the rounds of the world's press – Willy Brandt kneeling before the Warsaw Ghetto Memorial. At that moment I knew that I would be grateful to him for the rest of my life.

The first time that I met Willy Brandt after his genuflection in Warsaw was in Nuremberg towards the end of January 1990. Already bearing the marks of his grave illness, he had come there to honour the ninety-year-old Hermann Kesten, the writer, the Jew and the emigré. I tried to thank Willy Brandt with a few awkward words. He asked me how I had survived. I told him, as concisely as possible, that in September 1942 Tosia and I had been taken by German soldiers, along with thousands of other Jews, to just that square in Warsaw where the Ghetto Memorial now stands. There, I told him, I had last seen my father and my mother before they were driven on to the trains for Treblinka.

When I had finished my brief account one of us had tears in his eyes. Willy Brandt or me? I no longer remember. But I remember very well what I thought when, in 1970, I saw the photograph of the German Federal Chancellor on his knees. I thought that my decision to return to Germany in 1958 and to settle in the Federal Republic had been the right one. Fassbinder's film, the historians' dispute and Walser's speech, all of them important symptoms of the spirit of the age, have since done nothing to change my mind.

41

''TIS A DREAM...'

Today is 12 March 1999, Tosia's birthday, the day on which her eightieth year begins. We are alone, it is very quiet, it is late afternoon. She is, as always, sitting on the black sofa beside one of our walls of pictures; behind her are the portraits of Goethe, Kleist, Heine and Fontane, of Thomas Mann, Kafka and Brecht. On the little chest by the sofa are a few photographs – my son Andrew, now fifty, professor of mathematics at the University of Edinburgh, and Carla, his daughter, nearly twenty, studying English language and literature at the University of London.

I am sitting facing Tosia, doing nothing different from what I have done for the major part of my life – I am reading a German novel. But I find it hard to concentrate and put the book down on the low table. For a moment I step out on to our spacious, but too rarely used, balcony. The weather is fair, the sun is setting; it is a beautiful, perhaps as always a little too beautiful, and indeed solemn, spectacle. I cannot recall ever having watched the sun set from this balcony, even though we have lived here more than twenty-four years. Am I indifferent to nature? Certainly not. But I find what many German writers have found – it soon bores me. Now, too, I begin to feel a little restless and return uncertainly to our living room.

Tosia is reading a Polish book – poems by Julian Tuwim. I sit down very quietly, I do not want to disturb her. Is she searching for her youth, for our youth, in poetry? We shall soon have been together for sixty years. Time and again we have tried to forget our sorrow and to suppress our anxiety, time and again literature has been our asylum and music our refuge. As it was once in the ghetto, so it has

391

remained to this day. And what about love? Yes, there have been times when Tosia suffered a lot. There have also been far less frequent occasions when I suffered. About eight hundred years ago Gottfried von Strassburg said in his *Tristan*: '*To whom love never sent pain / to him love never gave happiness.*' We have both suffered a lot of pain and been endowed with much happiness. And whatever else may have happened, nothing has changed about our relationship.

It is still very quiet, hardly a breath is heard. Tosia glances up from her book and looks at me with a smile, questioningly, as though she senses that I have something to tell her. 'D'you know, just now on our balcony as the sun was setting, it came to me how to end the book.' 'Oh,' she says, pleased. 'How will you end it?' 'With a quotation.' I pause; she smiles again, this time – it seems to me – a little ironically. 'You think that surprises me? Well, let's have it. What's the quotation? 'A simple couplet from Hofmannsthal,' I answer. She is getting a little impatient: 'All right, but which? Come on, tell me.' I hesitate for a moment, then I say: 'Very well, the book will conclude with the lines:

> *'Tis a dream, cannot really be true*
> *That we are here together, we two.'*

42

THANKSGIVING

Every book has its history. Mostly, of course, this is of no interest to the public. For that reason I will only say a few words about the genesis of this autobiography. The idea was first suggested to me by my wife Tosia a few days after our escape from the Warsaw ghetto in 1943. I did not follow it up at the time and I have resisted other suggestions put to me by various people over the years and decades, including my son Andrew Alexander. The reason was fear. I did not wish to relive it all in my mind. Moreover, I was afraid that I might not be up to the task.

Not until half a century later, in 1993, did I change my mind and decide to produce a record of my life. Now the autobiography is here, and the time has come for me to thank all those who have aided its progress with advice and encouragement, with their expectations and their curiosity – and at times, fortunately, with all kinds of warnings. I wish to thank my friends and colleagues, especially Ulrich Frank-Planitz, Volker Hage, Jochen Hieber, Hellmuth Karasek, Salomon Korn, Klara Obermüller, Rachel Salamander, Stephan Sattler, Frank Schirrmacher, Matthias Wegner and Ulrich Weinzierl.

I am obliged for important suggestions and information to three Warsaw authors – Jan Koprowski, Hanna Krall and Andrzej Szczypiorski – and to three scholarly institutions: Yad Vashem, Jerusalem; Żydowski Instytut Historyczny, Warsaw; and Institut für Zeitgeschichte, Munich. Last but not least I would like to thank Franz-Heinrich Hackel, the publishing director of Deutsche Verlags-Anstalt, for his confidence, his suggestions and advice, and for his indefatigable zeal. I finally have to thank my secretary, Frau Hanelore Müller, who has patiently assisted me over the years.

M. R.-R.
Frankfurt, July 1999

INDEX